From Jerusalem to Kashmir:
The Secret Life of Jesus in India

Jozef Banáš

Jozef Banáš
From Jerusalem to Kashmir: The Secret Life of Jesus in India

Text © 2013 by Jozef Banáš
Editor © 2013 by Anna Lackovičová
Jacket photo © 2013 by Peter Frolo
Jacket design © 2013 by Viera Fabianová, Richard Guzman
Slovak edition © 2013 by Ikar (original title: 'Kód 1 – Tajomstvo zázraku')
Translation © 2013 by Petr Kurfurst
Proofreading © 2013 by Sean Jones © 2020 by Cornelia Merk

English Edition © 2020 published by Hybrid Global Publishing, 301 E 57th Street, 4th Fl, New York, NY 10022 USA and co-published by Global Slovakia, Bratislava Slovakia
Foreword © 2020 by Dr. Clint G. Rogers; Dr. Zuzana Palovic; Cornelia Merk

No part of this book may be reproduced or transmitted in any form or by any means electronic or mechanical, including photocopying, recording or by any information storage and retrieval system, without permission in writing form from the publishers. Jozef Banáš has asserted the right to be identified as the author of this work.

Manufactured in the United States of America, or in the United Kingdom when distributed elsewhere.

All rights reserved.

Library of congress cataloging-in-publication data available upon request.

ISBN 978-1-951943-22-6
ISBN 978-1-951943-23-3 (eBook)
WWW.GLOBALSLOVAKIA.COM

GLOBAL SLOVAKIA
OUR FUTURE IS GREATER THAN OUR PAST

Jozef Banáš (1948) is one of the most translated contemporary Slovak writers. Author of a number of bestsellers, Jozef has collected an array of prestigious national and international awards. His impressive record counts 37 books that have sold a total number of 320,000 copies and have been translated into thirteen languages globally. His success is no coincidence.

Dan Brown has described Jozef Banáš as a seeker of truth, and the Dalai Lama blessed his efforts to bring people together.

After the eclipse of a busy career in diplomacy and politics, Jozef Banáš turned his sharp focus to writing in 2006. He has been bringing history and its iconic characters to life ever since in his trademark documentary style novels. Every year Banáš publishes a new literary masterpiece. His work includes the #1 bestselling novels Code 9 and its sequel Code 1 about the secret life of Jesus in India that have become the subject of much heated debate both home and abroad. His semi-autobiographical novel Jubilation Zone, documenting love and friendship beyond the Cold War, is the most translated Slovak literary work to date.

Jozef's creative and spiritual home is Slovakia, a mountainous country with a rich history located right in the very heart of Europe.

www.jozefbanas.com

Motto

I want a human of flesh and bone, like you.
Not an angel, not a machine. Oh my God.
May he cheer or be to pieces blown, like you,
should he lose a fight or the wrong way plod.
I want a human who will stay one,
both in joy and when he may pine,
even in penance, even on cloud nine.

Miroslav Válek

In a time of universal deceit - telling the truth is a revolutionary act.

George Orwell

Acknowledgments
I am sincerely grateful to the guardian angel of this book – Mrs. Anna Lackovičová for her expert comments, and Mr. Ľubo Fellner for creating excellent conditions during my three Indian expeditions.

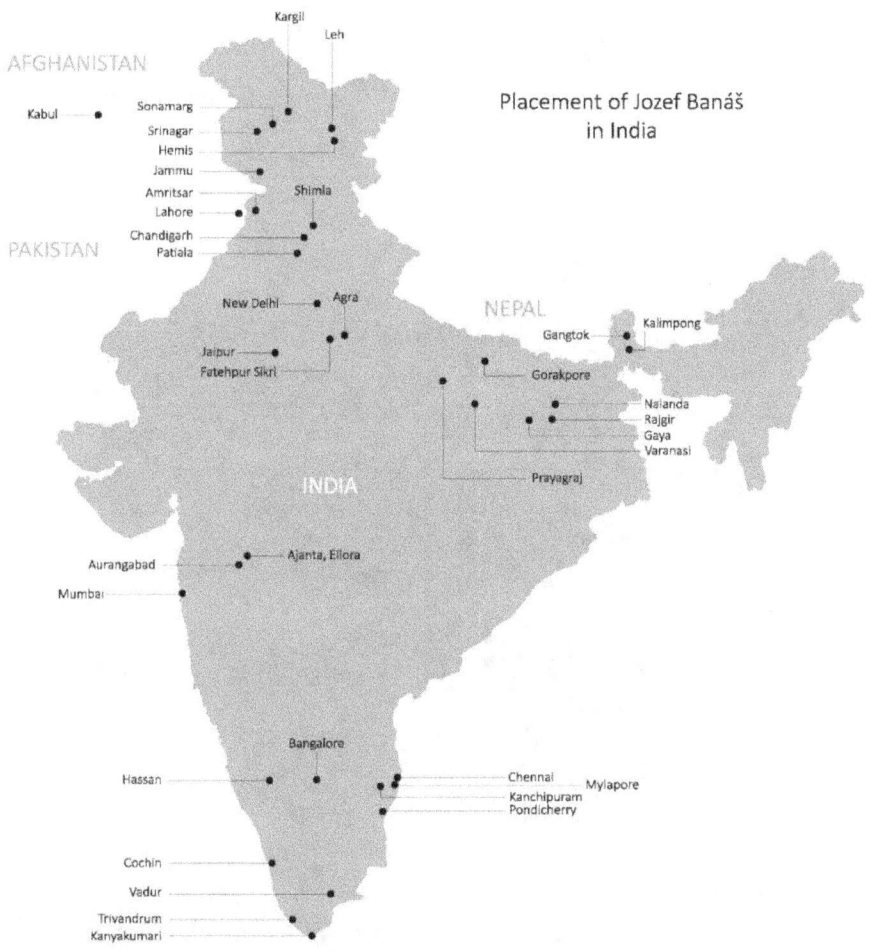

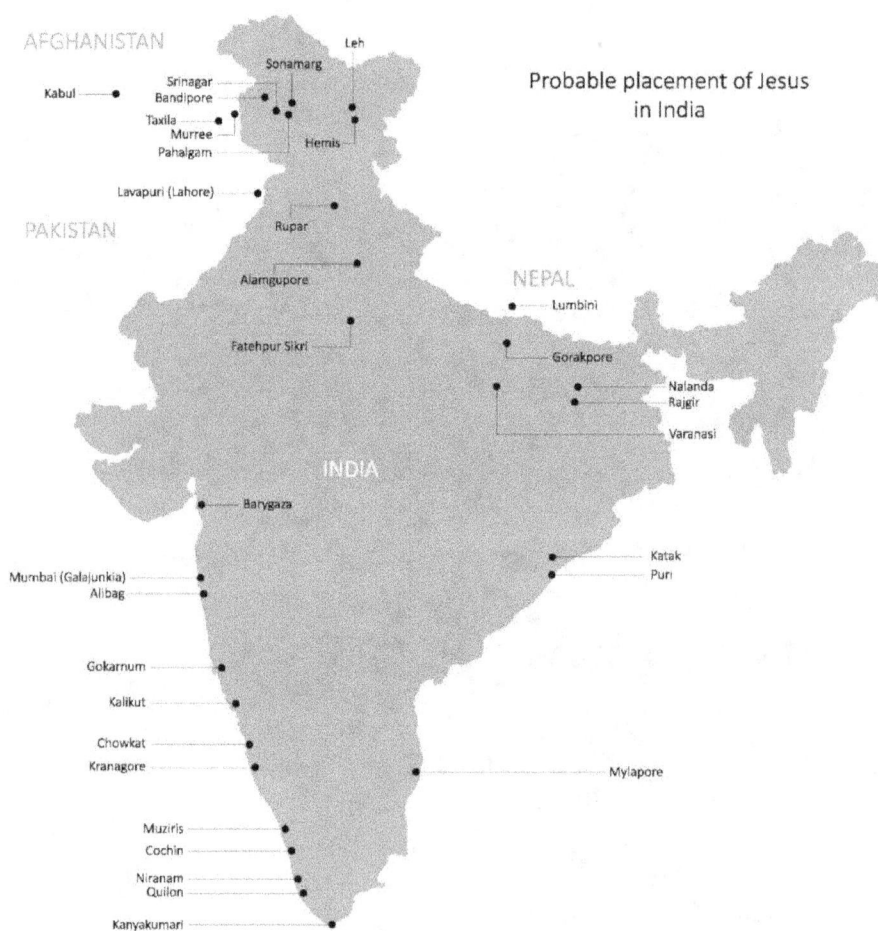

What If One Story Can Change the Way You View the World and Your Entire Life?

As someone who spent a lot of time in India and a lot of time studying Jesus, I'm excited about how this book, *From Jerusalem to Kashmir: The Secret Life of Jesus in India*, by Jozef Banáš could change your life forever.

Reading it brought back to my mind an unexpected conversation I had during one of my first visits to India...

"I love and respect Jesus," world-renowned healer Dr. Naram said, as our car swerved through the crowded streets of Mumbai, India. We were headed to pay respects at a nearby temple before a busy clinic day.

"Really?" I asked. For some reason it caught me off guard to hear him say that. I grew up in a conservative Christian home in the Midwest, USA, while Dr. Naram came from a totally different part of the world, growing up as a Hindu in India. Now he was part of an unbroken lineage of master healers that goes back to Jivaka, the personal physician for Buddha, with many famous patients, including the Dalai Lama, Mother Teresa, and Nelson Mandela.

I was trying to make sense of what Dr. Naram said in context of what I believed. I wondered, what did he know about Jesus? So I asked, "Why do you love Jesus?"

Dr. Naram replied, "He became a master of the art and science of healing. He mastered many ancient healing practices. For that reason, he is my senior, my teacher. There is so much I can learn from him."

Since I loved Jesus, I was somehow touched that this famous Indian healer also loved Jesus. It was fascinating and a little confusing, however, to hear the different reasons why.

"Did you know Jesus came to India?" Dr. Naram asked me.

"No, I've never heard of that before."

"Our ancient records share how he spent years in India, learning and teaching."

I was aware that the Bible had no record or account of Jesus for a significant period of his life. From the time Jesus was 12 years old until he was nearly 30, there was an absence of any account in the scriptures on where he was or what he was doing.

During the three years I lived in England, I'd heard legend of him visiting there. I'd grown up in the USA hearing accounts of Jesus' visit to the American continent. I'd been taught that when Columbus originally arrived on the shores, some native American tribes thought he was the 'great white God' returning. Although Columbus definitely wasn't that, I found it interesting that the native people had a traditional teaching that there was a 'white god' who had visited them in the Americas, and it was said he would come again. But I had never heard of him visiting India before.

I had wondered many times what actually happened to Jesus during all those years that are unaccounted for in the Bible. Why is there so little information on where he was or what he did during that long period of time? Was it possible that for at least part of that time, he had travelled to India and learned from the great sages and saints there?

In a strange way it made sense to me, as many of the things I'd witnessed Dr. Naram do were things I'd previously only heard of Jesus being able to do. During the ten years I spent with him, I'd seen people declared legally blind by their doctors who now were able to see without glasses, people in wheelchairs now walking, and those who were not able to speak for their entire lives now speaking. I'd seen people with all kinds of chronic and acute health challenges from diabetes, to arthritis, to infertility, to severe cancer now claim their problems were gone, thanks to this ancient healing science. I'd even seen cases where people said they had 'evil spirits' in them who were able to operate normally after being treated by Dr. Naram.

These looked like miracles to me, which I attributed to some special power in Dr. Naram, but he said it was healing based on an ancient science.

I was very skeptical to begin with. As a university researcher I questioned everything. And as a Christian, I felt cautiously protective. I didn't want to accept that it was possible for other people to do what Jesus did.

Then my dad fell ill, and in an effort to save his life, I began to go deeper into what Dr. Naram was doing. One thing led to another, and I ended up living in India and traveling the world studying with him for more than ten years (from 2009-2020). In the process, I documented thousands of cases of 'miraculous' healing, and the secrets of the ancient science behind them, which I shared in a TEDx talk and put into a book, *Ancient Secrets of a Master Healer: A Western Skeptic, an Eastern Master, and Life's Greatest Secrets.*

Perhaps the biggest shock came when after many years of Dr. Naram's training, I began to do many of the same things for people. It altered the way I saw myself and all of life completely. Could this be part of the same science that Jesus came to India for?

I remember one of the first times I experienced this. We were in Frankfurt, Germany, and Dr. Naram asked me to help a woman with severe back pain. The pain was so extreme that she could barely bend. Simply by putting my hands on her back in a way that activated certain points that balanced her internal systems, her pain disappeared in about two minutes. She was so startled when she could bend over and touch her toes with no pain. I was surprised, too, that I was an instrument in helping her receive this gift. Throughout the day, Dr. Naram sent me one person after another, with physical, mental and emotional challenges — and with each I was able to use the ancient science to help them.

But then came a man in a wheelchair who was paralyzed on his right side and had not walked for 3 years. Dr Naram promised him that "Dr. Clint will help you walk." I went in to speak with Dr. Naram, and in a concerned voice I asked, "But how?" Without any worry in his voice at all, he just instructed me what to do. Within a few minutes the man was up walking, his wife in tears, and the doctors at the clinic watching in amazement.

I escaped to the bathroom. With tears in my eyes, I looked in the mirror, barely able to comprehend what was happening. Then I closed my eyes and said a prayer, thanking God that this ancient technology had been preserved by this lineage of masters and still existed on the earth today. I felt overwhelmed and I was in awe.

About a month later I was invited to speak at an event in Texas to an audience of martial arts instructors. At the end, I felt inspired to demonstrate what was possible by asking a couple people who were in pain to come up and I would help them. Everyone watched in amazement as the people who came up regained mobility and their pain went away. The 1-hour presentation turned into a 4-hour session, as person after person wanted to come up to be healed. My friend, Jeremy, who attended with me said, "The only thing I can compare that to is when Jesus started healing people one by one."

When I got this book about 'the secret life of Jesus in India,' I was extremely curious. As I read the pages, that curiosity turned into joy. Although this book is a fictional account of what may have happened during the unaccounted years of Jesus, it is obvious that the author, Jozef Banáš, has done extensive research and put his whole heart into the writing. While I was reading each chapter, I felt like I was unlocking secret keys to one of the most important stories of all time, which ultimately points to the power all of us have within us. An incredible power fueled by love.

The Bible quotes Jesus speaking about this power in you. "Very truly I tell you, whoever believes in me will do the works I have been doing, and they will do even greater things than these." (John 14:12)

Jozef Banáš has given the world a great gift with this book. You may agree or disagree with the content, but that is not the point. Even the author does not claim the narrative to be true. He says, "My ambition was to write a story, not a history textbook; to inspire contemplation, not to convince; to invite a search for the truth, not to own it."

And Banáš has done exactly that. As you begin reading, set aside everything you think you know for a moment, and simply enjoy the journey you take with this narrative of Jesus, along with the story of the modern-day seekers of truth in this book, Michal and Marika.

And as you contemplate the possibility of what may be true for Jesus, also consider what might be true for you.

Mumbai, India - June 2020
Dr. Clint G. Rogers
International Bestselling Author of *Ancient Secrets of a Master Healer: A Western Skeptic, an Eastern Master, and Life's Greatest Secrets*

Jesus: The World's Most Celebrated Messiah and Least Known Migrant?

The thought of Jesus living in India seems implausible to many, even sacrilegious. The most popular figure in history and the moral foundation behind one of the greatest civilizations on the planet is seen and cherished as a symbol of the Christian West.

The fact that he was born a Jew in a turbulent Arab Middle East is already difficult enough to integrate in the Euro-American mindset. It does not sit well with the image of the blue-eyed blond Jesus who looks at us from church walls and books. For the most part, it is as if the life story of Jesus has been devoid of its context.

But Christ was not born in a void. He was born and raised in a region that had been at the crossroads of worlds for millennia. This is where civilizations, cultures and belief systems came together thanks to prominent trade routes. Historians of the past speak of Jerusalem as the center of the Earth.

If Jesus was indeed a historical figure, born with a tremendous spiritual connection, agile mind and expansive consciousness, it seems only natural he would yearn to discover what lay beyond his 'known' world. Especially since that world was connected to the faraway lands of many cultures and kingdoms.

Jozef Banáš' powerful documentary novel narrates the lost years of Christ that the Bible does not account for. Spiritual seekers and historians alike have been striving to fill this gap in Jesus' historical timeline for centuries.

Banáš' detail-rich portrayal of the 'unknown years' reads akin to a movie script. The story parallels two journeys. A 21st century couple, beset by a health ordeal, set upon a pilgrimage to the Holy Land in search of Jesus' healing. The second animates Jesus' life from over 2,000 years ago as it follows the destiny of a boy growing into a man. It unveils a real flesh and blood human who followed a calling, faced earthly hardships and eventually rose to become the prophet we so cherish.

With more than a quarter of a million books sold in Banáš' native Slovakia located in the heart of Europe, it is astounding to discover just how popular his depiction of Jesus' life in the Far East is in the Catholic country.

Statistically about one in every eight households owns one of Banáš' many bestselling novels - each pushing the envelope and challenging the status quo in their unique way.

I first got interested in Jesus' travels as a migration scholar and during my visit to the Himalayas. As an avid researcher, my goal was to understand the value of return migration in knowledge transfer. My passion for migration led me into the heart of some of the best universities in the world - from a Master's in the Netherlands, to a PhD in the United Kingdom, I studied this topic under the sage counsel of the world's best experts.

In the process, I read through countless theories, dug up a vault load of data and recorded hundreds of hours of conversations with migrants, in an attempt to explain the phenomenon. This is when I came to appreciate the story of the world's most celebrated man – and its least known return migrant.

Jesus is an archetypical embodiment of The Hero's Journey described by Joseph Campbell. This global monomyth has shaped the collective imagination across eras, cultures and beliefs. The pattern is simple, yet profound. Under the guise of adventure, the hero leaves, transforms and resurrects, only to return home a wiser and more experienced human, ready to share the seeds of what he learned about the world and self.

Jesus was a man who left, learned and returned with new wisdom that eventually formed the foundation of an entirely new belief system.

To me, he represents the blueprint that I spent many years exploring and that I presented in my book *The Great Return*. From time travelers to culture shifters, I explored what happens when – the lost daughters and sons of Slovakia choose to defy the brain drain theory and return home.

The fact is that migration has been an indispensable part of the human story going back to the cradle of human humanity in Africa. Our ancestors moved across land and water in search of something – food, shelter, safety and procreation.

Eventually, the hunter-gatherers settled down to farm on the land, but our thirst for knowledge continued to drive us to cross rivers, lakes, plains, mountains and oceans – this time in the pursuit of trade, but also wisdom and understanding. We have been departing and returning ever since in a powerful universal rite of passage.

Historically, a man was not a man without having once proved himself through the cycle of going and coming. Men and later women were expected to leave home in order to grow – as hunters, traders, warriors or wise men/women. However, the rite was only completed once one returned. Just as Jesus did.

Of course, the migration trajectory of Jesus' life in India has been academically studied. Most popularly is the work of German scholar Holger Kersten (1983). His research was built on the work of the Russian journalist Nicolas Notovitch (1894), who first made the claim in the West that Jesus learned from the Buddhists and Hindus.

I would like to commend the exceptional work of Jozef Banáš for not only shedding light on this important narrative. But for doing so by brilliantly weaving together historical sources, spiritual wisdom and his own travel expedition – to explore a much lesser known perspective on the man we celebrate as the messiah today.

Bangalore, India – July 2020
Dr. Zuzana Palovic
Migration Scholar and Author of *The Great Return*

Was Christianity Built on a Lie?

To say that my relationship with God, Jesus and the church was strained from the very beginning is putting it mildly. I was educated, or should I say indoctrinated, in Kindergarten and primary school by Roman-Catholic nuns and priests in the 1960s and early 1970s. God, I was told, was my *Heavenly Father* who was *just and loved me in eternity*, but at the same time, because Adam and Eve had disobeyed God and fallen from grace, I had been born into 'original sin'. I was a condemned sinner and could only reach eternal life by the grace of God. I felt I was judged and punished for something I hadn't done. Then, even worse, I was told that Jesus sacrificed his life for me to redeem me from my sins. I was a little child and couldn't understand why someone else had died for me, long before I was even born. What had I done? But deep inside I still felt guilty. This narrative didn't make sense to my childish mind and left me confused and fearful.

Going to church every Sunday filled me with dread and resentment. I never felt that this was the house of a loving father, but rather a place where priests created an atmosphere of fear with their preaching from the pulpit. As I got older, I began to wonder why a religion that was built on Jesus' teachings tried to keep its followers in fear. Later still, I learned in my history lessons how Christianity had killed millions of people in the name of God, and I struggled even more to reconcile Jesus' teachings of love and compassion with the Catholic Church's actions to secure their power. I formally left the Catholic Church when I was 17.

Like most people who were brought up with the Bible I was aware of Jesus' lost years, but I never pondered where he could have been or what he might have done during all these years. And, as I had been told that he had died at the cross, I also never even considered the possibility that he might have survived crucifixion and lived to a ripe old age. That is, until I read Jozef Banáš' book, *From Jerusalem to Kashmir: The Secret Life of Jesus in India*. My inquisitive and analytical mind immediately went into overdrive.

The last account of Jesus as a child comes from Luke. According to him, Jesus had such a profound knowledge and understanding of the scripture that *he could talk with the teachers in the temple* at the age of 12. So, why would a boy at the verge of manhood, who was obviously interested and educated in the scriptures, be content with working as a carpenter for so many years before starting his missionary at 30? Isn't it much more likely that he wanted to continue his studies to satisfy his curiosity and gain more wisdom? Again, in Luke 2, we find: *And Jesus grew in wisdom and stature, and in favor with God and men.* So, Banáš' argument that Jesus traveled to foreign countries during these years has considerable merit, particularly when we look at the similarities between Jesus' teachings and the teachings of Buddha.

My own spontaneous healing in 1998 after suffering from excruciating pain for nearly eight years sent me on a quest to find out what had caused this 'miracle'. My research showed that there are certain 'ingredients' that are always present in those healings. One of them is the patient's belief that the healing is going to happen, which Jesus depicted by saying, "Your faith has made you whole." I also discovered that using the right techniques and modalities, such as pressure points, mantras, herbal remedies, foods, or detoxification at the right time led to all kinds of healing miracles. Many of those miracles I read about resembled the miracles that Jesus performed in his time. So, if those miracles can be brought about by using certain techniques and modalities, a logical question is then, where did Jesus learn them?

Banáš also highlights a few verses in the Bible that describe the events around the crucifixion. Reading them with the idea in mind that Jesus didn't die at the cross, you may find evidence in the Bible that supports this theory. For example, according to John 19:39, Nicodemus brought 75 pounds of myrrh and aloe to the grave after Jesus was taken down from the cross. These two herbs have excellent medicinal and antiseptic properties, which makes it very likely that Nicodemus and Joseph were treating Jesus' wounds and not using the herbs to embalm his body. We also have to ask why this medical preparation became known as the *ointment of Jesus* if it wasn't used as a healing agent in the grave? I admit that I had heard of the ointment before, but I never made the connection or realized the significance of its name.

Before I started to help people heal their body, mind, and spirit after my own healing, I worked as a translator and proofreader, and sometimes I still do, like for this book. In my training, I had to study linguistics, which is the science of origin, roots, history, and significance of words. So, the fact that so many names of towns, places, and temples in India and Kashmir bear a stark resemblance to the names in the Torah or are directly related to Jesus' name, are a strong indicator to me that not only the Ten Lost Tribes had traveled to these countries but Jesus as well. Why would a region or a town use Jesus' name if he hadn't been or lived there? They certainly didn't name a place or temple after him because they had just heard of him. Just think about how names for our streets, places, buildings, and airports are chosen today. Don't we name them in memory or reverence of a famous person that is relevant to this area? Jesus must have left such an impression on the people living there that they found him worthy enough to name a place or a building after him.

Throughout the book, Jozef Banáš makes a compelling case for the probability that Jesus travelled to India and Kashmir, not once, but twice. The author has put a tremendous amount of work and research into writing this novel, and the result is a thought-provoking yet plausible account of what might have happened during Jesus' lost years and after his disappearance from the grave.

Reading the book with an open mind will make you question the narrative we have been told for nearly two millennia. Banáš stresses that the book is a novel and not a historical account of what really happened, and each reader will have to decide for themselves what they can accept as possible truth and what they will dismiss right away. He invites us to search for our own truth. And sometimes, this truth cannot be found on the internet, in history books, or in a novel; it can only be found within our hearts.

Paradise Island, The Bahamas – September 2020
Cornelia Merk, co-author of *Revolutionize Your Health – How to Take Back Your Body's Power to Heal*

Table of Contents

The Armor of Dogmatism	xxi
Sibyl's Prophecy	xxiii
Chapter 1, The Miracle in Cana of Galilee	1
Chapter 2, Templum Hierosolym	7
Chapter 3, Mysterious Dream	11
Chapter 4, The Prophet's Judgment	17
Chapter 5, You Must Go to the Grave!	21
Chapter 6, You Shall Not Kill	25
Chapter 7, Secret Angels	29
Chapter 8, The Wisdom of the East	35
Chapter 9, The First Miracle	39
Chapter 10, A Weird Hunch	45
Chapter 11, The Wailing Wal	49
Chapter 12, The One We're Awaiting	51
Chapter 13, Unum	55
Chapter 14, The Blood of the Innocent	61
Chapter 15, The Mysterious Card	67
Chapter 16, Royal Teaching	71
Chapter 17, The Tiberias Surprise	75
Chapter 18, An Unknown Stranger	79
Chapter 19, I Will Wait for You	87
Chapter 20, The King of Peace	91
Chapter 21, The Forgotten Glasses	97
Chapter 22, Shalom	105
Chapter 23, A Wish God Doesn't Get That Often	109
Chapter 24, Incident with the Prince	115
Chapter 25, Church Shootout	121
Chapter 26, Solomon's Wisdom	125
Chapter 27, A Strange Fragrance	129
Chapter 28, Cosmic Energy	133
Chapter 29, The Fake Grave	141
Chapter 30, The Feast of Death	149
Chapter 31, I believe!	153
Chapter 32, A Time Will Come, You'll Find Out	157
Chapter 33, A Doctrine Based on a Lie	161
Chapter 34, A Failed Test	165
Chapter 35, A Key to the Secret	169
Chapter 36, The Supreme Inquisitor	179
Chapter 37, BRHM	185
Chapter 38, The Vatican Agent	191
Chapter 39, It Won't End Well for You	201
Chapter 40, Fear	207

Chapter 41, The Lost Tribes	217
Chapter 42, Footprints in the Stone	221
Chapter 43, Burning at the Stake	227
Chapter 44, Lotus Christ	237
Chapter 45, Attempted Murder	243
Chapter 46, The Devil	247
Chapter 47, To Live Love	251
Chapter 48, Operation Roza Bal	257
Chapter 49, The Price of Death	261
Chapter 50, Do Not Fear!	267
Chapter 51, False Prophets	271
Chapter 52, The Hearts	275
Chapter 53, You Shall Become God	281
Chapter 54, Afraid to Tell You	285
Chapter 55, An Unpermitted Wedding	289
Chapter 56, A Murderous Conflict	197
Chapter 57, A Perfect Prophecy	305
Chapter 58, Jews in Kashmir	311
Chapter 59, God Won't Help Us	317
Chapter 60, The Countdown	325
Chapter 61, The Time Has Come	327
Chapter 62, God Bless You	337
Chapter 63, A Surprise	341
Chapter 64, The Crunch Is Coming	345
Chapter 65, Pilate's Proposal	351
Chapter 66, Shoes Off in the Grave!	355
Chapter 67, Ibis Ad Crucem	361
Chapter 68, The Figure in the Tomb	369
Chapter 69, I'm Giving You Two Weeks	375
Chapter 70, The Royal Bloodline	379
Chapter 71, The Escape	389
Chapter 72, You'll Snuff It Lying Down!	393
Chapter 73, Joachim and Boas	397
Chapter 74, A Cruel Confession	403
Chapter 75, Moses' Grave	407
Chapter 76, A False Charge	413
Chapter 77, The Way of Love	417
Chapter 78, Code 1	425
Chapter 79, The Cornerstone	431
Chapter 80, The Secret of the Miracle	439
Epilogue – One More Thing I Wanted to Tell You	443
Bibliography	445

The Armor of Dogmatism

What chokes and smothers modern-day Christians the most is the dogmatism of their own church organizations. It reduces the believers' own thinking, feeling and wishing like a straitjacket and, on the collective scale, it works like ice covering the churches' frozen fields. The rule of dogmatism means that Christian people's feeling, thinking and wishing are to be governed by church dogmas and instructions. Faith is under-stood not in the sense of Jesus-like living; rather, faith is agreement in ideas that affirms and conforms to the "divine authority" of the church. In such an approach, the question of truth becomes a question of power, represented by the church's authority. Dogmatism does not permit believers to seek and find God in their own virtuous ways, even at the cost of error and doubt. Quite to the contrary, believers are supposed to accept that the church doctrine has given them the whole truth, which is why any doubt is declared to be an offense to God's majesty. Instead of being allowed to ask questions, believers are forced to make themselves questionable. Such an attitude blocks personal growth and keeps believers immature. Fear of questioning the imposed dogmas leads them to questioning of their own personality and latent neurosis. Instead of salvation preached by Jesus in the sense of healing and joy, this spreads a fearful, dismal, pathological existence, which is in obvious contradiction to what Jesus strove for.

Prof. ThDr. Karol Nandrásky
Biblical theologian and philosopher (excerpt from his book *Jesus and the Present*, 2010)

Sibyl's Prophecy

That day, the Sibyl, Queen of Sheba, whose real name was Mikhalda Kumana, summoned her loyal ones and told them, "The messengers whom I sent to the north of our country brought me news that a very wise and just monarch lives far away from here. His name is Solomon. A man will arise from his land who will bring the whole world light when the sun celebrates solstice a hundred times. Even though he will suffer the greatest abasement, defamation and torments in the city of Jerusalem, he will elevate its glory. Priests who profit and gain from erroneous readings of laws will revolt against him. They will accuse him of lies and blasphemy and will be no better than worldly rulers. When they acquire power and wealth, they will forget about him; they will fight amongst themselves not for truth but for the power of gold and will cease to fulfill what they set out to do. The priests' status will be greater than that of their worldly rulers; their pride and arrogance will grow with their power. Only with their approval will kings and princes sit on royal thrones; only with their consent will royalty marry. The hegemony of the priests will cause much evil. The Messiah will become a shield for committing vices. That is why the Queen of the South will stand on trial with this race and condemn it, because she has come to hear Solomon's wisdom from the ends of the earth and, behold, here is HE, greater than Solomon."

1   The Miracle in Cana of Galilee

Had Tomáš known what would happen to him in Cana, he might have been more responsible. But had he been more responsible, a new miracle wouldn't have happened in that biblical town. The heat was intolerable as early as seven in the morning that day. He set out from Tiberias in his old Fiat before noon.

While Israel was gripped by temperatures unusual for early April, it was surprisingly cold in Slovakia. It had been raining for three days now, and Marika was annoyed because she had to fire the two young men she had hired to dig out the old, half-withered shrubs defacing the way to their house while Michal was away in Košice. Michal couldn't part with the shrubs. Parting with old, needless stuff was her husband's constant problem. He spent so much time and energy moving them from place to place! Half the garden was covered with old junk which he was convinced would 'come in handy one day', the living room was filled with souvenirs he'd collected on his countless travels. Recently, the more tired she felt, the more vigorously she got rid of stuff that disrupted positive energies according to feng shui. She risked Michal getting mad when he found out. But then she'd thrown out a few jugs, lockets, oil lamps and other pieces of junk inconspicuously from time to time without him noticing. His furious reaction when he discovered she'd thrown out a rock that he'd brought from Jerusalem shocked her. He had a real fit of hysteria. Wrathful, he ran to the trash can and rummaged in it for nearly an hour without a blush of embarrassment in front of the neighbors until he eventually found his souvenir as if by miracle.

"Do you know what this is?!" he yelled at Marika almost out of his senses, but with visible relief.

"An old useless rock that was filling up the shelf and collecting dust. I wish you'd at least dusted it."

"This is the symbol of Unity!" he interrupted. "The primordial home of us all!" Marika stared at him in a state of shock. "UNUM! You can't understand that. It's the most important symbol of any I have! Please don't ever do that again! Understand?! Don't touch my stuff! I insist on you not doing that! You do cleaning in your room, but leave my study alone," he shouted with unusual sharpness.

"No need to go all mad like that over your symbols! You keep collecting them on your trips, covering the house with them, there's hardly any room left to walk. And don't forget your study is also the living room where we have guests."

"All right, all right," he said, calming down, "but symbols are crucial for our lives. They transfer energy from holy places to our homes. This rock is not just any rock; it was given to me by the Coptic archbishop Athanasius in Jerusalem. He gave Tomáš the same rock," he explained with an odd expression on his face as he put the rock back in its place.

"You never told me you went to a Coptic priest with Tomáš," Marika wondered.

"Tomáš took me to see him. They're friends. Archbishop Athanasius studied at the patriarchal seminary in Maadi near Cairo, and he's considered one of the greatest living sages. Did you notice this?" He took the rock again and gazed at it in awe. He was showing her some lines, incisions in the rock she hadn't noticed before. "Look, this is the numeral one, the symbol of unity. And this, when you look closely, are the letters J and B. I don't know exactly what they mean but they're related to the east and west."

Marika studied the rock attentively. "The man in this little picture here, sitting in the lotus position, looks like Christ." Michal nodded. "But why would Christ sit in the lotus position?" She shook her head over the indistinct, faded outline of the seated male figure.

"Maybe that's the symbol of union between the east and west. The archbishop said that according to some legend there's a statue of Jesus in the lotus position somewhere in the east, making a sign with his hand. He said this rock shows the path to him."

Marika smiled furtively. She couldn't wrap her head around the fact that Michal, an educated man, had so much respect for all sorts of superstitions and legends. In fact, the inclination to believe in them was hers more than his. Despite this she apologized with a serious face. "I'm sorry, I couldn't have known it was so important to you. Forgive me."

"This rock is extremely valuable to me. As I said before, there are two. Totally identical. They were given to the archbishop by his predecessor who in turn received them from his predecessor. They're said to originate from India. They're unity rocks and they only work if two people touched by the same issue think about them at the same moment. It's said to be capable of miracles. After all, you could see for yourself."

"Michal, Miško… you know how much I love you but… I'm sorry but sometimes I feel you take your superstitions too far. Yes, I know faith was crucial in my… er… healing, but that doesn't mean I was helped by some rock which you prayed to here, and this Tomáš of yours in Israel, although he's a priest…"

"Did I hear you correctly? Are you blaming me for being superstitious? You, who meditates by a cross with a crucified Jesus every evening and morning?" But then he halted himself. "Sorry… maybe…" He wouldn't finish. He was now sitting by the computer and looking through incoming mail. Suddenly he almost jumped. "That can't be possible!" he exclaimed, staring at the screen and breathing heavily.

"What's the matter?" Marika called from the kitchen. "Has Adelka written?"

"No."

"She hasn't in a while. We should call her. Can you open Skype?"

"Yes, I can, but first take a look at this." He pointed at the email he'd just opened. It was from Tomáš.

"Sorry, I'll read it later, I must finish the soup now."

Michal stared at the computer screen in fascination. The message from Tomáš seemed to confirm that the rock really worked. The face of the gracious archbishop Athanasius, who'd given him and Tomáš the two mysterious rocks the year before, emerged from his memories. "They are keepsakes. They bring luck. But only if they are together. They do not have to be together physically; it is enough if their two owners are together mentally. When you have a problem or if a disaster or sickness is upon you, just think of this symbol. Unum. The principle, the path, and the goal." The archbishop smiled enigmatically as he handed them both identical flat rocks, about four by four inches each.

"Unbelievable, they're totally identical," Michal shook his head.

"They look like natural stone, but they are made of jasper from near Sarnath, the holy place where Buddha gave his first speech. If these rocks are in the right hands, they can bring those who own them to absolute awareness. They just must not be handled by anyone else. If either of the rocks gets into wrong hands, their power will be lost." It fully dawned on him that what Marika had surprised him with a moment ago he had already discussed with Athanasius.

"What's absolute awareness?" he'd asked the archbishop.

"That is the hardest thing we must undergo. It is understanding of one's self. Such understanding is a medicine; it liberates us, reminds us of what we once were when we were still in the light, when we stood at the beginning of things in unity, when we were human, perfect, pure as children."

"How can you attain such awareness?"

"That is a secret that will reveal itself when you find its symbol."

"Symbol? What symbol? And where do I find it?"

"Legend has it that there is a statue of Christ in India that Thomas the Apostle made and placed into Jesus' grave. Supposedly, it is Jesus in the lotus position. Just like this outline." He pointed at the barely perceptible silhouette of a long-haired man at the back of the rock.

"Thomas the Apostle in India?" Michal stared at him in surprise.

"Thomas is the patron saint of India, and he was the supreme spiritual representative of the Syrian Christian Church of Malabar, which is still widespread in Southern India today. It split from the Roman Catholic Church. It's even called Mar Thoma," Tomáš, the brand-new owner of an identical rock, cut in.

"Mar Thoma." Michal looked at his friend. "Thomas' Church. Named after you."

In a shaking voice, Michal shouted from the computer, "A miracle happened in Cana of Galilee!"

Marika watched him with one eye and noticed that he seemed absent-minded. "That's really some news you've got there... Everybody knows Jesus performed his first miracle there – turning water into wine."

"I didn't mean that one." Marika looked at him intently. "Tomáš writes that he was driving his old Fiat from Tiberias to Nazareth this morning. It was a hundred and four degrees in the sun and the asphalt on the road was scorching. Tomáš never checks his tire pressure and so unsurprisingly they were overinflated. He had an appointment in

Nazareth, but he was late as usual, so he was doing ninety miles per hour on the highway. His tires overheated on the blazing hot road and…"

"Oh my God, I hope he's all right," Marika exclaimed in fear.

"His front right tire burst."

"What happened to him?"

"Nothing fortunately. The tire burst just as he stopped at a red light at an intersection in Cana of Galilee." Then he frowned momentarily. "Marika… do you remember what time it was when I came with that rock from the trash can?"

"A minute past twelve."

"Are you sure?"

"I am. The man next door had just turned on the midday news on his radio at full blast."

"That can't be right," Michal contemplated. "Tomáš' tire burst exactly at that time."

Marika walked over to her husband and wiped her wet hands on the apron. She ruffled his hair and said quietly, "This morning, as I was praying, I don't even know why, but I remembered Tomáš. I prayed for his good health and that he may do well."

"Why? You don't even know him."

"I know what the guy means to you. You're my husband after all."

2   Templum Hierosolym

Mary's parents Joachim and Anne couldn't conceive a child for a long time, and Joachim swore that if God endowed them with a child, then they would raise it to be pious. When they had a girl, they named her Mary – based on the Hebrew Miriam, meaning *long-wished-for child*. As a three-year-old, they took her to a relative, the high priest of the Temple of Jerusalem, who instilled within her devotion to God. She was brought up in a girls' institution beside the temple. The school raised obedient temple servants as helping hands to perform tasks that weren't among the duties of Jerusalem's clergy. At the same time, the future servants were given an education. Mary often went to the Royal Stoa, where she learned religious ceremonies alongside other pious women. Deprived of her parents' guidance after their death and with a religious education which gave her next to nothing for life in the real world, she didn't have a clue about sexuality and love. That was why she puzzled over how and when she could have conceived when her aunt – her mother's sister Elizabeth – told her one day that she was in a certain condition. Only then did she begin to understand these things. She spent three months considering what to do to avoid ignominy while she stayed with her aunt, who was herself pregnant, and her uncle Zechariah in the village of Ain Karem not far from Jerusalem. In fact, she was at risk of being stoned to death for adultery. She eventually took to heart her aunt's advice to marry the widower Joseph, a renowned carpenter from Nazareth. The widower Joseph, who had sons Joseph, James, Judah and Simon and daughters Lydia and Lysia, wouldn't rush into a new marriage, but he agreed in the end. They married the year Emperor Gaius Octavius Augustus completed the eighteenth year of his rule. Mary was sixteen, Joseph thirty years older. He only learned that his fiancée was pregnant when she was in her fourth month. Five months later, they obeyed the Emperor's order to set out from Nazareth to Joseph's birthplace, Bethlehem, to fulfill their duty in the census, decreed in order to update tax registers.

About a million Jews had lived in Palestine for over half a century after the conquest of Jerusalem by Pompey's legions; they existed in the peace imposed by Rome. Cruel and scheming King Herod the Great ruled Judea, and as he wasn't even a Jew, he was hated by the population. But Rome was content with the peace in Palestine, a peace Herod secured through fear and terror. One of his first actions after he rose to power was to execute forty-five men out of the seventy-one-headed Sanhedrin, the Jewish judicial council. So afraid was he for his position that he had his two elder sons strangled out of fear of conspiracy, and his wife Mariam, their mother, put to death soon after. He issued an order to have another of his sons, Antipater, murdered five days before his own death. At the close of his life, the alcoholic ruler still managed to burn alive two popular rabbis – Judah and Matthew – along with forty of their followers.

At the peak of his rule he began an extensive reconstruction of the Temple of Jerusalem in an attempt to appease the public at least a little. To prevent laypeople entering the prohibited areas, he had a thousand priests trained as stonemasons and carpenters. The temple was completed in a record-breaking eighteen months. However, the reconstruction wasn't enough to satisfy Herod's delusions of grandeur, so he had it expanded, employing about eighty thousand workers from all over Palestine, who would work on the project long after Herod was dead. Master carpenter and stonemason Joseph of Nazareth spent many years working on the temple's construction. Although he was an old man now, he was still called to the site from time to time because he was a noted expert and advisor on temple and palace construction not only in Galilee, but also Phoenicia, Decapolis, Samaria and Judea. Shortly before the winter solstice on the 24th day of the month of Kislev, in the Jewish year 3761, he was again on the construction site. He was there by request of the royal grand master builder, who learned that Joseph was passing through Jerusalem on his way to Bethlehem, where he was headed along with his wife Mary and servant Ruth because of the census. The demanding construction of a wooden vault, on which the pillar stones rested, was managed by master Yohannan, but he too had to leave for three days, going to Jericho for the census. Joseph wasn't exactly ecstatic about the invitation as Mary was pregnant and about to give birth any moment.

However, he was persuaded in the end, and so he was there when they completed the construction of the gigantic pillars, the biggest ever built. King Herod donated a locket to each of the best masters to mark the occasion. It was shortly after noon when the grand master gave Joseph the locket on behalf of the King. Joseph was nervous because he had promised Mary and Ruth he'd come home to Ruth's aunt's house, where they were spending the three nights of their stay in Jerusalem, right after noon.

Joseph said his goodbye after the ceremony and hurried to get his wife. The grand master lent him a horse-drawn wicker two-wheeler for carting vegetables, to be returned on the way back to Nazareth.

Compared to the donkey which they had made the one-week trip from Nazareth on, the horse and cart was real comfort. Joseph wrapped Mary in a linen blanket and then he and Ruth joined her on the cart. They stored a waterskin, wineskin, some spare dresses and garments, a leather bag with flatbreads, dried goat meat, cheese, dried figs, and pomegranates and set out on the journey. The journey from the Temple to Bethlehem was a gentle, uphill trip of about four Roman miles, but it meant about two hours for the elderly mare.

As soon as they left the city via Zion Gate and hit Hebron Road, it started sleeting. Upon entering Bethlehem, Mary indicated to Joseph and Ruth that the child was beginning to ask for the light of day. Joseph hit the slow mare with a thick stick to speed up. They went from inn to inn, from house to house, but they were all occupied by people arriving in the city for the census. Finally, someone took mercy on them: Apsafar, an innkeeper. He put them up in his stables, cut into a rock behind the inn, for a few silver talents. As soon as they put some thick linen blankets on the straw Mary went into labor. Joseph and Ruth didn't even notice that it had stopped snowing. The child's cheerful cry was heard in the stables at the moment when an unusually bright star appeared in the clear night skies.

Mary had given birth to her first son. They named him Joshua ben Joseph. Joshua the savior, son of Joseph. As a keepsake for her son's birth, Joseph gave Mary the precious locket he'd been given by the King that day. It was made of a peculiar metal, with a six-point star on the obverse and two columns linked with an arch with the barely visible words, *Templum Hierosolym*, or Temple of Jerusalem, on the reverse. It warmed Mary's hand nicely in the cold stables.

Puloas, a tax collector, brought three mysterious strangers dressed in splendid, richly ornate robes into the cave. They had come to visit the newborn child. Nobody knew if they were with one of the numerous caravans passing via Bethlehem or if they had arrived with the intention of seeing the child. They dismounted from their horses, walked over to the crib and introduced themselves as wise men from Persia, Egypt and India.

The one they called Gastaphar (and whose real name was Gondophares) put gifts on the cold floor and spoke words that none except his two companions understood. "We have journeyed from distant lands and have brought your child gifts that represent the three values of human life in this world. The symbol of matter – gold; the symbol of mind – incense; and the symbol of spirit – myrrh. Let them accompany him on the road he is destined to take."

Mary allowed the strangers to cradle the child in their arms. At first, he tossed himself about restlessly in the warm arms of the sage Gondophares from the faraway city of Takshashila under the flanks of the Himalaya, but when the benign man pushed a drop of the myrrh resin in his tiny palm, the child stopped weeping and peacefully fell asleep. Upon witnessing the scene, Balthazar and Melchior looked at each other and smiled because they comprehended the mystery. Then they bowed with reverence before both Gondophares and the child. Mary accepted the gifts thankfully and, not knowing how to repay the wise man, she pushed Joseph's locket into his hand.

3 Mysterious Dream

That Saturday night would turn out to be the night when the most mysterious thing to happen in Marika's life occurred. It began with Michal's late phone call. He was calling from Košice, telling her that the forty-five-year school reunion had gone well. He was in high spirits and seemed to have forgotten the incident with the souvenir from Jerusalem. "We're taking the night train back with Kajo and Jožo, we'll be in Bratislava at seven in the morning."

"Don't eat on the train. Mrs. Lörincová has brought fresh eggs, you'll have some delicious scrambled eggs for breakfast." She was trying to be cheerful but failed. The lump in her breast was draining her good humor and energy. Since she had discovered that the cancer had returned, she tried hard to drive all dismal thoughts away; she didn't want to sadden Michal. Sometimes, when he lost his temper, she felt like reminding him of her suffering, but he was the guy with whom she had been walking down the path of her life for more than thirty years. "Excellent. I'm looking forward to the scrambled eggs and especially to seeing you. I love you," he remembered to add, as he always did when he was away from home. "Go to bed now, it's almost midnight. Bye."

Moments on her own always offered her an opportunity to stop, think, and go over the past days, months and years. That night, however, she had a lot of things on her mind. She couldn't fall asleep, so she listened to Chopin's piano concertos, which normally worked perfectly, but they didn't help this time. *The lump, the lump, the lump...* She played a CD with the sound of rain. The pitter-patter of raindrops falling on a lake surface put her in a strange mood. She went to the bar in the living room, poured herself a shot of fernet and sat in a deep antique armchair that Michal once brought from an antique shop in Nová Baňa. They had it mended, and it turned out to be a nice piece of furniture.

She settled down comfortably, opened the window slightly and lowered the sound because she felt the rain was whispering a little too loudly. Eventually, she turned off the player completely, but the sound of raindrops didn't subside. Only a while later, when half asleep, did she realize that the sound came from outside, where a violent downpour had started. *Funny, there hadn't be a cloud in the sky before.* Her sleepy glance strayed around the living room, one part of which was for guests and the other was Michal's study. It occurred to her that she'd never before sat in Michal's study alone like this. The shelves of his large bookcase were lined with Tibetan prayer flags, a bust of Socrates, a dried olive twig from the Garden of Gethsemane, an old pewter oil container he'd brought from somewhere in Turkey, a Chinese coolie's cap, and other souvenirs that reminded him of his travels around the world. He liked travelling, meeting new people, cultures, palaces, and most of all huts, where, as he himself put it, real life was to be found. She regretted she didn't travel with him, but her fear of flying was stronger than her desire to see foreign countries. She was all the more pleased to listen to Michal's stories and see his excellent photos when he returned from each trip. She found the flat rock she'd thrown out recently on the shelf with the five volumes of *The History of the World*. She gave it a long stare, as if something in it was attracting her.

"This is the symbol of Unity, the primordial home of us all," Michal's excited words resounded in her ears. She took the rock into her hand; it was small but surprisingly heavy. She noticed an equilateral cross with the horizontal line at a peculiar slanting angle. There was some lettering next to it, probably in Hebrew. The script was quite identical to that on the menorah, the seven-armed candleholder standing next to it. Michal had brought it from Bethlehem. The only word inscribed in Latin characters that she understood – *amen* – was in the bottom right corner. On the reverse of the rock she was surprised to see the six-pointed Jewish star and the famous symbol of Buddhism – yin and yang, the meaning of which Michal had explained to her several times. It expresses the illusion of duality that causes all the human suffering. The ultimate goal of Buddhism is to eliminate duality and restore unity in the world. The white dot at the center of the black lobe and, likewise, its opposite, the black dot at the center of the white lobe mean that either of the aspects of duality contains a seed of the opposite aspect. All that is good contains a seed of evil, and all that is evil contains a seed of good. Together, good and evil make a unity. Next to the symbol, there was some writing in a language whose script reminded her of curved Indian letters. At the center of the lettering was the barely visible outline of a long-haired man sitting in the lotus position that she'd noticed before. It seemed to her that his right hand was raised. The rock must be very old; the outline of the sitting man was barely perceptible. It was interesting that she noticed it immediately the first time she held the rock, even without Michal pointing it out. She was tossing the strange rock in her hands and thinking about her husband. Esotericism and mysteries had always been his hobby and he'd started taking an ever-keener interest in spiritual matters since his expedition to China, Nepal and India. In the bottom right corner, in exactly the same place as the word *amen* on the reverse, there was another symbol that she recognized thanks to Michal's explanation. It was the *Om*, or Aum, the most sacred syllable in Buddhism, symbolizing the infinite unity of the universe. She started repeating it to herself until it eventually seemed to her as if she wasn't saying om, but omen, or even amen. She realized how very similar in pronunciation these two mysterious words were. *As if they had a common root.* She put the rock back in its holder, where it had been inserted, and then she noticed that there was even some lettering on its bottom. It was in English. She turned up the light and read: *I remember, my brother, that when your sun rises, mine sets, when you are born, I die. J.* And another sentence right after that: *I remember, my brother, that when your sun sets, mine rises, when you die, I am born. B.* There was a single word next to the sentences: UNUM.

The rain was getting stronger, but the mysterious stone unsettled her more than the rain. She felt a gentle prick from her breast lump, so she poured herself another fernet. She felt better than she had in a long time. Moments spent with Michal rushed through her head. Undoubtedly the most beautiful moment had been half a year before, when she told Michal after he returned from his one-month expedition in Tibet that she'd fasted while he was gone and her breast cancer, which Michal hadn't even known about, had disappeared. She'd never forget the look on his face when she showed him all the medical confirmations and blood analysis results a few days later. There wasn't a trace left of cancer. Likewise, she'd never forget the night when he'd brought a bouquet of red roses and proposed to her. However, an uneasy feeling, a sense of the anxiety she had had when the little lump first appeared in her breast, had entered her soul recently. Thanks to prayer, a belief in the power of healing, and a forty-day fast she had avoided the operation and the cancer had gone, much to the physicians' astonishment. The advice of her friend Ľubka, who'd been through a similar ordeal, turned out to be effective. However, she abandoned the meat-free diet after some time and treated herself to a cigarette here and there. Her prayers and meditations became increasingly sparse. The lump in her right breast raised a warning finger…

Both the fernet and the rain began to take effect and Marika's mind plunged into sleep. In a half-dream state, she suddenly saw a strange case made of leather. It was immediately familiar to her: a leather casket with her mother's jewels. After her mother's death eight years ago, she'd put the casket at the bottom of a deep drawer in her desk, over time forgetting it. She came across it about a year ago while cleaning. That was when she first found out she had cancer. Michal was getting ready for a long trip to Tibet and Nepal, his dream journey, and she didn't want to thwart it. She knew he'd cancel the trip if she told him about the disease. Her friend Ľubka recommended a forty-day fast and getting rid of all old, needless things that prevent the flow of positive energies around the house. That was how she found the case with her mother's jewels and the precious locket. Since she never liked wearing jewelry, she put the case in a safe place and forgot about it over time.

The clock struck two and the monotonously pattering rain eventually put Marika into an uneasy sleep. She dreamed about her favorite kitten Heňa, which she used to play with as a child, but her mother spoiled her fun, as if on purpose, by calling her inside whenever she spotted her cradling the kitten. The kitten came to their yard less and less often until the day when a big black tomcat appeared.

The kitten left and never showed up again. The tomcat now appeared again, in her dream. She drove him away, but he only hissed at her. Then she was floating on a peculiar narrow boat down a very long, endless channel cut into deep rock. The channel was full of water, the passage was very narrow, and she was very afraid because she hated confined spaces. The channel then discharged into a lake; the moon was full; the moonlight illuminated the peaceful lake surface. She tried to row but no matter how hard she pushed the oar the boat remained stationary. A guffawing woman was standing behind her and hitting her on the back with a long stick, trying to move her on. She felt she was putting all her strength into the rowing, but the boat wouldn't move. After a while, she turned around and noticed that the stranger was her mother. She smiled, smoking cigarette after cigarette. She sat down next to Marika, put a pack of cigarettes on a low table and blew smoke in her face.

"Cancer's bad, that's what you deserve, shlomo…" she said maliciously, although her mouth was shut with only the cigarette clamped tightly between the lips. Marika waved her arms around, trying to blow the smoke away from her face. When it entered her lungs, she realized it wasn't smoke but some strange smell, a heady scent of roses, essential oil and lavender. Her mother was laughing, smoking and yanking her onyx-black hair from time to time. Yanking her hair was her mother's habit, but it humiliated Marika; all the kids in the yard mocked her for it. She began to suffocate; she coughed; she was terribly afraid that she would die. Her mother grinned in her face and kept repeating, "Cancer's bad, that's what you deserve, shlomo… Cancer's bad, that's what you deserve, shlomo…"

She tried to drive away the dream image of her mother, a mother with whom she'd never had a nice relationship until the day she died from cancer. She waved her arms around her, kicked, but her moves went right through the apparition's jeering face. She wanted to call for help, tried to scream, but her mouth wouldn't make a noise, only a muffled wheeze, as if she had lost her voice. She tossed about in her armchair, sweat breaking out on her forehead. And then the sound of a broken plant pot was heard. She twitched violently. A shattered pot with a sansevieria was lying on the floor. She realized that she must have hit it while she was struggling with her mother's apparition, and it broke on the parquetry. She gasped heavily; her mother's apparition had vanished, the night was over, the dream was gone. She opened her eyes.

Michal was standing over her. Her heart was pounding, but her husband's kiss on her hair calmed her. She hugged him firmly.

"Oh my God, is it morning already?"

"The fast train from Košice arrived on time and Jano drove me. What have you been doing here?"

"I couldn't fall asleep, so I listened to some music... I didn't drop off till early in the morning."

"You must've had a bad dream." He brought a broom from the kitchen and started sweeping the dirt and shattered shards. He straightened suddenly, smelling something; he sniffed and shook his head. "What's this fragrance?" Marika nodded. "Can you smell it too? It's like some essential oil. No, it reminds me more of roses..."

"It seems more like lavender to me." Marika inhaled the intense fragrance.

"Did you put on some perfume?"

"It's probably something outside..."

Michal went over to the window. Fresh morning air drifted into the living room from outside. He took a deep breath. "The air outside is fresh and clean." He gave her a suspicious look.

"How could I have put on perfume; you just woke me up?! Plus, I never had perfume like this."

"Yeah, that's weird. It's incredibly intense. It reminds me, wait... Where on earth have I smelled this?"

Marika took a deep breath. "I dreamed about my mother. For the first time in my life. She was smoking all the time, blowing the smoke in my face, only it didn't smell like cigarette smoke. It was this exact scent."

It suddenly dawned on Michal. When he realized where he'd smelled the fragrance before it made his flesh creep.

4 The Prophet's Judgment

The boy was circumcised according to Jewish custom in Bethlehem eight days after he was born. They went to Jerusalem after the circumcision staying with Ruth's aunt again. Mary and Joseph returned to the temple thirty days after the boy's birth, where they sacrificed two doves. A priest dressed in a white robe with a colorful belt performed the obligatory prayers and finished the rite of cleansing, followed by Jesus' salvation ritual for five shekels. After the payment, the priest raised the child above his head, holding him toward the shrine for a while before handing him over to Joseph. He in turn handed him to his mother. After this ritual, they were allowed by Jewish law to leave Jerusalem and they returned to the house on Marmion Road in remote Nazareth.

The boy grew, and, in spite of trying hard, Joseph couldn't win his stepson's heart for a long time. He'd have given anything for a single smile, a single display of filial love. It seemed as if someone had told the boy that Joseph wasn't his true father. No big or interesting job offers came so Joseph and the boy had to work hard repairing farm tools; only occasionally did they get to make some furniture in the joinery shop. The earnings hardly sufficed to sustain the family. An artisan's status was similar to a slave's in the eastern provinces of the Roman Empire at the time. Fortunately, Herod Antipas – son of Herod the Great – began a grandiose renovation of the capital of Galilee, known as Sepphoris, which had been destroyed by Romans in the immediate aftermath of his father's death. The town's renewal became the driver for the economy of Lower Galilee, which was one of the most densely populated areas of the Roman Empire at the time. Herod obtained money for renovating the town and other major construction projects not only from taxes but also from abundant sources of hardened resin on the coast of the Dead

Sea, as well as some leased tin mines in Cyprus. The modest cottage in Nazareth was shaken with excitement when Joseph was summoned to renew Sepphoris. He would take his son with him from time to time. The town of ten thousand lay on the important trade route of Via Maris, running from Syria to Egypt. Although Nazareth was only a ninety minutes' walk, the boy disliked the proud and rich town, full of hated Roman soldiers, who the conceited Sadducee priests and two-faced Pharisees curried favor with. The young villager looked with incomprehension at the townsfolk in lily-white togas promenading on streets paved with marble and limestone, leading to their majestic villas; their richly ornate silk robes scented with perfumes and expensive spices imported from China and India.

He preferred to avoid the place if he could. Instead, he studied the Torah in a modest synagogue, which was just a large cave in the rock rising above the center of Nazareth. His mother, herself educated in a temple school, was very fond of the boy's interest in education. She encouraged him and taught him herself. The boy, eager for knowledge, was filled with joy over David's psalms as well as Solomon's instructive statements. Rabbi Berechiah of Nazareth supported Mary with her son's religious education, and the synagogue warden, chazzan Elijah, also developed a liking for Jesus.

During morning and evening prayers he carried the scroll with the inscribing *Shema Yisrael* on his forehead and arms as his parents had taught him. As a seven-year-old boy, he knew the Israeli prophets' books by heart, and he had a particular liking for listening to adults disputing in the synagogue. They argued about how much a woman should be subordinate to a man, in which cases divorce was possible, as well as metaphysical topics so typical of Jewish scholars. Although Jewish boys were guided to debate and boldly present their opinions from early childhood, Jesus' unusual wisdom still surprised the elders.

During one such disputation he listened to a pointless controversy about whether it was unconditionally necessary to observe the exactly defined time for the lighting of candles before the start of a sabbath. This was possible when the sky was clear because the moment when the sun set could be determined accurately, but those present had a violent row about how to determine the sunset accurately when the sky was overcast. The dispute ignited when Jesus asked to speak. Everyone looked at the boy attentively, expecting one of his typically unconventional opinions.

He came up to the Torah table, bowed, and began speaking in a voice that was surprisingly strong for a nine-year-old boy.

"The Lord absolutely doesn't care if our sacred day starts a moment earlier or later! I mean the sabbath was made for people, not people for it!"

"Don't be blasphemous, God introduced the sabbath for Israel to give it a time to rest," his neighbor Amon interrupted him sharply; he'd had a long-standing dispute with Jesus' father over a patch of land by the caves.

"Of course, for Israel to have a time to rest, not to slave. Rabbis have made Jews slaves of the sabbath! They've achieved it with numerous instructions that they themselves invented, claiming they're from God." A murmur ran through the gathering.

"Why don't you quote a rabbi?" someone called to him.

"Because I have an intellect of my own, given to me by God, just like a rabbi." Jesus' speech fundamentally differed from the legislators and Pharisees, who always made circular references to the laws of the Mishnah, the Jewish collection of laws tried and tested over centuries.

"He speaks as if he had the right to interpret the law. But only rabbis have that right," Amon protested.

The men were accustomed to Jesus' straightforward talk, but they considered a young boy mentoring adults to be too audacious. Chazzan Elijah tried to calm him with a gesture, but Jesus continued boldly. "You look for the law in your books of writings, but you look in vain because writings are dead. Life is the law. Moses was given the law from God not as writings, but as living words. God's law is inscribed in everything that represents life. It's in the grass, trees, rocks, rivers, fish and birds, in earth and fire, but most of all, it's in you, because God loves everything that lives much more than your writings, which contain no life and which you made up by yourselves!"

"Don't be blasphemous, stop it!" someone yelled.

The boy went on dauntlessly. "God wrote his laws not on pages of books, but on the pages of your hearts, your souls. He gave you eyes and ears so you could see his deeds and hear his words, but you block your eyes and ears and listen to the words not of God but of priests, who have stood up in front of him and blocked him out. Man is the author of writings, but God made life and its beauty."

A hubbub and a stir broke out. "Well put," someone said. "Verily, the boy's right," another supported him.

"Stop him from speaking blasphemy in the house of God!" yet another yelled out.

However, with an extraordinary calmness that succumbed neither to praise nor to reprimand, Jesus spoke in a voice they couldn't but listen to, as if some magical force attracted them to him. "You don't enter the house of God yourselves, and you obstruct those who wish to!" The young boy from Nazareth grew so angry that, unwittingly, he shifted from Aramaic, which was the general language, to Hebrew.

"Stop, don't blaspheme any more, the Lord hears you and he won't forgive you for these words," Amon tried to stop him, likewise in Hebrew. "How dare you? I'm not going to listen to this," he raged and was preparing to leave. "I'm not going to participate in such blasphemy against the Lord and our prophets! A nobody, whom I'm sure we all know very well, an illegitimate bastard, will not lecture us." Other men nodded in agreement and followed him out.

Suddenly, Jesus stood in front of them with surprising boldness. "You say you know the words of the Torah by heart, but either you lie, or you deceive yourselves. What I said were not my words, but words of Isaiah about the guilt and punishment of Israel. If you judge me, you judge him. Which one of you has the right to judge a prophet?!"

5 You Must Go to the Grave!

It seemed that Michal wouldn't be going on the trip at all. He felt that everything was going wrong.

He had felt a strange uneasiness in his soul since the morning, like some unpleasant premonition. Something was telling him that he shouldn't leave home now, that he should stay with his wife. At the same time he couldn't wait for Tomáš and his night-time rambles down the alleys of the Christian, Jewish, Muslim and Armenian Quarters of Jerusalem, visits to the remnants of Solomon's Temple, the Wailing Wall, the Via Dolorosa, the Church of the Holy Sepulcher, the Citadel, the Mount of Olives, the Garden of Gethsemane, Mount Zion, Damascus Gate, and many other sights. But he felt that something was not right with Marika. His mood was also dampened by the fact that the travel agency had informed them that they would stay in Bethlehem instead of Jerusalem. It was still relatively close to Jerusalem, but he knew the conditions in Israel well enough to know that Bethlehem is in the Arab- occupied territory, which is separated from the areas inhabited by Jews with a wall that's taller and much more impenetrable than the Berlin Wall was in its time. The city is internally controlled by Palestinian police but walking there and back through the checkpoints inside the five-meter-tall wall is almost impossible. If he insisted on walking down the streets of Jerusalem's Old City at night, he would have to take taxis, which are incredibly expensive in Israel. And most importantly, his frequent crossings of the border might be suspicious to both sides, and he might be denied passage. Eventually, despite the heavy-hearted feeling, he decided to cancel the tour. The agent wasn't very happy either, but since the agency had violated the contract (changing the place of accommodation arbitrarily), they crossed him off their list without any cancellation fee.

Walking home from the travel agent, his humor was almost at its lowest ebb. He couldn't have suspected that the news he'd hear at home would spoil it completely. He was reluctant and unable to believe what Marika told him. When his wife had told him after his return from Tibet that she'd cured her cancer there was hardly a happier man on earth. His beloved wife's face smiled again, and her eyes were rekindled with their characteristic sparkle and cheer. The previous Christmas was the most beautiful they'd had together. Even Adelka and Hans arrived from faraway Sudan. His happiness would still be perfect if he hadn't started to notice that his wife was somehow devoid of energy, tired. Her weariness had escalated over the last two months; she'd done less and less of her favorite swimming and when she came back from the pool, she went to bed immediately. She also started to complain about constipation, she couldn't concentrate, stopped going out, even to her favorite teahouse. Her face had a portentous, fateful expression. He'd had a bad feeling but had been afraid to voice it out loud. He'd failed to muster the courage to ask her. Today she told him the terrible news.

When he came home, she was sitting at the kitchen table and rubbing her red eyes. "Have you been crying?" he asked, unsettled.

She sat silent for a while, then she started speaking slowly, "I have cancer."

Michal felt an electric shock run through him. He'd suspected he would hear those words one day, but wouldn't admit it to himself. He refused to even consider the idea that his beloved one could get that nasty, awful, repugnant disease again.

"You got rid of it!"

"It's back."

"How do you know?"

"I found a small nodule on my right breast by accident..." she said heavily and wiped her tears quietly.

"When?" He took her hand and stroked it gently.

"A month ago."

"After we shifted to raw food? You lost a few kilos and I thought it was because of that," he sighed.

Marika nodded. She was too ashamed to admit that sometimes she would secretly treat herself to her favorite Csabai sausage and she couldn't resist a cigarette while he was away on a business trip. "I thought it would go away, just as it went then. The weight loss stopped, even the stool got better, the nodule stopped growing. At least I thought so. The fatigue came back about a month ago…"

"But you held out so bravely, I didn't notice a thing," he lied.

"The worst thing was that it started to hurt. The pain grew stronger and longer."

"And then you shifted to raw food exclusively again."

"Yes, but it seems… it seems it doesn't help. I've seen the professor. He confirmed it was back. The cancer's back. He recommends an operation…"

She burst into tears. Michal embraced her and stroked her hair. He could have wept as well. He didn't know what to say, how to express himself so he just stroked her hand. The great joy that had entered their home after she had defeated the malicious disease turned out to be premature. "Oh well, we'll fight it. We'll be stricter on raw food – and I promise you will get through it. Imagine, I just read somewhere that not only Christ, but also Solomon and Buddha took the forty-day cleansing fast. We'll fight, and we'll overcome this disease. As if I had known… I just went to cancel the tour this morning."

"The trip to Israel?" He nodded. "But you can't do that! Michal, you must go!" she said in an unusually resolute voice.

"I'll go some other time. When you're better. Now I must be with you." He stroked her and kissed her on the eyes.

"But it was your dream trip, it's very important to you."

"There's nothing more important than you."

"Michal, fasting for forty days isn't easy but I'll try it again, only, it's more important to me that you go to Israel. You must go!" She raised her voice so much that he gave her an uncomprehending look.

"Why would I have to?"

"Because… you see… because of me."

"Because of you?" She nodded.

"Why?"

"You must go to the grave!"

6 Thou Shall Not Kill

Life in Nazareth, with a population of about three hundred, went on at its monotonous pace, with only the occasional stamping of the Roman soldiers' horses or stirrings from the hated tax collectors, referred to as customs officers, breaking the peace. Uprisings broke out in many places and thirty thousand Roman legionaries, mostly mustered from among Jews, Samaritans, Galileans and Syrians, who supervised over peace in Palestine, had a busy time. The largest part of the military was deployed in Syria; Judea had to make do with a tenth of the numbers deployed there.

Jesus and his siblings liked to sleep on the flat roof of their house, which the father and brothers had fixed only recently. He had his own nook there, which he missed so badly in winter when they all slept in the same room. Their whole family lived in a single room, divided into two areas. The lower area was home to their domestic animals, of which the young rams Ben and Shlomo were Joshua's favorites. They all ate and slept together in the elevated area of the room, on mats spread on the cold floor. Adjacent to it was a small kitchen with a fireplace and a kettle, several clay jars and a few pieces of tableware. They washed outside the house to prevent the clay in the room from becoming mud.

Spring was drawing near and the roof had to be reinforced with a new layer of clay and rolled compact before the rainy season. They lay reeds on wooden beams and topped them with thick layers of mud, which soon hardened to stone under the pitiless Palestinian sun. The boy couldn't wait till the spring, when life in the village moved to the roofs, where people ate, slept, talked to their neighbors, prayed, and even danced. With some palm leaves and four sticks, Jesus made himself a shelter from the blistering sun in one corner. He liked to sit in there, observing life in the yard and the adjacent village lanes from up above.

He watched women collecting water from the well with jugs and watering their gardens. He also liked watching the animals running around the yard. Artisans worked outside the houses in the street, attracting customers to their workshops in the process. His father too had part of his workshop in front of the house. Nazareth was renowned for its good carpenters and Joseph belonged among the best. He used to be a tekton – planner or architect of large projects.

Unfortunately, his best times, when the town of Sepphoris was erected, were over, and his strength was slowly waning too, so he had to make do with minor repairs of wheels, carriages, carts and coffers. He even rejoiced over the occasional order for several wooden beams to be used for crosses from the Roman administration. It wasn't his favorite job, but he had seven hungry children to feed. Along with vices and anvils, he had carpentry tools laid out on wooden workbenches, and chisels of various sizes, saws and axes were hanging in brackets on the wall. Although Joseph was very particular about tidiness, the stone-paved floor of his workshop was constantly strewn with sawdust and shavings. According to tradition, the father tried to encourage his son to take up the same profession as he himself had, but the restless Jesus didn't like the monotonous work in the shop; when he wasn't at school in the synagogue, he helped his mother milk the goats and sheep and watched her as she made cheese from the milk. He liked grinding grain in the stone mortar; his mother turned the resulting flour into new dough together with a pinch of salt and a bit of yesterday's dough, used as the leaven. Sometimes he himself would mix it and put it away for a few hours to rise, then formed flat breads and put them into the bread oven in the yard. He and his father had built it from stone, which was abundant in the yard outside his carpentry shop.

What he liked the best though was going to school and the synagogue. He was the most gifted pupil of the bet ha-sefer, the primary school in which his mother had enrolled him at the age of five, as tradition commanded. The teacher – chazzan Elijah, popular with the children – wrote the twenty-two letters of the Hebrew alphabet on a wooden board covered with wax at the start of the lesson; they would all repeat them. Jesus had long since known them, so he read the Torah, which Elijah illustrated with many interesting similes for them, by himself. At the age of ten, he went to the upper class, known as the bait Talmud – or the House of Wisdom, as the adults called it – where learning of the Torah was extended with learning of the Mishnah, a set of laws explaining the

Torah. The pupils debated fiercely with the teacher, and the blue-eyed son of Joseph the carpenter excelled in asking questions. The children would often laugh out loud when he confused the old chazzan with his queries.

Hillel, the famous rabbi and teacher from Jerusalem and a friend of rabbi Berechiah, arrived in Nazareth. The old wise man stayed in the school for a few days, debating with the pupils. "I can't believe my own eyes and ears, my dear friend. Who is that boy?" Hillel asked his colleague Berechiah in disbelief.

"He's a son of Joseph and Mary; she used to stay at the Temple School in Jerusalem for some time. Their son is the prophesied 'God with us' – Emmanuel, but we call him Jesus. He's so wise for his age that there have been rumors he's not from this world. He's the best pupil I've ever had in the House of Wisdom," Berechiah praised the boy.

"So, you are a son of Joseph the carpenter, of David's lineage." Hillel stroked Jesus' curly hair once he came at his bidding. Jesus was silent. "Aren't you proud of being of that lineage?"

"They say I'm not his son."

"You're King David's descendant, as is your father!"

"Everyone extols David for having killed the Philistine Goliath, but they don't mind my father and all his ancestors originating from David's adultery with the wife of Uriah – who he had killed to be on the safe side," the boy raged.

"You know about such things?"

Jesus didn't reply to Hillel's question; instead, he asked about something that didn't give him a moment's peace. "Teacher, we're taught the Ten Commandments. Why did my father have to cut a lamb's throat yesterday if Moses says in the Commandments 'Thou shall not kill!'?" the boy burst out.

Hillel stopped to think; he wasn't accustomed to his Temple students asking him such questions to which even his friend Berechiah often couldn't find an answer. Chazzan Elijah didn't want the rabbi to struggle with Jesus' question, so he started reading. "Moses speaks clearly: Whenever you want to, you can kill and eat meat in any of your gates, with the blessing of the Lord, your God."

"But that means Moses contradicts himself. Which scripture is the right one then?"

"When God said, 'You shall not kill!' he was referring to people. Killing animals is permitted."

"Chazzan Elijah, I wonder whether you aren't distorting God's Commandments. The Scripture says clearly, 'You shall not kill!' not 'You shall not kill a human being!'"

"My boy, don't blaspheme. Does the Scripture not teach us that God gave Moses the Ten Commandments on two tablets of clay on Mount Sinai? Are you questioning God himself?" Elijah raised his voice.

"I'm not questioning God. God is the most impeccable good, which is why He commanded people not to kill," Jesus answered calmly.

"Sacrifice to God is an obligation for a Jew," Hillel tried to appease him.

"Doesn't Moses say, 'You shall bring God all that He commands you to: your offerings combustible and for killing, your tithes and levies, and the best of the gifts that you have promised to your Lord? What is it you don't understand here?" Berechiah asked him.

"We don't pay the tithes to the Lord but to priests of the Temple of Jerusalem. The temple that High Priest Annas has turned into a private marketplace and exchange office!"

"Stop blaspheming, or I'll have to invite your father before the council in the synagogue," Berechiah rebuked him.

"Leave the boy alone, what he says has its logic. The Law really only says, 'You shall not kill'," Hillel shook his head.

But Jesus stood there sad and sighed heavily. Berechiah felt sorry for him. He went to him and gave him a friendly pat. "All right then, I won't tell your father anything," he soothed the boy, "but be careful about your tongue. Your reputation is bad enough as it is for your constant criticism of the Scripture." Jesus burst into tears. "Come on, Joshua, you're a man, you won't cry for an animal."

"I'm not crying for an animal. I'm crying for your hypocrisy."

"Son, you are very well-read and wise for your age. Have you heard about my Academy?" Hillel asked him suddenly.

Jesus wiped his tears on a sleeve and sat up. "Of course I have."

"And would you like to study there?"

"Hillel's famous academy of law and thought?" The rabbi nodded. "But I'm too young for that," he objected.

"Who we admit is decided by the senate, of which I am the chairman. What do you say? Will you switch to my Jerusalem school if I arrange it with your parents?"

Instead of a reply, the boy threw himself in the rabbi's arms so violently that he nearly knocked the old man over.

7 Secret Angels

In an inconspicuous building on a street in Rome, aptly named Via dei Cherubini after a particular choir of angels, the headquarters of one of the most influential secret services in the world is located. It is subject to no parliamentary control, it does not report to any democratically elected government, and its greatest advantage is that no one assumes its existence. While passing by the mysterious building, people only whisper in fear that it is the seat of secret angels. Who would have thought that the institution entrusted to disseminate Christ's gospel, with all his goodness and love needed a secret service? If it has one it proves that something may not be right about the dissemination of God's word. Or maybe that's not even the point. Secret services have always been, and will always be, a fundamental instrument of powerful institutions such as states, big multinational corporations or giant firms, which need such services to protect their power and undermine others'. The SIV – Servizio Informazioni del Vaticano – has only a little over a hundred members, mostly recruited among Jesuits and Benedictines, but they are perfectly trained. To the outside world they have no ranks, addressing each other with dignity as brothers.

Three of them – brothers Maximilian Hausser, Carlo Toti and Felix Kruger, employees of the fourth department specializing in combating heresy – were quietly sipping Mauro coffee, something of a domestic brand among the SIV staff, in a patio shaded by a giant plane tree. The weather was lovely, and no one was in a hurry. They were in a good mood, which improved even more when the fifty-something Maximilian, the oldest of the three brothers who had been recently promoted to lieutenant colonel for outstanding merit in combating heresy, said with a smile: "So, this Michal Kráľ has checked out of the tour. A few days before the departure. Odd, don't you think?" He looked at his two colleagues.

"Why odd? They were supposed to stay in Jerusalem and the plans changed, so he gave it a miss," Carlo dissented.

"I don't like it. What if he found out something at the last moment?" Maximilian thought out loud.

"You mean from this Dvoran?" Felix burst out.

Carlo Toti gave him a surprised look and turned back to Hausser. "You've been overly suspicious since you became lieutenant colonel. At least I can go on holiday."

"Remember, we used to have ranks in Global Power. I'm brother Maximilian now," Hausser frowned. Then he added more calmly, "This guy is no ordinary tourist. Have you forgotten what he did to us when we were still with Global Power?"

"That was different. He had the perfect organization backing him then, now he's alone and I'm certain he doesn't know anyone on the tour."

"Excellent, that means a shorter shift for us," Carlo lit up.

"Not quite. Our friends in Mossad also confirmed they had intercepted communication between Kráľ and the rebellious priest."

"This Tomáš Dvoran?" Carlo asked. The lieutenant colonel nodded. "The one we put the screws on to collaborate?"

"Yes. But Mossad information confirms he isn't lying."

"Are you saying we cooperate with Mossad?" Felix said in a surprised tone, joining the discussion.

Maximilian and Carlo laughed heartily. "Dear brother Felix, you really are a novice and you show it. Otherwise you would know that the Vatican and Israel have a great understanding when it comes to intelligence matters. After all, why not? Our top bosses are all Jews," Maximilian smiled.

"But Popes aren't Jews!" Felix protested.

"Hitler had Jewish blood as well. You never know… And who says Popes? I'm talking about Jesus, Mary, Joseph, Peter, Paul, Jesus' disciples… Even your Judas was a Jew." Felix gave a bitter smile. "When the Holy Father visits the Middle East, Israeli boys help us a lot. We've also lent them a hand. Have you heard about the Meir case?" Felix shook his head. "Mossad owes us a favor since that case."

"Well, I haven't heard about that one, and I've been in service for some time," Carlo nodded.

He passed the answer to Brother Maximilian – or Lieutenant Colonel Hausser, a one-time deputy to the chief commander of the Vatican Guards and successor of Alois Estermann, who was unmasked as a former spy of the East German Stasi and found dead alongside his wife on May 4, 1998. Hausser began, "One day in January 1973, an unregistered airplane took off in Paris in the early morning. It was supposed to fly to somewhere in Africa, but it made an unexpected layover in Rome. An inconspicuous car with Pope Paul VI's personal secretary was awaiting the airplane on a remote taxiway. The Pope asked for a brief meeting with the Israeli Prime Minister Golda Meir, travelling on the plane. Although the meeting was strictly classified the Palestinians learned about it. Two Fiat station wagons approached the plane, carrying five men from the Black September Organization armed with Russian surface-to-earth missiles. They were determined to destroy the plane along with Prime Minister Meir."

"Isn't Black September the group responsible for killing the eleven Israeli athletes at Munich in 1972?" Felix asked.

Maximilian nodded and continued, "But they didn't know they were being followed by Mossad agents, who had been informed by our Brother Angelo Casoni. While they were being handcuffed, Mrs. Meir had a nice thirty-minute talk with the Pope and then left for Africa. Well, all kinds of things happen in our job," he smiled.

"Hell, if that's all true…" Felix shook his head.

"I don't see what is so surprising. Pope Pius XI even signed a concordat with Nazi Germany which ordained a bishop's vow of loyalty to the Nazi regime. When Nazi Germany was defeated, the Vatican successfully intervened to prevent the war criminal von Papen, head of the Catholic Center, from being tried before the Nuremberg tribunal. It was the Vatican that protected war criminals, smuggling them safely to exile. 76 percent of the SS, the murderous Nazi military group, were practicing Catholics."

Felix took a breath and tossed some soothing whisky down his throat. "Let's say I didn't hear any of that."

"Dear Brother Felix, do you know what the SIV actually is? Look at the symbol of our institution. Its centerpiece is the monogram IHS. It may mean Iesus Hominum Salvator – Jesus the Savior of Humans, but it can also be altered to Iesum Habemus Socium – Jesus is Our Ally. It's the symbol of the Jesuits, the Pope's most loyal servants. Or, to be exact, the Pope's soldiers. Jesuits were the Church's military secret service, searching for heretics above all. We've essentially continued their mission to this day, and we've been fulfilling it successfully together with our Dominican brethren. Dear Felix, you still have a lot to learn with us." The lieutenant colonel smiled and slapped the novice on the shoulder. "But let's get back to the point. Although Král' seems to have come to his senses since he came back from Nepal and India, I wouldn't underestimate him. We monitor and analyze each step he takes, his statements, articles, interviews that he gives; they're full of malevolent statements aimed at the Vatican, the Holy Father and some of the clergy."

"He makes fun of faggots and pedophiles in the cassock, I quite like that," Felix laughed.

"Dear Brother Felix, when we pursued him through Himalayan valleys and Indian mosques back with Global Power you weren't in service yet. This guy is extremely dangerous. He maintains contact with so-called peace powers, who are nothing but a conglomerate of scumbags trying to upset the established existing world order. And do you know what the fundamental pillar of stability in this fragmented world is? Our Catholic Church! That's why I won't allow anyone – anyone, do you understand – to even faintly threaten the stability of the Holy See! We have enough problems as it is, there's no need for enemies outside as well."

"What terrible plans does this former rocker have up his sleeve?" Felix asked.

"Well, just you tell him," Maximilian invited Brother Carlo Toti.

Toti fumbled for words for a while. "How could I... We think they aim at uniting the world's religions. Their motto is UNUM. It means One. Oneness is their basic mission. Its symbol is the number one. It's a long-term project; we found out they call it Code 1."

"The Church has been in real danger since its establishment. There've been so many reconcilers of religions, and there will be, pah... Don't exaggerate, gentlemen," Felix laughed cautiously. "Why would they bother us, combaters of heresy?"

"Probably the two things seem close to them. It must be serious when the most elite section of our Servizio has been entrusted with it," Maximilian said gravely. "Brothers, can you imagine what would happen if these scoundrels really united one day? What implications it would have for the Holy See and for us? Christianity would be done for!" he added, banging his fist on the table.

"But really, you can't be serious about this," Felix protested.

"We're dead serious about it. The point is Jesus' grave in Srinagar. That is – supposed grave," he corrected himself smartly. "We have information from Dvoran that they speak about the possible existence of such a grave in all seriousness. After all, Kráľ has declared publicly that he's going to try to visit the tomb. Do you understand what evidence from Roza Bal would mean for us?" Hausser lifted his eyebrows menacingly.

"From what?" Felix inquired.

"Roza Bal is the name of the tomb in which Christ is buried according to statements by multiple experts. So far, we've managed to eliminate every attempt to collect any samples for DNA analysis. So far..."

"We nearly went down in '78," Toti remarked. The novice Kruger gave him an uncomprehending look. "London Muslims held a world conference *Deliverance from the Cross* in June. It was attended by over fifteen hundred people from all around the world."

"All mad, I'm sure," Felix objected.

"You're wrong. The congress was chaired by the former chairman of the UN Security Committee, Pakistani Foreign Minister Zafarullah Khan. Fortunately, we managed to prevent the attendance of the principal witness Professor Fida Hassnain, head of the archaeological center of the government of Kashmir, the only one to have examined the tomb. The government took away his passport at the last moment. The Kashmiri government compensated for it a little later by giving the old gentleman a state medal."

Hausser tapped his fingers on the table nervously. "We mustn't underestimate Kráľ. What he did to us in Tibet with his buddies, those wretches, must be a warning to us. One of our best people disappeared mysteriously and the other one had to be... Ahem... But we'll destroy them right at the root and whoever collaborates with him! We won't leave any of them standing, I swear! Or my name isn't Hausser!" he yelled in a fit of anger. His thick, slightly grizzled eyebrows rose and fell in with the rhythm of his wild gesticulation.

Carlo and Felix sat silent and waited for his anger to subside. Once he calmed down, he tossed a shot of whisky down his throat and breathed heavily. "What does J.B. stand for?" Felix asked quietly.

"May I?" Carlo looked at the lieutenant colonel questioningly and was given a nod. In a calm tone, Toti began to explain for his younger colleague. "When King Solomon had the temple in Jerusalem built, he put two columns by the east gate. To the Jews, the columns represented a royal, indestructible power, joined by an arch symbolizing the heavens. They called the arch shalom – peace. The temple builder Hiram installed the bronze column 'J' – Joachim – to the right of the gate, and the column 'B' – Boas – to the left. They say the initials were derived from the names of Jesus and Buddha. The columns symbolize the two greatest personalities in history and teaching. When the two columns are symbolically joined again, the longed-for UNITY will prevail in the world. Everything will again be joined in ONE – human races, religions..."

"Understand? Do you get this?" The lieutenant colonel nearly pounced on Felix. "These cockroaches have the unification right in their symbol. The initials J.B. are cursed!"

Felix smiled. "Interesting what you're saying. There is only one thing about it, they couldn't have known anything about Buddha, or Jesus, in Solomon's times; they didn't exist back then."

"And what about the prophets in the Old Testament? Jesus didn't exist in their times either and yet he was prophesied! No, no, dear Felix, don't laugh this off, or I'll eventually think you're some kind of a secret angel amongst us..."

"I'm sorry, boss, I don't get you."

"I'm saying you're one of them too!" the lieutenant colonel said and looked Felix in the eyes speculatively.

"I insist on you not saying that, commander!"

"Alright then, enough for today. Since Král' has cancelled his trip to Israel I'm tentatively calling off our plan. Carlo, you can go on your holiday. If anything happens, Felix here is in charge of the matter while you're gone."

Carlo smiled. He flew out on his long-wished-for holiday in the Bahamas the next day.

8 The Wisdom of the East

The week's toil was interrupted by the yearned-for Friday sunset, initiating the sabbath, the Jews' mandatory rest from any work. The blowing of the shofar, used by the chazzan to announce the end of work, was Jesus' favorite sound. He would stand on the roof and twist his head up to the sky longingly, waiting for the first three stars to appear and the sharp notes of the ram's horn to summon people for prayer. He had experienced few such moments in the last three years: he spent most of the time in Hillel's academy in Jerusalem and only came to Nazareth for vacations or certain holidays. Nazarenes didn't hide their jealousy of their talented compatriot, a student at the elite Jerusalem Academy, which hosted not only Jews but also Greeks, Phoenicians, Armenians, Egyptians, Moabites, Nabateans, Babylonians and Persians; there were even a few young Indians among the students. Once he reached thirteen years of age and was admitted as a full member of the religious community, he was allowed to read from the Scripture in the synagogue. In the ceremonial rite of Bar mitzvah, he pledged himself to the law, which meant that if only nine men came to the synagogue, he could add himself to make ten for the service to start. From the age of thirteen, responsibility for his actions passed from his parents to him. Although Jesus was an 'academic', he would spend Saturday services, when worshippers gathered in the synagogue and occupied the pews along the stone walls, alongside his peers on the floor, which was pleasantly cool, especially in the hot summers. A lectern with a seven-armed menorah stood in front of the wall facing Jerusalem. The room, lit with the menorah candles and olive torches, looked magical. Jesus listened to the Torah reading, translated from Hebrew to the generally used Aramaic after every three sentences. Since the dispute with his neighbor Amon four years earlier, he felt that some of the men, even his friends, shunned him now. They certainly did so at their parents' bidding. Some Jewish fathers and mothers incited their children to turn against him because of his friendship with some Samaritan boys, who made up a non-Jewish minority in Nazareth.

"Everyone who was born as a Jew will enter the Kingdom of Heaven automatically," the rabbi said in a calm voice. The entire gathering listened to him carefully. "Pagans first have to convert to Judaism to be entitled to the Kingdom. The Scripture says that Abraham sits by the gate of hell, intercepts every Jew that has been sent there and saves him."

"And what if that Jew is a bad person?" Jesus' excited voice resonated in the synagogue. The men looked at him in surprise. "Will he go to the Kingdom of Heaven even then? The Scripture in fact teaches us that only good and brave people will enter our Father's Kingdom. Who is more likely to enter the Kingdom, a bad Jew or a good Samaritan?"

"Well," rabbi Berechiah pondered this difficult question, "I think that because we are the people chosen by God, it is more likely that a bad Jew will enter…" he replied unconvincingly.

"But then you deny the words of the Scripture, which encourages us in almost every word of every psalm to be good. Do the Proverbs not say that the bad ones will stray outside the Kingdom?" the young boy asked passionately.

Everyone in the synagogue turned their eyes on the nervous rabbi who evaded a reply. "Dear Joshua, stay behind after the service, we'll talk." Being an Essene, he found it unwise to stray off topic; deep in his heart he agreed with Jesus, but he knew that most of the listeners were Pharisees and a handful of Sadducees, and he didn't want to make them angry. The men were ostensibly displeased by Jesus' questioning and wouldn't let him say the Haftarah, excerpts from books of prophets, normally a great honor for every young man. Quite to the contrary, they asked him to leave the House of Prayer. Once the service was over, the rabbi came out of the synagogue and sat next to Jesus, who was sitting on the steps deep in thought.

"Don't bother yourself with it, they have the right to do that. And, after all, it wasn't the first time it happened to you."

'They're hypocrites,' Jesus thought. *'They go to the synagogue not to communicate with God but because it's the custom. They sit up front so that others can see them. They say the Lord's Prayer, but they*

understand none of it. They think the louder they shout the words of the Scripture the sooner the Kingdom of Heaven arrives. Yet they sin as soon as they leave the synagogue, insulting God with their plea to Him to lead them not into temptation – as if God was evil and tempted people! The priests interpret the Lord's words not the way he meant it, but the way that suits them. They frighten us with sin all our lives, but I refuse this interpretation. Constant remorse makes people ill instead of enjoying life, singing and rejoicing.'

He leaned over to the rabbi, who embraced him like a father. "I've been thinking of many things that bother my soul. Tell me, were Adam and Eve the first people that God created?"

"Of course they were."

"But the Scripture says that when our Lord marked Cain on the forehead, he left his presence for the land of Nod east of Eden."

"Correct."

"But the same Scripture says that in the land of Nod Cain met his wife, who conceived and gave birth to his son Enoch. Where did that woman come from if you say that Eve was the first one?"

"Hillel told you that his Academy will teach you to think, but he didn't tell you that a thinking person has trouble for life."

"So, you don't know either…"

"What's this you have against priests?" Berechiah tried to change the topic. "I'm a priest too. Would you say I deceive?"

"Tell me teacher, is the Temple in Jerusalem God's temple?"

The rabbi knew the boy's way of thinking, and he immediately asked himself what his question was driving at. "You mean, is it meant for worshippers or merchants?" Jesus nodded. "I know, it's terrible what the priests have made of the temple. They've turned the whole area into a private trade zone."

"I learned in the Academy that the revenue from the moneychangers' business and the sales of sacrificial animals go to High Priest Annas," Jesus shook his head in disgust. "My brothers and sisters couldn't have soup because our parents had to sacrifice turtledoves to the temple. That's unfair; God will punish Israeli priests for that one day."

Berechiah said nothing, because he knew the boy was right. People – Essenes in particular, as well as many Sadducees and Pharisees – had expressed growing displeasure with the disgraceful abuse of the temple for priests' enrichment.

"Priests command us to listen to them and their decisions on who shall go to the Kingdom of God after death. I think they are preventing us from building the kingdom here on earth. Giving love is enough."

The rabbi smiled and stroked Jesus' hand with kindness. "You're a great idealist, but you're right. If we gave out love instead of hatred, we would all be happy. Only it's not that simple. To teach people to give out love is probably impossible," he contemplated.

"Why? All you have to do is set an example."

"You're my young savior of the world," the rabbi smiled.

"Only life is real, only love is eternal, and nothing can destroy it. They teach us about a punishing and merciless God, but I think He's kind, benevolent and forgiving. God doesn't want to punish us; he wants to help us. God can't force his way into our hearts by punishment, because by doing that, He'd infringe on our freedom, which he gave us at the creation." The rabbi looked at him silently. "That's the words of our dear rabbi Hillel."

"I hear his condition is serious."

"It seems that the rabbi's return to the Father has slowly begun. He lies all day; he can no longer walk. But still he's our most beloved teacher," Jesus said in a sad voice.

"He's our nation's greatest living sage. You couldn't get a better teacher." The rabbi gave him a friendly pat on the shoulder. But Jesus showed no signs of joy. "Do you have a problem?" Berechiah asked.

"Erm... how should I tell you... Yes, rabbi Hillel and his Academy are great, only... well, we keep repeating the Psalms, the Proverbs, the Talmud endlessly. It's fine, but I'd like to know more. I feel that wisdom is not only in Jerusalem and our prophets' books. I'd like to learn more."

"What do you mean in particular?" Berechiah looked at him.

"The Wisdom of the East."

9 The First Miracle

Marika pressed Michal's hand so tightly that her fingers went white. "You must go to Jesus' grave," she stressed.

"But Marika, why does it make you so agitated? I'm not going now; I'll go another time."

She was silent, then said quietly, "Another time may be too late. Michal, please, do it for my sake. For the sake of my sickness." She thought for a while and then said resolutely, "I've felt better in the last few days, I haven't been so tired, I'll go with you."

"You know it'd please me more than anything, but even if we wanted to, we can't anymore. I cancelled and there are no more free places on the tour."

"I'm sure you can get one more place!"

"It's pointless staying in Bethlehem. But if you insist, maybe my place is still free. If you feel well, I can give the travel agent a ring right now."

"Well…" she hesitated for a moment. "No, I'm not going without you. I wouldn't dare to."

"Tomáš is there. He'll take care of you; he has contacts, he knows everyone in Israel. He can arrange the best doctors if something should go wrong."

"No, no," she considered. "I'm not going without you. Michal, Miško, please call the agency and tell them you've changed your mind."

He looked at her in astonishment. "Why does Jerusalem matter so much to you?" She rubbed her palms together nervously as if she wanted to tell him something but wasn't sure if confessing her thoughts to him was the right thing to do. "Don't worry, our faith in you overcoming this illness will get you through it. Maybe the one up there just wants you stronger than others so he's put a heavier burden on your shoulders than on the rest's. Take the disease as a challenge. God seems to be giving you a real helping. I think he knows what that's for. Maybe He has a purpose for you; he needs you to be strong. Marika, you must have faith and you'll succeed! You've healed yourself once, you will heal yourself again," he tried to convince his wife, but he wasn't sure if she could muster enough inner strength, willpower and faith once again.

"If I had healed myself, I wouldn't have fallen ill again. I'm not strong enough for another forty-day fast. I don't think I have it in me. I feel, I feel… I've lost trust in all these alternative methods." She cast her eyes down and tears slowly rolled down her cheeks. "And the doctors have recommended chemotherapy, radiation and all their usual methods. I've decided not to undergo that. It just doesn't make sense. They haven't saved anyone yet, they only torment people pointlessly."

"It came back because you reverted to a meaty diet." She shrugged. "You didn't protest either."

"I thought… I thought you're an adult and you know what you're doing," he said quietly. "But that doesn't matter, we won't give up. We'll go on a meat-free diet again, this time we'll be strict about it." Suddenly there was a flash in his eyes, as if he remembered something important. "And besides, I'll get you some special medicine from Tibet. They say it's a miraculous traditional cure for cancer. It's been used successfully to save thousands of kids after the Chernobyl disaster." He was trying to encourage his wife, but she stared at him with a bitter smile of futile comprehension and gratitude. "I'm absolutely serious."

"Okay, Miško, I'll give it one more try. Raw food. Totally raw. Just vegetables, fruit, tea, juices, nuts, cereals. It won't be easy, but I'll give it a go. But I have one request for you." A strange glow emanated from her moist eyes.

"Great, excellent," Michal rejoiced. "I'm with you all the way and I hereby declare I'm going on a raw food diet." He came up to his wife and kissed her on her hair, which was showing ever more grey strands. "I'll do whatever I can for you. What do you want?"

"Let's go to Jerusalem. Please register for the tour again. I want to meditate by Jesus' grave." Michal pondered for a moment. "You can do that peacefully only at night, if you're very lucky. Tomáš writes the place is crowded with tourists by day. And we won't be able to get from Bethlehem to Jerusalem at night."

"It's meaningful, even if I should only spend five minutes by his grave," she said, excitedly. "You may find it weird, but something's telling me this place is the key to me getting better. I apologize, Michal, I must seem like a superstitious old hag, but... I can't explain why, I just feel that my condition can only improve if I engage in deep, wholehearted mediation by Jesus' grave."

"Marika," he reproached her kindly, "but Jesus' grave is not in Jerusalem!"

"I know they say he rose to the heavens. But at least the tomb where he was laid to rest is there." Michal realized that a person in her position is ready to believe in anything that could be of help. Maybe the Church of the Holy Sepulcher was a placebo that would really help. "I don't understand it much, but if you believe in it..."

"Sorry, I do believe. And I'll also put my prayer in the Wailing Wall."

Michal was going to object, but he realized Marika had said the amazing word 'believe'. He smiled. "I believe it, too."

She looked at her husband and then slowly took his hand in hers. "They say... they say... that if you put your wish in the Wailing Wall God will surely fulfill it for you. Back when you were in Tibet and I cured myself of cancer..." She wanted to add something, but Michal interrupted her.

"...you were helped by your will, raw food and the fast that Ľubka advised you to try. You yourself said that she'd cured herself in the same way. Only you made a little mistake after that."

"I didn't tell you the whole story. It just so happened that Ľubka was traveling to Jerusalem at that time and she put my prayer in the Wailing Wall. I believe... that is, I believed, that I was cured not only by the raw food but by the prayer as well." She observed her silent husband. "Don't you meditate, don't you pray? Isn't your room full of all kinds of symbols? The meaning of rituals is not logical but symbolic. They symbolize our desire, faith and hope."

"But Marika, to believe in some kind of miraculous cure by means of a slip of paper in a wall... I'm sorry..."

They both fell silent. Then Marika continued, "Back when I had the disease the first time, Ľubka took my slip of paper to Jerusalem. She put it in a crack in the Wall and..."

"It couldn't have helped that much, as it came back," Michal said in disgust. "Ľubka's has returned as well," she said quietly.

"What?" Michal almost exclaimed.

"She told me a week ago."

"And what's she gonna do?"

"She's resigned to it. She's going to have an operation and then chemotherapy." Michal said nothing. "I know what you're going to say. I'm not going to have any operation! No way. Once they meddle with your body metastases get into your blood and you're done for. No thanks! I believe faith works. I believe! There's just been a mistake. I think I know where…"

Michal gave her a questioning look. "Where?"

"Ľubka should've gone to Jesus' grave instead of the Wailing Wall." She slowly reached to her neck and unclasped a locket she was wearing on her neck. Michal had never seen it. She handed it to him. "Look what I found. It can't be a coincidence."

Michal studied it with interest. "What is it?"

"A locket. I found it in my mother's forgotten casket, in her suitcase. When you came back from Košice, in that dream I had… I dreamed I saw a casket of jewels in an old suitcase under the basement stairs. I'd forgotten where I'd put it. I only found it thanks to the dream."

"Marika, please forgive me, but this is mad!"

"Michal, did you smell the strange fragrance in the room when you came back?" He nodded. "There you go! Where did the fragrance come from? In that dream my mother was in our living room smoking all the time… and blowing out that fragrance."

Michal stared at her for a long time. "Are you saying that…"

"I'm not saying anything, only that we could both smell the scent of roses and lavender very clearly." Lost in thought, Michal turned the locket over in his hand. A strange warmth emanated from it in spite of it being made of metal. "Warm?" Marika asked with a smile. He nodded. "They say it's made of a strange metal; nobody knows its composition."

"Have you had it tested?"

"No, my mother told me not to."

"Why did you never mention it to me?"

"I wasn't allowed to." Michal gave her a puzzled look. "Sorry, it has nothing to do with trust, but that was simply what my mother told me. As she gave it to me on her deathbed, she just said, 'This will help you find your goal. But you can only show it to your dearest person when you feel you have a serious problem, a really serious one.'"

"What's this nonsense?! What's your serious problem? You've got over it once, you'll make it this time, too!" Michal turned the strange, circular claret-colored locket, less than an inch in diameter, in his hands. One side featured a clearly visible six-pointed star, the reverse showed two vertical lines and an inscription in tiny, illegible letters. "The Jewish Star of David... Was your mother a Jew?" Marika nodded. "But you're a Catholic."

"I was baptized."

"Why did you never tell me?"

"You didn't ask."

She looked at her husband, who was wondering what to say. "They say I'm a quarter-Jew too," he laughed. Marika was relieved. "I remember now, I was given a similar symbol once by a mufti at the Taj Mahal... It's just a few hundred miles from Kashmir."

"What's Kashmir got to do with this?" she asked in surprise.

Michal steered away from her question. "I'm not sure if it was identical. But it certainly had the Star of David on it. What does the writing say?" Marika handed him a magnifying glass. Michal could barely contain his excitement. The reverse of the locket displayed two columns, joined with an arch, which seemed identical at first sight, but careful observation informed him that they differed. One had vertical lines, while those on the other one spiraled. Looking even more closely, he noticed letters on both the columns. He went hot and cold all over. There was a letter 'J' on the left-hand column and a 'B' on the right one. Over the columns was an arch that connected them, bearing an inscription, *Templum Hierosolym*. "I never knew you were interested in such things."

"I'm your wife," she replied with a smile.

"And Templum Hierosolym?" He tried not to show his excitement. "The word *templum* would clearly be a temple, or church."

"Right you are. I've looked it up on the Internet. *Hierosolym*, or *Hierosolyma*, may look like an Ancient Greek word, or at least its first part, which means holy. *Solym* denotes peace, just like the Hebrew word *shalom*. The root is the same as in the name Solomon."

"So Templum Hierosolym is the Temple of Jerusalem."

Marika nodded. "Solomon's temple. The only part left of it is the Wailing Wall."

Michal's cell phone rang. He glanced at the display.

"The travel agent's calling." Marika looked at him with hope in her sunken eyes. "Yes? Kráľ speaking." He listened to the voice at the other end and his face lit up with a smile. "That can't be true. Really? That's fantastic! Hang on, my wife must hear this, I'll put it on speakerphone."

Marika listened. "Hello, Mrs. Kráľová, an incredible thing has happened. Your husband asked us a week ago if you could go on the tour as well, but unfortunately, it couldn't be arranged because the tour was full. But now that the volcano in Iceland erupted and flights were cancelled, we had to make the trip a day shorter, so the departure is on Wednesday instead of Tuesday. A few people, including your husband, have cancelled their registrations."

"So, you have free spots?" Marika exclaimed excitedly.

"We do. For both of you."

"That's great news."

"It's even better than that. A lot of airlines have canceled their flights because of the eruption, so a lot of travel agencies have cancelled their tours, meaning hotels in Jerusalem have become vacant. Our group will therefore stay in Jerusalem, not Bethlehem. We'll be at the Victoria hotel. That's a five-minute walk from Damascus Gate. From there, it's three minutes to the Church of the Holy Sepulcher, and five minutes to the Wailing Wall."

"That's excellent. I'll be at your office in an hour! And thank you."

"Amazing, Michal, that's amazing." She jumped up. "It's a miracle!" She hugged her husband and kissed him ardently. "I love you."

"And I love you. Don't worry, it'll all be fine. I feel it's no coincidence that the volcano in Iceland has erupted just now. I'm beginning to believe we'll manage to get to the Church of the Holy Sepulcher for the Saturday night meditation."

Marika put her hand in a drawer furtively and took out a slip of paper. She handed it to Michal. "Do you want to know what I'm asking God for?"

"What's this paper?"

"My wish, ready for a crack in the Wailing Wall."

"No. It's your secret."

"But I don't have any secrets from you," she smiled. "So, do you want to read it?" She pushed the slip under his nose.

Michal unfolded the slip slowly. His mouth opened in surprise when he saw it.

10 A Weird Hunch

The sun began to ascend and was reflecting off the white clay cottages built of adobe bricks and mud. Mount Carmel, which had been appropriated by the Romans and re-named Mare Nostrum, on the coast of the Mediterranean Sea, could be seen in the west from the small hill on which the synagogue stood. Jews referred to the sea as the HaYam HaTikhon. Mount Tabor loomed in the east. The rabbi and Jesus sat next to each other and observed the landscape.

"Your words are peppered with not only rabbinical wisdom but also that wisdom endowed to you by the heavens. Just like myself before, Hillel teaches you the Scripture, Jewish laws given to us by God. That's why we're the chosen people. But I haven't taught you this natural wisdom," the rabbi mused.

"This wisdom is one and everywhere. I'm just trying to open the window to my soul to let the wisdom in."

"Yes, that's easily said, but what hand is strong enough to open the soul's gates and let truth in?"

"It's the hand of love, which opens people's hearts for truth, compassion and understanding to work inside them. Teacher, I think all religions stem from the same source, originate from the same God. I don't think our Judaism is exceptional in any way. At the Academy I've come across some Indian Vedic treatises, and they teach the exact same moral principles that we know. I don't think that we Jews are the only people with the right to call ourselves chosen. Everyone who honors God's commandments is chosen, whether they're Indian, Chinese or Persian. What makes us Jews better than others that would justify our pride in being 'chosen'? I think Buddha is a son of God just as Moses, Elijah, Isaiah, Jeremiah and all our prophets were."

"If, as you say, our prophets were at least as wise as the eastern ones, doesn't it suffice to take interest in the Scripture only?"

The boy pondered for a while. "At the Academy I've come across Buddha's conversation with his disciples on Vulture Peak shortly before his death. It's the most amazing thing I've ever read"

"More interesting than our Scripture?"

Jesus didn't reply. "It's called the *Lotus Sutra*. They say it was written in Kashmir…" Then he thought for a moment, wondering whether to tell his beloved rabbi. "And I also wanted to tell you that… that I've read the *Skanda Purana*."

"What's that?"

"One of the eighteen Hindu holy texts. Something like our prophets' books. There's a lot in it that's similar. It speaks about their god, whose properties make him almost identical to our Jewish one. Only… only their God is several thousand years older."

"There's only one God, so he can't be older."

"Well, I meant to say they've communicated with their God for several thousand years longer than we have."

"Does their God have a name?"

"His name is Jagannath. India's greatest temple in Puri is consecrated to him. The city has a great temple school. And the city of Takshashila has a university, which has taught the Vedas, Ayurvedic medicine, philosophy, astronomy and mathematics for seven hundred years. And, above all, they study Buddha's teachings there." The boy stared at his teacher with his eyes aglow.

The rabbi spent a long time sizing up the boy. "I'd rather you didn't tell others about these things. And thank you for the trust you have in me." He began to understand where the boy had got ideas and formulations that didn't exist in the Torah or its interpretations.

"Rabbi, there's one more question. Ahem… Moses' journey from Egypt to Palestine took forty years…"

"Yes."

"Funny. Where did they wander? I mean, it's just over three thousand stadia. However slowly they walked, they should have made it in less than four months." Jesus shook his head.

"Erm… well… I admit this hasn't crossed my mind before. But that's what the Scripture says!"

"That's what I mean! The Scripture says they left Egypt and travelled for forty years. I've calculated it. In that time, two generations of Jews would have comfortably walked roughly to the river Ganges under the Himalayas in Northern India."

"You can't be an ordinary young man. It appears to me you've come from elsewhere."

"One more thing I wanted to ask about… In the Scripture, the Lord says to Moses that the country He's giving him is a country of hills and valleys, drinking water from heavenly rains, a country with abundant spring and autumn rains, and…" he broke off, adding a moment later, "We only get rain in winter, Romans are building aqueducts now, and they had to transfer water from Lake Tiberias and the River Jordan to our fields in Judea, even Decapolis…"

"So you assume Israel is not the promised land?"

"The only country east of the River Jordan that matches the Lord's description is… well, Kashmir in the Himalayan foothills. It is, in fact, even called the Promised Land or Heaven on Earth." Joshua looked at the rabbi with his deep eyes, waiting for his response.

The rabbi scrutinized him, unable to reply to his logical argument. For a moment, he seemed to radiate an unusual warmth and light that couldn't be attributed to the hot Palestinian weather and the play of the sun's rays.

"The capital of Kashmir is Srinagar. And Takshashila is only about a week's walk from there. In fact, it's in Gandara, a friendly neighboring kingdom."

Berechiah pondered. He felt Jesus' determination to go east was irreversible, but still he attempted to sway him. "Dear Joshua, I've known you since you were a little boy, and I know you're a man of action and resolution. I feel that deep inside you've decided to leave. I know your resolution to go east is irreversible. I wish you success, only you should remember your old father's worsening condition. It's your filial duty to take care of him at the close of his earthly existence and to help your mother."

"Father has four other sons from his first marriage, I'm not his eldest son," Jesus objected. "My father is elsewhere," he added enigmatically.

Berechiah went silent for a while but then continued. "And our precious teacher Hillel isn't in good shape either. You know you're the most precious gem of his Academy. I'm afraid if you left now, it would break the rabbi's heart and... I know your heart's dragging you east, but... erm... I have a compromise proposal for you. In the Jordan Valley, near Ainon and not far from Salim, is Dositheos' monastery."

"I know, I've heard about it," Jesus sat up. "Dositheos also taught my cousin John and Simon the Magician."

"And there are scholars from the East there – from India and Tibet. Why don't you first try him?" Jesus thought for a moment, saying nothing, but eventually his face gave a wide, grateful smile. "Think about it. It's becoming a little too warm, I'd better be going. Shalom." The rabbi stood up and left.

When Joshua was helping his mother grind grain in the mortar that evening, she came up to him, concerned. "Is something bothering you? Have they been unkind to you again?"

He gazed toward the north, where the majestic Mount Hermon, covered with perpetual snow, loomed in the distance. It was too far from Nazareth, but Jesus closed his eyes and could see not only Mount Hermon, but the tall, snow-covered tantalizing peaks of the Himalayas, which he'd read of in the Lotus Sutra, rise before his sight.

His mother watched him, her heart pounding. A weird hunch entered her heart. "I feel you're not quite content at the Academy," she noted.

"I've decided to leave it."

"Does Rabbi Hillel approve?" she asked in surprise. The boy said nothing. His worried mother walked up to him and stroked his hair gently. "Where do you want to go?"

"To a monastery."

11 The Wailing Wall

The morning of Wednesday, April 21, 2010, offered more hope for Marika than any for a long time. Two backpacks full of maps of Israel and Jerusalem, basic hygiene supplies and a handful of summer T-shirts stood leaning on each other next to the bed where she was enjoying a little lie-in. When her hand inadvertently touched her right breast and felt the lump her mood worsened. She snuggled Michal as if searching for a haven from the disease. It occurred to her that she was alone with her body and her sickness, but together they made two in the world of love. She was glad to know she had a man beside her who had his weaknesses like every other man, but one she could always rely on. She got up quietly, turned on the computer and read an email from Adelka in Sudan. She wrote that everything was as usual. It seemed that they had gotten used to the place, even though she had the feeling that her daughter was keeping something back. Hans and Adelka had been posted with an international Doctors Without Borders team in the Doro refugee camp in the Upper Nile state, housing about ninety thousand refugees from the Blue Nile state, a number which was still rising. She knew her daughter and was aware that the situation must be a lot worse than she had described. She often couldn't sleep because of it, and sometimes she wondered whether her cancer wasn't also caused by her almost permanent worrying about her only child. She couldn't forgive herself for not pleading with her more and letting her go to Sudan. She knew, however, that it would be futile telling Adelka to come back; she wouldn't obey anyway. So she just prayed for Adelka's safety during those three years she was away. Michal woke up to the hissing of water boiling in the kettle. Usually, he'd cuddle his wife and kiss her nape every morning; today, he kissed her on the mouth. "Hopefully it'll all work out well," he smiled.

Marika embraced him firmly. "Will you have Jasmine or Darjeeling?"

"The jasmine scented one." He sat by the table and took the leaflet with the tour itinerary. "I think we'll change the itinerary a little."

"Why?"

"A visit to the Holy Sepulcher is only scheduled for Friday, and I feel you should go there sooner."

"If you're referring to my health, I'm fine. When I'm in the Holy Land, I'd like to see Lake Tiberias, Capernaum, Nazareth, Bethlehem and the Dead Sea as well."

"I thought you'd rush to Jesus' tomb first." He looked at her in surprise.

"Of course I will, that's why we're going. But I don't want to be there with a crowd. I'd like to spend some more time there. It would be wonderful if we managed to get there on Saturday night. I've dreamed about this – being with you in Jesus' tomb in the rotunda at least a while. Just the two of us."

It occurred to Michal that the Church of the Holy Sepulcher was commissioned by Emperor Constantine at the suggestion of his mother Helena more than three centuries after the crucifixion of Jesus and none of the relics left in it had anything to do with Christ. The important thing, though, is that people believe that they are real and that this belief helps them. "I don't want to spoil your wishful thinking, but I asked Tomáš. He said it's almost impossible. He's been in Israel for six years and he hasn't made it among the few chosen ones that are let inside on Saturday night. But a miracle may happen!"

"You'll see it will happen. I believe it."

"If the worst comes to the worst, we'll bribe the monk who selects people for the night meditations," Michal laughed. "And when will you slip your prayer in the Wailing Wall?"

"We can go right after we arrive. If things go as planned, we should be there early in the evening." And, after a pause, "Do you have everything? The belt pack, the belt, the torch, the cell phone, the money, the credit card, the spare glasses?"

"You can cross off the spare glasses from your careful list. Look," he took off his glasses. "They've been on a chain since yesterday. Just make sure I don't go to bed with them."

She gave her husband a loving look. "I think… I think I am starting to feel happy. Do you know what I can see when I close my eyes?" Michal shrugged. "The Wailing Wall."

12   The One We're Awaiting

As Jesus was approaching the town of Skythopolis, known as Beit She'an in Hebrew, from whose walls the dead bodies of King Saul and his sons once hung, he looked back once more. He gave one last look to the Samaritan synagogue, the Roman temple with its splendid colonnade, amphitheaters and baths, and turned into the Jordan Valley under Mount Gilboa, toward Ainon near Salim, south of Beit She'an, where Dositheos taught. In the distance, he saw a house that wasn't built according to Jewish custom. The gate was open, so he entered the courtyard.

Men and women with shaved heads, wearing sleeveless red linen robes, with one shoulder bare and sandals on their feet, were walking around the courtyard. Nobody paid attention to him; it was clear that the residents were accustomed to seeing strangers. There was a big door directly opposite the gate, wide open as well. He looked for approval to enter, but the residents ignored him, busy with their own matters. One was washing, another was doing laundry, yet another was cooking something over a fire. Steady sounds were heard from within the room, as if someone was hitting a large drum. When the drumming stopped, some indistinct male voices started singing. He listened. *Om mani padme hum...* The singing was followed by more drumming, then again, the hushed tones of chanting. Oil lamps were burning everywhere; the room was dim, although the sun was shining outside. The center of the hall was dominated by a statue on a pedestal. The statue was of an unknown man, though it could also have been of a woman. The beautiful, slightly plump face with very wide slanting eyes over which there was a dot in the middle of the forehead, looked ahead speculatively. The figure smiled enigmatically. Lamps were twinkling in front of the statue; reflections of their flames shimmered on the stone pedestal, scattered with flowers. The statue made a fascinating, almost magical impression on Jesus. He stood there for a long time, looking at the unknown serene face, which no doubt represented an unknown deity.

"That's Buddha." A monk with a shaved head stood next to him and spoke in excellent Aramaic. "The man who changed the lives of millions in the East," he added with a mysterious smile. "Do you want to be our student?"

"What religion is taught here?"

"No religion is taught here."

"What then?"

"Wisdom. Sophia," the monk replied and took a long look at the newcomer. Jesus' evident discomposure seemed to amuse him. "Are you a Samaritan?"

"No. I'm from Galilee."

"What, then, are you doing in this region, claimed by your fellow believers to be more soiled than a grave, and its people dirtier than pigs?"

"Don't attribute to me hatred that I don't profess," Jesus replied. "And you, are you Samaritans?" he asked inquisitively.

"Some are. But me and a few others are from far away, India, Nepal, the Himalayan foothills and the lower Ganges valley. Our ancestors – Buddhist monks – came here more than two hundred years ago. They had been sent out by the enlightened Emperor Ashoka, one of India's greatest rulers and one of the wisest people that Earth has ever borne. Some of our brethren went to Syria, Egypt and Greece; most are in Alexandria, where the famous Alexander the Great of Macedonia had brought them. There are even Jews among them, known as Essenes. Some of them arrived from the desert monastery of Qumran, situated in the rocks above the Dead Sea. They came here because they'd heard the teachings we'd brought were very familiar to them."

"What will I learn from you?"

"First and foremost, that everything is everlasting, that life continues without end, and that the spirit survives the body in which it dwells. The physical death of every human being is followed by a resurrection of the soul, which reunites with the universal spirit that dispatched it to the body. There it awaits another journey. This is repeated until the soul reaches nirvana, or paradise, thanks to its virtuous life and purification. You will learn about reincarnation, which is the foundation of both Hindu and Buddhist teachings. You will learn that persisting in rigid ideas and rituals is folly."

Jesus gave him an examining look. "What else?"

"We've heard from your merchants arriving along the Silk Road that your people are awaiting a messiah. Some are convinced he has come. We found that interesting and came to understand your people. We've been observing them for many years, but the religion that it professes has disappointed us. It gives you anxiety, not peace. It's not about a kingdom of heaven, but a kingdom on earth; it's about matter, not spirit."

"My words exactly," Jesus replied in comprehension. "What God do you have?"

"We have no God, because we're convinced that the divine dwells inside each of us."

His words made the veins on Jesus' temples swell. His breath quickened. The Buddhist was saying exactly what he thought.

"And Dositheos is your teacher?"

"He too."

"And who above him?"

"Buddha is the greatest authority."

"I've heard about him. He's the one who was supposed to become king, but he left the royal palace, set out on a path of virtue and taught people how to end their suffering." The man gave a scrutinizing look. They said nothing for a long while, feeling there was too much they'd like to talk about.

"Is John, son of Zechariah and Elizabeth of Ain Karem, here as well?" Jesus asked eventually.

The man nodded. "He mentioned that a son of Joseph, the carpenter of Nazareth, is about to arrive. Are you the one we're awaiting?"

"Yes."

13 Unum

Passengers on the scheduled El Al flight from Bratislava to Tel Aviv were waiting to be questioned by the security staff of the Israeli airline company. The twenty members of the Pantour travel agency tour were queuing in front of three desks in a side area of the entrance lobby, to which El Al agents called them one by one. Everyone had been questioned except Marika and Michal, who were just waiting for their turn. Eventually, they were invited to the desks, separately. They were given the standard, identical questions at first.

"What is your objective in Israel?" the obliging agent asked Marika in passable Czech.

"Visiting Christian sights."

"Are you traveling with an agency tour?"

The question surprised her: it must have been clear to the official that she was travelling with the group. But she remembered the guide's warning not to show surprise or irritation, that it was more of a psychological checkup, and that it was up to the agent's discretion whether to allow them aboard the plane or not. A bad night's sleep might mean the end of their trip, and, if given the wrong stamp in the passport, a ban from Israel for up to three years. She replied obligingly, "Yes, with this group."

"Do you know anyone in the group?"

"My husband."

"Nobody else?"

"No."

"Do you have any relatives in Israel?"

"No."

"Friends, acquaintances?"

"Erm... my husband has a friend there."

"Do you know his name? Address?"

"Tomáš Dvoran. I don't know the address; my husband will know that."

"Okay, we'll ask him. Is this your first trip to Israel?"

"Yes."

"Has your husband been to Israel?"

"Yes."

"When?"

"Last year."

"Did you plan your holiday for a long time?"

That made her a little uneasy; the official watched her.

"Well... my husband did, I decided at the last moment."

"Why?"

"I got better."

"Do you have a serious disease?"

She replied unconvincingly, "Not really."

The man turned her passport in his hands for a moment. "Have you visited an Arabic country?"

"No."

"Where in Israel are you going to stay?"

"Erm... at a hotel in Jerusalem. My husband knows exactly."

The man smiled. "Hopefully he does. How you women rely on us!" Marika felt a little relief. "How much money do you have on you?"

"None, my husband has all the money." She looked toward Michal, who was just being interviewed similarly by another agent.

"So, your husband has the credit card too?" She nodded. "Allow me one last question: did you pack your luggage yourself, or did someone help you, except your husband of course?"

"I helped him," she smiled.

"Thank you, Mrs. Kráľová, you may go now." He handed her the passport and walked up to the agent interviewing Michal. He stopped and stayed respectfully back; he didn't know the man interviewing Michal. It was his first day here, but he knew from experience that it wasn't one of their guys, but a Mossad secret agent.

The officer was very obliging toward Michal; he even seemed to apologize to him for his embarrassing questions. "Well now, that seems to be it. I wish you a nice stay in Israel." As he handed him the passport, he asked as if as an afterthought, "But you dropped out of the tour?"

"I did."

"Why?"

"My wife… ahem… she didn't feel well, so I decided to stay at home."

"Did she get better so fast that you both rebooked again a few days later?"

"Well, yes."

The officer scrutinized him for a good long while. Marika, cleared already, stood back and watched them. The man turned Michal's passport in his hand, making Michal sweat a little more with each move. The airport PA announced the last call for boarding the plane.

"You do realize it's only up to me if I let you on the plane or not?"

Michal was going to say something, a vein on his forehead swelled a little out of nervousness, but he managed to control himself. "Sure."

"So then, there you are," the officer handed him the passport with a good-natured gesture. "Take good care of yourself," he added in a strange tone.

* * * * *

The airplane ascended into the sky over Bratislava and headed south. About an hour later, Michal turned to his wife. She was gazing at the azure surface of the Aegean Sea; large and small vessels could be seen plowing through the water among a multitude of islands. A sense of security and peace ran through her body as he took her hand in his. She smiled at him and put her head on his shoulder.

"What are you thinking about?"

There was a silence for a while, only disturbed by the hum of the aircraft engines and a baby crying somewhere at the back. "I wanted to tell you I went to see a nice lady before the departure. Her name's Mária, like mine. She reads tarot cards."

"Marika, I hope you don't believe in these fortune tellers!"

"They're no fortune tellers. She explained to me that the tarot is… erm… how should I put it, a gate to an inexhaustible well of wisdom and love which exists in the universe and in us as well."

"And why did you go and see her?"

"Because... because I wanted to know what that dream about my mother meant. You see, it's been recurring."

"But Marika, this is all nonsense."

"Michal, this is no nonsense. I had the same dream last night. We were on a boat and she was driving me somewhere with a stick and blowing smoke in my face..." Michal rolled his eyes. "You smelled the fragrance yourself!"

"Just admit it, I'm not gonna kill you or anything, I mean, we all have our weak moments. Even I sometimes have a smoke." Michal forced himself to smile. He remembered that unusual fragrance and how it didn't seem funny at that time.

Marika stared at him in a state of shock. "You smoke?!"

"Tell me you don't! I understand and I don't blame you for anything. Sometimes I'm gone, you get depressed, so you have a smoke..."

Marika raised her voice so much that some fellow passengers turned to her. "I swear, I swear to you I didn't smoke that night! Understand?!"

Michal knew his wife wasn't lying to him, so he just asked quietly, "So where did the fragrance come from?"

"My mother was a heavy smoker and she died of lung cancer."

"You aren't really trying to tell me it was her who smoked there... Sorry, I am interested in mysteries and esotericism, but this is not possible. No, no... don't even start with that."

"What was the fragrance then? And why lavender and not cigarette smoke? As if she was hinting at something. You see?"

"And the tarot gave you an answer, huh?"

Marika started speaking after a while. "The tarot is about examining yourself. You see, all diseases originate from our attitudes to ourselves and the world around. My starting point is that if God is universal love, he doesn't want to punish us but rather show us the way. A disease is a kind of signpost along the way, only sometimes we don't understand it correctly."

"I agree that faith is paramount. What then is the tarot good for?"

"To me, faith means reliance on God and the whole universe being on my side. Everybody tells me I have to fight the disease. But I feel that's a wrong approach. I don't want to fight; I want to understand it, or to be more precise, to understand its message. God only does his job after we've done ours. I think the tarot will... erm... I was gonna say it will help me with this understanding, but in fact it has helped me already."

Michal gave her a surprised look. "You've understood something?"

"That I'm not supposed to change the world, just myself."

"How are you going to achieve that?"

"By loving myself."

"Isn't that selfish?"

"Loving yourself means loving others above all. Only by giving do you receive; only by sowing good do you reap good. If that's your starting point, then clearly my disease is the harvest of something I sowed wrongly."

"But what kind of God is this that sends suffering down upon people?"

"We call it upon ourselves. If I had loved myself the right way, I would never have eaten the flesh of slaughtered animals, or eaten cakes, drunk coffee and alcohol, smoked; I'd have done more sports and, most importantly, I wouldn't have stressed myself out so much. I knew all these things were harmful, yet I was doing them for such a long time. I've been thinking about where I made mistakes to get sick and I think the tarot has helped me find that point. It's really a mirror – when you look in it, you can see nothing but yourself. You can't deceive a mirror." Marika felt that her enthusiasm for the tarot wasn't getting through to her husband, so she tried even harder to explain it to him. "The tarot won't tell you what the future has in store for you. The cards only describe your inner feelings for you, help you find your purpose and mission here on earth, and find a way that you are to follow. Usually we start looking for the way when we experience trouble."

"Will you finally tell me what those cards told you?"

"That I'm selfish."

Michal gave his wife a surprised look. "You, selfish? I don't know anyone who helps others and gives out more than you."

"It may seem that way, but the point is why I do it..." Marika speculated. "I don't do it for others but to satisfy my own ego."

"Now you've lost me completely."

"Look, Miško, do you know what cancer is? The disease occurs when cells of a body decide they won't serve the whole. Instead of being a part of the whole system, where each component – the heart, the liver, the kidneys – has its role, cells start building their own realm. This is a tumor, and it threatens the whole body. Instead of working for the whole and reinforcing unity, they each go their own way."

"Reminds me of people somehow," Michal stated.

"Exactly. People too concentrate on their career, families, money, houses, property, not thinking about others. We don't think as 'WE' but rather as 'I'. And our doctors... well... they don't treat a person as a whole but only their parts. They don't remove the disease but only its symptoms."

"Do you wish Adelka was here with us?" he asked unexpectedly. He knew their daughter's absence was her greatest trauma. He often felt that if she were with them and they had a grandchild from her, Marika would be happy and wouldn't have cancer.

"Why are you asking?"

"Sorry, sometimes I feel you are fixated on her more than is wise..."

"Is it a bad thing for a mother to worry about her only child?! You should think of her more. You don't even know what's happening to her, what she's doing, what worries her..." she accused him, suddenly out of breath. But she calmed down quickly. "Forgive me... I didn't mean to be mean. Yes, I've been thinking of her, I've been worried about her. I pray every day for her to be safe. I wish the three years would go by quickly so we can be together again..."

"...making up Unum," Michal said under his breath and smiled.

"What did you say?"

"I'm sad too because they aren't here."

14 The Blood of the Innocent

Jesus was standing on the fifteen steps running in an arch to the Temple, ending by the splendid Nicanor Gate in the western wall of the Court of the Women. Since his departure for Dositheos' monastery he only came home before the Passover to commemorate the departure of Jews from Egypt with his parents at the Temple of Jerusalem. He was watching the crowding pilgrims who couldn't wait to enter the Court of the Israelites. When he pictured that the marvelous building was almost a thousand years old and that the wise king Solomon had begun it in the year four hundred and eighty after the Jews' departure from Egypt, in the fourth year of his reign, a sensation of bliss flooded his heart. However, the temple that the young Nazarene was watching now belonged to Herod, not Solomon. Herod the Great had begun rebuilding it about thirty years ago. Scaffolding was still protruding toward the sky on parts of the walls because a segment of the western wall had collapsed and had to be repaired. Roman soldiers were on top alert during the Passover festival. Since the anti-Roman uprising during the Passover in the year of Herod the Great's death, the Roman governor summoned extra military reinforcements to Jerusalem to be on the safe side.

Nobody except the priests was allowed to see the inside of the Temple, or even the Court of the Priests. Jesus and his parents were walking across the vast Court of the Gentiles where even non-Jewish pilgrims were allowed to enter. The boy was listening to the mixture of languages spoken by Jewish pilgrims from Greece, Phoenicia, Mesopotamia, Alexandria, Galilee as well as distant Rome. He also watched those who exchanged various domestic and foreign coins for shekels of Tyre, the currency most appreciated in the Temple because it was minted from pure silver. Roman coins were banned from use in the Temple. The courtyard teemed with merchants selling animals and birds for sacrifice. In the general chaos merchants, craftsmen and peddlers were offering their wares, haggling and shouting their prices in loud Aramaic. Jesus observed disgustedly the faces of people defiling the holy ground of the Temple. He watched as the priests, Levites and church guardians helped to turn that sacred place into a mere trading center. The trading and money-changing continued even in the Court of the Women where non-Jews were not admitted. The thirteen shofar-shaped cases of the Temple treasury were evenly distributed along the courtyard perimeter. Pilgrims threw monetary donations in them; they were then collected in the Room of Shekels. Every adult Jewish man was required to pay an annual temple tax of half a shekel.

Flocks of ravens were hovering over the temple, trying to catch their share of the huge amounts of animal sacrifices. During the festival, blood from the murdered animals literally cascaded down the wooden and stone drains and into the Kidron brook, turning its water red. Five thousand rams, goats, cows, oxen, hens and pigeons were sacrificed every day.

"So then, my boy," his father interrupted his contemplation, "let's say goodbye to your mother. She'll wait for us here, in the Women's Courtyard, and we'll go to the Court of the Israelites."

"Be brave, my son, and control yourself." His mother kissed him on the forehead and followed the fleecy wool of Ben, the lamb that Jesus was carrying in his arms, with sadness in her eyes. Since he had sacrificed his first Ben in Nazareth as a little boy long ago, she bought a young ram from the shepherd Aron every year and always called him Ben, which means son.

"Why isn't mother coming with us?"

"You're asking like it's your first time," his father rebuked him nervously. "That's how tradition lays it down," he shrugged. He grabbed the boy by his arm, and they walked slowly down the long stone-paved corridor toward the Court of the Priests. Although they'd been to Jerusalem many times, Joseph felt that Jesus was extraordinarily agitated today. As he grew older, he became more squeamish about blood, and so his father was concerned about how the boy would tolerate the sight of the mass of blood and dead animal parts on the jagged stone altar standing at the center of the Court of the Priests. The four edges of the altar were adorned with animal horns. The Sanctuary facade rose behind the altar.

"Father, do you believe that the Sanctuary houses the rock on which Abraham wanted to sacrifice Isaac?" Jesus tried to talk away the dramatic moment that was drawing near.

"So they say," his father said in a slightly irritated tone as they approached the Sanctuary. Instead of the honor and awe that would be appropriate for the holy place, this courtyard too was filled with noise and commotion. Some were singing prayers, others pushed forward the lambs, rams, even cows they were leading to the sacrifice. A remorseless massacre took place in the holiest place of Israel every day. The father and son approached the priests and Ben, the little lamb, cuddled up to the boy as in apprehension of what would come.

"Why must we sacrifice animals to God?"

"Why are you asking every time?" Joseph replied irritated. "The Torah commands us to. But don't worry, your Ben will go to heaven. God likes sacrificial animals that come to him willingly."

"Ben isn't coming willingly!"

"Don't be afraid. You'll see, when the priest speaks the word of God out loud, the lamb will calm down and accept his fate with joy," he said, trying to appease him in a somewhat unconvincing way; he was sorry for both his son and the lamb, all the more because it could grow into a mighty ram and provide the poor family with a means of subsistence. Then came the moment. Joshua, who had tears in his eyes, stroked the animal, played with its little black ears, and kissed it on its black snout. The animal cuddled even closer to him in the hope of protection. But Joshua was incapable of that. Moved, his father allowed him to play with the lamb a little longer. Slowly they approached the long line of pilgrims carrying lambs in their arms and drew closer to the hooded priests who stood opposite and each held a golden or silver bowl. The air was filled with sharp notes of blowing shofars and the helpless shrieks of animals having their throats ritually slit. The chain of priests extended all the way to the altar. The closer he and his father got to the priests, the more Jesus trembled with tension. His father finally took Ben and handed him to a priest, who examined him carefully for any defects, then muttered something and covered his eyes with his ears. The animal awaited the death sentence with a surprising serenity. The priest held the lamb's ears for a while, then produced a sharp knife and handed it to Jesus' father, who cut the lamb's artery with a swift movement; blood spurted out. Jesus' legs began to tremble; the priest held up a bowl into which the blood poured. When the lamb's blood was drained, he handed the bowl to another priest, who in turn passed it to another, and so on until the blood reached the altar, where it was all poured out.

"Shall we be going?" Joseph asked compassionately. But Jesus couldn't detach his eyes from the dead Ben and other carved up and dissected bodies. "Come on, you know we breed the lambs for the sacrifice which cleanses our dwelling and our souls and erases our sins," Joseph appeased him.

"That's nonsense. We cannot erase our sins with any animal sacrifice. The priests made that up!"

"They're also sacrifices for good harvest, our good health, peace and calm," his father objected unconvincingly. The boy looked back once more and watched the fire blazing away on the stone altar: it was burning parts of bodies of the previous sacrifices. One of priests was throwing entrails, fat and kidneys in the fire, but putting the flesh aside. He also put Ben's hide aside. According to tradition it belonged to the priest.

"What are they going to do with the meat?" the boy asked.

"If we want to, we can take part of Ben home and eat him…"

Suddenly the boy's face twisted itself in a grimace; he could hardly breathe the air sated with the reek of blood and roasted meat. The people had given up fighting off the swarms of flies feasting on the shreds of flesh, bones and curdling blood. He couldn't control himself anymore and grabbed the nearest priest by the neck.

"Can you not hear the death cries of the animals, the bleating of lambs and the anxious fear of doves that you murder wholesale?! Can you not smell the terrible reek of burnt flesh?! The Temple is meant to be a place of union between people and God. How can people encounter God where rivers of blood run?!" Jesus was shaking the priest ferociously and his father was trying to get him off.

"What impudence! How dare you lecture priests and rabbis about what people need!" the priest wheezed, looking for support among the others. Old Hillel, the chairman of the Sanhedrin, was sitting on his sedan concealed in the crowd and watched Jesus, who hadn't noticed him in his righteous angry rapture. The rabbi was over one hundred years of age and felt that his days were coming to an end.

The present day might be his last one, so he decided he wouldn't miss the opportunity to see his favorite former student when he heard Jesus had come to the courtyard.

The boy was still raging. "Are you telling me it's important for a person's virtuous life on earth how many times a kid is boiled in its mother's milk? You have elevated meaningless rituals above life. Moses' law says you shall not boil a kid in its mother's milk!" he yelled.

The priest was trying to appease him. "It used to be common among the Canaanites to separate the first kid from its mother, milk the mother goat and then boil the kid alive in its mother's milk, but this kind of sacrifice is no longer practiced by anyone!"

"And how does that differ from the sacrifices you practice here? What difference does it make to the kid if you boil it alive or chop its head off?!"

"God has commanded us to act in this way. This sacrifice effaces sins!"

"What's an innocent animal got to do with our sins? And don't tell me lies! Isaiah says, 'Don't make any more futile sacrifices.' The incense sacrifice is repulsive to me!"

"I guess you're not quite in your right mind," the priest reprimanded him more lightly and made up his ruffled tunic.

"Do you think you know more about God than these priests do? The Temple really isn't a place for immature boys to showoff and boast about their wisdom!" said rabbi Shammai, Hillel's deputy and leader of the ultra-conservative wing of the Sanhedrin, supporting the priest. He was attracted by the dispute and came to have a closer look.

Jesus' eyes met with Hillel's at that instant. "Teacher Shammai is right. There's no need to show off. Modesty suits the wise more," Hillel said.

Jesus went quiet. He held the sage Hillel in high regard. Before Hillel got to lead the Sanhedrin, he travelled around Judea preaching, and Jews welcomed him almost as a new messiah. They loved him for his moderation, kindness, patience and prudence. He tried to accommodate everyone and be helpful with advice and deeds at any time. A remarkable thing about him was that he wasn't a Jew by origin: he was born in Babylon and only converted to Judaism later. In spite of his old age he still tried to appease people and give them strength and courage. That was one of the reasons why Hillel had very soon become not only a teacher to the young Nazarene but also a lifelong role model along with

Berechiah and Dositheos. Bursting with joy at seeing his beloved teacher, he walked up to him and bowed in respect. Jesus realized that when Israel finally lost the rabbi they would be like a sheep without a shepherd, so he used the simile.

"Sheep need a shepherd like people need a spiritual teacher," Hillel replied.

"I want to be like you one day." The boy looked in his eyes with admiration.

"I don't think you'll be like me. You'll surpass me. The animal sacrifices are terrible, but the sacrifices of our lost brethren are even worse. They are scattered all over the world, from Cyrenaica and Lydia to Cyprus, Phoenicia, Syria, Babylon and Hyrcania, Kerala and Mumbai in India, searching for someone to bring them back to their homeland."

"Those families have been abroad for over five centuries; they have properties there and offspring, many even non-Jewish…"

"I didn't mean bringing them back to Israel but to the Lord's House."

"How can that be done?"

"You will go to them."

15 The Mysterious Card

Michal's gaze was fixed on the back of the seat in front of him. Marika watched him for a while; she felt something was vexing him.

"Have a problem?" Michal didn't respond. "Hello? Did you leave the steam iron on?" she tried to joke.

"What did the cards tell you?"

"You really shouldn't worry about me; you'll see, everything's going to be fine." She pointed at her heart. "I feel it here, the solution is in Jerusalem. In fact, I don't just feel it, I know it." She thought for a moment and went on, "The tarot card told me that my journey to love starts in the east." Michal looked at her in surprise. "So, we're right in going to Jerusalem."

"I'm afraid it's south more than east... How did the card tell you that?"

"Are you genuinely interested?" Michal nodded. "I don't understand it so well myself that I could explain the principle of the Major and Minor Arcana, which make seventy-eight tarot cards together. I drew the Six of Swords out of the Minor Arcana."

"What does that mean?"

"You can have a look, here it is." She handed him one of the cards with a peculiar reverse – a sky with the twelve signs of the zodiac. Michal turned it around and gave it a long hard look. A woman was standing on an unusual narrow boat; the hood of her dark blue cloak covered her hair. The boat was floating eastwards on a peaceful lake surrounded by tall mountains covered with snow and the woman was wielding a long, peculiarly shaped oar, reminiscent of a heart. There was an outline of a fort on one of the peaks. The moon was full, the lake surface was totally calm, and above the boat was a vast area full of stars, giving the impression of cool, fresh air, which the woman was inhaling deeply. The shoreline with little cottages, extending into the distance, could be seen in the background behind the boat. The boat was protected by six swords and the prow of the boat depicted a female face at the center of a circle, radiating what looked like the sun's rays. Michal spent a long time gazing at the card in concentration. Then he handed it back to his wife before saying, "Hm, the woman reminds me of Mary."

"Which Mary?"

"Jesus' mother. I don't know why, but my grandmother used to have a similar picture in her prayer book which I used to read to her. She had it as a bookmark."

"Well, I hadn't thought of that," Marika smiled.

"And did the tarot reader explain the meaning of your dream about your mother?"

"In the tarot, you understand many things only after some time. The earth is matter, egoism, rigidity. The reader said it symbolizes the mother. We even call her Mother Earth. And the word matter itself is derived from the Latin *mater*, which means mother. It's *Mutter* in German. I'm supposed to leave my mother, break free of my dependence on her, and breathe new air, as clear as possible. My mother's cancer was due to her dependence on me. When my father divorced her, I was one year old, and I was everything to her. When I left her, she couldn't handle it. So, the tarot reader essentially told me the same thing you did."

"Maybe she could have told you one more thing..." Marika looked at her husband questioningly. "I apologize, but sometimes I just feel that...well, it seems from the remarks you sometimes make that you are upset by and you regret not knowing who your father is...."

Marika sat silent for a long while. "Yes, I never saw my father, he never showed any interest in me... and, yes, I'd like to know him. He didn't even come to my mother's funeral. I know nothing at all about him. I've no idea if he's still alive, if he married again, if I have any siblings, if..."

She recovered in an instant and tried to turn the conversation away from this unpleasant topic. "The tarot reader said swords symbolize lightning, that is fresh air."

Michal couldn't take his eyes off the card; it fascinated him. "This oar's strange. It really looks like a heart. It's all weird. The woman has an expression of agitation in her face, but the lake's totally calm, without a ripple. The woman holds the oar not vertically, but parallel to the boat, so that it won't work even if she dips it in the water. She's rowing, but the boat isn't moving. I've seen oars of various shapes: square, round, ellipsoid, but heart-shaped? Where are these cards from?"

"They're a reprint of some older ones from Florence. The tarot reader sold them to me. She said the painter lived about a hundred years ago and traveled around the world a lot."

"He must have meant something," Michal thought.

Marika took the card from him and looked at it carefully. "I think I've got it. The woman is on the way, she keeps trying, but her boat won't move."

"Of course, she's holding the oar wrong."

"But it looks like she isn't aware of that. She's trying, but she's making a mistake she doesn't know about…"

"Do you think you're making a mistake?" Marika nodded sheepishly.

We'll land at the Tel Aviv airport in ten minutes. Will passengers please fasten their seat belts? When they touched down, they went through a check similar to the one before the departure, only shorter. They only breathed a sigh of relief when their passports were stamped with *Ben Gurion Border control. Visit permit.*

A coach with a driver and a Slovak guide named Karol was awaiting the group outside the airport. In addition, Marika and Michal were awaited by a likeable, long-haired forty-something year old man, who hugged them both mightily. "So, this is your amazing wife," he said.

"This is Tomáš," Michal introduced his friend to Marika.

"I thought as much," she smiled.

"I know everything from your guide: you're staying at the Victoria hotel, that's by the Muslim cemetery near Herod's Gate. I've stayed there too. The owner is Massoud, a very polite Arab."

"We were supposed to stay in Bethlehem, but everything got mixed up because of the volcano eruption, so we're staying in Jerusalem," Marika explained.

"I know. You've been lucky. You can hardly get any accommodation in Jerusalem at this time of year, there's normally thousands of tourists everywhere. But many tours have been cancelled after the eruption. The place was insane at Easter, the Armenians fought with the Greeks in the temple again, but that's become almost an Easter tradition by now," Tomáš laughed.

He had no difficulty persuading the guide to be allowed to accompany them to the hotel; they knew each other and Tomáš sometimes guided Slovak tours himself. Although he lived in Tiberias, Israel being a small country meant dashing off to Jerusalem was no problem for him.

"I'll drive you in my car, we'll be faster, and we can talk on the way." Being a gentleman, he took Marika's backpack and led them to his car.

"Your infamous Fiat?" Michal inquired.

"I can tell you, all the saints were with me that day. But don't worry, I've been checking my tire pressure since then."

The sun was hot even though it was nearly six o'clock. Tomáš stepped on the gas and got on the freeway. "There are no turns, so we'll be there in less than an hour." A lively discussion ensued so they didn't even notice that a black Volkswagen Passat was following them the whole way.

16 Royal Teaching

The peculiar thing about Dositheos' monastery was that not only was its main gate open, but all the doors of the two-story building were open as well. It was inhabited by both men and women, some long-haired, some shaven; the long-haired ones wore white robes, the shaven ones wore red, sleeveless robes, with one shoulder bare and sandals on their feet. It was a community of people who had sold their belongings and donated the proceeds to the whole community. They sowed, plowed and reaped crops together; they cooked and took care of the communal property; and most importantly, they studied, prayed and meditated together as commanded by the *Order of Unity*, inscribed on a parchment almost seven feet long.

Jesus was the youngest student at the monastery, and he soon became popular for his strenuousness, fairness and wisdom so unusual for his age. He befriended them all, but was most fascinated by the Buddhist and Hindu monks, who'd brought from their distant homelands medicinal techniques, the use of meditation and concentration for improving one's health, along with other ideas from ancient Hindu Vedas as well as instructions on the proper life taught by Buddha and since tried and tested over five centuries. He acquired not only their wisdom but also their language. He listened to stories from the Vedas and, above all, verses from the most scared Hindu book – the Bhagavad Gita, which means as much for the Hindus as the Torah does for the Jews. The amazing thoughts of the Bhagavad Gita were in agreement with many thoughts of the Jewish Scripture. That fascinated him enormously. He was even more fascinated by the fact that the verses recited by the monks had no place for the words hatred, punishment, wrath, revenge, murder – words that the Old Testament was literally riddled with. While Jews ostentatiously flaunted every single act of compassion, Hindus kept it to themselves and their God. Jews had a systematic way of materializing God's words, while Indians sought for the ways of the spirit. At a time when Israel was busy satisfying its material needs, the cedar groves on the Himalayan slopes witnessed the creation of the verse of the Indian Bible in which the god Krishna holds a conversation with the archer Arjuna about the meaning of life and death. Listening to the monks, Jesus tingled with excitement and couldn't get enough of the breathtaking ideas of love of one's neighbor. Krishna's advice to Arjuna became inscribed in his memory; it reminded him of King Solomon's *Song of Songs*:

When you rid yourself of pride and selfishness and when you learn asceticism, you will see everything in unity.
The earthly world was not created as a vale of tears, but as an improvement workshop for humans.
You will be redeemed by nobody but yourself.
A wise person is not pleased with good things and offended by bad things.
A little love for a person is more than a lot of love for humanity as a whole.
Maybe what I cannot change is meant to change me.
God is pleased not by the amount of work we do but the love with which we do it.
One's own way, however imperfect, is better than someone else's perfect way.
Nothing is more certain than death, and yet we live as if it did not exist. When you forgive someone else's sin, God will forgive you two of yours.
Failure is a teacher as good as success.
Free yourself.
Three gates lead to hell: the gate of desire, the gate of wrath, and the gate of indulgence.
A person is the result of self-discipline.

This is the path of the royal teaching, the most important of all the Vedic teachings, the most beautiful thoughts of Buddha, the splendid point of Moses' teaching, the sole truth, the monks emphasized to Jesus. Their words were like a life-giving nectar; they cleansed him like crystal-clear mountain water, filling his mind with warmth. Unlike Jews, people in India didn't consider themselves to be the apex of humanity, the chosen nation, but God's children, loved by God equally with all other beings. What he had missed in Judaism was the selfless love which he felt while listening to the verses of the Bhagavad Gita. He literally felt in his young soul the nutritional value of this divine fare, which captivated his heart more and more. He understood that there is no goal, only the way. He realized that the hypocritical Galilee and Judea were too confining for him. He increasingly opposed the perpetually repeating strict rituals. They made them waste precious time, which they could have spent repairing the monastery devastated by an earthquake forty years before. But Dositheos' monastery wasn't perfect either. The support of the Buddhist monks, who performed the morning prayers facing to the east thus angering the Jews who faced the Temple of Jerusalem, further led to Jesus' fall into disfavor. Not everyone was willing to make the vow of poverty as the Indian monks had done, and many Jews disliked the eastern monks' introduction of the Indian solar calendar instead of the one following the Jerusalem Temple prescription, although the former was much more accurate. However, what irked young Jesus the most was the monks' unnatural separation from the people. He was annoyed that instead of demonstrating their belief in God through acts of help to their neighbors, they only concentrated on self-improvement within the monastery walls. He refused to continue the monastery's antiquated rules for which he found support among the Buddhist monks. He was a man of freedom and a supporter of reason. He drifted increasingly farther away from the Jewish monks and became ever closer with the Buddhist and Hindu monks from Kashmir and India. His desire to get to know their countries and try to find his lost ancestors, about whom the monks had told him a lot, was burning in him and he couldn't resist it. He decided to follow the path of the royal teaching.

17 The Tiberias Surprise

After check-in and a quick snack, the group converged in the lobby of the Victoria hotel where their guide Karol welcomed them, introduced all the participants to one another, and showed them the itinerary. The following day was to include Lake Tiberias, Peter's house in Capernaum, the site where the feeding of five thousand took place in Tabgha, and the site of Jesus' first miracle in Cana of Galilee. The day after that the group was to visit Nazareth and Jericho, and the whole of Saturday would be dedicated to Bethlehem. The tour participants who were in Israel for the first time felt the hair on the back of their necks as they heard these holy New Testament names. The full-figured Mrs. Žáková from Galanta and her similarly curvaceous daughter made signs of the cross on themselves at the sound of each of these biblical names. Many of the others clutched firmly at rosaries and various amulets.

"What a religious trip this is going to be," Tomáš leaned over to Michal. "Fake churchgoers the lot of them. You'll see the hustle when they arrive in Bethlehem. They'll roll about on the ground and kiss marble dirtied by thousands of shoes next to a hole in which Christ is said to have been born," he smiled. "I don't like these hypocrites. At home they backbite, lie, drink and steal and then go to confession. Or they come to Jerusalem and buy all the flasks with the oil in which Christ was supposedly anointed. They don't even find it odd that they would have used hectoliters of oil."

"Calm down," Marika rebuked him; they were on first-name terms by now. "Everyone has their own path to God. If fake oil helps them find salvation, so be it."

"Since our friend Tomáš Dvoran is a priest in Tiberias, he'll guide us tomorrow," Karol informed those present. "You couldn't find a better guide of the Lake Tiberias area in all of Israel. He's a very well-read man, he's studied theology, archaeology and ancient history in both Rome and Jerusalem, and besides Italian, he has also mastered Ancient Greek, Latin, Hebrew and even Aramaic – the language spoken in Galilee in Christ's time." The people smiled at Tomáš and nodded in admiration.

"Please don't over-praise me. History is something of a hobby to me, but that's all." He blushed a little.

"We'll see about that tomorrow. I haven't come across a single question on biblical history that you couldn't answer," Karol added.

A debate rolled out on the coach on the way to Lake Tiberias. People asked the trickiest of questions and Tomáš gave interesting replies to them. He also told many biblical stories, which earned him loud praise, particularly from the old women. After a visit to Capernaum, the participants decided to grab a bite to eat. The team of curvy ladies in the back seat (headed by Mrs. Žáková) produced schnitzel and ham sandwiches wrapped in paper napkins brought from home. Mrs. Žáková's daughter, wearing a T-shirt with a picture of Jesus, which barely covered her enormous breasts, gobbled up the sandwiches with a can of beer and belched from time to time. Her father, who sat in front of her, warned her to no avail, "You shouldn't eat so much, you'll have heartburn again." But the mother shouted him down, "She has to eat it otherwise it will go bad by tomorrow." When the daughter was finished, she was handed another sandwich with thick salami slices. Tourists who didn't have any provisions were just casting envious glances in their direction. Tomáš proposed going to a little-known fishermen's restaurant in Tiberias, fifteen minutes south of Capernaum. He warned that Peter's tavern was for locals but the atmosphere was unique so they should be prepared that it was going to be a little rough. His proposal was accepted unanimously, and it turned out he was right. The old-time fishermen's tavern decorated with parts of old boats, oars, nets, stuffed fish and, above all, lots of fresh flowers, really enchanted them. It was alive with noise and good humor. Locals, mostly older men, sat behind tables and played chess or dice. The guests praised the traditional tilapia – so-called Saint Peter's fish.

"I haven't seen a single fishing boat on the lake," somebody remarked.

"The government has banned fishing as the fish stocks have decreased dramatically," Tomáš explained.

"And this Saint Peter's fish we're eating came from where?"

"The Mediterranean, they're brought from Haifa," he informed and then added, "And what would you need boats for here? You can walk on this lake," he laughed, and several of the others with him. The older ones didn't laugh; they didn't understand the joke or at least pretended they didn't.

"Do you know why Christ walked on the lake?" Michal added. "Because he performed a miracle," Mrs. Žáková replied promptly. "Because Jewish ferrymen were very expensive," the heckler laughed.

"That's not true," Tomáš opposed. "Neither the miracle, nor the ferrymen. He had to walk because he couldn't swim." A handful of the tourists could hardly suppress their laughter by now. Mr. Hlavatý started singing the well-known folk song *"There's no use sending me to school, I won't be a priest, no use thrashing me."* The people were enjoying a great day full of experiences. The wine and the singing improved their mood even further.

"You should be ashamed of yourselves!" Mrs. Žáková rose from the table angrily, followed by her daughter and her flock of old sufferers. "You call yourself a priest! Well then, God help us," she blessed herself and walked out of the tavern. She waved her arm in disdain as she was passing by Tomáš.

"Now I've put my foot in it," the merry priest shook his head.

"Screw them, not even holy water can help those two," a man who'd been sitting on his own at the end of the table appeased him. "That's my wife, and she's got my daughter all crazed. Let's have some more wine, on me! This wine of Christ. Place the order, father. For all of us here," he asked Tomáš.

There was no need for much persuasion, although he realized it was quite hot and the wine would work twice as fast in such weather, but when he saw the encouraging looks in the others' eyes, he ordered two more jugs of red wine. "After all, not even the gospels say that when Christ and his companions arrived at somebody's home after a day's journey, they were welcomed with water. It was wine everywhere. Water is mentioned very little in the New Testament. The guy turned it into wine even in Cana of Galilee," the religious Galanta lady's husband laughed. "Now then, boys and girls, to your health! May this be a fine trip." He filled the glasses, and once more soon afterwards. "The wine is excellent. Is it local?" he asked Karol.

"It's brought from nearby Cana. They say it's leftover since Christ's time."

"Did he change so much water?"

"So he did, only there's no water left in Cana today," he added.

"Why are we sitting here then? Let's go to Cana," the guy suggested.

"Really, we should be on our way again. We still have to see the Mount of Beatitudes." Nobody wanted to leave the abundantly laid tables when Karol stood up and announced – to the disappointment of the merry group – that it was time to board the coach and continue to the nearby Mount of Beatitudes and from there to Cana. "If you need the toilet, I advise you go now, because there might be a slight problem with it on the hill," he informed the group and went to the lavatory himself. The toilets too were decorated traditionally: an old fishing net hung from the ceiling, oars in the corners, reproductions of old paintings on fishing themes on the walls. It was obvious that the whole area around the lake thrived off fish and the fishery tradition. After all, many of Jesus' disciples were fishermen from around the lake. Michal's turn was the last. As he was drying his hands, he cast his eyes to a corner where some old oars were fastened to the wall. They were of various shapes, but two of them made him go hot and cold. He couldn't believe his own eyes; the oars were old and moldy. A reprint of an old painting above them showed a boat with some fishermen wielding identical oars. He stood and gazed at the oars and the painting for a long time as if they were apparitions. Then he broke into a run and dashed onto the coach which was full of high spirits with only the Galanta lady and her group glowering gloomily. The driver had just started the engine when Michal rushed on. He was pale, sweating and trembling slightly.

"Are you alright? You look upset. What's the matter?" Marika was agitated.

"Come with me. Quick."

"Please, we must go now," Karol tried to halt them.

"Just a minute," Michal replied, grabbing Marika by the hand and dragging her off the coach forcefully. They entered the men's lavatory, disregarding the surprised looks of men relieving themselves in concentration over the urinals. "Take a look at this!" He took an oar and handed it to her. "And this." He pointed at the painting of fishermen. "What do you think?"

"Of what?"

"The shape of the oar."

Marika took it in her hand and gave it a long uncomprehending look. "It's heart-shaped."

18 An Unknown Stranger

Hillel's health worsened, so Jesus set out to see his parents in Nazareth to ask them to accompany him in visiting the elderly monk, adding that a lot of time had passed since the Passover. The sun climbed high into Jerusalem's sky, the air became hot and Hillel invited Jesus and his parents to his dwellings, located in a stone extension of the temple, where he was spending almost all his time in the pleasant shade. A young Levite loaded the table with dried dates, figs, grapes, flatbreads, leavened bread, biscuits, even a gourd of wine which remained untouched in such searing heat. The rabbi refused meat and encouraged his students to do likewise. He was eagerly interested in Jesus' progress with Dositheos. He couldn't be more amazed at how much his thinking had advanced since he left the Academy; he was no longer the boy from Nazareth seeking answers, but a young man, aware of his abilities, knowledge and the power of his faith. As if reading Jesus' thoughts, he laughed, "You shouldn't stay long at the monastery. You know how it is. A devil becomes a monk when he grows old. Look at this courtyard," the rabbi looked through the window. "It's paved over, detached from life, with not a single bird, tree or flower. Only the thorny fig shrub that has taken hold on a grain of soil in the rock. The place is sad, it reminds me of a tomb. And monasteries are the same."

"But the monks say one is not subject to temptation there and can thus concentrate on being in communion with God," Jesus protested.

"That's a manifestation of weakness. Strength is manifested by resisting temptation and speaking with God in a street filled with a noisy crowd. Everyone can resist temptation inside monastery walls." He washed his hands and followed the fruit he had eaten with a morsel of freshly baked bread, at the same time encouraging his guests to partake of the richly laden table, which they did timidly. "I feel Israel will soon feel too confining to you," Hillel ruminated. Both Jesus and his parents looked at him attentively.

"What do you mean, master rabbi?" Joseph asked.

"Wisdom isn't found only in the Torah and the Talmud. Wisdom also thrives in Persia, India and China. Your son deserves to be taught by the best. As well as our prophets he should familiarize himself with many other wise sages, Zoroaster, Laozi, Confucius, Buddha…" he suddenly broke off. "A noble guest from a faraway land is visiting me. Come with me to the courtyard, it will be my pleasure to introduce you to him," he said.

"Rabbi, it will probably be best to stay in the shade," the Levite suggested tentatively. Hillel pushed him away from the bed and made for the sedan with surprising speed. People drew aside reverently when he appeared in the courtyard. They suddenly noticed a drunken Levite, slouching on a step amidst the crowd, holding a jug of wine in his hand and shouting abuse at the passers-by.

Jesus looked at the rabbi, walked over to the Levite and took his jug, saying, "The Scripture says: you shall not consume intoxicating substances. Wine obscures your mind and makes you lose your senses." He started pouring his wine on the ground.

The man jumped up, snatched back the jug and yelled furiously, "This boy is arrogant and ill-mannered! I ask you, rabbi Hillel, to order this bastard from Nazareth out of the holy area! He's not going to distort the Scripture at will in our parts!"

Joseph moved forward in embarrassment to drag Jesus away from the yelling man. Anger seized Jesus. He grabbed the Levite by his linen belt, drew him closer and growled in his face, "It's you and hypocrites like you that distort the Scripture! Instead of spreading the Lord's word, you loaf around, take the front seats in synagogues, get drunk and overeat, compete for who has the biggest money pouch, do all you can to get people's attention, but you're not capable of explaining the Torah to the lowest pagan!"

"I won't stand for some illegitimate bastard insulting me and my friends! Any of them will explain the Torah to you instantly!"

"You don't have a clue about the true meaning of the Scripture." Jesus wrenched himself free so strongly that the Levite reeled. Breathless, the man looked at his friends standing behind him who were preparing to teach Jesus a rather more physical lesson. The temple guardians were getting ready to intervene. However, an unknown, thirty-year old handsome man with a darker complexion came forward at that moment. He had been standing in the crowd watching the dispute with interest. He stood in front of the aggressive Levite calmly but resolutely. "My name is Rav Anna. I'm a pagan and I've decided to convert to Judaism…if you can explain the Torah to me in the time it takes me to stand on one leg."

"The Torah? Explain the Torah in such a short while? But that can't…" the Levite argued.

"Can't be done? But you said that each one of you could explain it instantly," the stranger smiled. "Come on…" He stood on one leg and the crowd laughed admiringly at the stranger's daring. A few of the Levite's Pharisee friends tried to drive him away but, at the same time, six well-built men in similar garments and with short daggers in their belts stood up and approached the stranger. However, the stranger, standing on one leg, calmed his guardians with a smile and they retreated and watched the situation, ready to intervene. Rav Anna was smiling kindly at the Levite, who shrugged meekly, and he turned to Hillel with the same request. The rabbi gave him a roguish look, then he turned to Jesus and asked him, "Can you fulfill the stranger's request?"

"Is this your guest from far away?" Jesus smiled. Hillel nodded. The crowd fell silent in tense anticipation. Jesus approached the stranger and sized up the mysterious man standing on one leg, straight as a candle. He looked at Hillel, ran his eyes over the dozens of faces watching him, and said calmly, "Love your neighbor as you love yourself. That's the whole Torah. The rest is just commentary."

The crowd muttered, the stranger stood on both legs, smiled gratefully, walked up to Jesus and embraced him. "Thank you. I know the Torah very well but only now do I truly understand Abraham's legacy. I'd like to have a word with you."

"Who are you?"

"The great rabbi's guest. Can we go a bit farther away from these people?" The stranger led Jesus to some pleasant shade under the colonnade in the Court of the Gentiles. Hillel was looking at them and smiling contentedly. The stranger offered Jesus a soft brown ball before taking one himself and eating it. Jesus accepted his offer. "Halva. A traditional Indian sweet made of corn and sugar."

"Are you from India?" Jesus looked at him in surprise. The man nodded. "I arrived by ship in the winter."

"That must have taken you a year."

"Not really. Strong westward monsoon winds blow in the winter."

"Rav Anna means gracious rabbi in Hebrew. Are you a Jew?"

Rav Anna nodded. "I'm a royal prince, a descendant of one of the lost Israeli tribes. I was sent by my father, Indo-Parthian king of Gandara, known as Gondophares, who resides in the ancient center of Vedic and Buddhist science in Takshashila."

Jesus could hardly breathe from astonishment. "I've never heard about such a king."

"You haven't, but he knows everything about you. Since the first moment you were born. Perhaps your parents told you that at your birth three kings – wise men from the East – paid a visit. One of them was Caspar. He introduced himself to your parents as Gastaphar in Armenian, but his true name is Gondophares. He was still young when he visited Bethlehem..." the stranger smiled enigmatically. "He's also known as the King of Wisdom."

"Why have you come here?" Jesus looked at him questioningly.

"To meet you in person. My father got all his information about you from the Buddhist monks at Dositheos' monastery and from our good friend rabbi Hillel. You'd be surprised how much contact there is between such distances. Back when the star appeared over Bethlehem our sages and astrologers knew it was the birth of a successor of the Kings David and Solomon, kings of wisdom, whom we respect deeply."

"But how did you get here?" Jesus asked, not knowing how to respond to the prince's words.

"I arrived in Jerusalem from the Aelana port on the Red Sea."

"Did you pass through the lands of Edom and Moab, mentioned by Moses?"

Rav Anna nodded.

"I know," the boy broke in. "The road goes from Memphis and Heliopolis in Egypt via Clysma, Mitla Pass, the Egyptian fortresses of Nekhl and Themed in the Sinai Desert, to Aelana, from there it continues north via Edom, Moab, Philadelphia and Decapolis to Damascus and Palmyra, where it branches left toward Antioch, north toward Edessa, and east toward Babylon."

"Excellent! You really are exceptionally well-read," Rav Anna praised him. "There's a branch from Philadelphia that goes to Jerusalem and then to the port of Jaffa, but we managed quite well with my chariots. Have you ever been there?"

"No."

"And would you like to?"

"I would indeed."

"And further?"

"Where further?" Jesus asked.

"To India." Jesus was taken aback. The stranger noticed the unusual sparkle in his eyes and replied to him, "My friend, the great teacher Hillel has told me much about you. He is in awe of you..." he broke off.

"But what?"

"He's afraid for you. This country, ruled by Pharisees and hypocrites, may be dangerous for a man with such critical opinions of the Torah and the all-powerful priests. You are still very young, but already you are a great hope for the people of Israel."

"Rabbi Hillel is powerful and influential," Jesus said.

"That's true, but his old age... I'm afraid you won't stay under his aegis for long. Although we all wish him the best he is clearly running out of vigor. And then, I believe, your future lies in the east, not the west. That's why eastern sages came to your cradle. You'll be welcomed in King Gondophares' court at any time. Not only is India safe for you but it's also the cradle of learning."

"I know some of the Vedas out of your four collections."

"Yes, they've existed for more than sixteen hundred years. They're five hundred years older than the Torah. The *Bhagavad Gita* is the epic of epics. Those amazing, splendid ideas, such as: *Love your neighbor as you love yourself.*"

"I know," Jesus smiled. "The essence of Moses' and Buddha's teachings is identical."

"Would you like to know Buddha's teachings in more detail?"

"I certainly would."

"Well, then I invite you on a long journey. Did you know there's a university that has been teaching young people from all around the world in my father's realm's capital, Takshashila, for over seven hundred years?" Rav Anna asked markedly.

"I do," Jesus replied. "The Greeks call Takshashila Taxila. Even the famous military leader Alexander of Macedon stayed there for some time."

The prince added, "It was also the place of education for Chanakya, the famous scholar and Brahmin, the founder of the Mauryan Empire, and the chief advisor to King Chandragupta, whose son was the famous Buddhist King Ashoka. Even Jivaka, who treated Buddha for some time, studied there."

"One can pursue the study of astronomy, futurology, medicine, philosophy, Ayurveda, surgery, music, dance and most importantly, the Vedas and Buddha's teachings."

"Marvelous! Do you know this from Dositheos' monks?" Rav Anna looked at him in surprise.

"We also have Indian and Buddhist texts in Greek available at Hillel's Academy and the monastery." Jesus paused for a while, but then his eyes glowed and he looked at the prince candidly, "I'd like to visit your country."

"Splendid. My merchants will buy balm, perfumes, papyrus, Tyrian purple, bitumen, glass from Egypt and many other goods which we'll transport to Aelana, from where we'll set out to Orissa on my ship. You'll be my guest for as long as you wish. I'll be happy and honored if you accept my invitation. I'll give you the best charioteers in India, who will take you to my father in Takshashila in the Kashmiri foothills." Jesus went a little pale and silent. "Are you alright?" Rav Anna asked worriedly.

"Yes, I just feel like I'm dreaming."

"No, my friend, you're not dreaming. I'm not inviting you to my country for you to learn but to teach us."

"I'm teaching you? But I've only just turned sixteen."

"That's exactly the age at which students are admitted to Takshashila University," Rav Anna smiled. "You're a young man gifted by God and you have every chance of becoming one of the best that have ever walked this earth. Your way of thinking, arguing and speaking is totally identical to Buddha's. You say that when a blind man is leading a blind man, they both fall into the pit. Buddha said the same thing. You speak of faith that moves mountains; he spoke of the same faith. You liken priests to whitewashed graves that are full of filth on the inside, while

Buddha said to Brahmins that they were like raw wood inside and smooth on the outside. He too refused the Brahmins' bloody sacrifices like you do and criticized their hypocrisy like you do with your priests. There are so many incredible similarities between you that it can't just be coincidence." Rav Anna thought for a while and then added, "I've wondered whether I should tell you, but I think you ought to know this. In his prophecy in the ancient Buddhist text Lagvati Sutata, our most enlightened Awakened Buddha foretold that about five hundred years after him, a Metteia would come: this is Masiha, or Messiah, in Hebrew. We think it's you."

Jesus listened to him silently, then he asked pensively, "Why do you think I could be Buddha's successor?"

"You are Buddha now. In Sanskrit, it means intelligent, wise... But the main thing is... erm... you must have noticed that we Indians are of a darker complexion. In the Lagvati Sutata, Buddha said quite clearly that the new messiah would be a Bagwa Metteia. Bagwa means white in Sanskrit. And the time of five hundred years after Buddha is upon us now."

"You know, my friend, I admit that a visit to your country sounds very attractive to me, and I'd give anything to be able to go. Only... only I promised rabbi Hillel not to leave Israel while he lives. I feel it's my duty to be with him until his last worldly moment."

The prince pondered. "I understand. You've given your word, and one's word is not taken back. Still, though, I'll try to convince the rabbi to release you from this commitment."

"It's not the rabbi's commitment, it's mine! And I will fulfill it," Jesus said resolutely.

19   I Will Wait for You

The coach set out to the north and arrived in the parking lot below the temple on the Mount of Beatitudes less than fifteen minutes later. The afternoon was hot and the wine the tourists had drunk earlier was beginning to show. Karol hadn't even finished the organizational instructions when they rushed out to the souvenir stalls to buy crosses with little glass windows allegedly containing soil on which Jesus had walked; others bought stones cast in Plexiglas, purportedly original remnants of the Capernaum synagogue where Jesus had preached, and the less wealthy contented themselves with plaster casts of the Temple of Beatitudes. The most ardently devoted old woman in the Galanta group bought a bone in a tin case and showed it proudly to everyone. "That's an original bone of one of the fish that Jesus fed the five thousand with at Tabgha."

"That must have been expensive," Mrs. Žáková responded with naked envy.

"It was, but to have a bone that Jesus himself might have held in his hands..." she replied happily and kissed the tin case with reverence. Some others kissed it afterwards.

Karol invited everyone to the beautiful palm garden surrounding the temple. After a nice stroll, they gathered under some shelters which guarded them from the scorching sun. They sat down and continued the sociable conversation that had started at lunchtime. Karol asked Tomáš to familiarize them with the history of the place. Under normal circumstances, Tomáš' talk would end as it usually had in the previous six years he had been guiding Slovak tourists around Galilee. Perhaps he would again tell a few generally known stories and miracles from Jesus' life as they are told in the New Testament, they would drink another bottle of wine and they would go back to Jerusalem in a jaunty mood. Maybe because of the heat, the wine, the presence of Michal, whose opinions he was well aware of, or a look at the plastic bags filled with Christian souvenirs made in China and bought in stalls from Arabs, he recalled – as he often did at that time – the evil methods of the Vatican secret service which had been used to persuade him to collaborate; something in him resisted this time. Anger seized him. "You've bought souvenirs to remind you of your visit to the Holy Land. But I'm not sure if these trinkets and cheap knock-offs are what you should take back home from Israel." The hubbub subsided after this unusual introduction; they knew Tomáš a little by then and they thought he would crack another joke again. "I suppose we're all Christians here. Is there anyone who isn't a Christian?" No hands went up. "Excellent. Now I'd like to know how you know you're Christians."

"Silly question." The owner of the Saint Peter's fishbone shook her head. "We were baptized of course."

"Is that it?" They shrugged without answer. "Do you think having been baptized is enough for a person to be recognized as a Christian? That's the least you can do. After all, you have no merit in having been baptized. If you think you'll be redeemed automatically just because you're baptized, you're completely wrong!"

"The Scripture says that only the baptized will enter the Kingdom of Heaven," the lady from Galanta raised her voice.

"So, in your opinion those who haven't been baptized won't go to heaven?"

"They won't!" she replied resolutely.

"What do you think?" Tomáš turned to the others, "Who's more likely to go to heaven? A baptized waster or an unbaptized decent person?"

"A decent person of course," Mr. Hlavatý said, coming closer.

"Nonsense," the lady snorted. "Unbaptized people aren't even buried legitimately."

"Madam, do you know that the majority of people on earth aren't Christians? Where do they go?" Hlavatý asked.

"That's their problem, God only summons the baptized. Christians, Catholics."

"I beg your pardon, but are you really implying that God, the greatest force in the whole universe, the Creator, has chosen this tiny grain of sand that we call Earth out of the billions of planets that exist in the universe, and out of the multitudes of people that live on it he's chosen Christians in particular, and Catholics exclusively on top of that? What have Catholics done to deserve such preferential treatment from God?"

Some laughed heartily – Protestants surely. The lady got upset. "How can a Catholic priest ask such questions? It's in the Scripture and the Scripture is not to be questioned. All that's in it is truth and nothing but truth."

"There you go! The same Scripture says a righteous life is more important than baptism."

"What are you driveling on about?" another lady from the Galanta group butted in. "Baptism is the most important sacrament and you have no right to question it! That's blasphemy!"

"I don't understand why you're yelling at me, I totally agree with you," Tomáš protested. "Do you know how old Jesus was when he was baptized?"

"He was thirty," the lady replied sharply.

"And do you know why he had John baptize him?" They stared at him in silence. "I'll tell you then." Tomáš smiled faintly, produced a pocket edition of the New Testament out of his breast pocket and started reading. "Gospel of Matthew, 28: 19-20, Dispatching of disciples." The group of women from Galanta fell on their knees and made the sign of the cross upon these words. Tomáš continued, *"Jesus said to his disciples: Therefore go and teach nations, baptizing them in the name of the Father and of the Son and of the Holy Spirit, and teaching them to obey everything I have commanded you."* There was a moment of silence and Tomáš turned to the kneeling women. "Therefore, go and teach nations. Can you tell me how you can teach eight-day-old babies? No place in the Scripture speaks about baptizing infants. If the Writ is holy, it has to be respected! Baptizing babies means nothing: it's a betrayal of Jesus! A newborn baby can't make that decision itself." Tomáš was almost yelling. "Can you imagine how much stronger the Church would be if it only contained people who entered it based on their free choice, that is, adult people? The kind of people that John and Jesus' disciples baptized? I'll tell you what Jesus said about baptism in this very holy place. If you don't have the time to read gospels, at least read the Sermon of the Mount, please." He opened his book and read out: *"The true sons of God are those who have decided to follow me voluntarily based on their own free will, without any coercion whatsoever. God has given reason to all his children, which means ability of deciding freely. A person should choose their spiritual path voluntarily. I, Christ, offer people a path to the Divine Heart, but I do not force a single one to take that path. If you wish to be like me, I will help you. If not, it does not matter, I will wait for you."* Tomáš shut his book and cast a stern look at the silent tourists.

"Tomáš, I think you preach more convincingly than Jesus once did on this hill," Michal smiled, "I'm just afraid you won't get much love from people by shouting at them."

Tomáš said nothing.

"We should be going, time's moving on. There's still a long way to go to Jerusalem and we want to make a stop in Cana. I think Tomáš is ready to debate with you on the coach as well," Karol called out.

"I'm fed up with them. And myself," Tomáš muttered. Michal looked at him uncomprehendingly. "I'd love to pack my stuff and get lost somewhere in Tibet or a Buddhist monastery in Ladakh and care no more about this hypocritical world!" They were walking silently toward the coach on the heated asphalt when the gentleman from Galanta approached Tomáš.

"Excuse me, I wanted to apologize for my wife. She's a good woman and I love her. She's just… slightly disoriented. So am I, I must admit. But you opened my eyes today. I feel cleansed. I even think a miracle might have happened on that hill. It seems I've come to Israel specifically for this day. Thank you so much." Then others came to him and told him the same thing.

Tomáš smiled at them thankfully. His mood improved, and he suddenly felt he was the happiest person in the Holy Land.

20 The King of Peace

After a long stroll together in the pleasant shade of the colonnade, Rav Anna and Jesus returned to the staircase in the Women's courtyard, where rabbi Hillel and Joseph and Mary were awaiting them in the shade of the Nicanor Gate.

"Son, it's high time we set out, the sun's already high in the sky," his parents urged him. "Why would you be leaving in this heat? You can stay the night at my place and set out at daybreak," Hillel suggested. Mary looked at her husband: she was clearly in favor of this proposal. "Well, why not? Thank you for the generous proposal, friend Hillel," Joseph bowed.

"At least you'll have some more time to talk with my dear guest, Prince Rav Anna of Orissa." The stranger and Jesus' parents exchanged courteous bows.

"Master," Rav Anna addressed Joseph, "I'd like to put forth to you a proposal which I've already spoken about with your son. He agrees with it." He looked at the surprised Jesus. "Father Hillel approves of the proposal as well." Hillel nodded and gave Joseph an encouraging look. "I'd like to invite your worthy son to a visit of my country."

"India?" Mary almost wailed in fear. "But that's very far away. And what would he do there? He must complete his studies at Dositheos', and... help his father in the workshop," she searched for any reason to decline the prince's proposal.

"My dear prince, yes, I'm delighted with your invitation, but you know I cannot accept it at the moment," Jesus protested as well.

But Rav Anna continued calmly. "I deeply respect your parental instinct to protect this talented young man, but I assure you he'll be in the best hands in my palace in the city of Puri where the famous

Jagannath Temple is, and in my father King Gondophares' residence in Takshashila. My house, my servants, my friends and parents will all welcome him with open and caring arms."

"Do you want to go?" Mary turned to her son. Jesus said nothing. "Well, you see he doesn't," Mary implored.

"He does, only everything is in the hands of the great rabbi," Rav Anna looked at Hillel.

"I know what you mean to say. My time has nearly come, and I will not insist that this young man, the greatest hope of my people, should pass up the opportunity to go and collect the wisdom of the east at your kind invitation."

"Rabbi, thanks for the generosity, but I've given my word and I'll stand by it. Please let's talk about this no more," Jesus said.

"My son, just go with the prince, you'll be in the best hands," the rabbi protested. Jesus said nothing.

"And how are you going to get there?" Mary asked, encouraged by Jesus' silence.

"My ship in the port of Aelana on the Red Sea is just being loaded with goods and will set sail soon."

"But by God, the distance is enormous. No son or daughter of Israel has ever set foot there," Mary reasoned in fear.

"Dear mother, that's not the case. There have been Jewish settlements all along the coast of Malabar since the times of your famous King Solomon. There are synagogues there, in which your son will find devoted servants to your God Yahweh. The cities of Cochin and Kodungallur are the greatest centers of Jewish religion and culture in all of India."

"The books of the Torah indeed speak of Jews sent to the east by Solomon," Hillel butted in. "It is a known fact that Solomon made Palestine a trade hub between Africa, Asia and Europe and sent Jewish merchants to Tangier, Carthage, Cyrenaica, Memphis and even Nubia in Africa, as well as Cordoba in Hispania, Arleat in Gallia; the entire trade in Rome has been in Jewish hands. There are Jews in Adriatic Salona, Corinth, Babylon, Arabia, Persia, Bactria, but I've never heard of Jews reaching India in Solomon's times. Our wise king helped the Phoenicians – with whom his father King David had signed a treaty of friendship– finance their naval expedition past the Pillars of Hercules to

Tartessos in Hispania. He established Europe's biggest port in Gadir along with the Phoenicians, but I've never heard of King Solomon going east," Hillel said heavily. He wiped his sweaty forehead with a white cloth. But his hand only moved very slowly, so Mary herself volunteered to dry his cold forehead. The rabbi looked at her thankfully and continued refreshed. "Gadir was the key transshipment area for Celtic gold, copper and, most importantly, valuable tin, used to make not only our beautiful cutlery but also bronze. Can you imagine any army without bronze? Jerusalem was the seat of not only a wise king but also a skilled trader and financier, my friends," Hillel tried to smile.

"The port of Muziris, our most important one, located near Kodungallur north of Cochin in Kerala, was established by Jewish and Phoenician merchants. It's the center of spice trade," Rav Anna added to Hillel's words.

The old man awoke again and continued in a low voice, "The Torah says that King Solomon built his ships in Ezion-Geber, which is near Eilat on the Red Sea coast, in the land of Edom." Then he pointed at a place in the Scripture for the Levite who was standing by. "Read!"

The Levite's sonorous voice attracted passers-by. "Hiram sent his servants, sailors and sea experts to Solomon's servants on the ships. They sailed to Ophir whence they brought four hundred and twenty talents of gold and took it to King Solomon."

"Is this the same Hiram that was the Phoenician king and had a friendly relationship with Solomon?" Jesus inquired.

Hillel nodded, "The same that helped him build the Temple in Jerusalem, the most splendid and expensive structure in the world in its time. Can you imagine how much material its construction required? Wood, cement, asphalt, stone, granite, sandalwood, gold, silver, ivory. That was why Solomon sent Jews to India when the Temple construction started, to establish trading posts."

"I'm sorry, father Hillel, I'd like to correct you. The Temple was the most splendid structure in Palestine only, because India already had several of them by that time, such as the Jagannath in my city of Puri," the prince added good-naturedly.

The rabbi didn't respond; the men watched him uncomfortably. But inquisitive Jesus interrupted the silence, "And where is this rich land of Ophir?"

"The legendary country was a three day's voyage from the mouth of the Indus, north of our large city on the west coast named Mumbai. It was the main trading port with Arabia, Egypt, Israel, Oman and Babylon. It was part of the realm of the Buddhist King Ashoka three hundred years ago," Rav Anna replied.

Hillel watched Jesus whose eyes were aglow with zeal. "Do you desire to know the land where your brothers, the descendants of King Solomon live?" Jesus said nothing. "It's starting to get really hot, let's go inside," the rabbi invited them. He gestured to his servants, who lifted the sedan, and the whole group including the Levites returned to the pleasant shade of the rabbi's dwelling. He was pale and asked for cold water. He had difficulties drinking, and his lips were trembling.

"Rabbi, are you feeling worse?" Mary asked. Hillel forced a smile. "Shall we send for the temple doctor?"

"My children, I'm feeling better than I may have ever felt. I feel I can hear Archangel Gabriel playing the Lord's trumpet," the rabbi said with a smile.

"Rabbi…" Mary leaned over to him and wiped the sweat that pearled on his forehead.

"My dear little daughter, this is how you used to wipe my forehead when you were my favorite pupil at the temple girls' school. I took to you just like I took to your great husband and your son. I'm happy to have experienced in my earthly life the one who will soon bring us hope. But I won't be around when he does."

"That's what we fear the most…" Mary whispered, tears in her eyes.

"But why? My moment is coming, and you should rejoice. Only those who leave without hope should be sad. But I believe, I have hope. I've tried to use the opportunity that the Lord gave me as well as I could – to everyone's benefit. He who believes doesn't die," he breathed and asked for another cup of water.

"Rabbi, father." Mary took him by the hand and kissed it tenderly. Joseph, Jesus and Rav Anna sat by his bed without a word.

"When you realize our life is eternal, it changes fundamentally. The fear of death that accompanies us from birth suddenly disappears. Our earthly life is only a transformation of spirit into matter; death is life and life is death. We start dying the moment we're born. The birth of one is the death of another. It's just like the sun: it sets for one but rises for another at the same moment. But the sun is eternal: it shines and warms perpetually. Rejoice with me."

The rabbi asked to be taken out to the terrace. He lay on his mahogany bed, breathed serenely, and kept his eyes open until the evening star appeared in the sky. He gestured to Jesus to come closer. The boy kneeled by his bed and the rabbi put his hand on his head. They knew the end had drawn near. With his trembling lips he began to recite the extolling confession Shema Yisrael: "Hear, O Israel: The Lord is our God, the Lord is One. And you shall love the Lord your God with all your heart, all your soul, all your power, and these words that I command you today will be in your heart forever…"

His voice weakened, his lips stopped shaking, and his hand slid off the boy's head. He closed his eyes and never opened them again.

21   The Forgotten Glasses

Marika didn't feel well on Friday morning. Michal put his hand on her forehead: she had a fever. Although she was very keen on going to Nazareth and Jericho, just a few minutes before the coach was about to depart, she changed her mind and decided to stay in the air-conditioned hotel room.

Unsettled, Michal called Tomáš, who arrived at the hotel soon. The attentive manager Massoud offered to call a doctor, but when both Marika and Michal reassured him it was just a high fever, he left the room.

"Are you sure you don't need a doctor?" Tomáš repeated the manager's question.

"Tomáš, you're such a close friend of us that you know what's the matter with me and what I need. Hope. If you know a doctor who will give it to me, then call him in."

They fell silent. Michal tried to lighten the oppressive atmosphere. He turned to Tomáš with a forced smile, "You told the people some interesting things yesterday, only I'm not sure Jesus would praise you for how you told them." Tomáš looked at him with surprise. "If you want people to adopt your truth, you should say it to them with a little more kindness."

"Jesus too lost his temper sometimes when he saw too much stupidity around him."

"At least you have someone to use as an excuse," Michal laughed. "I guess Jesus would have forgiven you, but if your bishop heard what you were telling the people yesterday, I don't know…"

"I didn't become a priest for the bishop's sake. But you're right, I've been thinking about giving up more and more. I can't find the strength for more hypocrisy. You see, ordinary people don't pretend. One has more faith, another has less, but those of us who are just searching for it have the least of it. Yet we dare to teach it to people. As if you could teach faith!"

"I apologize, I get a feeling that ahem… I've never asked you, but I think you have a girlfriend…" Michal asked meekly.

Tomáš said nothing for a while. "I used to."

"Now you don't?"

With unusual sharpness, as if Michal had struck a sensitive point, Tomáš snapped back, "Can we not talk about this please?!"

"I beg your pardon. You shouldn't leave the Church. What will become of it when priests like you leave?"

"See! Even you expect miracles from me, yet I can't even give you hope."

The atmosphere became oppressive again, like the dust that falls on one's soul when it seems that that there is no hope, that life is futile.

"Tomáš, do you believe in reincarnation?" Marika asked all of a sudden.

Michal looked at his wife, surprised at what she was thinking about.

"Of course I do, otherwise our life would be pointless," Tomáš replied. "We're here to learn something, to understand and help our soul ascend to a higher level, which we complete in the next life."

"I don't believe in reincarnation," she said.

Tomáš pondered for a while. "Are you afraid of death?" he asked quietly. Marika nodded. "There you go, you've just proven you do believe."

"I don't understand."

"Why are you afraid of death? If you knew that everything ends ultimately upon death, that there's nothing after it, what would you be afraid of? The nothing? But you are afraid, so you believe that there is something afterwards, beyond. That's natural, only there's no need to concentrate on death too much, because then you give up living. He who's afraid of death is afraid of life too. Death is with us in every instant, it's like stars in the daytime sky. We don't think they're there, but it's only us being unable to see them. When you go to sleep at night, you leave for a spiritual world. Rest assured, my beautiful friend, and expect your next life as placidly as you expect your next inhalation, the next day, the next year. As much as we don't know what comes after death, we don't know what came before birth. It seems the same to me.

A human being is an odd creature. It goes to sleep preparing for the next day, planning for summer, holidays, next year. Why don't we prepare for death in the same way?"

"How could you prepare for death?" Marika asked.

"By living courageously, keeping God's law. But you know that," Tomáš smiled kindly. "I know, it's easy for me to say but… I'm sorry, if I was in your shoes and I learned…" he fell silent, as if considering whether to finish what he was saying.

"Learned what?"

"…that I had cancer. I'd probably sit somewhere in total silence and ask myself what worse could happen to me…" Both Marika and Michal watched him attentively. "Death… So, if you thought like this, you'd also realize that you have the same thing ahead of you as we all have. It's not long since I realized in Cana how close to death I was. And since then, I've been trying to make friends with death. Suddenly, my life has become incredibly beautiful. I'm no longer afraid."

The voice of a muezzin summoning people for prayer in a nearby mosque was heard in the room.

"I'm sorry." He took Marika's hand in his, putting his other hand on her hot forehead. "You've got a fever."

"It makes sense what you're saying," Michal admitted. "Only I'm afraid it's not what Marika wants to hear at this point." He looked at Tomáš, sitting by the headboard of his wife's bed, and he realized it looked like he was giving the Last Rites. He was taken aback by the idea, almost in fear.

"What's this locket of yours?" Tomáš asked suddenly and leaned closer to Marika's locket protruding from her blouse.

"Hey, don't you lean that close to her, you're a priest, you could be tempted," Michal laughed.

"Another reason why I want out of the Church," he replied, smiling. "But this locket Marika has is really interesting. I think I've seen something like it in David's Museum in the Citadel. Funny…" he scratched the back of his neck nervously. Michal observed him and found something strange about his friend.

"Take a look at it if you want." Marika took off her locket and handed it to him.

"Where did you get it?"

"From my mother."

"It looks very old. Where did your mother get it?"

"I've no idea."

"Can I borrow it?"

"What for?" Michal sat up.

"We'll go to the synagogue in Wilson's Arch. That's a synagogue basically on top of the Wailing Wall. My friend Simonides is the rabbi there, a very wise and worthy man. He's from the ancient lineage of rabbi Hillel's. They say there isn't a wiser rabbi in all of Israel. I think he will know what this is."

"That's an excellent idea," Marika lit up. "While you're there, Michal, you can put my message in the Wall?"

"You'll put it there yourself," Michal objected.

"You take it and put it in there. They say a wish has a greater chance of success if inserted by a close friend." She didn't wait for an answer and pressed the slip of paper into Michal's hand.

"Is it the same thing you showed me at home?"

"I've added something."

"Can I read it?" Marika smiled roguishly. Michal unfolded the paper and narrowed his eyes. "Where are my glasses?"

"I really have no idea. Why do you take them off your neck? Didn't you get that chain just so you wouldn't have to search for them all the time?" Marika reproached him.

The telephone rang at that moment; the reception clerk informed them that Mr. Kráľ had left his glasses at the reception desk. Michal stood up to fetch them, but he realized he wouldn't be much use in the lift without his glasses.

"Damn, the numbers in the lift are so small I can't read them without my glasses. Tomáš, would you come get them with me?"

"Why both?" Tomáš jumped up readily. "I'll be back in a minute."

Michal gave him an appreciative look and returned to Marika. Tomáš ran down the stairs, taking two at a time. He picked up the glasses at the reception desk, and although a man was just getting in the lift and gesturing him to join in, Tomáš headed back to the emergency staircase. Surprised, the man just shrugged. After making sure that there was no one else in the mezzanine, he went to the window, took out his special smartphone equipped with the latest photographic and optical technology. Michal's thick horn-rimmed glasses were child's play for his cutting-edge device. He scanned both lenses instantly using a synchronized scanner and determined the refractive power, which was shown on the display: plus two and a half diopters on the left eye, plus three on the right. He also photographed and measured the gilt chain and measured its length accurately. Tomáš then laid the glasses with the chain on the smartphone and the display showed their exact weight. He hesitated for a moment before mailing all the photos and measurement readings to the SIV headquarters. He felt like a scumbag betraying a man who trusted him absolutely. He cursed the fact that his passionate love affair with Veronica had been discovered by the bishop. He had no doubts that the bishop was tipped off by one of his gay friends who always tried to convince him that he was one of them, only he hadn't tried it yet. The bishop presented him with a choice: either the end of his clerical career, or have the other option explained to him by father Pietro, in charge of special affairs in the diocese. In exchange for the bishop turning a blind eye to his relationship with Veronica, father Pietro asked him to collaborate with the secret service. It wouldn't be difficult, just a tiny favor from time to time. Replacing Michal's eyeglasses was one such favor. He cursed both himself and the day he fell into father Pietro's clutches. He tried to delude himself with the fact that he was doing it for the Church's good, but he knew he was deceiving himself. His love for Veronica eventually turned to nothing because she left for Brazil with her parents. He swore he'd run away somewhere far off on the first opportunity, far enough for the Pharisees of the Vatican to keep their dirty hands off him.

*****

He returned to the Král's' room less than four minutes later and handed the glasses to Michal, who was sitting by his wife's bed. He thanked him, putting on the glasses to read her expanded wish. "What's that?" he asked in surprise. "Why, it's all in Hebrew," he frowned.

"I had a friend from the Israeli Embassy write it for me. For the Jewish God to understand my wish better," she laughed.

"Well, I don't think these glasses will help with this. Will you tell me what it says?"

"I will one day."

He looked at his wife with diffidence. "You don't trust me?"

"Michal," she said with a rebuke.

Tomáš was finding the scene awkward, so he butted in. "Marika's right, there'll be an awful crowd by the Wall in the evening. Remember it's Friday and the Jewish Sabbath starts at sunset. All the Orthodox Jews of Jerusalem will be there. You'd be better putting the message there during the day. The rabbi won't have time to see us in the afternoon either. So we'll be back for lunch and I'm inviting you for a glass of wine in the evening," Tomáš smiled and squeezed Marika's hand encouragingly. "You'll feel better by then. Don't worry, I trust we can get to Jesus' grave when it's quiet and deserted." Tomáš tried to keep up the smile.

"Tomáš, are you alright?" Michal looked at his friend, whose behavior was unusually nervous. He nodded unconvincingly.

He felt relief when Marika turned to him after that. "You said yourself you've been here for six years, but you haven't succeeded."

"Yes, but the need to be by the grave has never been this urgent…"

"I also believe we'll succeed," Michal stroked Marika's sweaty hair and turned to Tomáš. "Shall we go to the restaurant you mentioned? Near the Ecce Homo?"

"Why not, we can, but we'd have to sip fizzy water."

"Why?"

"It's in the Muslim Quarter, it'd be pointless trying to get some alcohol. We'll go to my favorite tavern on David Lane in the Armenian Quarter. It stocks excellent Armenian wines, and it's just a few paces away from the Wailing Wall. The Sabbath will be an experience you won't forget. Alright?" He looked at Marika with a smile. "Don't worry, everything will be fine."

"I don't doubt that," Marika said, smiling sadly. "I know how much Michal was looking forward to rambles around Jerusalem, so the two of you go and come back for lunch. We'll have it together at the hotel."

"Oh no, I've got a good book, I'll stay with you in the room," Michal protested.

"Miško, just you go, both of you go. I'm really not that ill. Really. Plus, I'm curious to hear what the rabbi says about my locket."

"No, I'll wait with you until lunch and then we'll see. We'll have lunch at the hotel and if you feel better then we'll go to the Wall together," Michal insisted. In the end, they agreed Tomáš and him would walk to nearby Damascus Gate and come back in a while.

When they came back after about an hour, Marika was asleep. She was still asleep an hour later, so they had lunch at the hotel without her. In the afternoon, they went to a nearby marketplace and bought some fresh grapes, figs, pomegranates and, most importantly coconuts, which Marika never tired of. They entered the room with their arms full of fruit just as she woke up. The deep sleep had obviously done her good. She was smiling with a sparkle in her eyes that hadn't been there in the morning.

"How are you feeling?" Michal asked and put his hand on her forehead. The temperature had gone.

"Excellent," she smiled. "Have you looted a fruit kibbutz?"

"Are you coming with us to the city? The sabbath starts in the evening, and that's an experience," Tomáš said, trying to persuade her.

"I'm feeling well, but I think I'll still stay at the hotel. I want to be well for tomorrow, when we go to the Old City. But you go."

"Are you not even having dinner with us?"

"I think a fruit fast will do me good today. And if you put my message in the Wall during the sabbath, maybe my wish will get to God faster," she smiled.

"So then, we'll just go to the Wailing Wall and will be back soon," Michal nodded.

He cleaned and washed the fruits for her, put them in a bowl on the bedside table, and set out for Damascus Gate via the marketplace with Tomáš. In the dense crowd of Muslims doing their shopping they didn't notice the two inconspicuous men walking behind them.

22 Shalom

After Hillel's death, members of the Hevra Kadisha burial society arrived with his only brother Shebnah, who tore his clothes according to tradition. They started preparations for the burial, which took place in the afternoon of the same day. Jesus, Mary, Joseph and Rav Anna attended. They left after the meal of condolence. They went across the Women's Courtyard between the Wooden Hall and the Nazirites' Hall, then across the Court of the Gentiles between the stone balustrade and the Sanhedrin meeting hall, before arriving in the section containing lodgings for guests to the Sanhedrin. As it was getting dark, the prince accommodated them in his rooms for the night. After dinner and a ritual bath, they sat in the spacious lobby with an exquisite mosaic floor and abundant flowers in Egyptian glass vases. The large window faced an expansive terrace full of almond trees with parrots sitting in their branches. Rare peacocks were strolling among the trees. Although they had been expecting the beloved rabbi's passing, the moment of death made their souls sore.

The prince's personal butler intruded at every turn to keep him informed on the status of preparations for the next day's departure from Jerusalem. They were all thinking about the same thing: Jesus' journey to India, unimpeded now that Hillel had died.

The prince turned slowly to Jesus' parents. "My country is home to wise, kind and god-fearing people, just as yours is. It will be of enormous benefit to your son and the whole of Israel that this talented boy acquires the wisdom of our Vedas and our enlightened Gautama Buddha."

Mary looked at her husband meekly. He said nothing. He stood by his son a moment later and stroked his curly hair. "I know you're eager for knowledge and understanding of the mysteries of life and death. I know you're not happy living in a world of dogmatism, preferring to go and search for the truth. If you're decided, set out now, as that is the meaning of your life."

"Yes, father, I will search for the truth."

"We too have a lot of lies, deceit, hypocrisy, thievery, murders and suffering. But perhaps because we can understand the causes of suffering thanks to our Great Awakened, we are more able to help others as well. Please accept my invitation as a gift not only to your son but to the people of Israel too. Staying in the land of Buddha will be of great help to him on his way," Rav Anna reassured the parents.

"When will he come back?" Mary wanted to know.

"I intend to show him Orissa, Rajagriha, Benares, Nepal, Lumbini, Tibet, Kashmir, Takshashila University, and other holy sites; I think about four or five years. But don't you worry, you'll be informed about him at every turn via my merchant friends."

Mary's face frowned at the idea of her youngest son leaving her for so long. "Mary, didn't the rabbi say our son would be in the best hands? That the prince's family is the most virtuous?" Joseph tried to convince himself more than his wife. He walked over to Mary, trembling with tears, and embraced her lovingly.

"Can we go then?" Rav Anna asked. Jesus stood by him resolutely.

"But he has nothing with him, he's not ready for such a big journey," Mary protested.

"He has all he needs. My servants have purchased the necessary clothes and footwear for him. We have food and drink galore. My friends will take care of his security on the way." He pointed at the bearded men standing on the terrace nearby, wearing long white cloaks under which they had swords and daggers, mighty turbans on their heads and colored chains on their forearms. The men bowed politely. Jesus' father stood by him after a moment of silence. His grey hair was fluttering in the wind. "My son, there's nothing left to do but say goodbye. My time too is drawing near, I don't know if I will ever see you again. Even though I have no merit in you coming to this world, I love you like my own son. In fact, you've grown on me more than any of my own children. I give you my paternal consent to go."

After a long time, Jesus embraced his father and kissed his calloused and wrinkly hand warmly. He felt sorry for not having become closer to this kind and benign man.

When stars rose over Jerusalem, none of the Nazarene family could fall asleep, so Joseph and Mary talked about their son's long and dangerous journey until the dawn. They parted peacefully in the morning.

"Shalom," the father stroked the son's hair.

"Shalom," Jesus replied.

"Is it true that shalom means peace?" the prince asked. Jesus nodded. "And Solomon means the king of peace."

"We're going to search for it together," Rav Anna smiled.

Joseph stared at the young men as they departed. Suddenly, he was grasped by an inexplicable sadness. The moment he realized it might be the last that he saw of his son, Jesus turned around and waved goodbye to his parents.

"We sail from Aelana, the port from which King Solomon sailed to India a thousand years ago," Rav Anna said.

"Prince," Jesus turned to him in deep thought, "you said Ophir used to stand at the mouth of the river Indus." Rav Anna nodded. "The Indus rises in Kashmir, doesn't it?"

"It does. Why?"

"It is possible that the Jews and King Solomon might have reached that country?"

"Wait for the surprise."

23 A Wish God Doesn't Get That Often

On the way to the square by the Wailing Wall they were overtaken by many Orthodox Jews, wearing wide hats with long, wavy sidelocks sticking out under them. They were wearing kaftans and black socks, hurrying from the Orthodox neighborhood of Mea Sharim toward the Wailing Wall via Damascus Gate. At the crossroads with Via Dolorosa they intermingled with crowds of Christians hurrying to the Church of the Holy Sepulcher. Outside the entrance in the square by the Wall they had to undergo a security check, after which they entered a wide area in which crowds of Jews and rubbernecks from all over the world were thronging. The area by the Wall was divided into a women's and a men's section, and photography was strictly prohibited.

"Do you think we'll manage to get to the Wall?" Michal asked, disconcerted.

"No problem. Only we have to put on a kippah. They're in that box over there." Tomáš pointed toward the narrow entrance to the Wall. They both spent another moment observing Jews performing their rituals associated with the start of the sabbath by the Wall. The area by the Wall was filling with both men and women as the sunset was drawing nearer. Some of the men were praying, meditating with the Torah in their hands, repeating parts of it out loud and swaying back and forth; others were talking sociably, some were singing, others dancing, smiling, greeting God with their eyes upwards, giving him thumbs-up as a sign of appreciation; others were arguing with Him, persuading Him.

"I think I'm beginning to understand why the Jews are the chosen people," Michal smiled.

Tomáš pointed out to him promptly, "Notice how they communicate with God." Michal visualized images from Christian, Muslim and Buddhist shrines that he had visited. Everyone in them knelt or even lay down. "The Jews worship God with dignity," he thought out loud. "I haven't seen a single one kneeling. Now I understand why God roots for them more than for others. He likes people self-confident."

They mingled among the Jews and rubbernecks; nobody paid attention to them. They were making their way toward the Wall when suddenly a man peeled off a group of debating Jews and shook hands warmly with Tomáš. "My dear friend, what a coincidence! What brings you to Jerusalem?"

"I'm guiding tourists from my country. Allow me to introduce you to my friend, Mr. Kráľ." Michal went up to the man and shook his hand amicably.

"I'm rabbi Simonides. Welcome to the Wailing Wall. We are pleased at your demonstration of respect by visiting this holy place. If you care, I will gladly invite you to the synagogue. It's actually a continuation of the Wall under this arch. It's named after the British officer Wilson, who discovered it in the 19th century. It served as a western access gate to the Temple Mount in Christ's time," the rabbi started explaining enthusiastically. "Please, come in, Slovaks are especially welcome in these parts. We'll never forget how you helped us with the arms supplies in 1948 – you were still Czechoslovakia back then. It will be an honor to guide you through the synagogue."

The rabbi set out and the two delightedly followed him. As they entered the rabbi slowed down and explained the tasks the Jews were performing, basic information connected with the sabbath, and showed them rare books stored on tables which the men were free to browse.

"What brings you to the Wall?" he turned to Michal.

"Curiosity as well as… well… my wife gave me a slip of paper for me to put in the Wall."

"Have you done so?"

"Not yet."

"Remember to do that."

"And besides, we've also come… erm… to see you in fact," Tomáš butted in. "We have this object. It belongs to my friend's wife, and I think it's interesting." He handed the locket to the rabbi.

The rabbi took it in his hand, turned it over and shook his head. "Yes… yes… interesting indeed. Let's come over here, farther away from the hubbub." They moved back between long rows of libraries, where there were fewer worshippers and sat down by one of the tables laden with books. "It's a very valuable locket. Very powerful. It dates back to Herod's times. Strange. Do you know how your wife got it? It really is an antique. You'd get a lot of money for it. If you ever decide to sell it, I'll buy it for our synagogue immediately," the rabbi proposed.

"I had no idea my wife had such a valuable thing."

"How much for it?" the rabbi asked.

"We're not selling it," Michal replied with a smile. "I'll give you ten thousand Euros."

"No, it's a gift from her mother."

"Is your wife Jewish?"

"She used to be."

The rabbi nodded with understanding and examined the locket closely.

"Such lockets were given as royal accolades in Herod's time. This is incredible." The rabbi opened a drawer in one of the tables and produced a magnifying glass and examined the locket with it. "It features two columns. One with a letter J, the other with a B. Interesting, interesting… There's an interesting section of the New Testament – the Epistle of Jude. He was probably Jesus' brother. Jude mentions how Jesus' ancestor Enoch prophesied a great disaster that would destroy humankind if it lived immorally and impiously. He foretold hurtling sea waves and a huge fire that would destroy the world. To preserve at least the most important knowledge that humankind had gained until then, he decided to store it in two columns. One was made of marble so that no fire could devour it, and the other was from the vegetable resin laterus, which no water could wash away. These columns survived the flood. Fragments of one of the columns were found during the construction of Solomon's Temple about three thousand years ago. It was reconstructed and erected by the eastern gate. Another was built beside it, and the two columns were linked with an arch in the middle of which was a keystone called *Shalom*. That means peace, as well as happiness, success, divine bliss. The right-hand column was called Joachim, symbolizing the clerical, spiritual power; it was toward the east. The left-hand one was named Boas, after King David's forefather, and it symbolized royal, secular power; it stood toward the west. The Shalom keystone was the symbolic connection between the two pillars of power. The symbols of secular and spiritual power have been separated as a consequence of the actions of hypocrites, which is the reason why the world is evil today: everything that's separated is evil. In contrast, everything that's united is good, and everyone who unites is good. Boas is lined with spiraling ornaments, Joachim with vertical," the rabbi said and smiled. "Now look at your locket."

"I know what's on it. A Star of David and the two columns, B and J, on the back of the locket. The words Templum Hierosolym are over them. They look Greek because *Hieros* means holy in Ancient Greek. And the word *solym* is actually your shalom, peace," Michal said.

"Or Solomon." The rabbi thought for a moment and then added, seemingly to himself, "There are two places in the world where Jesus preached, and both are gripped by contention, unrest and war instead of the peace he wished to establish. He was born in one of them and died in the other. They are like the two columns – Boas and Joachim, the birthplace and the place of death, connected by Solomon, king of David's lineage, the same family as Jesus, the king of peace." He came around and turned to Michal, speaking more loudly, "Do you have any idea how your wife's mother came by it?"

"No, and my wife isn't sure either."

"Did she wear it?"

"Only recently."

"And for how long?"

"A few weeks."

"Is your wife sick?" Michal and Tomáš looked at him in surprise.

"She has cancer. She recovered from it once, and it came back again…"

"Evil energy radiates from the locket. It probably absorbed it from a person who wore it before."

"Her mother wore it."

"Did she die of cancer by any chance?" the rabbi asked.

Michal nodded. "How do you know?"

The rabbi evaded an answer. "Your wife carries within herself her mother's cancer. I don't know how she influenced her, but I think they weren't very fond of each other. You said your wife asked you to put her plea in a crack in the Wall."

Michal nodded. "Do you know what the significance of this Wall is?"

"It's a fragment of Solomon's original temple, the only part left after the destruction by Babylonians and Romans later on."

"That's right, but what's the significance of people from all over the world coming here to tell God their wishes, even writing them on slips of paper and inserting them in the cracks of the Wall?"

The rabbi shrugged. "The Temple was God's seat and according to our tradition, the Wall is the place nearest God, which is why our wishes reach him more directly."

"A nice story," Michal nodded.

"Well, you see, being a people chosen by God, we must be closest to Him," the rabbi smiled roguishly. "And it probably works, since even your Pope has put his wish in the wall." He pondered for a while and then asked Michal, "Do you know what your wife's wish is?"

"I don't."

"Didn't she show you?"

"She did, but I didn't understand it." The rabbi looked surprised. "It's written in Hebrew."

"Your wife speaks Hebrew?"

"No, she doesn't."

"So, she had someone write it for her. And she didn't tell you what it means?" Michal shook his head. "And you didn't want to know?"

"I admit I did, but I didn't question her."

"Your wife's seriously ill…" Michal nodded. "But if she didn't want you to know what her wish was, she'd have asked you explicitly not to read it. But she gave it to you to read, although she knew you wouldn't understand it… strange." He shook his head for a moment, then looked Michal deeply in the eyes. "Will you show the paper to me?"

Michal handed it to him. The rabbi read it carefully and frowned. Then he asked, perturbed, "Why didn't your wife come here in person?"

"She's here."

"She's in Jerusalem? And she hasn't come to place her wish in the wall herself?" he asked in surprise.

"She didn't feel well. She's in bed at the hotel."

"She had best come and see me." The rabbi handed him back the paper. "As soon as possible. But, of course, not sooner than tomorrow after sunset," he added and grinned broadly.

"Why? I'll place it in the Wall myself."

"Your wife's condition is very bad. Believe me, she doesn't have much time left."

"What did she write?" Michal asked, disconcerted.

"A wish God doesn't get that often."

"Can you... ahem, share it with me?"

"It's a wish she doesn't need God for. I can fulfill it myself."

24 Incident with the Prince

After having said goodbye to his parents, Jesus and Rav Anna, accompanied by guards, rode their horses to an inn near some purifying baths. The large courtyard was congested with carriages, neighing horses, oxen and mules. The caravan, composed of about fifty fully laden carriages, was so long that the last one had only just left the city when the front end arrived at the southern foot of the Mount of Olives. Passing the hamlet of Bethany, the caravan continued toward Jericho. Even though it was only shortly after noon when they arrived at the river Jordan, they decided to spend the night in that beautiful place. The next morning, they continued on the Jerusalem road until it joined the main road toward Aelana under Mount Nebo. Jesus looked at the hill, which stood at about two thousand six hundred feet tall and whose summit faded away in a mist. He recalled the words of the Book of Deuteronomy – the event when the Lord led Moses to this hill and said to him mysteriously, "This is the country that I'm giving to your progeny, but you will not enter it..." Jesus had long before pondered over these peculiar words with which God denied Moses entry into the chosen land. He was supposedly buried somewhere here. Supposedly... The Israelites' most important prophet, and no one knew where he was buried. How could that be? 'Could he be buried somewhere else?' Jesus wondered.

The chariot, drawn by two mighty Nisean horses, began to accelerate. "Can we slow down a little?" Jesus asked the prince who had taken the whip from the driver and was briskly cracking it down on the horses. The chariot was bumping and bouncing on the stony road and the horses' manes were flapping in the wind, caught by the same enthusiasm that seized the prince. After they came down from the hills, they joined the main road, which was much more comfortable than the one they had taken from Jerusalem. Rav Anna was holding the reins firmly in his hands, showing Jesus the speed at which the two-wheeled chariot could run. They had exchanged their luxury coach for it in the morning. They had overtaken a slow caravan of fully loaded camels, carriages drawn by oxen, big Asian onagers, donkeys and mules. Only the fast military chariots were horse-drawn. They were rushing along, followed by a chariot with two soldiers who stayed close to the prince.

"Slow down, please, I'd like to soak up the image of this hill for as long as possible; it's holy to us," Jesus insisted.

But the prince rushed on, exhilarated by the speed the horses reached on such a good road. Jesus watched him and wasn't sure whether the prince was demonstrating his strength and youthful vitality or his pride and arrogance. Mount Nebo was receding from view and Jesus raised his voice a little.

"More slowly, please!"

But the horses were running at a swift gallop along the dusty highway, the chariot was bouncing in a wild rhythm, and the wheel axles were going through the wringer. Jesus vainly tried to make the driver slow down. The animals neighed, feeling that the charioteer was losing control over them as well as himself. Jesus, feeling a sense of foreboding, finally snatched the whip and the reins from the prince's hands, loosened them and the horses slowed down to a gentle trot. The prince frowned at him in anger; Jesus nearly took fright at his disdainful, wrathful look, one that he hadn't seen in him before. Suddenly, there was a creak and the right wheel tore off.

The chariot tipped over and the two men landed in the road's dust. The soldiers behind them stopped immediately and ran to pull them up from under the broken carriage. Fortunately, the riders and the horses were not injured apart from a few scratches. They both sat in a shady spot by a rock and were panting heavily.

"I apologize," the prince said softly. "It was like I was out of my senses."

"Luckily, the Lord was with us," Jesus smiled. "Had the wheel snapped off while we were in that wild gallop…"

Rav Anna was silent, then he said apologetically, "I'd like to be in the port and sail home as soon as possible. I'd like to see my father and mother, brothers and sister again soon. I miss them somehow…"

"That's how life goes. Some return to their homes, others leave theirs."

"Do you regret having left your home?" the prince asked and passed a waterskin to Jesus.

"Thanks." He drank thirstily. "I left home a long time ago: I wasn't born on Marmion Road. They say mother gave birth to me in some stable in Bethlehem during a census. When I wanted to know more about my birth, they passed over it in silence. I know Joseph is my stepfather, but who my real father is my mother never told me. I suffered for it all my childhood. Everyone in Nazareth knows I'm illegitimate, and I was mocked a lot for it."

"Does it trouble you?"

"No, it doesn't. I feel my father was the man who brought our people to the Promised Land."

"Moses?"

Jesus nodded. "Yes. That's why I asked you to slow down. We were passing by Mount Nebo, on which the Lord showed him Kanaan, which he was only allowed to look at. He'd been leading his people all the way, but they were led to their country by Joshua."

"Your namesake," Rav Anna smiled.

Jesus didn't react to that and continued. "But the people didn't believe that God meant well for them; they contravened Him, disobeyed Him, pretended they were following His laws but were instead following the priests' rules. So, God punished my people. He had many taken captive, and they then scattered around the world. The problem with us Jews is that we don't know for sure where our true home is. Rabbis say home is where your belongings are, so they drag their valuables around with them all the time to give them a feeling of home everywhere they go; but the more they travel and trade the more distant that sense of home becomes. Their home isn't anywhere."

"He who has his wealth in his heart is at home everywhere, said…" Rav Anna spoke. But Jesus interrupted him, "King Solomon."

"I was going to say Buddha. It's Buddha's thought."

"It's King Solomon's words. He lived five hundred years before Buddha, so Buddha must have got it from him, not the other way around," Jesus objected.

"Well, we're not going to quarrel about that, are we? What matters is that we've kept these beautiful words," the prince said forgivingly.

"It would be even more beautiful if we could live them," Jesus thought out loud. Then he looked back toward Jerusalem.

"I bet you're thinking about your Jewish brethren scattered around the world."

"Over there, past the mountains and the Dead Sea, is Judea; past that is Samaria and Galilee with Nazareth. I believe my people will return there one day. They'll surely return," he added more firmly as if to convince himself. "I shall bring them from a distant land and gather them from the ends of the earth…"

"That sounds almost like an oath." Rav Anna looked at him in surprise. "Those are words of the prophet Jeremiah."

"My friend, we have a long way to go, and the soldiers are waiting with a spare chariot, let's go." They went over to the soldiers, who were waiting with a new chariot and horses. The journey continued via the towns of Medeba and Dibon where the Israelites had encamped during the Exodus. On the fifth day, they made a daylong stopover in the city of Petra, the capital of the Nabateans' kingdom. The animals, the drivers and the soldiers all welcomed the rest. Laughter and singing resounded throughout their camp. Life in the city, home to twice as many people as Jerusalem, was vibrant and the people there lived a brisk pace. Rav Anna had visited the city before, so he guided the Nazarene boy eagerly around palaces built inside unusual rock formations, supposedly unsurpassed anywhere in the world. He explained to Jesus that Petra was one of the oldest cities in the world, established fifteen centuries ago. Moses had passed it all those years back, leading Jesus' ancestors out of Egypt.

Shortly before noon on the seventh day, as they were descending the western slopes of the Wadi Rum highland, Jesus caught a glimpse of a vast body of water. "That's the Gulf of Aqaba, a part of the Red Sea. Our goal – the port of Aelana – is just ahead of us," the prince explained.

Jesus looked in awe at the two tall beacons standing on either side of the wall guarding the port entrance. "Magnificent," he feasted his eyes on the breathtaking scenery.

"They say it's the second biggest port of Palestine after Caesarea. The southern breakwater is thirteen hundred cubits long and a hundred and eight cubits wide. It was built using a new material formed from volcanic ash mixed with sand; it's called concrete. It's an amazing technique: the materials and cement are poured into wooden molds, in which they harden to stone. We've been using this technique for about a thousand years in India. The pyramids in Egypt are bonded with cement as well," Rav Anna smiled, took a deep breath of cool sea air and put his hand on the young Nazarene's shoulder amicably. "The sea's ahead of us now."

Their caravan of carriages, horses and camels queued up on a pier, where the prince's giant ship was lying at anchor. Jesus had never seen anything like it. The young Indian, moved by the sight of the ship said, "It's called *Orissa*. After my country. It'll take us on the long voyage home." Jesus silently observed the huge ship. It had many sails, masts, and ropes along which sailors were clambering, preparing the ship for departure. Long queues of longshoremen carrying sacks, baskets and crates of goods on their backs were entering the ship via two wooden gangplanks. Others were lowering them into the hull using cleverly designed make-shift hoists.

"It's a merchant ship with a huge displacement hull as we're carrying heavy cargo. Mostly bitumen and copper," Rav Anna explained. The two young men walked to a gangplank and boarded the ship. Two soldiers kept pace behind the prince. Overseers supervising the loading operation bowed respectfully before the prince and his friend. The two young men stayed in the prow, where a smaller sail was attached to the front mast.

"It's more helpful for steering than increasing the driving force. That comes from the main sail," the prince explained.

"If the wind is good, how long will the voyage take?" Jesus asked.

"We're only carrying non-perishable goods. I intend to show you a few cities on the west and south coast of India. They're interesting Israelite settlements."

"But you want to be with your wife as soon as possible," Jesus objected.

"Of course, but I haven't been to those cities myself. Also, I'm fulfilling my father's orders."

"How did your father know I'd agree with going to India?" The prince said nothing. "Dear Rav Anna, I'm very grateful to you for taking me with you and I'll obey every word you say."

"Nobody's going to obey anyone. We're free people. We don't hurry… So I think two or three months before we arrive in Orissa." He looked at Jesus and asked him, "You're a carpenter's son. Try to guess what timber this ship is built of. You know wood, don't you?"

Jesus ran his palm on the wood and said without a hesitation, "It's cedar. God's tree. It has the ability to concentrate cosmic energy. Only this is a bit odd. Its structure is denser compared to ours."

"You do understand wood," Rav Anna smiled. "It is cedar, but Himalayan cedar. The best quality in the world, stronger than Lebanese. It grows at elevations of almost ten thousand feet, which is why it's the hardest. Perfect for shipbuilding. Our God Shiva meditated mostly in cedar forests. They're magical, medicinal trees mostly grown in Kashmir." Jesus thought about something for a while. "Come, I'll show you your cabin." Accompanied by the captain, the two went to the stern section, which contained the sleeping quarters. "This one's yours," the prince pointed at the closer cabin. "It's the same as all the sailors have, only you and I have preferential treatment: we each have our own."

"It'll be my first time sleeping alone and in a bed."

"Another thing I'd like to point out to you is these boards. They're made of cork. Do you know what they're good for?" Jesus shrugged. "In the event of a disaster, if the ship foundered in a storm, this board will keep you afloat on the surface for a long time."

"Let's hope we won't need them."

"Let's."

Jesus hesitated for a moment, thinking whether he should turn back after all. It wasn't that he was afraid of the long journey, but he couldn't forget the unexpected wrath that had glinted in the prince's eyes at that strange moment below Mount Nebo. But that disturbing memory was eventually overshadowed by the enticing vision of faraway countries.

25   Church Shootout

"Did you get it?" Michal asked Tomáš deep in thought as they were returning from the Wailing Wall to the hotel.

"Rabbi Simonides is known for his love of metaphors. I've got to know him over the years, and I have a good feeling from him. Optimistic even. But I'm still curious what he's driving at."

The Friday sun had set and the sabbath was beginning: Saturday, the seventh, festive day, when life in the Jewish part of Old Jerusalem grinded to a halt, shops closed, Israeli families decked their tables with white cloths, and women lit a candle for each family member so that their families could peacefully engage in relaxation, social meetings and play as commanded by the Torah. The Victoria hotel was in the Arab quarter, where life went on at its usual pace. Michal and Tomáš, who were still being followed by the two unknown men, crossed the Arab market and entered the hotel running up to the second floor quickly. Marika, in a surprisingly good mood, was sitting in an armchair with her tarot card in her hand; she put it down on a side table when they arrived.

"So, how was it?" she welcomed them merrily.

The fruit bowl was full of peels and pits. "You seem better," Michal rejoiced.

"Adelka called."

"How is she?" Michal asked inquisitively.

"All's well. I've even spoken with Hans. They were both in an excellent mood, teasing me about possibly becoming a grandma."

"That would be great," Michal hugged his wife.

"You know I'd love to go out and eat some delicious food."

"Great idea. So, we'll give my Armenian tavern a try," Tomáš suggested.

"The rabbi would like you to pay him a visit tomorrow after the sabbath is over. He wants to tell you something serious."

"The rabbi, tell me something? Which rabbi?" Marika asked, confused.

"My acquaintance. Rabbi Simonides, a great guy, very respected," Tomáš explained.

"But how did you meet the rabbi, and what have I got to do with him?" Marika asked bewildered, rising in her dressing gown while combing her hair.

"We met him in the synagogue by the Wall and… I gave him your wish slip to read before I put it in the Wall."

Marika suddenly stopped. "He told you what it says?"

"No, he didn't. Only when he read it, he said he needed a word with you. He said you don't need God to fulfill that wish, he could do it himself."

"Is that all he said?"

"He knew you were ill and that it's probably from your mother."

"You know cancer's not contagious."

"I meant owing to your mother," Michal corrected himself.

Tomáš got a text message, read it and frowned a little. "Excuse me, I have to go down to the reception desk, there's someone there to see me. I'll be right back." One of the two guys who'd been following them was waiting for him at the front desk. He gestured to Tomáš to follow him out of the hotel, where he covertly handed him an envelope. They exchanged a few words and the guy made off. Tomáš went back up to the Král's' room. Marika and Michal were on the terrace and took no notice of him. Michal's glasses were lying on the coffee table. They were absolutely identical to those that Tomáš quickly took out of the envelope. He put them on the table while simultaneously picking up Michal's originals, which he hid in his pocket. He went out to the terrace and put on a casual smile. "It was the rabbi's secretary, confirming the rabbi is expecting us on Sunday. And now, allow me to invite you to dinner. The restaurant is just a fifteen minutes' stroll from here."

"Perfect," Marika replied excitedly. Tomáš and Michal exchanged encouraging looks. "Just one moment, please, I have a request." They went into the room and Marika took her tarot card from the table. "Have a look at this, please. You know the Sea of Galilee well; doesn't this picture remind you of it?"

Tomáš sat down and examined the card for a long time.

"I'll go and get dressed in the bathroom. But I'm listening to you," Marika said, leaving the door open.

Tomáš gazed at the mysterious picture. "Hm, weird. What's it supposed to represent?"

"It's the six of swords, a tarot card. Do you know the tarot?"

"I've heard about it, it's some kind of card reading or whatever…"

"I'll explain it to you at dinner," Marika shouted from the bathroom.

"There aren't any tall mountains directly over the Sea of Galilee, but they could be a symbol of Mount Hermon, which is about thirty miles north of the lake and is covered with snow most of the year. I'm not sure if it can be seen from Tiberias. And the castle? The only castle ruins I know about is the former crusaders' castle Belvoir, but that's just opposite, to the south. But maybe the artist intended it to have a symbolic meaning rather than one describing reality." Suddenly, his face lit up. "But the oars look authentic. They date back to Jesus' time, but haven't been used since around the 16th century. Hm… the woman's very interesting. She makes me think she's in a hurry, but the boat's not moving, see, there aren't any ripples on the surface, the water's quite still. What kind of image is that?"

Marika walked into the room, wearing an evening dress. "Oh," Michal called in appreciation, "You look magnificent."

"A woman sailing away from land, eastwards, along a lake surrounded with snowy mountains, rowing with an oar that was used in Jesus' time…" Marika pondered.

"Marika, what's this?" Michal asked all of a sudden. He put on his glasses swiftly. Tomáš watched, a momentary flash of worry quickly subsided when he was sure Michal hadn't noticed anything. The glasses were a perfect duplicate of the originals. "The woman's head is covered, but hell… wait a minute."

He put down the card and shot out of the room. He was back a moment later, carrying a magnifying glass. He examined the card with it. "She has a tiny, almost invisible dot on her forehead." Tomáš and Marika leaned over the card. "It's hard to spot even with the magnifying glass," Michal shook his head.

"Funny, such dots are only worn in India. They're called tilaks," Tomáš noted. "Interesting, interesting," he shook his head. "What did rabbi Simonides tell us?" He turned to Michal.

"He told us a lot, but the most interesting for me was what he said about Jesus. That both places where he preached are gripped in war and strife instead of the peace he wanted to create. Jerusalem is one place where he preached and obviously there's war and tension. But where is the other one? Capernaum? Nazareth, Jericho, Tiberias, Caesarea? None of these places are suffering war and fighting," Michal ruminated.

"Maybe he just meant it symbolically," Tomáš suggested. "The woman has an Indian tilak on her forehead, she's sailing east, but in fact she's standing in one place. What a brain teaser," he smiled. "But I have a feeling we'll solve it… Wow, it's past five!" he said glancing at his watch.

"Oh my God, the time just flies! I have a suggestion. Let's have a look in the Church of the Holy Sepulcher at least for a moment, then go for dinner," Marika proposed.

"A good idea, it's just fifteen minutes from here, and the tavern is less than ten minutes' walk from the church," Tomáš agreed. At that moment noises and screams were heard from the corridor: female voices were yelling and there was stomping on the stairs.

Michal went out into the corridor, where he very nearly crashed into an excited Mrs. Žáková, who had gone to the Church of the Holy Sepulcher along with other ladies after they came back from their trip to Bethlehem. "Shooting! There's been a shootout in the Church of the Holy Sepulcher! Incredible! A man was killed, I saw him being carried out of the church with my own eyes!"

"A regular shootout like in a western movie," another lady was shouting. "People nearly trampled each other to death. They were running out of the church, out of their minds…"

"Police came, locked the church up and cordoned it off with tape… Unheard-of, they're even shooting by Jesus' grave now…" The ladies were shouting over one another and informing everyone about the dramatic event they'd just witnessed.

26 Solomon's Wisdom

Since the loading was delayed and the ship's departure was not expected for another two days, Jesus followed the prince and his bodyguards into the harbor. On their way to a large tent erected for passengers waiting to board one of the ships headed for Arabia, Africa or India, they passed by half-naked slaves, who were dragging heavy packs of wool, leather, kegs of bitumen and other goods on their backs. There were tables with decanters of water and wine, teapots, bowls of fruit, dried goat meat, fish and other invigorating dishes for the journey. The prince and Jesus walked past a group of elderly men and women sitting comfortably in ebony chairs laid next to a flock of camels that were laying quietly on the stone paving of the harbor in the shade of the huge tent.

"They're Berbers. They're traveling to Berenice, from where they'll continue to the Nile as a caravan," Rav Anna said. They were obviously wealthy as they were served by black slaves. Although it was hot, the men had their heads wrapped in some kind of scarves; the women were wearing long, whitish wraps on their heads, thrown over their left shoulder. However, one of the women differed markedly from the others. She was wearing a purple dress exposing her shoulders, lots of ivory and pearl jewels on her chest, and gold bracelets on both her wrists. The scarf on her forehead was much more ornate than the other women's. It flowed down to her shoulders and exposed her pitch-black hair from time to time as a gentle breeze blew through the tent. She pulled her hair aside occasionally to drink from a goblet handed to her by a slave who constantly cooled her with a fan made of palm leaves.

Rav Anna noticed the enchantment in his young companion, who couldn't tear his eyes off the beautiful woman. "She's the Berber princess Mariam from the desert kingdom of Siwa in Western Egypt. Only she has the right to wear the ruby diadem with five sapphire lions on her head," he explained to Jesus, who seemed to feel ashamed for staring at the mysterious beauty.

"Are we going to Berenice as well?" Jesus asked.

"We'll make a stop at Adulis, the main port of the Axumite kingdom. We'll load ivory from Azania there."

"I thought Aelana was the biggest port in the area," Jesus tried to talk away his embarrassment.

"Berenice and Myos Hormos on the coast of Egypt are the most important ports of the Roman Empire trading with India, Africa and China, and Adulis in turn is the key trading port with slaves and ivory." The prince tried to continue his explanation for his young companion but noticed Jesus wasn't listening to him. Fascinated, he was looking at the princess, barely fifteen years old, who gave him a shy smile. Something quivered inside the young Nazarene; an emotion unknown before entered his heart as it beat faster than usual.

"Just don't fall in love now," Rav Anna warned him amicably and led him farther into the tent, where a group of soldiers was waiting. They took some refreshments and slowly set out for the ship, which set sail two days later.

Jesus was standing on the deck and the wind was playing with his hair. He was gazing at the receding shore. Rav Anna put a friendly hand on his shoulder. "What are you thinking about, my friend?"

"I still can't believe I'm traveling to India."

"You'll meet wise people and learn sciences that don't yet exist in your country. I think you'll like my country so much you won't feel like going back," he jibed. "The Malabar Coast in Kerala will be almost like your spiritual home. Wise King Solomon sent Jews there to establish trade posts."

Jesus was looking at the calm sea, gulls from the receding shore hovered here and there. "How come you know so many details of Jewish history?"

"The Torah speaks about it. The second wave of Jewish settlers was at the time of Assyrian captivity of Jews after the destruction of the northern kingdom, when many of the captive Jews from the ten tribes of the northern kingdom were sent east. The Assyrians applied the policy of mixing nations in their empire, as did the Persians and Alexander the

Great after them. The third wave was after the Temple was destroyed by Nebuchadnezzar and the southern kingdom was defeated. Several thousand Jewish merchants and craftsmen settled in Cochin at that time."

"Do you think we'll have a chance of seeing that place as well?" Jesus asked.

"Of course we will. And Kodungallur north of Cochin. It has the biggest Jewish synagogue in all of India."

"I didn't know that," Jesus admitted. "I can't wait. I was taught at Hillel's Academy that King Darius I instituted Aramaic as the common official language throughout his empire, which was a great advantage for the Jews because it was the most widespread language among Palestinians. Romans spoke Latin, and Greek was mostly used in the ports."

"Naturally," the prince smiled confidently. "After Phoenicians, Greeks were the best sailors. Darius sent the Greek geographer and sailor Scylax of Caryanda to investigate the options for further navigation from India to Red Sea ports. Scylax had a fleet built in the mouth of the Indus that arrived in the port of Suez twenty-nine months later. That enabled the Persians to expand tremendously. When Darius I died five hundred years ago his empire extended from the Balkans to Kashmir."

"I'd never have thought Jews and Greeks would get that far," Jesus shook his head. "Where did you learn all this?"

"At Takshashila university."

Jesus' eyes lit up. "I know it teaches Vedas, Ayurvedic medicine, philosophy, astronomy, mathematics and Buddha's teachings, but I had no idea it also teaches Jewish and Greek history."

"Naturally, because Greek and Jewish teachers teach there," Rav Anna smiled. "You'll be surprised to learn the extent of India that the Jews and Greeks have seen. Takshashila is on the western slopes of the Pir Panjal Range. Kashmir stretches from its eastern slopes."

"I know," Jesus replied in deep thought.

27   A Strange Fragrance

In spite of it being a sabbath, many of the souvenir shops in the Jewish Quarter were open.

"How come they're open? It's their holiday," Michal asked as they were hurrying excitedly down the streets of the Jewish Quarter to the Christian part of the city. The sun had sunk below the buildings and the sabbath was nearing its end, but they didn't dare to disturb the rabbi.

"That's simple. The shops belong to Jews, but the staff are Arabs, so everything's alright," Tomáš smiled. In the tavern, he read out loud the Saturday English-language issue of the *Haaretz* daily of April 24, 2010, with a big headline on the front page: *Police shoot attacker at Church of Holy Sepulcher*. There was talk everywhere of an Israeli police officer having severely wounded a tourist in the Church of the Holy Sepulcher in Jerusalem.

According to Radio Israel, the man was still in critical condition in a Jerusalem hospital. "A police spokesperson said that the man had drawn a knife in the church and attacked a plain-clothes police officer, who had asked him to leave the church because it was closing for visitors. There is no information about the attacker's nationality yet." He added that the attack was not politically motivated."

Tomáš put the paper aside. "The waiter said it was a Ukrainian worshipper who'd put a knife to the nearest woman's throat threatening to kill her if he wasn't allowed to Jesus' grave in the rotunda. It happens from time to time that a fanatic panics when they find out that the queue outside the entrance to the confined area of the alleged tomb is proceeding so slowly that they don't have a chance of getting in before the closing hour. Many visitors save money all their lives to get to this holy site. When their plan blows up a few yards before their goal, they lose their minds. They don't get a second chance: they know they'll never save up for another trip to Israel again. He was in fact a poor fellow," Tomáš noted deep in thought.

"We'll wait till sunset and accompany you to the synagogue," Michal turned to Marika. "You'll talk to the rabbi and Tomáš and I will meditate by the Wall in the meantime."

"I have a feeling that we might be lucky today. The Israeli media have turned it into a huge issue and, knowing tourists, they'll want to stay in tonight because of the commotion. There's visibly fewer of them this year because of the volcano," Tomáš laughed. "We still have plenty of time before sunset; let's go to the church, and if we don't get to the night prayer session inside, you'll go see the rabbi. And if we're lucky by the grave – and something tells me we might succeed tonight – you'll see him tomorrow," Tomáš suggested.

Marika and Michal liked his idea; and indeed, when they arrived in the small square outside the entrance to the Church of the Holy Sepulcher, there were surprisingly few people in it.

"It's looking good so far," Tomáš smiled. "I am not sure if you know but a member of the ancient Muslim family of Joudeh has been sitting on the bench by the church entrance day after day since the times of Sultan Saladin. It was he who decided more than eight centuries ago that the Church of the Holy Sepulcher would be guarded by Muslims to prevent Greek, Roman and Armenian Christians from quarreling. Others got involved in the dispute over the claim to the tomb in the n19th century: the Syriac Orthodox Church, the Copts and the Ethiopian Orthodox Church. They're at such odds with each other today that Jewish police have had to assist the Joudeh family in pacifying the fighting Christian monks and sometimes even pilgrims too. While the eighty-something Abdul Quader Adib Joudeh used to open the church by himself, today he has an assistant, Wajih, who takes a long ladder through a tiny hatch in the door from a Greek, Roman or Armenian priest when the bells ring in the morning. He first opens the bottom lock, them climbs the ladder about ten feet high and opens the top lock. The ritual is repeated in the evening, only the locking procedure is reversed.

"The critical moment starts on Saturday evening, shortly before six in the evening, when the church is closed until midnight. For many this is the most exhilarating part of their stay in Jerusalem. The Greek,

Roman or Armenian priest picks about fifty lucky individuals out of the throngs crowd who will be allowed to stay in the church until the first minute of Sunday when the gate opens on the stroke of midnight and the first mass starts in the rotunda by Jesus' grave, followed by other masses performed by the different church groups at exactly one-hour intervals. To get into the church on a Saturday evening is a matter of incredible chance and luck because only a few dozen out of several thousand are picked. I've been living here for six years and I've never succeeded," Tomáš pointed out. "It's nearly six o'clock, let's go in. This is very odd, normally there's a crowd at this time of day, and today there's hardly anyone. They're probably all really scared."

As soon as they entered, the gate-closing ritual started just as Tomáš had described it. A Greek Catholic monk recited a loud invitation calling for those who wished to stay for the night meditation to enter. He was himself obviously surprised by the small number of churchgoers, so he repeated his invitation several times in a raised voice. The mighty gate shut a moment later, the Greek monk stuck a ladder out of the window, which Joudeh's assistant took from the outside, a key rattled in the lock, and a silence fell.

Along with about twenty others, Michal, Marika and Tomáš found themselves inside the vast Church of the Holy Sepulcher, the holiest place of all Christians.

"This is a miracle indeed," Marika shook her head.

"It is," Tomáš affirmed.

Marika's face suddenly furrowed in concentration. "Michal, Miško..."

"What is it?"

"Can you smell the fragrance? This whole stone is smeared with something aromatic." She pointed at a stone slab on the ground near the church entrance.

"It's the stone on which Jesus was laid after they took him off the cross. At least that's what legend says," Tomáš smiled. "It's precious oil of spikenard, used by Mary Magdalene to anoint Jesus' feet. It's made of a rare valerian that grows in Tibet and Kashmir."

"But... it's... it is..."

Michal's face lit up. "It's the fragrance that was in the room the day I came home from Košice."

"Yes, it's exactly that fragrance."

28 Cosmic Energy

Jesus was still immersed in thought when both he and Rav Anna noticed agitation and uproar on board. The ship's captain came running up to them and said something to the prince excitedly in Greek, a language that Jesus didn't know.

"Go to your cabin, please; pirates are approaching the ship." The prince grabbed Jesus under the arm and led him to the cabins.

"Pirates? Since when have there been pirates in the Red Sea?"

"Since they defeated General Pompeius' fleet in the Aegean Sea. They became bolder and bolder and started looting even in the Red and Arabian Seas. But we're ready for them. We have weapons that the local freebooters haven't dreamed of." The prince remained remarkably calm.

"I'd like to stay on the deck and help with the fighting," Jesus said.

"Do as you will but keep to the west of the bridge. Their ship's coming from the east. Meaning we don't even have to go around them."

Concerned, Jesus watched the preparations for the clash with the mighty pirate galleon, which was approaching the Indian ship fast, powered by at least a hundred long oars. It was a slender, lightweight vessel, much faster than the heavy merchant ship *Orissa*. The captain held a brief council with the prince, and then went over to his men, who were awaiting the pirates' arrival with surprising composure. The galleon drew so close to the ship that the Indians could recognize the faces of the men on board. They were an adventurous rabble from Arabia, Zibbit, Aden, African Dafili, Dangali, Dobas, Eritrea and Lacca. They included numerous former slaves, who took remorseless revenge on any rich man they got their hands on in addition to pillaging. Jesus expected the warriors and other crew members, armed with bows, lances, axes, special discs with sharp spikes, swords and daggers, to stand up defiant in defense. Instead, the captain had a white flag raised on the mast.

"Are we surrendering?" Jesus asked, surprised.

"You'll see," Rav Anna appeased him.

When the pirates noticed the white flag, the men gathered on the deck and let out victorious cries. They brandished their sabers and got ladders ready to climb onto the much higher deck of the *Orissa*. When the pirate ship drew even nearer, bamboo pipes about ten feet long appeared in four portholes just below the *Orissa*'s deck and began pumping out a fume under pressure. The pirates didn't notice it at first, their eyes fixed on the higher deck. But the fume became so dense after a while that the pirate ship couldn't be seen. The western wind carried clouds of the dense smoke toward it, and it became almost completely shrouded in the yellowish mist. Surprised, Jesus realized after some time that the uproar and shouting on the pirate ship had ceased. The cloud of smoke was filled with a strange, ominous silence. The prince, the captain and the soldiers gathered on the deck and watched in suspense the thinning clouds of smoke, which had stopped spouting from the portholes. When the smoke dissolved after a short while, the captain smiled contentedly. The sight of the pirate ship was horrifying. Dozens of dead bodies were lying on it, some still twitching in death throes, and a few were floating on the water. Those who attempted to swim away from the ship were easily picked off by the prince's archers. A victorious cry broke out aboard the *Orissa*. Both sailors and soldiers hugged each other. The captain gestured to the steersman, who was holding a lever in each hand and pulled at them to turn the two side rudders almost perpendicular to the ship's hull, which changed their course toward the pirate galleon. A moment later, they lowered two ladders off the *Orissa*'s deck, and men specially trained for close combat descended them onto the pirate ship.

"Fancy coming along?" the prince asked Jesus. Jesus didn't reply; he was curious, but he was afraid of seeing the dead pirates. He was standing next to the prince, watching the men on the other ship with a frown. "If someone finds them, they'll think God has punished them. They're all dead without a single wound. Nobody will ever find out how these men died."

"I don't understand," Jesus shook his head.

"I told you you'd meet people and see things in my country that you in the west haven't dreamed of. You've adopted a lot from us, but we guard the important secrets. This weapon is one of those secrets. As you spend some time in my country, you'll get to know others, much more important."

"I don't want to learn to kill people," Jesus protested.

"There's no need for that. You'll learn to cure people, using the most amazing techniques. But if we hadn't had our weapons here, you'd be dead by now. We never use them to attack, always only in defense."

"What was the smoke from?"

"It's our secret weapon. I only know it's a mixture of tar, sulfur and some strong poisons, whose composition is only known to initiates. When you become one, all the secrets will be unveiled to you too." Frowning, Jesus was just shaking his head. The military commander had returned from the pirate ship and reported something to the prince. "They're all dead," the prince repeated dryly for Jesus, who showed no sign of joy. "We didn't attack, we just defended ourselves," the prince explained.

"You don't know who those people were and how they became who they were," Jesus protested.

"They were brigands and deserved death," the prince replied.

"But what if they were just poor people forced to pillage because of their poverty? You come from a rich family and you've never had to steal. Maybe they were former slaves who'd escaped their masters."

"My friend, you should stop trying to find only the good in everyone. Yes, man's essence is good, but circumstances don't always let us show the good. Should I have been merciful with the brigands? They would have killed us all."

"You didn't give those people a chance. Maybe there were many captives among them who were forced to kill. Maybe they were waiting for your soldiers to defeat the pirates and for you to then set them free. What if there were innocent men among them?"

"I can't rule that out, but unfortunately, they had bad luck."

"If I knew there was one innocent man among ten guilty ones, and I didn't know which one he was, I wouldn't have the right to kill any of them."

"That's a splendid thought, but it only holds theoretically. In a battle, you don't have the time to tell which of your enemies hate you out of conviction and which were only forced to hate you. In a battle, you simply have to defend yourself. If someone hits you, you have to hit him twice. That's the law of life. I know, it's merciless, but only the strongest survive."

"Only… you didn't defeat them with fighting but with a trick. You flew a white flag and they lowered their sabers. But then you drew yours."

"My soldiers drew no sabers," the prince replied nervously.

"And what was the poisonous smoke?" Silently, Jesus watched the sailors as they descended the ladders onto the pirate ship. They took whatever they found on its deck. There was quite a bit: amphorae of wine, magnificent Babylonian carpets and embroidery, carefully stored in sandalwood crates, ivory, silk, and most importantly, chests filled with gold and silver jewels, alabaster vials of rare oils, purple dyes, all probably stolen from a merchant ship.

"Why are you taking this aboard?" Jesus asked.

"Why should we leave it for strangers? Other pirates perhaps… It would be of no help to the robbed ones, it will be to us," Rav Anna replied.

"What are you going to do with it?"

"Don't worry, we'll give it out to the poor when we come home," Rav Anna smiled. Jesus stared at him and felt bad. He'd witnessed a robbery for the first time in his life, and he could do nothing to prevent it.

"Have you ever seen the inside of a pirate ship?" Rav Anna asked him. Jesus shook his head. "Come then, let's take a look." Jesus wasn't too eager, but the prince was pulling at him, so he went over to the ladder. Soldiers and sailors helped them descend onto the pirate galleon's deck.

"Please, have the things returned. They aren't ours, they don't belong to us," Jesus made one more attempt at persuading the prince.

"No, my friend. Don't confuse mercy with stupidity. They are ours! It wasn't us but them who wanted to assault and rob us. That we have better weapons is our advantage. God wanted it that way."

"You're an upright man and I know you'll keep your word," Jesus resigned. He was trying to calm down but wasn't succeeding much. His agitation got even stronger onboard the other ship, as he saw the multitude of dead men. They stepped over them in silence; the prince was guiding him into the inside of the ship. The prince's bodyguard checked every cabin, corner and corridor first and only after making sure it was safe did he let the prince in. When he emerged from the largest cabin, he came up to the prince and whispered something to him nervously.

The prince asked Jesus to wait outside. He came back a moment later. His face was gloomy. He came up to Jesus and said quietly, "I couldn't have known they'd taken captives on board." He stepped aside. Jesus entered the cabin. About ten women were lying on large sofas. None of them moved. The prince entered and the guarding soldier alongside him. It was the group of Berber women who the prince had seen before in the huge tent in Aelana waiting to board with their husbands and children. "They'd been captured for sex slavery," the prince noted.

Shocked, they stared at the dead bodies. The young Nazarene had looked death in the eyes before, but so far it had mainly been dead animals. He hadn't seen so much human death. His whole body was trembling. He couldn't restrain himself and came closer to the dead women. He closed their eyes, one by one, stroked their hair, and tears ran down his face. Suddenly, one of the female bodies moved slightly. The men noticed it and went over to the women, who showed no signs of life. But another hand moved and the mouth of a woman lying underneath the dead one gave a soft moan. They took the dead body off her and nearly stopped breathing in surprise. A beautiful woman with a ruby diadem with five blue sapphire lions was staring at them with half-dead, piercing green eyes. Princess Mariam! Jesus' heart pounded.

"Quick, get the doctor, run!" the prince commanded the soldier, who ran up to the deck and shouted the prince's order over to the *Orissa*. "Don't you worry. Our doctor Pancha is a vaidhya, an Ayurvedic priest-doctor, master of cosmic energies. Nobody will get her back to health if he doesn't. He's brought people back to life when they were in the other world more than once. Everything's going to be alright," the prince appeased Jesus, who couldn't conceal his distress.

The ship's doctor ran into the room a few seconds later. He applied three fingers to the princess' hand, measured her pulse, and whispered something to Rav Anna in a hushed voice. Jesus watched the two in suspense. He leaned over to the prince with a question in his eyes; the prince said unconvincingly, "He has to relieve a blockage in her liver and kidneys. He needs urine for it. As much as we can get," the prince interpreted the doctor's instructions. He turned to a soldier.

"Quick. Ask men, especially the younger ones, who haven't drunk alcohol and eaten meat to urinate in a jar. Go," the doctor ordered the soldier. Meanwhile, the doctor's assistant – the medicine maker – arrived in the cabin. The doctor gave him some instructions. The man helped unbutton the princess' dress and immediately began to massage her chest with a liquid that he'd brought in an alabaster vial. Meanwhile, the doctor compressed spots on the lifeless woman's head and scruff and massaged her temples. The sailor ran in a moment later, carrying a jar, and handed it to the doctor.

"Gentlemen, could you please leave us alone now? We need some quiet," the doctor asked both the prince and Jesus. "I think the girl's going to live, but it's worse than I expected. The poisonous gas was extremely powerful."

He looked at the distressed men. He applied an enema, which introduced the fresh urine into her body. At the same time, he massaged her liver area with it vehemently. Jesus and the prince left and walked about outside the cabin without a word. The doctor's assistant came out a moment later and asked the prince to enter. Jesus wanted to follow them, but the assistant gestured to him to wait. Jesus couldn't take it after some time and entered anyway. The princess didn't breathe. The doctor's gestures indicated resignation. Sweat was running down his forehead. The prince urged him loudly to do something, but the doctor just took a few deep breaths and sat down on the princess' bed helplessly. Her eyes were dim.

Something inside Jesus snapped at that point, as if a strange, unfamiliar force was leading him. *Yes, I'll give it a try*. He went over to the bed, pushed aside the doctor, who didn't resist, leaned over the woman and put his ears to her aquiline nose. He could sense no breath. He closed his eyes and prayed out loud, "Oh, Father, the only hands you have are these. They are yours to guide. With these hands destroy all the krimi that have entered her body, all the evil substances that poison her like tentacles; destroy them with the force of mantras and your endless energy, drive the krimi out of her head, lungs, blood, muscles, liver and kidneys. All the krimi spreading through the body, now listen to my voice. Your growth has come to an end, your end is nigh!" Then he chafed his hands and applied them to the princess' heart. The prince, the doctor and his assistant watched him tensely. Every splash of a wave on the ship's prow, every screech of a gull that had forgotten to return to the shore could be heard inside. Moments seemed as long as eternity. Jesus' eyes were closed, his hands were trembling a little, and he whispered something unintelligibly. The princess startled after a while and began to breathe slowly. She opened her eyes and looked around. He watched her face. She had a tiny black dot on her left cheek. When she noticed Jesus' head leaning over her, a hint of a smile appeared on her face. The dimples in her cheeks were giving her a mischievous expression.

"Drink, please, drink," she whispered in a velvety voice. They handed her a cup of water, which she drank thirstily. Rosiness was returning to her face.

"Miracle, that's a miracle," doctor Pancha shook his head. "She was dead. You recited our mantra. Where did you learn it? You in the West cannot know our word *krimi*, denoting evil substances in the body." He looked at Jesus inquiringly.

"I learned this and other mantras from Buddhist monks in a monastery in Palestine."

"That's very well possible, but mantras don't help by themselves. I've returned many to life using cosmic energy, but this woman was too far gone. Her aura was almost extinct. But you did it," the doctor shook his head uncomprehendingly.

"Yes, she was dead, but according to the rabbinical teaching, the spirit of a dead person hovers over the body for three more days, only then will it recede to the higher spheres; it goes to Sheol. There's still hope even on the third day. Properly directed cosmic energy can perform miracles. As she'd only died a while before, there was great hope."

"I know all that you say. I even said the same mantra, yet I couldn't do it," the doctor said not understanding.

"The only difference is between your faith and mine."

"No, my friend, the difference is you love her," Rav Anna smiled.

"Can I have your hands, please?" Jesus extended his hands silently. The doctor examined them for a long time, sniffed at his palms, and eventually applied them to his forehead. He closed his eyes and whispered a mantra. Then he turned to Jesus. "My spirit has never met with such a powerful energy. Your energy field shines like a sun. Who are you?"

Jesus didn't reply. He stood up, walked over to the door, turned toward the shocked men and gave them an enigmatic smile. "Every plant not planted by my father can be uprooted, you just have to believe it." He went out onto the deck, to its highest point in the prow, and there he stayed for a while staring at the sun sinking into the sea.

29 The Fake Grave

They were walking around in the dark, empty, mysterious church. "Little can be seen of the magnificent original temple because each Christian Church extended it in an effort to get as close as possible to Golgotha. So, the church interior as well as exterior has become an assortment of chapels, smaller and larger churches, monasteries and altars. Since the fire of 1808, when the whole interior was destroyed, the Christian Churches have been blaming each other for the disaster. The Greek Orthodox Church blamed the Armenians for starting the fire, on purpose in fact, to change the established order in the church. The Armenians, on the other hand, declared that the Orthodox priests had got drunk, set some wood on fire and then tried to put it out with hard liquor," Tomáš started speaking, but he noticed that Marika and Michal were barely listening to him. They were fascinated by the genius loci – like everyone who entered the place. "Let's go to the holiest spot now – Jesus' grave."

As they were entering the rotunda, Marika and Michal, in beatific awe, took each other by the hand. At the center was the Chapel of the Holy Sepulcher, twenty-six feet long, twenty feet wide, and twenty feet high; the place of Christ's alleged resurrection, the fourteenth and last station of the cross. The chapel portal, lined with tall, mighty candelabras, guarded the entrance to a small corridor, a confined space with a holy stone.

"This is incredible," Tomáš shook his head. "People will fight and risk their lives to be allowed to spend at least a minute in this place. I've seen fights, injuries caused by umbrellas, cameras, handbags and knives. Now it's all for us and a few others."

When they bent over to be able to enter the tiny room of the tomb, they felt a strange shivering. Nobody was disturbing them, nobody was pushing them, the deep silence was only broken now and then by the murmur of a pilgrim praying softly. The shimmering light of bulbs was creating a mysterious atmosphere. Marika had wished to see this place for at least a few seconds, and to be able to touch the holy stone; now her and about twenty other visitors had almost three hours in this huge church, the holiest place of Christianity. A Greek Orthodox mass would begin at midnight, followed by an Armenian at half past two in the morning and a Catholic one at half past six. It was Saturday, April 24, 2010.

Tomáš entered the tomb first, followed by Marika and Michal behind him. None of them dared to utter a word out loud. They were on their own in a place which only a lucky few ever got to see on an ordinary tour and even then, for no more than one or two minutes along with the noise and hustle of other eager visitors. Nobody, however, was rushing them now, so they could fully devote themselves to Marika's longed-for meditation in the holiest place for all Christians. She put her sweater on the cold stone floor and sat on it. Michal pulled up next to her.

"I'll leave you alone. I'll guard the entrance to make sure nobody disturbs you. When you're done, it'll be my turn," Tomáš whispered and left with a serene expression on his face.

They freed their minds; it was surprisingly easy, as they knew nobody would be intruding on them for at least an hour. They were both experiencing this miracle with all their heart and soul, it felt just as they had always imagined it. Obviously, it was something new to them. In reverence and humility, they held each other's hands and said nothing. Marika rested her head on the marble slab protecting the stone on which Christ's body had been laid long before when they took him off the cross and closed her eyes. The holy atmosphere, the blazing candles, the magic of the place (regardless of whether it was real or only in her head) elicited a strange euphoria in her mind, blended with a total despondency over the return of her cancer. She was going to ask God for help, but it suddenly seemed trivial to her, and instead of prayers she apologized for her lack of faith – for begging with the Almighty, He who knows what each of us needs the best. At first, her mind was distracted by the various kitschy fake flowers, holy pictures, inscriptions in Greek and Russian, and pictures of saints that previous suppliants had stuck in the tiny room in a hope that they could win God over with postcards. *I hope He accepts them, as they know no other path to Him.* She looked at scenes from the life of Christ, turned into silver pictures lined with candles and flowers. The huge withering bunch of lilies must have been put there by a great sinner.

She began to feel drowsy in the peaceful atmosphere of the place; she begged, prayed, meditated, not knowing whether she was in a dream or in reality. "We're here to learn something. Reincarnation is the only meaningful explanation for our life." Tomáš' words from the previous day's debate flowed through her head. She realized that in spite of her fear of death, instilled by a generation of parents and priests, a person's soul cannot disappear, only the person can change. Life is an incessantly flowing stream of light, an inexhaustible energy, like water in a well; at times there is more and at times less, but it is always replenished. It is like an apple that first develops as a blossom and only later becomes a fruit that brings rewards, rewards that become subject to the law of death. However, the blossom opens again the following spring, becomes a fruit bringing again fresh rewards.

She wanted to live like everyone else, only she was asking whether she was the right, healthy and useful fruit. Did she bring joy and rewards to the world around her? It is clear what the purpose of an apple is. But what was her vocation? She was nearly sixty years old, but did she know the meaning of her life? Had she understood anything? Had she sought enough? Hadn't the creator inflicted this disease on her just so that she could finally realize that she wasn't going down the right path? Since He had let it return, perhaps she hadn't understood His intention, and so she had to walk her path of suffering again, providing she had the time and will for it. Why was she afraid? Where did the fear of this natural inevitability stem from? What is more natural: death or life? Can the one exist without the other? And are they not the same, as indicated on Michal's rock? As the sun set for one, it rises for another. One dies physically at some point, their mortal frame comes to an end, but another arrives in the physical world at the same instant. The individual changes, but the whole remains. And that is the point. An individual's life only makes sense as a whole and in unity. Living for oneself, separated from others, is pointless. She imagined how she would live if she knew she was the only person in the world. Who would she live for? Tomáš was right: 'nothing' cannot exist. Only something can exist. And so, even death is a part of something, it is not nothing. She would stop being afraid when she was certain that all her life, every instant of her earthly existence was heading toward the fulfillment of God's law. Only its fulfillment in our daily lives rids us of the fear.

She realized death was evil because she'd been told it was since her childhood, at home and in the church, where she'd gone with her grandmother compulsorily. Why aren't animals afraid of death? Why do they die without death throes, unless of course their death is caused by human violence? Why do people talk about the struggle with death as something inevitable and equally important to life? Don't people start dying the moment they're born? Why do plants, trees, fruit, and the whole animal kingdom die with dignity and in peace, resigned to what's inevitable? Why are only human beings, the only creatures with an intellect, so bound to this material world?

Marika wasn't sure if she was asleep or awake, but she felt unusually good and lightweight. A pleasant warmth was running through her body, a feeling that her beloved husband was there with her. He and also Tomáš outside were giving her strength and assurance. Why had the cancer come back? Her eyes fell on an inscription written by someone on a postcard with Christ, stuck to the stone. *You will not get out, until you have paid the last penny...* Why do I want to know at all costs where you're buried, my Lord? Why is it so important to me? Isn't it much more important for my cure that I work on myself? What is so important about me heading east that you had to make my cancer return? Isn't this the very path to which you've sent me? Michal was in India last year and searched for you in Fatehpur Sikri. Maybe he did it to help me. We even both felt for a while that your bones were really there. But we must have been mistaken. Your final resting place no doubt lies where the need for reunification is the most urgent. All my life I've been forcing my sacrifice on others and was unhappy when they didn't want to accept the sacrifice as I thought fit. Perhaps even Adelka went to Africa to be finally left alone by me. I've become dependent on my idea of helping others and terrorizing my dearest ones with my kindness. I thought I was sacrificing myself, and instead I was just feeding my ego. And when people around me didn't want to accept my idea of help, I fell ill.

"There are two places in the world where Jesus preached, and both are gripped by contention, unrest and war instead of the peace he wished to establish. He was born in one of them and died in the other. They are like the two columns – Boas and Joachim, the birthplace and the place of death, connected by Solomon, king of David's lineage, the same family as Jesus." Michal was ruminating on the rabbi's words. He was sitting with his eyes closed by the slab on Jesus' grave and holding the hand of the person dearest to him in the world. How much he wished to help her! He'd do anything to help her get over her disease. However, he felt that this wasn't the right place for her cure. It's not a place of peace but a place of strife.

Marika didn't perceive time. She felt the warmth in Michal's palm and opened her eyes. She looked at him and noticed he was gazing at a picture of Christ lying on the stone slab, brought into the tomb by a zealous pilgrim. She too gazed at it. It was a different Jesus, not the one whose picture she'd seen many times in her life – from her childhood prayer book to pilgrimages her grandmother had used to take her on. This Jesus was different. He wasn't standing but sitting in a strange position. His legs were crossed, his eyes half-closed, his toga, thrown over his left shoulder, was covering his lap and legs, bent in the Buddhist lotus position. She could feel his gaze, as if he were hypnotizing her. She was looking at him, and something strange, unknown, joyful was entering her heart. The ring and little fingers of his right hands were bent, pointing downward, while the middle and index fingers and the thumb were pointing upward. His left hand was extended, and the index finger formed a circle with the thumb.

"It's a symbol of eternal duality, his divinity as well as human essence. I've seen many such pictures in Tibet."

"It's even on that rock of yours. What does it mean?" Marika asked in a whisper.

"It's an Indian mudra, known as the cincihna mudra. The gesture stands for understanding a grain of truth," Michal whispered.

Suddenly, Marika burst out unexpectedly, "The oars we saw in Tiberias…"

"… are in fact a symbol of his heart. Isn't that amazing? Hearts drive us…" Michal added.

"Yes, an oar… Michal, I think I'm slowly finding out why I'm not moving on and why my disease is back. Michal, Miško…" Marika's eyes were aglow as if she had a high temperature but when he touched her forehead it was cool.

A noise disturbed them in their meditation. A moment later, they realized it was half past eleven and the Muslim guard had unlocked the church, since the Greek mass would begin soon. They walked out.

Tomáš was awaiting them outside the tomb, smiling. "Now this will be an experience." The picture they saw shocked them. Coptic priests were praying behind the rotunda, and crowds of Russian Orthodox believers were whistling at them. They, in turn, were the target of hissing by Syriac priests, singing some worn-out mundane songs, droning and mocking the Greek Catholics and making fun of their prayers. Faces were slapped here and there, and the Greek monks had a hard time pushing out the mass of wild Russian Orthodox Christians who were elbowing their way to Jesus' grave in a furious desire to take a picture of themselves in front of it. *This really isn't a place of peace,* Michal thought. Marika didn't perceive the shouting, slapping of faces and nudging. Her eyes were glittering as she stared absent-mindedly.

"What are you thinking about?" Michal asked her.

"I think I understand why I'm ill. And I have an idea of how I can get over it. Can we meet this rabbi?" she turned to Tomáš.

"It's midnight, I don't think it's the best time for a visit," he smiled. "But the rabbi will certainly be in the synagogue tomorrow before noon."

"Okay, I'll go and see him. I think it was pointless looking for the tomb of Jesus in the Church of the Holy Sepulcher."

"Why?" Tomáš asked.

"Because that's not where Jesus is buried."

"Of course not, but then, where is he?" Michal asked.

"The Church states that Jesus rose to the heavens, you know," Tomáš smiled.

"You can't believe such nonsense. That's against God's law. Even the Church dignitaries know exactly that Jesus never rose to any heavens, but they can't admit it because that would ruin their terrestrial power immediately – the most important thing to them. That's why they hate and persecute anyone who tries to find Jesus' true grave," Marika ruminated and then she added softly, "There are two places in the world that suffer constant unrest. They're both associated with his work. I think I'm getting it. We spent three hours in the church and a lot of things became clear to me. That card... The woman is sailing east, but the boat is actually standing still, she's in a lake and has an Indian tilak on her forehead… The statue of Christ in the Buddhist lotus position… He didn't bring peace but swords. There are six swords on the boat… This isn't his true grave. The rabbi promised to answer this question for me?"

"He said you don't need God for that, that he could do it. You wished to know where Jesus is buried?" Michal looked at her in surprise.

"Yes, I asked God in Hebrew to tell me."

"So, this was the prayer that I put in the Wall?" Marika nodded. "Is it that important to you?"

"More than you think."

"I think I'm beginning to understand you," he said, moved by her great despair and even greater faith.

30   The Feast of Death

At noon they carried the princess on a sedan on the top deck. She was smiling. Her face was no longer so pale, and her breathing was calm. She sat next to the doctor and the prince in the shade of the bridge. The sea breeze was ruffling her hair like ripples on the Red Sea. Jesus was sitting opposite them, watching this mysterious beauty. An interpreter was translating her story from her Berber dialect into Aramaic. She'd been accompanying her mother and her entourage during their stay at the Dead Sea, where she'd gone to cure her joints. Shortly after their departure from the port of Berenice, they were attacked in the open sea by the pirate galleon on their way home. The pirates killed all men, children and old women, including her mother, and took the young women on their ship. She had no idea where they'd wanted to take them; perhaps somewhere back to their base. Having learned that everyone except herself had died after the poisonous gas attack, she didn't even weep. She asked the prince to take her to Adulis, where her father's caravan was waiting to take them to Siwa. Naturally, the prince gave his word that he would do as she had asked, so the *Orissa* dropped anchor in Adulis out of the blue two days later, where they handed the princess over to her father. Those two days were the most beautiful in Jesus' life so far. The sailors, soldiers and merchants all noticed the unusual change in the young Nazarene's behavior. His eyes were ablaze with happiness and longing. It appeared to him that Mariam was harboring an equal affection for him. Neither of them knew the other's language, but love is intelligible in any tongue. For two days, they were smiling, singing; Jesus even played a flute borrowed from one of the sailors for her. On the other hand, the moment of their parting after the ship anchored in Adulis was more cruel than any he'd known before. He would never have thought that love was such an amazing force.

The princess' father, King Masinissa, refused the carpets, embroideries, gold and silver in sandalwood crates, silk, salt and other goods originally stolen by the pirates that the prince wanted to hand over to him. The king donated them to Rav Anna as a sign of gratitude for having saved his daughter's life.

As the ship was leaving the port of Adulis, Jesus and the prince were standing on the deck and waving goodbye to the group of grateful Berbers. "Beautiful, isn't she?" the prince nodded his head appreciatively.

"Beautiful."

"I admit I was a bit sorry when she said her father was waiting for her in Adulis. I'd have taken Mariam to Orissa because of you," the prince smiled. He was watching the pensive Jesus. "I guess you've fallen in love." He hugged him amicably and together they waved goodbye to the group standing on the pier from which they were moving away. The princess, waving a blue scarf, was slowly diminishing, disappearing in the sea haze like a fairy rising to the heavens. Jesus closed his eyes and daydreamed of being in the embrace of the most beautiful woman he'd ever seen in his life. He felt as if a strange primal force took him by the hands and lifted him so that he was floating lightly, very lightly through an infinite space. He flew over the sea, landed on the pier next to her, and looking into her eyes he could see the whole universe in her eyes, a universe in which she was reflected.

The coast had disappeared beyond the horizon and it started to rain. The prince invited Jesus to his cabin. "Have you known a woman?" he asked. Jesus blushed a little and just shook his head. "Don't forget that the perfect harmony between a woman's and a man's body is an amazing thing, but the perfect harmony between their souls is much more joyous. You Westerners speak of lovemaking, but we speak of union. Union means unification. Are you listening to me?" Rav Anna asked.

"I'm trying to," Jesus smiled.

"I'm talking to you about unity and harmony, and you're thinking about the princess," the prince rebuked him amicably.

"I've broken free from her now. I'm listening to you attentively."

The prince smiled contentedly. "Breaking free is the fundamental precondition for human happiness. There are two types of people on earth. The first – the vast majority – are bound, unrealized, unawakened, seeking pleasures of the body and matter. They collect possessions, women, power, glory. They're invited to the feast of death. The others – a minority – are awakened, open-eyed, seeking pleasures of the spirit. They're the beacons of humanity. They're invited to the feast of life and will come to paradise. Everyone is invited to this feast, but few will be chosen." Rav Anna stopped talking and noticed Jesus wasn't listening again. "Are you thinking of her?"

"I beg your pardon?"

"I said, are you thinking of her?" Jesus nodded. "So you've not broken free after all."

Jesus said nothing. "You'll meet her if God wants you to. If not in this world, then in the other one. If you're meant to walk beside her, you will. Don't be unhappy."

"I'm not unhappy. I believe I belong to those invited to the feast of life."

"Sure, I'm quite hungry myself by now. Let's have something to eat."

31   I Believe!

Marika and Michal couldn't fall asleep for a long time after coming back from the church. Images of the crowd thronging in the rotunda, monks beating each other on the head with long clubs, noise, holler and stench from the number of candles and torches were passing through their minds.

"You asleep?" she asked, listening to her husband's disturbed breathing.

"Impossible."

"Me neither."

"How are you feeling?"

"Ok."

"Not good then," he embraced her in concern. "I think you have a temperature again."

"I'm fine, just excited." She fingered the lump in her breast in the dark. She was reluctant to admit it was growing. She didn't want to upset her husband, so she told a lie, "I think it's getting smaller."

"Wait," he took a thermometer and slid it under her arm. "When we're back, you'll see the professor to make sure it isn't growing."

"Michal, whether it's growing or not, I'm sick of all these doctors and professors. How will they help me? They'll cut off my breast and that's that. It may last for a while, but once you have metastases in your body – which I do – it shows up somewhere else after some time. They don't cure you, they just postpone your end," she burst out. "If they knew how to help me effectively, they'd have done it the first time. I don't believe all this radiation, cutting and chemotherapy saves anyone. To the contrary, they weaken your body so much it doesn't have the strength to fight the disease. The metastases got into my bloodstream when they took samples from my tumor."

"Why, you told me you didn't have the biopsy," he looked at her suspiciously.

She didn't reply. "If anything can save me, then it's making room for healing energy to take effect."

"What then, did you have it or not?"

"I did, they talked me into it…"

He thought for a while. "How are you going to achieve this making room for healing energy to take effect?"

"Fast again, to help the body not waste energy on food processing, to make the cells eat each other. It's quite simple. Tumor growth is encouraged by proteins. When you cut the input of nutrients containing proteins, the body can't do without them, so the blood starts eating everything in the body that contains proteins. And that's the cancer cells above all. As a result, the cancer eats itself."

"You believe this?"

"I believe."

"But you believed in a cure the first time too."

"Not enough. And my belief was wrong. Meditation, activation of the spirit at the right time in the right places is a major part of the belief. Jesus' grave is the right place for me."

"Why?"

"Because I feel it. Maybe it's a placebo, but I believe in it. It may be a bedroom, a forest, a church for others. For me it's His grave. I believe the place where his bodily remains are has a healing power." Michal smiled. "I know it may seem ridiculous to you, but I've sown the seed of this idea of the healing energy of His final resting place in my mind so deeply that I want to see it at all costs."

"But we're here. In Jerusalem."

"You know perfectly well he's not buried here."

"Where is he then?" Marika sobbed. Michal hugged her. They were both lying quietly and staring at the ceiling lit by a dim night lamp.

"Tomorrow – today, in fact – I'll see the rabbi. If he gives me an answer to my question, we'll go there."

"Hold on for a few days and you'll see."

"What?"

"See if it helps you."

"Miško, but they say themselves that this is not where Jesus is buried!

This is just where they put him in the grave and then he got lost somewhere," Marika objected.

"When do you want to see the rabbi?"

"Tomáš said before noon. We can go and see him all together."

"You don't want to be with him alone?"

"I think I know what he'll tell me. I'd like you to hear it as well."

"Yes, I'll come with you. I'll do anything in the world for you. I want you to live with all my heart. Very much… Marika… we must succeed… You will be saved. I believe it. I believe!" Tears started rolling down his face. They were tears of hope.

32 A Time Will Come, You'll Find Out

After the unforeseen delay in Adulis, the captain shortened the stopover at Eudaemon (Aden) to only one day, during which an ebony chest filled with pearls was brought to the prince's cabin from the harbor. The captain held council with weathered Arab seafarers, who advised him to set sail as soon as possible as the summer was beginning and the south-western monsoon wind was gaining force. Jesus was sorry about not being able to stay longer, because the city was, according to legend, the birthplace of Adam and Eve's sons Cain and Abel. The ship gained unexpected speed after leaving the port thanks to the favorable wind. Before leaving the Erythraean Sea, they stopped over in the port of Moscha in Mascat where they replenished their supplies of water, fruits and vegetables. After that, they sailed for several weeks across the Erythraean Sea for the port of Barygaza, a major Greek trading post.

"So, welcome on Indian ground," the prince bowed before him as they disembarked on a pier in Barygaza. Rav Anna took a tiny locket from his bosom, opened it, dipped his right middle finger in a deep red dye contained in the locket, and made a dot on Jesus' forehead. He made one at the center of his forehead with the same finger then. "The tilak is a symbol of divine happiness and victory. We bear it on the Ajna chakra. We call it the third eye. It links the spiritual forces of God and man."

"I'd like to know more about chakras."

"Don't be impatient. You've come to India to learn all this, but above all, you've come to acquire patience," the prince said to Jesus in an appeasing tone, and then they took a stroll around the port in the company of soldiers. "Northwest of here, in the majestic delta of the Indus, the legendary land of Ophir was once located – the ancient trading partner of

King Solomon's empire. However, its glory and wealth have long been covered with dust following the raids of many barbarian tribes. New, richer and more powerful realms have overshadowed its bygone glory. Barygaza is the most important port in the area today," Rav Anna explained to his young companion, who listened to him attentively.

After unloading the crates of bitumen, they loaded some sandalwood and the ship continued to Alibag. They arrived after a five-day voyage. The history of the port, one of the most important on the Malabar Coast in King Solomon's times, was similar to that of Orissa. Barbarian tribes had largely destroyed it and only a part of the old town remained. Jesus' heart started pounding as its contours appeared on the horizon. Rav Anna had described the dramatic landing of the ship carrying Jewish merchants sent by King Solomon a thousand years earlier. The ship had foundered shortly before reaching the coast, but it was towed to the coast successfully despite being badly damaged. The Jews had set up their first trading post on the western coast of India and developed an active religious life.

"While my men unload the merchandise, we can go have a look at Gallayunkya, so you can have a first touch of real Indian atmosphere. We can go to the synagogue too if you want to."

Jesus agreed zealously. The shortest way from Alibag to Gallayunkya was by sea. The prince hired a fast trireme with three rows of oarsmen, which arrived in the port later that day. The sailors put down a gangplank for Rav Anna, Jesus and their bodyguard to cross to the pier. The prince beckoned to the servants, who brought a sedan, and invited Jesus to get in.

"Are they going to carry us on their shoulders?" he asked.

"What else?" Rav Anna asked, surprised.

"I'm sorry, my dear friend, I'll respect your custom insofar as it doesn't humiliate people. I can just as well walk on my own feet through the city."

The prince frowned momentarily but masked his annoyance quickly. "It won't be that easy. You haven't seen the streets of an Indian city. We can take a horse carriage if you don't mind that."

Jesus agreed and they got on a coach, which set out into the noisy, narrow streets of the old city. The Nazarene couldn't stop looking around; his senses were ecstatic with a massive overflow of emotions. The noise, hubbub, shouts of drivers, cows' mooing, monkey shrieks and peacock squawks were all mingled with the hollering of vendors of numerous brightly colored spices, fruit, vegetables, fabrics, leather bags, sandals, pots, sticks and a deluge of other merchandise. He was overwhelmed by the temples, built by the enlightened Buddhist King Ashoka two and a half centuries before. Rav Anna also took him inside a synagogue, since Gallayunkya was also a well-known Jewish trade center. Jesus couldn't resist the excitement.

"And to think we're not even on Malabar Coast yet! I'm so looking forward to the Jewish settlements there and their synagogues," he enthused.

"We're a little late. I'm afraid the winds will reverse, and our onward journey home will get complicated. We'll load all we need in Barygaza, and the supplies, which we'll replenish in Muziris, where we have to unload some tin, will last us all the way to Mailapur," the prince said.

"I'd be very grateful if we could stop over in Cochin for at least a day. It's the oldest Jewish settlement in India and I long for a meeting with the rabbi."

"They say the Cochin community is at odds with each other."

"That doesn't matter to me. I don't know if I'll ever see these places again, and I'd like to bow to the descendants of the Judean tribe," Jesus begged.

"I'm not happy about your proposal. I must admit I'd like to get home as soon as possible."

"Prince, maybe my insistency isn't tactful, but I feel a stopover in Cochin will be useful for you and your ship as well."

Rav Anna said nothing; his face indicated displeasure with Jesus' insistence. He wasn't used to anyone pressing him. After a week spent in Gallayunkya, they returned to the port of Alibag, where the *Orissa* was ready for departure. The ship continued south, where they made a brief stop in Mangalore in the country of Karnataka, since several of their water casks had burst unexpectedly and they needed to replenish the supplies quickly. They whiled away the time with discussions, playing chess and card games. The soldiers, with whom Jesus made friends during the voyage, shared with him the secrets of martial arts and wrestling. He contested them in arm wrestling and was improving in fencing too. The majestic *Orissa* was sailing south not far from the coast, along the Jewish settlements of Gokarnum, Kalikut, Mandagora, Byzantium, Togarum, Chowkat, until they arrived in Muziris in the mouth of the Periyar river, the largest port of the Malabar Coast and important trading place with Rome, Alexandria, Axum, Palestine, Arabia and Phoenicia. Almost all the trade in pepper, cinnamon, cassia, cardamom, ginger, perfumes and muslin had shifted to Muziris after the downfall of Ophir. The prince's ship only stayed for two days while they replenished the food supplies and the sailors had a quick break in the city's inns and brothels. They grumbled a little, because the prince had promised them a several weeks' stopover in the city, full of attractive little taverns and entertainment establishments.

"We'll berth longer in Cochin," the prince decided after a conversation with the captain, who alerted him to the rain clouds crossing from the mainland toward the sea. Although the *Orissa* was a strong ship and could carry a huge payload, it began to rock like a nutshell on the growing waves.

"It isn't looking good. I don't understand why those two military galleons are sailing so far out in the open sea." The captain observed the outlines of two ships disappearing on the horizon; they'd been anchoring with them at Muziris.

Jesus smiled contentedly. Cochin was the most important Jewish colony on the entire coast. The two ports complemented each other. While Muziris, dominated by Greeks, focused on the spice trade, the Jewish Cochin specialized in diamonds, pearls, ivory and Chinese silk. Jesus was looking forward to a break in the city, whose name came from the Hebrew term for a synagogue seal.

As the majestic *Orissa* was nearing the coast, he was standing on the prow and inhaling deeply the air coming from the mainland. He'd been silent and pensive since their departure from Adulis.

"Are you thinking of Mariam?" the prince asked him. He nodded. "Pain weakens the bodily strength but strengthens the spiritual one. The one above knows precisely why He sent the Berber beauty on your path. You fell in love and love unfulfilled is the greatest suffering. I'm sure it's of a great significance to you, only it hasn't been revealed to you yet." Rav Anna fell silent and gazed into the distance. Then, as if to himself, he added, "Only love fulfilled brings more suffering."

"Are you in love?" Jesus asked.

"She's waiting for me in Puri. She's the most beautiful and kindest person in the world. I haven't seen her for a year now. Or my sons. But my father sent me out on the journey, and my father's wish is my command."

"Did you have to go? I mean, your captain could have brought you bitumen, wine and Dead Sea salt."

"I'm bringing home something much more important."

"What is it?"

Rav Anna smiled secretively and patted Jesus on the shoulder. "A time will come, you'll find out."

33 A Doctrine Based on a Lie

Storm clouds were hanging over Jerusalem before noon on Sunday. The bus for the Tel Aviv airport was departing at four, so they still had almost the whole day ahead of them. Marika wasn't very eager to leave the hotel; she wasn't able to reach Adelka in Sudan on Skype. The computer was very slow and other hotel guests were waiting for it, so she eventually gave up and contacted her by cell phone instead.

"Why are you calling her all the time? It's always the same story. Whether she's well, whether Hans is alright, whether she has enough clothes. As if it was freezing in Africa! I mean it must be getting on her nerves by now. Sometimes I feel you obsess too much over her."

"That's just like you. You could show more interest in her. She's your only child after all!" Maria replied frowning. She was scuttering beside her husband, who was walking briskly down the street leading to the Wailing Wall, chewing on some pistachios. At last, they met Tomáš just in front of the checkpoint onto the square by the Wall. There were substantially fewer Jews there than the day before, but more tourists. Since the synagogue under Wilson's Arch was in the men's section and women weren't allowed in, Tomáš first went to see the rabbi on his own. A moment later, he brought him over to Marika and Michal. The rabbi was dressed casually in a white shirt and black trousers. Tomáš introduced him to Marika, whom the rabbi welcomed like an old friend.

"Unless Mary minds that you'll learn her secret, it'll be my pleasure to invite you to my favorite kosher restaurant," he smiled affably.

"No, quite to the contrary, I'll be very glad if we're all together. You know, I must admit I think I kind of know what you're going to tell me, plus I'm not feeling quite well…"

"The restaurant in the Ben-Zvi Center is the best one in Old Jerusalem. Even their air-conditioning is kosher," he laughed. "Please, follow me."

There was a soldier with a machine gun on his shoulder outside the entrance, which made it clear that it wasn't just any old restaurant. When they entered, the waiter bowed low before the rabbi and led him and his guests to a separate parlor. The rabbi washed his hands ceremoniously, and the others followed him. He blessed the meals that the waiters brought and spent a while in prayer.

"May I ask you, Marika, if your husband and my dear friend Tomáš know what inquiry you addressed to our Lord?"

"My husband does, and I'll tell Tomáš as well." She turned to him, with her eyes lowered, and said, "I wanted to… that is, I want to know where Jesus is actually buried."

Tomáš didn't say a word, only gave the rabbi a surprised look. "Do you dare answer this question?"

The rabbi smiled, thought and then started calmly talking. "There are things that aren't mentioned for the sake of public interest, even though they should be mentioned for the sake of truth. But sometimes that is the way it goes; the truth doesn't always lead to goodness. My dear colleague certainly won't protest, I know his opinion."

He glanced at Tomáš and continued. "It is true, for instance, that Jesus was no Son of God, but it was passed by a vote at the Council of Nicaea on March 25, 325, chaired by Emperor Constantine. There were 217 bishops who voted for Jesus' divine origin; only three dared to protest. They were led by bishop Arius, who insisted that declaring a human being the son of God was heresy. The overwhelming majority of the votes were in favor of Jesus' divinity under heavy pressure from Emperor Constantine. Before the vote, the Emperor declared that Jesus' divine origin was the truth and that all other opinions were the work of devil. I've a strong feeling that even today, few people would dare to vote against the Emperor. The decision that day divested Jesus of his human character, tearing him away from the people, for whom he became an unattainable ideal rather than a beacon for those seeking. Let's admit that many find that quite convenient. People like moral models as long as they're at a certain distance from them. To be on the safe side, to not provoke them too much. They took Jesus from Jerusalem and moved him to Rome, a place he had never set foot in. At the same Council, a committee appointed by the Emperor chose four from among about eighty gospels, which were then canonized and became parts of the New Testament. The choice of gospels was allegedly down to a miraculous event: the chosen texts flew to the altar by themselves. The Church declared all the other gospels as heretic, and whoever referred to them would be thus condemned as a heretic, which in those days carried fatal consequences. What is more, a full eighteen years of Jesus' life – his childhood and youth – were left out of them. The Jews, and Muslims later on, disapproved of Jesus' godly origin. The Church turned the human Jesus into a God-human, mainly thanks to Paul. The Church has been caught in a dilemma since then: whether to follow Jesus' path of simplicity or Paul's path of power. The Popes chose Paul's path, and whoever disagreed with it was cruelly punished, especially a few centuries later, when the Church consolidated. Thousands of people following Jesus' path, not the Popes', were declared heretics and burned to death. That's why the Roman Church destroyed all testimonies depicting Jesus as a human being. Thus, the world's largest library at the time in Alexandria was destroyed in AD 391, during Emperor Theodosius' reign. It had contained unique testimonies about the life of the first Christians and the Church of Jerusalem. That same year, under Emperor Theodosius, Christianity became the state religion of the Roman Empire and Bishop Siricius was the first to use the title Pope. That crowned the greatest revolution in the history of humankind, started by Emperor Constantine: the oppressed Christians became the oppressors."

The rabbi exhaled; Marika and Michal were listening to him in breathless suspense. "The Vatican will not permit any attempt to prove the existence of Jesus' burial site. But none of the gospels makes any reference to the Ascension. If evidence was found that Jesus is buried somewhere like a common man, the Vatican would be done for. It would prove that the whole Church doctrine is based on a lie. Jesus' teachings, on the other hand, would gain momentum."

34 A Failed Test

The Cochin synagogue stood close to the coast, near the merchant port. The waves lapped up against its foundations when the tide was strong. Many ships were anchoring in the port, taking cover from the anticipated storm arriving from the mainland. As they were entering the synagogue, the wind was raising dirt and dust off the ground. They were glad to be inside. Rabbi Ezekiel Nobach, accompanied by the synagogue's chazzan and several important merchants, welcomed the prince and the young Nazarene reverently in the House of Teaching, which was part of the synagogue.

"It is a great honor for our community, our synagogue and myself to welcome this excellent young scholar, whose high repute has come from the Temple Academy in Jerusalem to our place," the rabbi welcomed Jesus. "Your astute ideas, brisk thought as well as your critical opinions of some of the vices among the Temple staff are of great interest to us, members of the Judean tribe, whose ancestors came here in King Solomon's times."

"Honorable teacher," a man sitting in the front row turned to Jesus, "I'd like to add to the rabbi's words that there are some amongst us whose ancestors left less than five centuries ago after Jerusalem was destroyed by the Babylonian King Nebuchadnezzar. And although we've been contributing, as our ancestors were, to the synagogue treasury with at least the same share as our first-settled brothers, it grieves us that our truth is not heard. We would like a greater share in the redistribution of profits flowing from our lucrative trade and a greater share in the power in our community." A hum ran through the synagogue, and Jesus recalled the prince's words. The relationships between the first settlers and descendants of new arrivals were evidently not good. The men stared at him and waited for him to take a position on their dispute.

Jesus began strolling down the aisle between the pews in his typical manner. He did so whenever he was angry. He hadn't even set foot on Indian ground properly, hadn't had time to greet his fellow believers joyously, and the first thing he came across was their mutual accusations. He had no intention to involve himself in their dispute.

"I don't understand your grievance," he turned to the man who'd been complaining to him. "You speak of your truth. But there is no your truth and their truth. Truth is one. It never changes. Everything in the world can be divided into truth and error. The truth is everything; it exists without a cause and is the cause of all thing. Error, it seems, is nothing, but it is also a form of a manifestation of everything." The men listened, frowning. "Everything that begins ends at some point, all visible things are only forms of manifestation, shapes; they represent nothing, therefore they must perish. The same goes for shares in power and profits. What are you actually disputing over? Meaningless, ephemeral matters?"

"No, it's justice we're after," the man objected.

"God is truth and justice, because He has been and will be, He will never change, never perish, He always remains the sole truth. Man only remains in truth and error. That's our role in this world: to seek truth by way of error. I don't know who of you are right and who are wrong. But what I know for sure is, as I look at you, you're at an age when most of you will no longer commit errors ten years from now."

"We're old and experienced enough, but we can hardly avoid errors," one of the men objected.

"If God is so magnanimous and will allow you to make errors, nothing's in your hands, everything's in His. Since man became flesh, he has contained both truth and error. The body is his tool for seeking truth. When you're not here, when you've died, when the error recedes, only truth will be left behind you. You'll be judged by it. But power?" He turned to the grieving man. "It's just a mirror image, a reflection of strength, it's nothing but an illusion. The real power is inside you. In how you can control your emotions and your reason. Rejoice when you're condemned, when injustice is done to you. The untruth of which you're accused of is your best training in self-control and patience, in the acquisition of the good. It's useful to learn how to endure insults and humiliation in order to subjugate your pride. For only those that serve are strong. Those who are served upon will not resist temptations. The real power is the manifestation of will in each of us directed by God. And the will of self-control is the strongest of them all. And if you can control yourselves, you will find a way to understanding. It is the rock on which you are to build your temple. It's the only thing that can protect you and empower you. You are living amongst foreign peoples, and instead of being united, you are trying to outdo one another. Let understanding be your power. Let it be your truth."

"Your speech is fine, but way too theoretical. You haven't helped us much in our dispute," the man protested.

"You're so far from home, and still disputing. Reconcile your dispute and agree amongst yourselves, because if you don't do it, the Lord will do it for you," Jesus rebuked them.

"We thought the Lord has sent you to us."

Jesus smiled bitterly. "Help yourself, and God will help you. The only hand the Lord has available is yours. You're all older than me – and I've come to India to seek wisdom, not to settle grown men's disputes."

There was a roar of thunder outside and the sky visible through the windows was criss-crossed by glowing bolts of lightning. A violent downpour started a moment later, quickly transforming itself into a devastating windstorm due to the wind coming from the mainland. Torrents of water were lashing the walls of the synagogue, it became dark, and the candles flickered as if frightened; some even went out. Sounds of ships crashing against the piers were heard from the nearby harbor; smaller boats cracked and splintered like toys on the concrete and stone blocks of the jetty. The crashing of waves and wailing of ships' bells were mingled with hollers and cries for help. The rabbi invited those present to pray for the rescue of those who stayed outside. Jesus cast his eyes down and left the synagogue without a word, alongside Rav Anna and the soldiers accompanying them. What they saw was horror. Although the rain was bucketing down, some of the ships, and even warehouses, hit by lightning were on fire. The men immediately mixed with fishermen and sailors who were rescuing their boats, cargo and above all their own lives. Dead and injured people were lying on the sandy beach, many with open wounds. Jesus, the prince and his soldiers were doing their best to help. They managed to revive many who seemed dead already. The people were pulling drowning men and fishing boats out of the sea selflessly, some were just lying inertly and panting in exhaustion. More and more Jews were coming to the nearby synagogue to pray along with the rabbi to the Lord to save lives and possessions. The cries of those drowning and begging for help were heard in the synagogue together with the wailing of the windstorm.

The storm subsided late in the afternoon. Those who saved themselves were sitting in fatigue on the ground with planks and pieces of broken boats lying about. Many were mourning the dead. The rabbi and his men came out on the synagogue porch and offered the tired and wet people some hot drinks. He offered some to Jesus as well, who pushed him away with a violent gesture. "Aren't you ashamed?!" he almost shouted at the Jews standing diffidently on the steps beside the rabbi. "Where were you when help was needed?"

"We prayed for the storm to subside. And it has, as you can see," the rabbi said angrily.

"You know where you can stick your praying! Your action was cowardly and contemptible!"

"Don't blaspheme! Praying to God is our duty, and especially when our brothers' lives are at risk," the rabbi snapped.

"When your brothers' lives are at risk, you ought to help them, not pray for them. Or do you really think you could have calmed the storm down with your prayers? Our Lord won't help a man before he's done all he can. God only takes over when human strength itself is insufficient. He ended the storm because he could see the exhaustion of those who were rescuing their neighbors. You rescued nobody, you were sitting in your warm and dry synagogue! With your cowardly praying, you let those you were supposed to help die! The best prayer is help where it's needed. You weren't praying but avoiding your duty. Remember, God will get even with you for this, because what you do unto others, God will do unto you. This storm was your test, and you failed it. Farewell, rabbi."

Jesus turned to the prince, "Let's get out of here."

35 A Key to the Secret

The mood got better as rabbi Simonides ordered some quality red wine. Only Marika was solemn, her face screwed up in pain every now and then.

"Excuse me, may I have a look?" The rabbi leaned over to her and pushed her right eye open, then her left one. He stared in her pupils and frowned. "Are you in pain?" She said nothing. "Tomorrow I'll take you to a good friend of mine, an excellent specialist in oncologic diseases."

"That's very kind of you, but we're flying home tonight."

"Then see your doctor immediately, please," he asked her. She nodded. "Are you interested in what I am saying to you?" They all nodded without hesitation.

"So, it's clear now that the discovery of Christ's final resting place is extremely dangerous for the Church, which knows it must be somewhere out there and is terrified somebody will find it." Almost breathless, they drank in every word the rabbi said. "However, the key to finding it is here, in Jerusalem. And now, pay attention, please. The key is Solomon's throne. In a figurative sense, but perhaps in a literal sense too, the term *Templum Hierosolym* was associated with it. Thus, not Solomon's temple, but his throne," he emphasized and turned to Marika.

"May I borrow your precious locket, please?" Marika took the locket off her neck and handed it to him. "I believe you shared with your wife what I told you the day before yesterday," he turned to Michal.

"I did."

The rabbi now turned to Marika. "There wasn't much fondness between you and your mother, am I right?"

Marika shook her head. "She was a domineering, even violent type. She could go berserk if something wasn't up to her expectations."

"We know those situations. And those types of people. I'm not totally sure, but maybe she too contributed to your disease. We're living in a time when almost one in every ten women suffers from this disease. Also, those bras are responsible for it as they compress women's breasts in an unnatural position. It's somewhat similar to men wearing their modern underpants today. What are they called? Ah, briefs. They compress the testicles, and then they wonder why they got cancer. It must be said, though, that genes don't play a major role here; the environment has more influence. Yours probably wasn't very good. You lived under constant stress. And I think you still do. Excuse me, where did your mother get the locket?"

"No idea."

"It really is an antique specimen. Extremely rare. It would be treasured even by the Rockefeller Museum. It's King Herod's commemorative medal. I don't know if any other object of similar value exists in Israel." He weighed the locket in his hand. "As you know, King Herod had the second Temple of Jerusalem built. About thirty thousand artisans from all over Judea, Samaria and Galilee worked on it, so we can't rule out that the carpenter Joseph of Nazareth was among them. Solomon had built the first Temple, though. It was the main assignment given to him by his father, King David. The construction works started in 960 BC, ten years after his accession to the throne. It was the most splendid structure ever seen in Jerusalem. A true residence of God, a dignified place for the Ark of the Covenant. However, Solomon didn't have a dignified place for himself to live, oversee his rule and worship God, so he had an artificial hill built east of the town to construct the temple on, facing the valley of the Kidron brook. He had a shrine built there in which he was buried later. The size of the temple was similar to that of God's Temple. It was six hundred and fifty feet from the southern colonnade to the northerly House of the Forest of Lebanon. It was three hundred and thirty feet from Solomon's house, inhabited by the king, and the house of his favorite wife Naama, daughter of the Egyptian pharaoh. Solomon was a king, and what's the symbol of kings?" the rabbi asked, looking at his companions, who were enjoying an excellent bean falafel with pita bread.

"A royal crown," Tomáš said.

"It is today, but in Solomon's time, kings decorated their heads with a diadem on ceremonial occasions. Are there any other symbols of royal power?"

"A scepter?" Michal replied.

"That too, but the most important symbol is the throne, isn't it? The most important part of Solomon's temple was the throne shrine, which was called Solomon's Throne. According to legend, it was a massive stone structure at the center of the temple with an octagonal base about fifty feet in diameter. There was a superstructure on the base, comprising the actual shrine with a small entrance to the mighty stone structure. There was a stone staircase to the top via the lower gate on the base and then to the shrine itself. So then, you, dear Marika, and you, honorable Michal, have inserted your request slip into the wall of the correct temple, but even if it did work in this way, it couldn't have been granted, because the key to Jesus' final resting place is not Solomon's temple, but Solomon's throne. The problem is that *Templum Hierosolym* could have meant the same thing back then.

"*Templum* means temple, but in the figurative sense, and with respect to Solomon's deification and the temple-like nature of the building, the same word could have referred to his throne as well at the time."

"Are you suggesting that my mother's locket is related to my wish?"

"Does it say *Templum Hierosolym*?" the rabbi shrugged. "Then it's clear." Marika and Michal exchanged surprised looks. "And now pay attention, let's make a brief excursus on Jewish history."

Michal glanced at the clock. "Rabbi Simonides, it's very kind of you that you dedicate so much time to us, only I'm afraid my wife isn't feeling very well, and we still have to pack…"

"Do you want your wife to get cured?" Michal nodded. "What I'm going to tell you is very important in the interest of finding Jesus' final resting place."

"Michal, please, stop interrupting. Plus, I'm feeling well," Marika said unconvincingly.

"My narration is also important for you to understand Jesus' actions."

"A Jewish rabbi interpreting Jesus' actions: if only the Vatican learned about this!" Tomáš smiled.

"Jesus was – and will remain – a Jew, even though this fact evidently hampers the Vatican," the rabbi replied. "So, Jesus' task, prophesied to him by the prophets, was not to redeem humankind, but to unify the Jews. The father he mentions so often is not God, but the father of the Jewish nation, Moses."

"You can't mean that," Tomáš objected.

But the rabbi continued calmly. "As a proper Catholic priest, you should always have your New Testament on you," the rabbi smiled.

Tomáš nodded and produced a thin book.

"Excellent. Now open Luke, please, and read sentence ten of chapter 19."

Tomáš leafed in the book for a while and then read out, "*For the Son of Man came to seek and to save what was lost.*" He tingled nervously.

"And now, please, Luke, chapter 22, sentences 29 and 30. They're Jesus' words as he parts with his disciples at the last supper."

Tomáš read again, "*And I confer on you a kingdom, just as my Father conferred one on me, so that you may eat and drink at my table in my kingdom and sit on thrones, judging the twelve tribes of Israel.*"

"Have I still not convinced you?" the rabbi smiled. Tomáš said nothing. "We rabbis are familiar with not only the Old Testament but the New one as well. And one more place, to be on the safe side. Matthew, chapter 10, sentence 5. It's Jesus' recommendation to his disciples."

Tomáš found the sentence and read it silently.

"Read it out loud," Marika shouted impatiently.

"*These twelve Jesus sent out with the following instructions: 'Do not go among the Gentiles or enter any town of the Samaritans. Go rather to the lost sheep of Israel.*"

There was a diffident silence.

"Can I pour you some wine?" The men nodded. Marika thanked him and poured herself some mineral water.

"We don't have much time, so I won't go back to Moses' time. I'm sure you all know that Saul became the first king of Israel in 1030 BC. His son David and, in turn, David's son Solomon, are credited with the glory of Israel. The southern part of Palestine was inhabited by two Jewish tribes – Judah and Benjamin, the northern part by ten tribes. The kingdom disintegrated into two states after Solomon's death in 931 BC: the southern, that is Judea with Jerusalem as its capital, and the northern, that is Israel with Samaria as its capital. Two hundred years of strife between the northern and southern kingdoms ensued, of which the Assyrian King Sargon II took advantage in 721 BC. Following an agreement with the king of Judea, he invaded Israel, obliterated Samaria and dragged the ten northern tribes to Mesopotamia. They repopulated the empty places with foreigners, who later became Samaritans. A similar fate befell the southern kingdom a hundred and thirty-four years later: Babylonian King Nebuchadnezzar destroyed Jerusalem in 586 BC and dragged the southern tribes into captivity in Babylon. The most important fact for our story is that not only Solomon's temple but also Solomon's throne was obliterated. When Persian King Cyrus defeated the Babylonians in 538, he allowed the people of Israel to return to their homeland. Only two tribes returned, though: Judah and Benjamin. The other tribes – Reuben, Dan, Naphtali, Gad, Asher, Issachar, Zebulun, Manasseh, Ephraim, and Levi – were lost. They say forever..."

"But that's impossible. There must be some traces of them. Such a mass of people can't just get lost," Michal objected.

The rabbi smiled. "There are traces, and there aren't... What's important: the prophet Ezra says in chapter 10 that all men of Judah and Benjamin gathered in Jerusalem after their return from Babylon. He doesn't mention anyone else. And as the custom goes, Cyrus' successors were contentious too, and so their country was occupied by Persian Emperor Darius I. His empire stretched from Greece all the way to India. Every king consolidated his empire by relocating prisoners of war above all to uninhabited areas. It's highly likely that Darius I populated the uninhabited eastern parts of his vast empire with Jews. I've been dealing a little with the issue of the lost Israeli tribes, so I can quote the English historian Malcolm. In his book *History of Persia*, published in 1815, he writes that many Afghanis living in the Azareth province during the reign of the Shanshabi dynasty named themselves Beni Israel, which means Sons of Israel. The captive population of the southern kingdoms had always called themselves Sons of Israel. Azareth is today's Hazara province in northern Pakistan, right on the border of Kashmir."

"Kashmir?" Marika exclaimed.

"Not only that. The old border of Hazara province extended beyond the Indus river and was a part of Kashmir."

"Oh my God, it's nearly half past two," Michal glanced at his watch with agitation. "We'll have to be going soon, it's an hour's ride to Tel Aviv."

"Hang on," Marika interrupted him. "I think rabbi Simonides still wants to tell us something important."

The rabbi smiled. "I'm not going to hold you much longer. I just want to add that ancient Greeks knew Kashmir, and even the historian Herodotus mentioned it, calling it a paradise on earth, and it's even drawn on Ptolemy's maps. Locals have many names for the beautiful, God-gifted country. Bagh-i-Suleiman is one of them."

"What does that mean?" Michal asked.

"Suleiman is nothing more than the Arabic translation of the name Solomon. Bagh is garden."

"So Kashmir means Solomon's Garden?" Marika exclaimed in shock.

The rabbi nodded. "It's the most beautiful corner of the world according to the Bible. Tall mountains with monumental, snow-covered peaks, many lakes, of which Dal Lake near Srinagar – the capital of Kashmir – is the most beautiful. The local fishermen have peculiar, long and narrow boats, known as shikaras…"

"…and heart-shaped oars," Marika exclaimed.

The rabbi gave her a surprised look. "You've been there?"

"No." She stared at the floor and then added quietly, "And there's a ruin of a castle or of some other structure on one of the hills over the lake."

"A hill looms over the city of Srinagar, with an ancient tumulus on it. It's called Takht-i-Suleiman."

"What does that mean?" Marika was barely able to contain herself.

"Throne," the rabbi replied quietly.

"So there's a Throne of Solomon in Kashmir?" Michal ruminated. The rabbi nodded.

"But that doesn't have to be after the Jewish king; it could easily be named after the famous Ottoman sultan Suleiman the Magnificent," Tomáš objected.

"The problem is that Kashmir is an almost exclusively Muslim country, but it has both Hindu and Buddhist buildings. However, the architecture of this particular shrine is totally unknown in Kashmir. It is reminiscent of the shrines of Jewish prophets, such as Ezra's tomb in Iraq or Ezekiel's in Kifli… Do you know what the case containing the Ark of Covenant is said to have depicted? Two angels with raised wings, touching each other. This later developed into the pointed arch, the architectural element that's the foundation of the Gothic style."

Michal shook his head in disbelief. "Templum Hierosolym. Show me the locket!"

He turned to Marika. She handed it to him. He weighed it in his hand for a long time. There was silence in the room, only disturbed by the singing of a muezzin, summoning Muslims to a religious service in a nearby mosque.

"Is this really true?" Tomáš asked a little impolitely.

The rabbi gave him a reproachful look. "There's another mysterious building in Kashmir. About forty miles south-east of Srinagar, near the town of Anantnag are the ruins of the Martand Temple. You know what's interesting about it? It's a near perfect copy of the Jerusalem Temple!"

"How do you know that if, as you say, it's only a ruin?" Tomáš objected.

"The temple was drawn accurately by the Greek geometrician and astronomer Apollonius of Perga in about 230 BC. Apollonius spent thirteen years in Kashmir as a student."

"In Kashmir 230 BC? A Greek? That's impossible. How did he get there?!" Tomáš was nearly enraged.

"Well, I told you Darius' and then Alexander's empire extended from Greece in the west to Kashmir and India in the east. Greece, the Palestine of Jesus' time and the foothills of Kashmir were parts of the same state."

"That's unbelievable," Marika said softly.

"But you still haven't answered my wife's question. Is Jesus' grave in Kashmir?" Michal asked impatiently.

"That you have to find out yourselves. We can only conclude with certainty that it's not in Jerusalem or any other known place on earth, unless you believe the fallacy preached by some dogmatists about Christ's Ascension. If you believe that Jesus was a man like any other, his grave has got to be somewhere. I told you the path to his grave is via Solomon's throne."

"But this Takht-i-Suleiman is his throne."

"Solomon's throne in Srinagar was a thousand years old at the start of the common era, and the one in Jerusalem would have been the same age, if King Nebuchadnezzar hadn't destroyed it. The one in Srinagar was repaired by a Persian master for King Gopadatta in year 54 of his reign, which would be the year 107 of the common era. The Persian builders found four inscriptions carved in two columns during the reconstruction works. Two of them are of exceptional interest to us. Therefore, I've brought their facsimiles. Here," he put a photocopy of an unknown script on the table, "it's Old Persian."

Tomáš laughed and syllabized, "*Dar een vagat yuz asaf dava-ipaikghmbar-imikunad. Sal panjah va chahar...* What does it mean?"

"Read the other one as well. You're doing quite well," the rabbi laughed too.

"*Aishan juzu paighambari-bani israil ast.*"

The rabbi took the paper and translated it, "The first text says: *At that time Yuz Asaf* – that's Jesus – *spread his prophetical messages. It was in the year fifty and four.* The other inscription says, *He is Jesus, a prophet of the Sons of Israel.*"

"If this is true, then..." Michal was going to say something, but the rabbi butted in.

"Those who've been to Yuz Asaf's tomb said it smells of lavender and Himalayan valerian and a prophetic light shines there that cures every disease."

"And where is the tomb?" Marika asked eagerly.

"My dear friends, that's all I wanted to tell you. The rest is up to you," he smiled.

"Rabbi, one more thing, please... What does *shlomo* mean?"

"It's a familiar form of the name Solomon."

"Shlomo is Solomon," Marika thought out loud. "Takht-i-Suleiman. That's what you deserve, Shlomo... My mother's mysterious sentence..."

"What are you saying?" Michal asked.

"That dream the other night... we smelled the scent of spikenard after it..." she said more to herself.

They were silent for a long while; they had many more questions on the tips of their tongues, but it was time to get up, and they valued the rabbi's precious time.

"Dear rabbi, it's been a great honor for me to have met you, and I'd like to give you this locket as a keepsake of our conversation. If it's of benefit to the people of Israel, I'll be very happy," Marika broke the embarrassment.

"Oh no, no, Mrs. Kráľová. I can't accept it just like that. It's a thing too precious and valuable. I'll be happy to pay you for it," the rabbi tried to protest, but Marika pushed the locket in his hand.

"Well, thank you then. In the name of the Sons of Israel."

"You mean the lost ones?" she asked.

"Those too. Will you go and search for them?"

"It seems we hardly have any other choice," Michal replied instead of her. Marika looked at her husband gratefully.

They shook hands. "One more thing," the rabbi halted. "I don't know how you knew the fishermen on Dal Lake use heart-shaped oars, but it's correct. There are only two places in the world where fishermen use such oars. The Dal and Nagin lakes in Srinagar and…"

"… the Sea of Galilee in Jesus' times," Marika completed.

The rabbi stared at her for a long while. They were standing hesitantly in the door which the waiter was holding open politely.

Marika eventually resolved to ask, "Rabbi Simonides, there are two places associated with Jesus' birth and death. He wanted to sow peace in both, but sowed unrest; he brought swords instead of peace. One of them is Israel. The other one is… Kashmir?"

The rabbi hesitated for a while, then smiled. "Correct."

"Buddhist Ladakh is part of Kashmir," Tomáš said softly. They felt he was going to add something, but then he realized something and went silent.

36 The Supreme Inquisitor

The meeting room at the headquarters of the Servizio Informazioni del Vaticano in Roma's Via dei Cherubini – Cherub Street, perfectly secured against any wiretapping, was slowly filling with staff of the fourth department working in the Heresy Combat Unit. Two thermos bottles on the massive table were holding the company's popular Mauro coffee. Brother Carlo Toti was hurriedly assuring someone on his cell phone that he was definitely coming to see the derby between AS Roma and Lazio that evening. He was looking forward to the match but still angry about the interruption to his vacation in the Bahamas and having to fly back to Rome in the late hours. He was sleepy and annoyed. The novice Felix Kruger was curiously examining the various recognitions, medals, framed letters of gratitude from popes and cardinals, carefully stored in showcases.

"I had no idea I was in such a noble organization," he smiled contentedly.

Toti switched off his cell phone, not amused. Felix's remark momentarily filled him with pride.

"My friend, you are part of a service that's had some memorable achievements. We've enlightened a few inquisitive journalists, we saved the Church from Hitler in the war, helped a few interesting people escape to safety via Croatia after the war, got Adolf Eichmann, the organizer of the holocaust to South America, only for two years unfortunately, then the Mossad boys tracked him down, but we also helped Stangl, the head of Treblinka concentration camp, Klaus Barbie, the butcher of Lyon, Gustav Wagner, deputy commander of Sobibor concentration camp, doctor Mengele of Auschwitz, SS general Fischbock, and others. We took care of Ustashe leader Pavelic, who sent half a million Jews and Orthodox Serbs to the other world."

"Why on earth did we do that?" Felix asked.

"I don't know if this requires much thinking. How would I explain…? Our historical relationship with the Jews is not among the best. Or the communists. The Nazis' relationship to these entities is similar to ours. Simply said, Hitler was a firm guard against Bolsheviks, whom we aren't fond of either. And then, these guys will be grateful to us, which may come in handy one day. You see?"

Felix said nothing for a long while. He was mulling over whether he'd done the right thing, changing his peaceful post of a provincial of the Jesuit Order for the headquarters of the Holy See intelligence service. But here he was now, at the HQ of one of the most successful secret services in the world, and his job was to carry out orders, not speculate.

"It looks like it's gonna come to the crunch today," Toti leaned over to him. "I've met a few people from the Directorate, the feared archbishop Falcone of the Congregation and that secretary of theirs, Farabutto."

"Looks a bit fishy to me. I think this Kráľ scares them a bit too much," Felix objected.

"It's come to the worst. As if Hausser had known. A few days after coming back from Jerusalem, this guy's flying to Kashmir."

"He wouldn't be taking his wife with him if he was going with a secret mission."

"That could be our great advantage."

"Why?" Felix didn't understand.

"Our enemies are easiest to exploit thanks to their wives and families. We put the screws on the wife, the guy comes clean right away. That's why we're the most successful network in the world," he smiled meaningfully. "There's only a hundred of us at the HQ, but we have over a million priests and monks in more than six thousand dioceses in the 174 countries with which the Holy See maintains diplomatic relations. They are our unique source of information. Most importantly, they're hard to squeeze because they have no kids… ha, ha…"

"How do they get their information?"

"From confessors as well, it's said."

"Abuse of holy confession?" Felix frowned.

"I can't say for certain, but that's what's said." As soon as he finished, lieutenant colonel Hausser entered the room and held the door open courteously for the archbishop, arriving with his secretary and another unknown man. He shook hands with Toti and Kruger convivially and said dryly when they all sat down, "Welcome to this special meeting, which I've summoned as the situation with the object of our interest – Mr. Kráľ – is becoming complicated. It's not critical – not yet – but we've got to be extra careful. You've read your dossiers; I'm not going to restate them. As there are some junior brethren here among us who don't know all the historic facts, we've also invited an expert from Global Power, Colonel Koggler from the United States, whose experience is priceless. He was among the close group of people involved in the Fatehpur Sikri operation. Moreover, the Colonel is a recognized historian and external professor of history at Global University. I'm glad to welcome Archbishop Falcone as well to our meeting, and Monsignor Farabutto, secretary of the Congregation for the Doctrine of the Faith. His institution's work is closely related to ours, supervising us, so to speak," the lieutenant colonel added with perceptible displeasure.

"I believe our guests will tell us some interesting things." His voice indicated a certain grudge that he had for anyone with a rank superior to his. He found it hard to put up with the fact that Koggler was a colonel although he was younger. On the other hand, he favored the straightforward and free-thinking American. He was pleased to see the nervous representatives of the Congregations, who were familiar with Koggler's opinions and were a little afraid of a clash with him. Hausser deeply hated assiduous inquisitors, as he termed them, who got in his way, but he had to respect them as they were the right hand of the Pope, on whom his career depended.

"We expect you to do so," Falcone grimaced. As Hausser gave no reply to his remark, he turned to Farabutto.

"Monsignor, the floor is yours." He settled in his comfortable leather armchair. Farabutto, roughly fifty years old, pulled a few dossiers twined with a yellow ribbon out of his scuffed attaché case.

One of the old school, Hausser thought. *He's a pedant, this is going to take a while.*

The secretary stood up, drew a dignified breath and started speaking in a deep, slightly husky voice. He made a somewhat comic impression as his second chin shook gently.

"Brethren, I'm glad to have an opportunity to speak, after a long time, on the ground of this important institute of intelligence services, extremely valuable for our common affairs of faith. Thanks to brother Maximilian for his invitation. Like your Servizio, our Congregation is not a large institution – it comprises twenty cardinals and archbishops as well as thirty clerical officials and secretaries, but like yours, ours is highly efficient. Since our foundation by Pope Paul III in 1534 – then known as the *Congregation of the Holy Office of the Inquisition* – we've had many fine achievements in combating heresy.

However, it has to be said that almost since the foundation of our Church by Saint Paul, the fight with apostates and heretics has been the daily bread for popes and many other loyal sons of the Church.

Thanks to the close connection between the Church and the State, heresy was considered a crime not only against the Church, but against the State as well. No wonder then that Emperor Frederick Barbarossa, devoted to the Church, was compelled to institute capital punishment for misbelievers. Unfortunately, it was of little help, so the Inquisition was established by the bull of Pope Gregory IX in 1231 as a highly effective tool against heretics. The Pope entrusted the performance of the inquisition to the newly established Dominican Order, who handed heretics over to civil power – just punishment – excellently in their service to the Holy Inquisition."

"What constituted heresy?" Felix asked.

"Even reading the Bible was considered heretic," the monsignor replied, showing his displeasure with being interrupted. "Thanks to the Inquisition, not only the Dominican Order but the entire Holy Church consolidated their material possessions, as a heretic's property was confiscated to its benefit. Dominican inquisitors carried out their tasks ardently. About a million heretics were sentenced to death in the following centuries, until the dissolution in Spain in 1848. The most common victims of inquisition were women charged with witchcraft. I'm not sure if you're aware that the greatest number of witches were burned in the Upper Hungarian town of Krupina, the last one in 1748. The stake was also the end of apostates such as Savonarola, Giordano Bruno, Joan of Arc and the Czech heretic John Hus. If the convicted were numerous, the sentence was carried out en masse after the end of the holy mass in a way known as the act of faith, or auto-da-fé. Just as people were burned, there were public burnings of books that contravened our creed of faith and were on the list of forbidden books, the *Index Librorum Prohibitorum*, which was in force from 1559. Thanks to it, we purged the world of more than six thousand books written by heretics such as Balzac, Descartes, Diderot, Voltaire, Dumas senior and junior, Heine, Kant, Sartre, Rousseau, Hobbes, Locke, Hume, Pascal, Spinoza, Zola, Flaubert, Gide, Kazantzakis and other malcontents. Unfortunately, the List expired in 1965, but fortunately there are our brethren of the Opus Dei, who have their own list. It includes the Italian Umberto Eco and his *Name of the Rose*, and the American Dan Brown and his *Da Vinci Code*.

Ferdinand II of the Catholic Habsburg dynasty, our close ally, whose intellectual vanguard comprised our predecessors the Jesuits, started the Thirty Years' War in 1618. The Habsburgs strove for reinstatement of Catholic domination in Europe. During the fights accompanying the ascent of Protestantism, five out of six cities in Germany were destroyed and the population dropped from nine million to four. Unfortunately, not even torture and mass murder that turned Central Europe into a ruin, nor the abundant amount of gold, brought by our brethren conquistadors from Peru to finance the Counter-Reformation, could turn Protestants back into the Church's bosom. But we're not giving up and keep on fighting."

Monsignor Farabutto sipped some soft drink. Hausser, who saw from the look of his colleagues how bored they were, took this opportunity to interrupt.

"I apologize, monsignor, we still have a lot of points on the agenda, could you speed up your historical excursus a little? Thank you," the lieutenant colonel ground out.

"Yes, my dear colleague, I'm nearly finished. To conclude briefly, the Holy Inquisition was renamed to the Holy Office in 1908 and has been known as the *Congregation for the Doctrine of the Faith*. We were very proud when Pope Benedict XVI, an associate professor of dogmatic and fundamental theology, ascended to the supreme Church throne directly from the supreme inquisitor's post. This gives us a great hope for the future."

37 BRHM

The wind turned east again after the storm, so the ship picked up a decent speed. Jesus was slowly forgetting his dispute with the Cochin Jews but was unusually solemn in spite of that. The prince knew he was thinking about the Berber princess they had left on the African shore far away. Sadness entered their hearts when they discovered in the open sea the wreckage of one of the military galleons that had left Muziris alongside them.

"I wanted to thank you," the prince tapped Jesus on the shoulder appreciatively. "Your insistence on heading for the port turned out right. We could have ended up like they did…"

They spent a long time examining the wreckage, among which the dead bodies of sailors and soldiers were floating. The prince sighed and called the captain. "The wind has again turned in the right direction. I suggest we let our boys rest at Kanya Kumari on Cape Comorin after the hard time in Cochin port."

"An excellent proposal, I was just about to suggest the same thing. Thank you, in the name of the boys too." The captain ran merrily to inform the crew of the prince's decision.

Rav Anna turned to Jesus. "It's the southernmost port of India on Cape Comorin, consecrated to the virgin goddess Kumari. The only port in the world connecting three seas: the Arabian Sea, the Indian Ocean and the Bay of Bengal. And excellent cheap pearls can be bought there," he added.

"I'll be glad for every experience that teaches me something," Jesus replied, smiling after a long time.

Two days later, both the sailors and the soldiers set out merrily to the narrow streets of the harbor marketplace on the cape where good money could buy beautiful, unusually large pearls of many different colors. These pearls thrived exceptionally in the warm waters of southern seas.

They returned to the ship after three days filled with music, singing and drinking to enter the port of Mailapur less than two weeks later. Jesus couldn't have known then that his most loyal disciple, Thomas, would settle in the city.

After the sailors replenished their supplies of water and fresh fruit, the ship entered the Bay of Bengal and headed northward.

"If the wind's right, we may be home within three weeks." The prince gazed toward the distant north; he spent increasingly more time on the deck as his home was drawing near. The excitement of almost being with their dearest ones again was spilling over to the sailors, soldiers and auxiliary staff. Neither chess nor the screeching of monkeys that they'd taken aboard back in Barygaza could take their minds off their wives and children, whose faces were becoming ever more reality. When the prince spotted the white pyramidal roofs of the holy temple to the Hindu and Buddhist god Jagannath in his city of Puri on the mainland, his heart pounded with excitement. He hugged Jesus and tears welled in his eyes.

"I'm back home after nearly two years. My Orissa, the land of India's holiest sites. Maybe this is a convenient moment for me to tell you who I am," he smiled enigmatically. "Come, let's sit on the prow together to keep sight of my country." They asked for some tea, and the prince began explaining amicably to Jesus.

"When Alexander the Great defeated King Porus on the river Jhelum more than three hundred years ago, he sent twenty thousand Greeks to Bactria, south of the Oxus river. Bactria then developed into the Greco-Bactrian Kingdom."

"Was Greek so widespread?"

"Indeed, it even established itself in your Palestine. The Greek culture came all the way here. Bactrian King Euthydemos and his son Demetrius crossed the Hindu Kush massifs and entered Indian Punjab on the foothills of Kashmir, where they established the Indo-Greek Kingdom, which only ceased to exist seventy years ago."

"Why did it cease to exist?"

"Because Menander, the last Greek king, decided to convert to Buddhism. But Greek influence has remained very strong in the area; a Greco-Buddhist culture has emerged. Mahayana Buddhism, above all, was strongly influenced by Greek philosophy. The Buddha's earliest statues bear clear signs of Hellenic artistic elements. The Kingdom of Takshashila joined the realm of Alexander the Great after his victory.

Your home – Palestine – was thus in the same state with the famous university."

"I very much long to visit it."

"My father has already arranged for you to be allowed to study there. Both the teachers and the students are awaiting you. But it will take some time before we get there. You can't become a student at Takshashila just like that. You have to gain some knowledge of the real world, our culture and traditions, and most importantly, you have to master our language. You have to learn all that before you can start your studies."

"I'm slowly beginning to understand your language, Pali. I learned some of it from your monks at Dositheos', but I've learnt a lot from your sailors on the way here," Jesus smiled. Then he added curiously, "You promised to tell me who you are."

"You see, you won't let me finish out of impatience," the prince rebuked him good-naturedly. "After the death of Alexander, Chandragupta Maurya, an important enemy of Alexander, established the Maurya Empire in the Indus river basin, which reached its heyday during the reign of his son, Emperor Ashoka, who converted to Buddhism at the age of 38 and is credited with its wide spread. The well-known Greek ethnographer Megasthenes also worked in his father's court. My father, King Gondophares, who rules the Indo-Parthian Kingdom and who is looking forward to meeting you enormously, is a descendant of King Ashoka, the most ardent propagator of Buddhism."

"Are you a descendant of the famous King Ashoka then?" Rav Anna nodded. "But you said you were a Jew. Was Ashoka, the propagator of Buddhism, of Jewish origin as well?"

"I have professed the Jewish traditions by myself," Rav Anna smiled broadly.

"How did you get to know them?"

"I reached the conclusion that Indians and Jews share a common origin. Abraham had a son, Ishmael, with his handmaiden Hagar, and a son, Isaac, with his wife Sarah, and your Scripture says that all the nations of the earth shall be blessed in his progeny," the prince added with a smile.

"How do you know our Scripture?"

"I studied it at the Takshashila university. It teaches all the wisdom and secrets of the world." Jesus listened attentively. "One of the secrets being that Indians and Jews had the same father."

"I don't think you're being serious," Jesus said, looking at him in a state of shock.

"Hm... it is quite a long story." The servant poured tea for them both. "Is it not odd that Abraham is the father of all nations according to your Torah and Brahma is the father of all creation according to our Vedas?"

"Interesting. Even their names are a bit alike."

"They are not only alike: they are absolutely identical. In the time of Abraham, his people began practicing circumcision, which they adopted from the Egyptians. A whole series of pharaohs' wives were Vedic princesses. Abraham lived about two thousand years ago, and our Vedas were written about six hundred years later. They were brought to us by sages known as Rishis..."

"... Oh," Jesus sighed, "but our Rishonim were rabbis who compiled the Talmud and the Siddur, our book of prayers..."

"Exactly. Do you really think such a similarity in names can be mere coincidence?" Rav Anna smiled. "One of our Vedas speaks about the man and the woman who were the first on earth. Their names were Ask and Embla..."

"We have Adam and Eve..." Jesus shook his head.

"It's very likely that Indian and Egyptian cultures influenced each other widely in the times of the pharaohs. Busy trade existed between India and Egypt. After all, your first prophet Moses was raised in the court of pharaoh Amenhotep III. Also, Abraham's wife's name was Sarah. Do you know what the name of Brahma's wife was?" Jesus shook his head. "Sarah too. Actually, she was Saraswati, but swati is only an ending denoting a female partner or wife."

"That's impossible..."

"The Scripture says: when Abram was ninety years old, the Lord appeared to him and told him – you shall become the father of many nations, you will no longer be called Abram but Abraham. And your wife Sarah shall become the mother of nations."

"But Sarah died soon afterwards," Jesus objected.

"Yes, but what we're forgetting here is that Abraham remarried shortly after her death. You just have to read it properly. After Sarah's death, he married Keturah. She gave him six more sons, whom he gave gifts and sent away from Canaan while he was still alive."

"Where to?"

"The Book of Moses says clearly, you shall go to the eastern land…"

Jesus said nothing, unable to speak. "It seems it's too much for you in one go," Rav Anna acknowledged. "Well, one last thing… I'd like to ask you how you write the name Abraham in Hebrew."

"We don't use any vowel letters in Hebrew. So, it's BRHM."

"Exactly. What's the name of the father of all Indians?"

"Brahma."

"So how would you write the name Brahma in Hebrew?"

Jesus looked at him in a state of shock. "BRHM…"

38 The Vatican Agent

When Farabutto finished, the archbishop applauded, and the others thumped on the oak table symbolically. Hausser stood, almost as if he were standing at attention, took a deep breath, a sip of water, and began speaking monotonously. Those closest to him knew that the monotonous speech was a mask, hiding his excitement and anger. He was known for his quick temper, and he seldom controlled himself when opposed with irrational arguments. Besides, he disliked the fanatical dogmatists from the Inquisition, which was the nickname they had for the Holy Office. He had lost his temper from time to time in the Swiss Guard and from there he'd been transferred to the intelligence service due to his merit. Whispering tongues said that the guard breathed a sigh of relief after his departure.

His voice trembled a little. "Dear gentlemen, our Church has had strong opponents since its foundation, who have insisted we are the root of all evil in the world. Not only us, they say, but all religions. They wish to unite them, which in fact means destroying them. It is an ancient idea, and very appealing for the masses of believers of every denomination. Picturing life on earth without war and conflict is very attractive. If I were more naïve, I would admit I'd like that picture as well. But historical experience teaches us that any attempt at bringing religions closer is unrealistic and it ultimately always turns out to be targeted against us – Catholic Christians. The reason is simple: we are the strongest, Jesus is the savior of humankind, there's one and a half billion of us. That's where our responsibility derives from," Hausser elaborated.

"I apologize, dear colleague, I'm a policeman and I like accuracy, so I'd just like to point out that there's one and a half billion Christians, including Protestants," Koggler noted. "That means that the remaining five and a half billion people on this planet are not Christians, so I'd be more careful about Jesus being the savior of all of humankind."

"Thank you," the lieutenant colonel replied coldly. Farabutto and Falcone exchanged angry looks. Hausser continued, "We're therefore responsible not only for the Church, but for the whole world and its stability. Can you imagine the disaster that would unfold if the position of the Catholic Church in the world was weakened? That is why we're extremely sensitive to any hints of activity contrary to our interests. Maybe some will find this Slovak guy harmless," the lieutenant colonel gave Felix a significant look, "but we have our own experience, and, of course, information. Our agent in Jerusalem – the priest Tomáš Dvoran – informs us that…" he broke off producing a dossier with encoded messages from Israel, "…let me quote, 'Under the pretense of curing his wife of an advanced stage of cancer, Michal Kráľ has decided to travel to Srinagar – the capital of Kashmir, where the tomb of Jesus Christ is supposed to be located – as soon as possible and visit local healers said to have miraculous powers, allegedly descendants of Christ. The Kráľs' are firmly resolved on visiting the tomb." He put down the paper and continued, "Dvoran isn't lying, his words are confirmed by a recording we received."

"Oh my God, lieutenant colonel, is this what you deal with? You can't be serious! I was of the opinion that the Vatican intelligence is engaged in meaningful matters," Falcone laughed sarcastically.

Hausser's left cheek began to twitch slightly. His colleagues knew that wasn't a good sign. In a kind of defensive pose, Carlo pulled his chair closer to the table. "I'm ninety-nine percent skeptical about this, sir… But the information, and more in the dossier, is really interesting. I hope you have read it."

"I have!" Falcone jumped up. "But this is inconceivable, unbelievable! Do you really admit that Jesus is buried somewhere on earth? Have you ever heard of the Ascension? You ask me if I have read your agent's report? Now I ask you, have you read Luke? Perhaps not. Let me tell you what he said to his apostles when he parted with them," the archbishop nearly yelled "*'Then he led them out to Bethany, raised his hands and blessed them. And when he blessed them, he moved away from them, and he soared to the heavens!'* This is the word of God! Are you contesting it?!"

"I am not. I told you I am ninety-nine percent skeptical."

"But you trust it one percent. You, one of the Vatican's highest intelligence officers, concede that Jesus did not ascend to heaven and is buried on earth? Do you have any proof?!"

The silence was interrupted by Carlo, "Excuse me, sir, but I must ask you what proof you have of Jesus having ascended to heaven." Hausser looked at his fellow gratefully.

"You've gone totally mad. Millions of people have acknowledged the Ascension for centuries, and now you contest it?"

"Millions of people acknowledging a thesis doesn't mean it's necessarily true. Millions of people acknowledged that the Earth was flat, at the center of the universe, with the Sun orbiting it."

Falcone yelled, "This is blasphemy! Gentlemen, I am shocked. Why, you're denying the foundation of our doctrine!"

"Archbishop, we're not denying anything!" Hausser, too, stood up, "we're just thinking rationally. Jesus not having a grave is no proof of him being in heaven. I believe it is bad luck that Jesus wasn't entombed in Rome. If he were, Rome would be the only Christian pilgrimage site. As it is, we must share that glory with Jerusalem, Bethlehem and Nazareth."

"How could he be entombed here if he was never in Rome?" the archbishop butted in.

"But we have Saint Peter's Church. Peter's remains are buried under it," Farabutto exclaimed convincingly.

Hausser was discomposed and reluctant to argue, so he welcomed Koggler's raised hand. "Colleague Koggler?"

"I beg your pardon, gentlemen, I know that it is not my turn to speak yet but allow me to share a little information with you." He turned to Farabutto. "Mister Secretary, you know very well that excavations have been made under Peter's Church but so far there hasn't been a shred of credible evidence that Peter or any other of Jesus' disciples are buried under it. So, I've had this question cross my mind: If Jesus isn't buried on earth because he's in heaven, why isn't Peter in heaven as well? In 1953, the archaeologist Bagatti excavated a 'Jewish-Christian necropolis' on the Mount of Olives, in a place known today as Dominus Flevit, including a first-century ossuary bearing the inscription *Simon bar-Jonah*. We know Peter's original name was Simon, and his father was a Jonah. If an ossuary with the inscription Peter, son of Jonah, was found under Saint Peter's Church, it would immediately become a site of reverence and pilgrimage.

But since it was found in Israel, it's been sitting unnoticed in a small museum past the Church of the Flagellation."

Koggler gave thanks for the opportunity to speak, and Hausser gave him a friendly look. He was puzzled for a moment, as he realized he was risking his chair by arguing with the ultra-orthodox archbishop, but then he said despite this, "I apologize, I'm a soldier, not an ideologist, and I'm not going to speculate about theological matters. Of course, I'm a Christian and of course I respect the doctrine of my Church. Unlike you, however, I'm responsible for the practical – not theological – defense of our Church. If you prefer theology, can you please tell me how come that the greatest miracle in the history of humankind, which the ascension of Jesus' physical body to heaven undoubtedly is, is only mentioned in Luke's gospel out of all the four gospels?"

"If I may, I'd like to add something to my colleague Maximilian. It's a known fact that the words 'and he rose to the heavens' are not included in all the editions of the Bible. For example, the *New American Standard Version* or the *Revised Standard Version* don't contain them at all," Koggler erupted.

"Leave me alone with these American liberalisms. And what about the Nicene Creed? Does it ring a bell?" Farabutto objected. "Doesn't it say exactly that? He rose to the heavens?" He turned to Falcone, who gave him a grateful look.

"If you're contesting the Council of Nicaea, you're contesting the divine origin of Jesus – and that's textbook heresy. All this, if you please, at the epicenter of the Vatican, in the counter-heresy department! That's unheard-of!" Farabutto curried favor with the feared archbishop, renowned for his uncompromising attitude to everyone and everything that even considered deviating an inch from the church dogmas.

"Gentlemen, I fully respect and accept the Council of Nicaea and all that was approved by it for the good of our Church. I'm a disciplined servant of God, but my responsibility is different from yours. Moreover, I apologize, I cannot afford to work with theses, or dogmas if you will. I'm an intelligence officer and evidence is all I accept." Hausser tried to control himself.

"So, you don't believe after all! Where there's evidence, faith no longer matters!" Farabutto exclaimed again.

"Gentlemen, do not mix my faith and conviction with my intelligence work. We are waging an ideological war with Islam, Jews, Buddhism and other religions. The position of Christianity is getting weaker while Islam is rapidly expanding; some surveys clearly state that Germany, France and other Christian countries will be majority Muslim within fifty years. We are living in pragmatic times, when people rely exclusively on evidence. If someone proves that Jesus didn't ascend to heaven but is buried somewhere on earth, Christianity will be done for. You are protectors of doctrines, it's your task to believe. I'm a protector of the Church power, I'm a policeman, and the primary task of a good policeman is to remain skeptical unless there is one hundred percent certainty. What will you do when the genetic code of the man buried in Srinagar is found to agree with the genetic code of Jesus Christ?! Your job will be over that very moment. So, please, don't meddle in our affairs!"

Falcone said nothing, but Farabutto tried to object, "Where have we come to, when a high officer of the Vatican secret service, who is supposed to believe holy dogmas, believes such profane methods as DNA?"

Hausser drew a breath and continued recognizably agitated, "A DNA test is a complete analysis of an individual's genetic code. Genetic information is stored in linear DNA molecules and recorded by means of the genetic code. I'm neither a chemist nor a biologist, but I know that DNA is analyzed not only to determine the paternity of children, but it's also been used to prove the kinship of people who've insisted they're descendants of figures such as Tzar Nicholas Romanov, Marie Antoinette, the poet Petrarch, and others."

"Those are people who lived relatively recently, but Christ lived two thousand years ago," Falcone objected, in a more peaceful tone.

"Permit me to add that DNA tests have proven people's kinship with pharaohs, and a certain Ötzi, a mummy found in the Austrian Alps, a man who lived three and a half thousand years before Christ."

"If I understand this right," Toti said after a while, "one's genetic origin can only be proven if the samples are compared to somebody or something."

"Exactly."

"So, to what would you compare samples, if any, of the man from the Srinagar tomb?"

"With the shroud of Turin, or people in the family of Ghulam Bashrat, the man from Kashmir known for his exceptional healing abilities. He insists that he's a descendant of Christ and his pedigree has been examined very deeply and thoroughly."

"How do you know this?" Farabutto asked, surprised.

"From our people in Kashmir."

"Who's that?"

"Former Afghan Mujahideen."

"Who?" Falcone almost exclaimed.

"Afghans from the LeT."

"What let?"

"L-e-T: Lashkar-e-Taiba. It's the military wing of the MDI – Markaz Dawa Irshad, translated as the Army of the Poor. It comprises chiefly Afghan and Pakistani fighters from Soviet occupation of Afghanistan. After al-Qaeda, LeT is the most dangerous terrorist group operating in South and Central Asia. Their hatred toward India is not only ideologically driven, but even more importantly it is a deeply religious conviction; their objective is to establish a universal Islamic caliphate. That's why they find India's ambition of becoming an economically dynamic, multiethnic and secular democracy absolutely anathematic. The Pakistani armed forces and intelligence service support them unofficially. Besides, the growing cooperation between India and the United States in security and counter-terrorist activities is a thorn in the Islamist radicals' side. As the US is the main sponsor of Israel, the LeT fighters refer to this alliance as an abominable Zionist-Hindu-Crusader axis. LeT's methods range from brutally murdering Indian groups to minefields to kidnapping foreigners, in exchange for hefty ransoms or the liberation of their fellow fighters. I wouldn't like to fall into their hands."

"And these people are our allies?" Farabutto asked in disgust.

"They work for us out of conviction, for ridiculous money. Their chief motive is hatred for Jews."

"What does the Vatican have to do with their hatred?"

"Well... they know relationships between Christians and Jews have never been... so to speak... ideal..."

A silence fell on the room for a moment. Hausser broke it quickly, "A third option is... erm... to compare the samples from the Srinagar tomb with those containing remains of Jesus' mother."

"Who?"

"Mary, the mother of Jesus."

"Now you've gone completely mad?!" Falcone exclaimed.

"Sir, there are numerous graves in Kashmir oriented east-west, the direction in which Jews buried their dead, but seven of them are considered graves of saints."

"I'm wondering what I'm talking about with you; only the Holy Father's orders prevent me from leaving this place as a way of protest." Falcone shook his head and drank some water thirstily. He smacked his plump lips, ruffled his dense gray hair and asked crossly, "You say in your dossier that Kashmir is mostly a Muslim country. How can you be sure that Muslims weren't interred west-east for space-saving reasons?"

"I am totally sure of that. All of those graves date from the first century and before. Islam didn't exist back then. Kashmir was a land of Buddhists and Hindus who are known to cremate their dead."

"So, you're saying that Jews were in Kashmir in Christ's time or even before?"

"Precisely."

"How did they get there?"

Hausser scratched behind his ear. "These questions really require someone with some expertise, so, I'd like to ask colleague Koggler to answer them. Would you be so kind, colonel?"

Flattered, Koggler smiled. "I must say, lieutenant colonel, that your historic knowledge is surprisingly good." Then he turned to the archbishop. "Experts say there are three possible explanations of how Jews got to India. According to the oldest theory, Jews were sent to India by King Solomon, the other says they are the lost Israeli tribes dragged to Babylonia by Nebuchadnezzar, and the third theory says they're soldiers and servants of Alexander the Great who settled there."

"They may have been on the coast, all right, but make it all the way to Kashmir? That's impossible. It's a known fact that even Alexander's army halted in front of the Himalayan slopes," Farabutto objected.

"The Greek philosopher and historian Philostratus remembers that the Greek Apollonius of Perga, a geodesist and geologist, studied at the university of Takshashila. As he was leaving the university after thirteen years, Apollonius wrote a letter of thanks to his patron, the sage Iarchus. Do you know what the letter said?" Then he produced a slip of paper and quoted: "*'Thank you for everything that you did for me; I arrived over land, and today I am returning home by sea, but I could even return by air if I wanted to, for that is the size of the wisdom that I have learned at your place.'*" The men gave him surprised looks.

"Koggler, sometimes I think you wish to be interesting at all costs. How could there have been a university somewhere at the end of the world five hundred years before Christ?" Falcone protested.

"Excuse me sir, but now you're letting Christian pride speak for you. The oldest European university was established in Bologna in 1088. At that time, however, Varanasi in India, previously Banaras, had universities dating back a thousand years before Christ. It's been proven that seven hundred years before Christ, there were first-class universities in the city of Nalanda in Bihar and in Takshashila at the foothills of Kashmir, about a hundred and twenty miles from Srinagar. The Sharda university near Delhi had the world's greatest library at the time. In Buddha's time, that is five hundred years before Christ, the university in Takshashila had about a thousand teachers and more than ten thousand students enrolled in it every year. The students were not only from India, China and Japan, but demonstrably there were students from Greece, Ethiopia and Britain as well. They studied mathematics, astronomy, philosophy, and above all, medicine. The Roman Empire hadn't even heard about universities at that time. India, not the Roman Empire, was the richest country of the world. The sixteen kingdoms that it comprised owned a third of the world's wealth. The most important kingdom in north-eastern India in Christ's time was Magadha, its capital being Pataliputra, known today as Patna, the capital of the state of Bihar. It's the oldest documented settled territory in the world. Three hundred years before Christ, the city of Pataliputra had a population of four hundred thousand. Rome only achieved that population size four centuries later. The primary task of parents in every wealthy Indian family was to provide their children with education. The *Jami-al-tawarikh*, or the *First History of the World*, written in 13th century Persia, says that Jesus left his homeland at the age of thirteen and went to India to receive an education."

The archbishop and the secretary made obligatory sneers at these words, but listened to Koggler attentively.

"What's even better is that Pythagoras himself was in Kashmir five hundred years before Christ to study eastern philosophy."

"Oh, please, stop making things up, I can't listen to it anymore," Farabutto sneered, appalled.

Koggler observed those present for a moment, thinking whether it made any sense to continue. In the end, he said with even more vigor,

"In the Indian state of Himachal Pradesh, northwest of the famous Kullu valley with its renowned skiing resorts, there's a remote Parvati Valley with a village at an elevation of about ten thousand feet known as Malana. All of the Malana Valley is administered by a board of eleven who only report to God. Locals say that they're the oldest democracy in the world. Historians have examined their laws and found out they're an exact copy of classical democracy in Ancient Greece. Malana has even been called Athens of Himalayas."

"Koggler, stop spouting nonsense," Farabutto rebuked him.

However, the colonel continued calmly, "Their religious and cultural customs and rituals are identical to those of Old Greeks. According to legend, they're descendants of Alexander's soldiers. They speak the Kanashi language, very similar to Old Greek."

"I have no reason to disbelieve you, colonel," archbishop Falcone sighed heavily, "but it's all somehow hard to believe and there are so many facts in what you say. I feel it's going to give me a headache."

"I don't intend to tire you with facts, but they are important for understanding the motivations of Kráľ and his people," Koggler said prudently. "Let me just add that the apocryphal gospel of Thomas mentions that Christ visited the part of Orissa in the Kingdom of Magadha, which was a center of Buddhism and Jainism." There was a long pause, then the archbishop said in a softer, almost resigned voice to the others, "Please, don't start with apocryphal gospels... erm..."

Koggler continued, "About forty miles east of the city of Takshashila, or Taxila in the modern tongue, and six miles as the crow flies from Rawalpindi, in modern-day Pakistan, there's the town of Mary in the mountains. It was known as Murree until 1875. A hill looms over the town, containing one of the west-east graves. Local Muslims have called the place Mai Mari da Asthan since times immemorial; it means 'Mother Mary's resting place'. This quaint place lies in the western slopes of the Himalayas, about twenty miles from the border of Kashmir. The English military engineer Richardson proposed to destroy the grave in 1898, as the place was ideal for constructing a military watch tower. But the plan wasn't carried through, because Richardson died of an unknown disease immediately after his proposal."

"You and your legends... Someone dies of a local disease unknown to the British, and you have a mystery. There is no evidence of Jesus' mother being buried there."

"There's no evidence of many things, yet people take them seriously," Koggler smiled sarcastically. "Science can only build on available, demonstrable sources. The Quran, for example, Surah 23/52 says, *'And we lodged the son of Mary and his mother in a high place, furnished with security and a spring'*."

"Oh my God, now you've opened the Quran! It's all just legend, and I'm surprised you're spending your time on it," Farabutto noted in disgust.

"There you go. Mary being taken to heaven, and her son ascending there, these are just legends, but a billion Christians take them seriously," Koggler smiled.

"But they're the foundation of our faith!" Falcone raised his voice.

"Faith can be built with what's known as public relations today. Some time ago, a mad old woman in Chicago found a crack in a tree in the shape of Jesus' mother, and today that tree is a pilgrimage site. Fast food stalls are making a tremendous business out of it. If the media got down to work and produced a legend that Mary really is in a grave, everyone would believe it even if it wasn't true," Koggler stated cynically. "After all, there's no evident of Jesus' resurrection or ascension – and they work."

"Your degree of cynicism is unheard of," Farabutto noted.

"Let the Vatican request the Government of Kashmir for permission to examine the Roza Bal tomb in Srinagar and ask the Government of Pakistan to conduct DNA tests on the alleged tomb of Mary, and all will be clear. Only it hasn't happened, and those that have tried to collect some evidence have been silenced. So, besides the shroud of Turin and possible descendants of Jesus, comparison of the samples with samples from Mary's tomb is the third option."

The archbishop ran his hand through his gray hair and added, "I hope the secret arrangement between the Holy See and the Governor of Jammu and Kashmir concerning the ban on entering the tomb is still in force."

Hausser smiled. "In Kashmir, a bribe will not only get you inside Christ's tomb, they'll bring it into your hotel room, sir."

The cardinal thought for a prolonged while, stirring his hair. Eventually he asked, "What are your, hm… security arrangements in Kashmir?"

"Perfect security arrangements, sir. Dvoran has replaced Král's glasses with ours, packed with the latest technology, so we know about every move he makes and every word he says. Dvoran is going along with them, to be on the safe side."

39 It Won't End Well for You

"At last, welcome to Orissa, a land of wisdom and scholarship, my brother. Welcome to Puri, its holiest city." Rav Anna, moved, embraced Jesus.

The majestic ship *Orissa* finally entered the port after the long detachment. Crowds of people were thronging the pier, with monkeys milling around them, peacocks strolling with dignity, and cows slumbering here and there. Two pairs of elephants were standing amidst the crowd; large platforms on their backs connected each pair. They were decorated with garlands, varicolored fabrics and an abundance of diverse flowers. Each pair of elephants was standing on an elevated mounting platform. The gangplank was brought and then first the prince's bodyguards disembarked onto the pier, followed by several soldiers, and eventually Rav Anna and Jesus walked out toward the elephants to the sound of pipes and drums. A beautiful woman with two young children was coming off one of the platforms to meet the prince. She kissed the prince's hand and he kissed her with a similar ceremonial air. Then he embraced his children. "This is our precious guest, Jesus, son of Joseph and Mary of Palestine. This is my wife Punita. It means holy in your language. And these are my sons Dev and Sanjan. The first means God and the other Creator." Jesus bowed and put his hand on his heart. Then Rav Anna and his family walked over to one of the elephant mounting platforms, and Jesus walked to the other one, accompanied by two courtiers.

"Do you think this is necessary?" he asked the prince. "You said your palace is not far from the harbor. Can we not walk?" At that moment, a group of ragged and dirty people of a dark complexion appeared. They were walking slowly, with their eyes turned to the ground, not daring to look at those they passed. They were clacking bamboo sticks together.

The crowds accepted the monotonous, unpleasant and sad sound with annoyance and repulsion.

"What's that sound?" Jesus asked Rav Anna.

"That's the Shudra. It's their duty to warn everyone of their passing with sound, so that nobody touches them. We call them the unclean."

"And if someone did touch them?"

"He'd become unclean like them and fall to their slave level." The prince's escort and bystanders were watching Jesus' conversation with Rav Anna. "They're descendants of the indigenous inhabitants."

"What are their rights?" Jesus asked.

"None. None at all. They're slaves determined by God to do the dirtiest work. Their fate is sealed once and for all."

"Who can set them free from these conditions?"

"Only death." The prince frowned a little after the questions; he wanted to get home as soon as possible. "Come, my friend, get on."

"I'd still rather walk."

"Walk? Impossible. I'm a Kshatriya, member of the ruling caste, and if my Vaishya of Shudra subjects saw me walk, not only would I lose their respect: they wouldn't understand it at all. Look at them!" The prince pointed at the men and women kneeling, or even lying on the ground, their faces pressed in the dust of the pier.

"I think we'd gain their respect just by doing that. As it is, they're only going to hate us," Jesus protested.

Rav Anna frowned. After a moment's thought, he came up to Jesus and, followed by his wife's longing submissive look, he explained to him nervously, "My dear friend, remember you're in a country where the great Brahma divided people justly into four castes based on their importance."

"I'm not sure God divides people according to any criteria. All people are equal before God."

"This division was made by the supreme Brahma! And we, his children have to respect his decision."

"God is the supreme justice and man is his reflection."

Rav Anna gestured for his wife that he'd be with her in a minute. "I'm sorry, although this is not the best place and time, I'll explain it to you. At the beginning of all life the great Brahma spoke, and the first man came out of his mouth. He was wise and his designation was

Brahmin, because he was like Brahma himself. A Brahmin is a revered priest and knows no labor. He represents God in all earthly interests. Another man came out of Brahma's hand and his color was red. His designation is Kshatriya, a fighter, a knight, king or prince, and his most honorable task is to protect the priesthood. A third man came out of Brahma's innards and his designation is Vaishya. His color is yellow, and his duty is to farm fields, supply the Brahmin and the Kshatriya with food. The fourth one came out of Brahma's feet; he was black and designated Shudra. He is of low ancestry and a servant to all the human races. He has no rights, he can't even listen to the Vedas, our Holy Scripture, and if he looks a priest or ruler in the face, he must die. The lowest of the Shudra are the Pariah, who clear away the ashes of the dead, sweep the streets, take away garbage and dung." The prince looked at the silent Jesus, who looked sadly at the people lying on the ground. "Why do you need the respect of these creatures? And now you must excuse me, I'm going to see my wife. Together we'll go to the palace, where a welcome with all due honors is awaiting you. My servants, soldiers, cooks and my serfs' wives are at your disposal." The prince set out to his elephants.

"Are these castes in all of India?"

"All of it. Except Kashmir."

"This is worse than Jerusalem. There, even the worst pauper may look a priest in the face without penalty."

"In my country, if a Shudra dares to look in the face of a king or prince, the ruler has the right to kill him on the spot."

"That can't be true," Jesus cringed.

"You want to see it?" the prince smiled.

"See what?"

"That it's true."

He didn't wait for Jesus' reply and halted before a boy lying on the ground next to his father. He kicked him hard. The boy looked at the prince in fear as he yelled at him in outrage. He gave an order to one of his soldiers, who immediately drew his sword. The boy's father hurled himself to the prince's feet, embracing them and kissing them, but taking great care not to look into his eyes. Jesus realized that the prince wanted the boy killed. He wanted to stop the soldier, but he had already sunk his sword in the boy's throat with all his strength. The boy's head rolled into the ditch and blood gushed from the lifeless body's arteries.

"What have you done to him? Why did you kill him?" Jesus grabbed Rav Anna.

"I wanted you to get used to the fact you're in India now."

"God will punish you for this!"

But the prince wasn't listening to Jesus anymore; he got on the elephant carriage full of expectation and joy over his return. The elephants set out at a dignified pace and walked amidst the crowd of kneeling and lying serfs toward his palace. Jesus looked at the receding elephants and an endless sadness entered his heart. He went over to the desperate father and wanted to comfort him. But the panic-stricken man jumped into the ditch to his son's lifeless body. This wasn't how Jesus had pictured his arrival in his dreamed-of India. The prince was already some distance ahead, however Jesus felt a stronger separation; he felt the prince's increasing estrangement from his heart. The two escorting soldiers and the driver were humbly awaiting Jesus' instructions to be able to follow the prince's elephants, who had disappeared in a bend of the road. Jesus hesitated for a moment, but then he stood up resolutely and came back down to the mounting platform. Watched by the soldiers and the crowd around them, which was staring at him uncomprehendingly, he went down the steps. "I wish to walk to the prince's palace on Indian soil."

In a state of shock, the commander of the escorting soldiers objected in a trembling voice, "Sir, that's not appropriate. That's a violation of our time-honored traditions."

"Then change them," Jesus smiled.

"Sir, they're traditions we were given by God."

"God only gives good things. Let's go." Jesus stepped out, and the military commander knelt before him swiftly and grabbed at his robe.

"Sir, please, keep me alive. It is my task to escort you to the palace with all due honors. If you walk, if you don't ride the elephants... then... I'll be dead before this evening."

"Is that your tradition too?"

The soldier said nothing. "Please... I've a wife and two children..."

Standing in deep thought, Jesus considered what to do. Then he moved on to the nearest man. He had no eyes, his face was littered with scabs, ulcers and swellings, and one of his ears was devoured by rot. Jesus looked over the man's wounds covered with white hairs, a clear sign of leprosy. Shocked, the people watched the stranger's peculiar behavior. Even the most humiliated Pariahs were raising their heads and observing the scene. Jesus took the man by the hand. "Come with me, I'll restore your health."

He beckoned to a soldier to help the man climb the stairs onto the mounting platform, but the soldier jumped back in terror. So Jesus braced the unsuspecting blind man up the steps himself. Then he invited the other cripples to come up to the platform. But none dared to. The people were watching the unusual scene in astonishment. They hadn't forgotten the ban on casting their eyes on a stranger, but this one didn't look dangerous. They even stood up in shock and looked as the elephants receded with Jesus sitting on the honorary platform along with the most humiliated person among them, riding to the palace with dignity while the elephants happily blew their trunks. Instead of shock, smiles were gradually climbing onto the faces of the people in the street. They smiled for the first time in their lives.

"This won't end well for you," a naked man covered in dust whispered at Jesus. He stood up and waved goodbye to the receding elephants. One by one, others took scarves off their heads, pulled white cloths out of their sleeves, and those who had nothing waved their poor, dirty hands at Jesus. He looked down at the people from the height of his platform and replied to their salutations with a smile. He had never dreamed of such a magnificent welcome to India.

40 Fear

After Koggler finished, there was a half-hearted, sporadic tapping of fists on the table.

"Does anyone wish to ask the colonel a question?" Hausser inquired obligatorily, making it quite clear with his tone that he would prefer if people didn't. "Before we move on to the next point, can the colonel please briefly sum up what we know about Michal Kráľ so far?"

"Thank you, lieutenant colonel," Koggler stood up.

"We're all brethren here, I'm Maximilian, but friends call me Max," Hausser corrected the colonel. "And today's not the first time we've met." He had known Koggler for a few years and knew that he was a professional and a pragmatist who only acknowledged facts.

"Thank you, Max. Incidentally, congratulations. I'm pleased to see you have moved. Do you remember our last meeting at the Global Power headquarters in Brussels? You were representing the Vatican Guard, I think you were a major back then. I nearly drove you mad by explaining that Jesus isn't buried in Jerusalem as well as the fact that he very probably didn't die on the cross."

"Don't you start that blasphemy again," Falcone and Farabutto exclaimed nearly in unison.

"Gentlemen, I'm an employee of a civilian organization and I stick to facts. If you furnish me with evidence that Jesus is buried in Jerusalem, or on Mars for all I care, I will apologize to you. If you're content with dogmas in your lives, that's your problem. I'm not. I've accepted Max's invitation because the issue of Jesus' last resting place is of extreme importance for the further evolution of human civilization. As the lieutenant colonel has said, if it's proven that Jesus isn't in the heavens… Incidentally, I'd like you to explain to me where the physical heaven is, because there must be a physical heaven if Jesus' physical body went there. If you have the answer, I'll be glad if you…" Koggler digressed, but picked up right away.

"What was I going to…? Oh yes. So, if it's proven that Jesus is buried on earth, a fundamental paradigm shift in human evolution will take place. I don't need to mention what that would mean to the Vatican. Gentlemen," he turned to the archbishop and the Congregation secretary, "I'd like you to pay your full attention to our colleagues at the SIV, because if the DNA of the remains from the Srinagar tomb and the DNA of the Shroud of Turin or people claiming to be Jesus' descendants are ever compared, and found to be identical, then all your allegations about the Ascension of Jesus will become highly relative indeed. I don't need to elaborate on the implications for the Church and for you personally. And you, gentlemen, surely know very well the truth regarding the Shroud of Turin, in which Jesus was wrapped when they took him off the cross. I know you know it, because we sent you those reports. And, of course, I assume it's also clear to us why the Vatican hasn't shared its opinion on this evidence. For the others, let me restate some of the basic findings. Starting in 1969, the Shroud was examined by a team led by the Swiss criminologist Professor Max Frei of the University of Zurich using the method known as palynology, or pollen analysis. Frei presented the results of his research in March 1976. He managed to identify forty-nine different plant species, including eleven which don't grow in Europe but originated from Near Eastern soils with a high salt content, typical of the area around the Dead Sea. There were species such as tamarisks, seablites and wormwood, plants that only grew in Palestine two thousand years ago."

"But really, how can you prove the authenticity of two thousand years old pollen?" Falcone asked.

"Pollen grains are 0,0025 to 0,25 millimeters in diameter and are wrapped in a double shell thanks to which they can survive up to thousands of years. It's well known that the excavations at Pompeii contained some wheat grains that were then sown and grew. As you know, Mount Vesuvius erupted in AD 79."

"I haven't heard of a piece of linen cloth that survived two millennia," Farabutto tried to support the contemplative archbishop.

"Then you've heard too little. Go and take a look at Egyptian collections in museums in London, Cairo, Paris, Berlin, and you'll find linen fabric in perfect condition, up to five thousand years old."

"What does that prove?" Farabutto asked nervously; he was obviously becoming displeased with the whole conversation. But Koggler continued, unfazed.

"On the Shroud, they also found traces of plants from around Istanbul and southern France, and eventually Turin as well. They're all places where the Shroud has evidently been. That piece of cloth, three feet and seven inches wide and fourteen feet and four inches long, also contains twenty-eight blood stains. Jewish law commands that a dead person has to be washed – with hot water – and then wrapped in canvas. The traces of blood and sweat clearly indicate that the body wrapped in it was not washed. Meaning that the Shroud did not hold a dead body."

"Oh, colonel," the archbishop sighed, "but that isn't proof of anything."

Koggler continued calmly, "If a dead body had been wrapped in the Shroud, there wouldn't be any traces of blood. Blood only flows as long as the cardiovascular system is working, that is, the heart is beating. And if Jesus had died on the cross, his body would have been stiffened in an unnatural position. However, a man in a straight position was wrapped in the Shroud."

"What you haven't said, dear sir, is that a committee of first-class Italian experts was set up by the Archbishop of Turin and following three years of meticulous study, the committee concluded without any doubt that the fabric dated from the Middle Ages," Falcone said triumphantly.

"Yes, but two cardinal members of the committee – the Egyptologist Silvio Curto and the ancient art expert Noemi Gabrielli – later took back their original statements. The symptomatic thing is – pardon me, gentlemen – that it was an Italian commission. The Shroud was later studied by an American commission, which proved the opposite. Dr. Michael Tite headed up the next examination of the Shroud of Turin, which was examined using radiocarbon dating. However, Dr. Tite confessed in October 1988 that a sponsor, whom he wished not to name, had given him a million pounds sterling to falsify the true results of the research which had proven that the Shroud dated from the first century.

When Cardinal Ballestrero of Turin tried to intervene in order to clarify matters, he was pensioned off to his great surprise. But perhaps you have more to say about that," Koggler smiled, sipped his soft drink, and continued in a peaceful tone, "My friends, my method of communication is that anyone who feels that something is unclear can interrupt me at any point and ask me. OK? So, feel free to ask."

Upset, the representatives of the Congregation for the Doctrine of the Faith said nothing; it was clear that the derisive comment was aimed at them.

"Everything you're telling us is absolute nonsense! If you're saying Jesus' grave might be in Kashmir, it's clear he didn't die on the cross," Falcone objected a moment later.

"Naturally. Do you have any evidence that he did die on it? I mean, if he had died on the cross, he'd have been buried on that same day according to custom. But he doesn't have a grave in Jerusalem," Koggler stated coldly.

"How could he have an earthly grave when he rose to the heavens?" the archbishop roared.

"I apologize, your Excellency, but it's embarrassing for me, an ordinary worshipper, to have to lecture an archbishop. It seems you didn't pay adequate attention to your Biblical studies…"

"You don't have to lecture me on the Bible, I know it far better than you do!"

"Perhaps not. Paul the Apostle says, excuse me…" To everyone's surprise, Koggler produced a Bible out of his briefcase, opened it and started reading. "The First Epistle to the Corinthians, chapter 15 on Resurrection, Verse 44: *it is sown a natural body, it is raised a spiritual body…*"

"Are you really suggesting that the archbishop hasn't mastered the Holy Book?" Falcone exclaimed sinisterly.

Koggler wouldn't be ruffled. "Even if Jesus rose to the heavens, it was only forty days later. That's what the Bible says. In the meantime, according to the gospels, he was spotted alive twelve times. If you don't know where and when, I'll happily remind you of the places in the New Testament describing his encounters with people who saw him alive, although it should perhaps rather be you reminding me," he added with sarcasm.

"You don't have to remind me of anything," Falcone retorted and began quoting from the gospels, "Mark 19:9, John 20:11 to 18, Matthew 28:9,10, Luke 24:34, Luke 24:13-31, Mark 16:14, John 20:19-23, 26-29, John 21:1-13, Matthew 28:16-20, Mark 16:15-18..."

Koggler smiled contentedly. "You could even quote Acts of the Apostles and the Pauline Epistles to the Corinthians."

"Only, dear colonel, he was resurrected when his disciples and the other people met him! He was a ghost by then!" Falcone exclaimed victoriously.

"Your Eminence, I apologize but you just said the Holy Book lies," Koggler smiled.

"How dare you..." the archbishop simmered with rage.

"The Holy Book, I beg your pardon, let me quote John, chapter 20:27: Then He said to Thomas, 'Reach here with your finger, and see My hands; and reach here your hand and put it into My side.' Could you put your hands on a ghost's body?"

"But you've intentionally left out another thing said in the same John. Let me quote: *Though the doors were locked, Jesus came*. That is clear evidence that he was a ghost!" Falcone shouted triumphantly.

"The problem is that Luke, for example, doesn't mention any doors being locked. Instead, he says, *'Touch me and see; a ghost does not have flesh and bones, as you see I have.'* Then, as you know, he too ate fried fish with them. So, honorable archbishop, I'm sorry, but you are defying the words of Jesus himself when he says he's not a ghost but a man of flesh and bones. Moreover, I don't know how a ghost could eat fish," Koggler smiled, and all the SIV men with him.

Falcone ground his teeth, and Koggler continued calmly, "Another thing you forgot to mention is that when Mary Magdalene, Mary of James and Salome came to the grave, they found the stone locking the entrance rolled aside. Can you explain why you would roll the stone aside if Jesus was a ghost without a body?" Koggler, who had shown himself as an excellent authority on the New Testament, continued, "Or doesn't Matthew, chapter 28:12 say that they gave the soldiers a lot of money and said, *'You are to say, His disciples came by night and stole Him'*?"

"So, it was the disciples after all; they took him from the grave and they must have rolled the stone aside," Farabutto countered.

"If the disciples had taken him from the grave, they wouldn't have been surprised, as the Bible says, when they met him in Galilee a few days later.

So, I guess he was taken by someone else. And, guardians of faith, can you explain why then Jesus walked – whether as a ghost or a physical man – around Galilee, Jerusalem, Emmaus and who knows where else for forty days, and then suddenly decided to rise to the heavens?"

"To fulfill the prophecy," Falcone exclaimed.

"Can you quote that prophecy?"

"I don't have the Old Testament on me," he said, making a lame excuse.

"I'll lend you mine with pleasure."

Koggler handed his Bible to Falcone. Falcone made an ostentatious gesture of refusal. Koggler smiled. "But I can quote more references directly from the Holy Book, whose observance your office supervises and whose disrespecters it punishes severely! Then please respect the Holy Book yourself! Let me quote John the Evangelist: *Nicodemus, who was incidentally a healer as well, brought to the grave a mixture of myrrh and aloes, about seventy-five pounds.*" Koggler smiled. "Boy, seventy-five pounds is a lot. An enormous quantity, highly exceeding the amount required for embalming. The important fact is that myrrh was admittedly used for embalming, but it was primarily a very effective cure for inflammations, wounds and infections. And aloe is not at all an embalming herb: it's been used as a strong antibacterial, to heal wounds and stimulate the immunity system. Can you explain why they brought healing herbs to the grave, not embalming ones, if Jesus was dead as you say?"

"It's impossible for anyone to survive crucifixion. It was the cruelest method of Roman execution," Falcone objected.

"I must correct you. Crucifixion was primarily a method of torture."

"What are you blathering on about? Are you indeed suggesting that the Jews and Pilate didn't want to put Christ to death?!"

"There are a sufficient number of well-documented cases of people surviving crucifixion. Just read Flavius Josephus' historical treatises. Thousands of Jews were crucified in Palestine during the anti-Roman uprisings. In some cases, the Roman commander was free to decide that some had suffered enough on the cross and permit them to be taken down. Taking a live prisoner off the cross was nothing exceptional. We know from the gospels that Jesus was crucified at midday on a Friday along with two criminals. He was dead three hours later. A young, physically fit man? Isn't that odd?"

"You're forgetting Jesus was flogged before, unlike the other two."

"Sure, but even flogged, he had managed to carry his cross up to Golgotha, so he had enough strength and will," Koggler replied.

"I don't see why you haven't quoted John and other Evangelists who say that soldiers arrived and broke the legs of both those crucified with him. But when they came up to Jesus and saw that he was dead, they didn't break his bones," Falcone smiled triumphantly.

"Yes, it was a late Friday afternoon before the start of the Easter sabbath, and law commanded Jews to bury the dead before the sunset, when Saturday began. That was why they broke the other two's shinbones: to speed up their dying, because then they couldn't stay on the wooden rung and would suffocate. Don't you find it odd that the merciless Roman soldiers who had flogged and humiliated Jesus, torn his clothes, put a crown of thorns on his head, now suddenly didn't finish him off when they had the chance?"

"Well, that's true, but why would they finish him off when he was dead? The centurion had pierced his heart with a spear," Farabutto objected.

"Mister secretary, now I am unpleasantly surprised. I thought an esteemed secretary of the Congregation like you would know the Bible really well. The gospels say, quoting from John, '*When they broke the legs of the other who were crucified with Him, coming to Jesus, they saw that He was already dead, so one of the soldiers pierced His side with a spear, and immediately blood and water came out.*'"

Farabutto felt ashamed and said nothing, and Falcone was fidgeting in his chair too.

"He pierced his side, not his heart. And do you know who the soldier piercing him with the spear was? Centurion Longinus, his secret sympathizer, who had commanded the whole operation in person on Pilate's orders. According to Gregory of Nyssa, Longinus later became the bishop of Cappadocia, whence he came. And let me reiterate what I've said once, this time quoting from the Bible: *blood and water came out*... Even children know that blood clots, so if Jesus had been dead, no blood could have come out of him!"

Farabutto didn't know how to react. Koggler caught Hausser's conniving smile and continued, encouraged. "I've mentioned that Jewish law commanded burying the dead in the ground before the sunset. Jesus, being a Jew, which I hope you will agree, thus had to be buried in the ground. However, as all the gospels say – let me emphasis: all the gospels, so they're perhaps right in this case – Jesus' body was not put in the ground but in a grave hewn in a rock. Meaning he probably wasn't dead…"

"Koggler, stop that blathering!"

"Moreover, the gospels say that Jesus was lying on a stone slab, meaning that his body must have been straight, not bent. But I've already said that."

"Excuse me, mister… erm…" Falcone interrupted Koggler.

"Koggler," lieutenant colonel Hausser calmed his colleague down, seeing that the archbishop was now passing into the low-blow level of insults.

"Koggler… Are you a Christian?"

"Yes."

"A weird one then."

"What makes you think so?"

"Well, you've been claiming things that totally contradict the teaching of our Church."

"Such as?"

"Everything you've told us this far."

"Your Excellency, my apologies, but I've given you at least ten pieces of evidence that you haven't refuted in any way, so I might instead ask you whether you're a Christian and whether your Church tells the truth about Christ."

"What?! Do you dare to say this to an archbishop, a former papal nuncio? A member of the Congregation for the Doctrine of the Faith? That's outrageous!"

"Sir, we too concern ourselves with Christ's teaching. It's the most amazing teaching in the world. It's a teaching of love and truth. I seek truth; you own it. I try to act like Jesus did. It's very hard, but I try. I didn't become a Christian because my mother had me baptized. Baptism is not enough for a person to be a Christian."

"So now you deny the importance of baptism as well? The fundamental sacrament and value of Christianity? How can you still claim to be a Christian?" Falcone gesticulated wildly.

"It's not me, gentlemen, it's you who deny the importance of baptism. The whole of the Church denies it."

"But you said yourself you were baptized," Toti protested nervously.

"But such baptism is meaningless. It's in stark contradiction to what Jesus said."

"This is insolence, I'm not going to listen to that," Falcone exclaimed.

"Monsignor, can you quote me a single place in the gospels that speaks about baptizing newborn babies?" There was a silence. "Well, I can quote you two places that mention baptism. First, Mark, *'Therefore go, teach nations and baptize them.'* The other quote is from Luke, chapter 16: *'And He said to them, Go into all the world and preach the gospel to all creation. He who has believed and has been baptized shall be saved.'*"

"There you go," the archbishop burst out. "You've disproved yourself."

"But Archbishop, in both quotes Jesus is clearly speaking about baptizing adults, not infants. Teach nations and baptize them. Can you tell us how you can teach newborn babies? He who has believed shall be saved. Can you tell us how an eight-day old baby could believe? Do you want to hear what Jesus said to that?" He reopened the New Testament angrily. "Matthew 21:16: *From the lips of children and infants you have called forth your praise!*"

"What are you blathering about? How could Jesus have known we would do it like this one day?" Falcone protested.

"Well, I couldn't have expected a better confession," Koggler laughed, but then he continued excitedly. "I became a Christian by realizing some things. Through my own free will. Through my own reasoning, which you cannot deny was given to me by God. He indeed gave us reason, and he did so in order for us to think and make independent decisions. Do you know why the Catholic Church, although a mass organization, is today empty and weak? Because everyone is a member merely due to a formal act, the baptism of infants, not because of their own decision. Your duty is not only to urge others to respect God's laws, but mainly to adhere to them yourselves. With your dogmas you prevent people from thinking! I suspect He didn't even anticipate, but knew exactly that you'd do that one day." He opened the gospels fiercely again. "Matthew, chapter 23:13: *'Woe to you, teachers of the law and Pharisees, you hypocrites! You shut the door of the kingdom of heaven in people's faces. You yourselves do not enter, nor will you let those enter who are trying to.'*" Koggler was breathing heavily.

"Do you wonder why the Muslims are flooding Europe? You have a wonderful mass organization, you ask governments for money for each of your members, but you don't care if the Church is strong internally. Can you imagine how great the Church would be if it only united people who joined it based on their own independent decision? Jesus said, *you shall build your house on a rock, not on sand, because the first storm that comes will take your house down.* His warning words are beginning to come true. Baptizing infants means building a house on sand."

"This is outrageous. You lecture an archbishop, a professor of dogmatic theology?" Farabutto tried to defend Falcone.

"Gentlemen, I'm not interested in your dogmas but in life as exemplified through Christ. A dogma is an assertion for which there is no evidence, so you could easily call it a lie."

"Please, colleague, moderate yourself," Hausser turned to Koggler.

"This is beyond my tolerance!" Falcone and Farabutto rose. "We're leaving. Such blasphemy on Vatican grounds is an impudence."

"Please, gentlemen, colleague Koggler may have lost control a little, I apologize for him. Colleague Koggler, excuse me, this debate is interesting, but we're not here to examine whether Jesus died on the cross or not. Our task is to defend the Church's interests."

"Which Church? That of Jesus or that represented by these gentlemen? The one that Jesus speaks of…" He grabbed the Bible heatedly. It slipped out of his hands and fell on the floor. He picked it up angrily, pulled out a bookmark, opened it and almost yelled out, "Matthew, chapter 7: *Beware of false prophets…* He's speaking about you!"

"Goodbye, gentlemen. Colleague Hausser, we'll talk again," Falcone said menacingly and moved toward the door.

"Archbishop, there's no need for you to leave. I am leaving," Koggler said resolutely, picking up his papers and tossing them in his worn briefcase before starting to leave.

"Gentlemen, I think this is all a big misunderstanding. We are concerned with a common matter. Nobody says the Church is flawless, but we're all on the same boat," Hausser was trying desperately to save the situation. "Let us calm down and act in the interests of solving our common problem," he called on both the Congregation representatives and Koggler. Falcone and Farabutto hesitated for a moment. Then they realized they might get into a very unpleasant situation without Koggler, so they eventually sat down again, their teeth clenched. Koggler too returned to the table after them. He watched the two men for a moment. Their eyes were cast downwards. If he could see them, he would see anger and powerlessness. Most of all, he would see fear.

41 The Lost Tribes

Although more than a month had elapsed since the unpleasant exchange of opinions on the pier, there was still some lingering tension between the two young men. Admittedly, the prince was twice as old as Jesus – he celebrated his thirty-second birthday after his return to Puri – but he was increasingly jealous of the Israeli youth. He was accustomed to being the center of attention wherever he went. Now, however, the prince's experiences from the distant lands evidently weren't of interest to his friends despite his more than two years' being away from home. The Nazarene was the topic of the day in both higher and lower society; wherever he went, he drew attention with his remarkably mature and wise speech. At first the prince accompanied Jesus to the Jagannath temple every time, but when he saw that the priests were more interested in his words than in listening to the prince's stories, he went to the temple less and less often. Jesus also had disputes with the priests as they obstinately defended the Indian caste division. The news of his unprecedented act of inviting a leper on his elephant spread through Orissa like wildfire, and it was even known in other cities in India.

"This country stretches from the Gondwana mountains in the west to the Bay of Bengal in the east, from the wild mountains of Jaspur in the north to Gasnjan in the south; our predecessor was King Ashoka, who introduced Buddhism almost three centuries ago. And nobody has even questioned the system instituted by gods," Mahajan, the temple superior, gesticulated during one of the many disputes between the priests and Jesus.

"Castes are not from God but from Aryans, who arrived in India fifteen centuries ago. It was they who introduced the division of people into more and less valuable," Jesus objected. There was a hum among the gathering.

Mahajan frowned. "Young man, we've admitted you with respect and esteem, but it is improper to blaspheme in the temple, the residence of our god Jagannath, the incarnation of both Vishnu and the Buddha. I must ask you to keep control of your utterances," he raised his voice. "Take care not to become arrogant. Be so kind and read what's written on the temple frontage."

"I know. I've read it. It's a splendid thought: *Lord, if you love me, grant unto me that I may be the last servant in the large human family.* It is a splendid thought, but I don't understand why you only put it on the wall of a temple and not inside your hearts."

"Law prohibits priests and rulers to come into touch with lower caste people."

Jesus pondered. "I'll tell you a story of a king who had four sons. He decided to divide his property among them. To the oldest and most ambitious one he gave the truth and bade him spread it among the people; to another he gave a sword and commanded him to protect property and land; to the third one he gave fields and herds and ordered him to take care of livelihood for the others. As for the fourth one, he let the three elder brothers to decide what to leave for him. They feared the youngest one, so they chained him to a rock. Years later, the father summoned his sons and asked them to present their bills. Although they had done good work, he saw what they'd done to the youngest brother. He tore the eldest one's priestly gown, took his possessions away from him and sent him to jail; he broke the second one's sword, took his possessions away from him and sent him to join his brother; he took the third one's possessions and sent him to search his conscience in the desert. Then he went and tore loose the chain on his youngest son's leg, and he gave him all his brothers' possessions."

The priests said nothing, except for the youngest of them: Lammas, who had been a supporter of Jesus since his arrival in the temple. "How can slaves and destitute people, whom we treat worse than cattle, free themselves from the unjustness of the priest, the ruler and the soldier?"

There was a hubbub in the hall. "Why would they? It's their fate given by God," Mahajan protested.

"When you open up your hearts for God, as the sunflower opens up to the sunshine every day, then the Shudra will be as free as the priest, the ruler and the soldier. Because even you, priests, soldiers, and even you, my dear prince, are not free, and you will not be free as long as one of you is enslaved," Jesus turned to Rav Anna, who was listening to the dispute in silence.

"Are you saying this to the superior of four thousand priests summoned by Vishnu to this temple? Are you saying this to the prince who has brought you to our country with the best intention, so that you could study and acquire the legacy of Gods, to study the laws of the Man and the Vedas?" the superior rebuked him and then he added warningly, "If you wish to stay in the temple hereafter, you will have to change your thinking."

The gathering was eagerly awaiting Jesus' reply. However, he stood up without a word and walked out of the temple. He sat on the steps and watched destitute people walking in a long line bringing sacrifices to the temple on their thin shoulders: goats, hens, fish, coconuts, rice, fruits, that priests took from them. Just like in Jerusalem.

Suddenly someone put a hand on his shoulder. "Let's go away from here," Lammas invited him.

"Where to? I fear it's the same everywhere," Jesus protested.

"Let's go to Cuttack. It's a two days' trip north from here. I have a lot of friends in the Chandi temple there, young monks and priests who think like you. They will join us. We'll travel around India and spread the truth."

"I'm a stranger here and I'm still too young. I don't even know your language properly; nobody will believe me. I have a lot to learn first. I'd like to go where the wisdom of true wise men is, not dogmatic priests."

"If you allow me, I'll accompany you. From Cuttack we will go to Rajgir in Bihar, the city where the Buddha meditated five centuries ago. From Rajgir it's very close to Nalanda with its famous university." Jesus listened attentively to Lammas' suggestions. "We'll also visit holy Banaras on the river Ganges, the city of science and culture, where I will introduce you to the wisest Hindu healer, Udraka. He'll teach you to heal miraculously."

"I've heard Banaras is not far from Lumbini in the land of the Shakyas," Jesus noted.

"With good horses we can reach the Buddha's birthplace in three days. It's a flat country, the Himalayan shields only rise beyond Lumbini."

"Alright," Jesus said resolutely. "I'll see the prince and ask him for his consent."

"I don't think he'll protest. You see yourself he's not very keen on your words."

"He claims to be a Jew, yet he disrespects our laws," Jesus sighed.

"He is of a Jewish origin, but he's a ruler and a friend of priests. They have always stuck together," Lammas smiled. "I hope he'll gives us horses and all we need for the journey. We'll set out together to look for your lost compatriots. Do you agree?"

Jesus smiled broadly. "I have no wish more heartfelt."

42 Footprints in the Stone

The day after they returned from Israel, Marika felt languid and had a temperature. Her armpit lymph nodes were visibly swollen. She immediately saw her doctor at the oncology clinic, who arranged an appointment for her with a recognized expert in oncologic diseases, Professor Schneider. Michal drove her to the hospital entrance, firmly shook her cold, slightly wet hand, hugged her and stroked her hair encouragingly. He felt as if he were parting from her. He left the car in a car park in a nearby square and sat in the Peasant's café. He thought naïvely that they'd run a few tests on his wife and let her go home. Two hours later, she called him to say that she'd be staying in the hospital for a few days until all the necessary examinations were undergone.

When he came to pick her up three days later, he saw it wasn't good. She only interrupted the agonizing silence in the car shortly before they reached home. "They made a mammography screening, hm… they examined the top part of my belly with ultrasound, even made a scintigram of my bones. The diagnosis is clear – a carcinoma in the mammary gland… I couldn't believe it, so the professor wanted to make a biopsy, which I refused this time…" Tears welled in her eyes. "They even ultrasounded my liver… I have metastases there… increased amounts of markers in my blood…"

"Calm down. We'll get home, have some tea, and think about everything quietly," he tried to appease her. His own nerves were all on edge. When the water boiled in the kettle, he made two pots of their favorite Biluochun as usual, and then they sat in the living room and sipped in silence.

Michal couldn't stand it any longer. "What exactly did the professor tell you?"

"He said I have to have an operation. He almost mocked me, said the meditation in Jerusalem was no help… As if I didn't know…" Then she burst out, "How can it be? Not only did I meditate, I ate only one hundred percent fresh raw vegetables and fruit, combined them with raw juices, herbal teas… He rebuked me for giving in to influences of some eastern medicine, for relying on some holistic medicine and… for not admitting that it is not helping. He said he wanted nothing but that I regained my health." She sipped on her tea nervously and then she flared up. "But I've gone to them before and they didn't restore my health. So, their medicine's probably nothing special too. Back then, as I was lying there, I came to the same conclusion. I don't remember anyone leaving that place healthy.

They were just a piece of intestine, lung or rectum lighter, after they had them cut off. That's all they can do. Cut things, irradiate people, poison them with chemicals! The professor even mentioned his concern that I don't have a source of necessary proteins, because they're only in meat, and rebuked me for not eating any… What doctor is that, advising people with cancer to eat meat?! To him, I'm not a human being with a soul but just a machine with replaceable parts, like a car. What a professor! He's a mechanic, not a physician! All they can do is cut things off, but not heal people!" She burst into tears. "I've done all I could. I've done a forty-two-day fast, which wasn't easy… I abandoned all cooked food; I've done massages and meditations… Why did it come back?"

Michal stroked her hair gently. "I guess… I guess you had too little faith… I'm sorry, I never trusted these things much myself, but since our visit to Israel I think faith is the main thing you need. I feel as if your faith was somehow mechanical, you know, our way, formal only, superficial, I don't know the right words for this. Despite all this, it seems to me that what's happening with you has a deep meaning. I think God wants you stronger. You know, I'm sorry, I don't have the right to say this, I am not the one being tested, maybe because God doesn't have any intentions with me. But he's pulling you as close to his mirror as he can. Maybe he wants you to take a good look, I mean a really good look. So far, you've only glanced into it and felt everything's okay. But the closer you are to the mirror, the better you can see yourself. I'm a little concerned that you're not totally happy with yourself inside."

"Oh please, don't lecture me now!" she flared up. She started crying a moment later. "Sorry, I'm sorry. I've said the Lord's Prayer, I've begged God for help, but somehow it seems to me as if I've been doing all that in some kind of hallway, as if I haven't reached the temple of my soul, as if something is preventing me from entering. Once, as a child, I lay in a haystack at my granny's; it smelled great; I was looking at the sky where some birds were flying up high, the sun was shining, and all I could hear was the wind and the buzzing of bees. I can still feel that wonderful feeling today; I was seized by a strange mood, hard to describe, a real euphoria, I suddenly felt I was flying. I felt incredibly good and I saw an angel then. He was very much like the one I had in a picture at home. I imagined him, crossing a bridge over a stormy river behind me, with his wings stretched, protecting me. You know the pictures, we used to have them in our nurseries as kids. 'Ever this day be at my side, to light, to guard, to rule and guide…' I was happy and healthy. Each cell of my body was feeling happy… Where has that happiness gone? Where did it disappear to?"

"I've read a book by the Indian physician Deepak Chopra. He says every cell has its memory, its organs, like a human being. A human being is just a cell in a larger entity, just like a cell is a larger whole of many small parts. A cell dies just like a human being, and when it dies, it passes its memory onto another cell that's being born. You've got to reach down to your cells. That's where your disease stems from."

"I feel the same way. I seem to be walking round the temple of my soul, its doors nearly opening any minute, but then something occurs that takes my mind away. I stop concentrating and I can't enter the door of the truth."

"I think you're doing it right, only it seems to me you're in the wrong place. I'll show you something. I've found this on the Internet." He took Marika to the computer, where he clicked away for a while until the screen showed some pictures that they spent a long while gazing at.

"What's that? Traces in the stone?" Marika asked.

"Just like it's customary to make a death mask of the face of important people when they die, it was apparently the custom in the east to make a death footprint. These are the feet of a man who died in Srinagar in the latter half of the first century. His tomb is in the basement of a shrine known as the Roza Bal. The sarcophagus is laid in the east-west direction. Only the Jews buried their dead that way."

"How did a Jewish tomb appear in Kashmir in the first century?"

"That's the question…"

"Are you saying it might be Jesus' grave?"

"All I'm saying is that his tomb is definitely not in Israel. It's nowhere else in the world either… But he's got to be buried somewhere… Take a good look at these feet."

Marika stared at the photo for a long while. "There are some odd lines on them, as if… They look like…"

"They're scars left by wounds…"

"But that's impossible… How could someone who'd been crucified get to Kashmir in the first century?" Marika's voice trembled with excitement.

"We'll go there and find out. Maybe he's the one you're looking for." He cuddled his wife more tightly and said in a firm, resolute voice. "I've called my friend Ľubo, a manager in a big travel agency. He has excellent contacts there."

"And what did he say?" she asked with interest.

"He's arranged everything. He wants us to come as soon as possible, and he's arranged an appointment for you with the best doctor who, allegedly, has miraculous abilities. A Doctor Bashrat. His son would be awaiting us in Srinagar."

"The capital of Kashmir?" Marika squealed with delight. "Do you think we'll even manage to see…"

"Ľubo said that if meditating in the Roza Bal tomb is important for your healing, he'll do everything to get us inside it," Michal smiled encouragingly. "We've been lucky. We don't even have to fly to Delhi, I've managed to get air tickets from Dubai to Srinagar. That'll make the trip at least three hours shorter."

Marika realized Michal was being serious. She was afraid of flying; she was always scared of the confined space inside the aircraft. "So you… expected the doctors not to help me?"

Michal was silent. "After our visit to Jerusalem, I really took an interest in what's inside the Roza Bal tomb. And I felt your decision to go there was clear too," he tried to steer away from her question.

"When are we flying?"

"The day after tomorrow. We'll take a bus to Vienna Airport at nine. We depart for Dubai at twelve, and from there we continue to Srinagar two hours after the arrival. We'll arrive after midnight. I think the time difference is five and a half hours." Marika said nothing. "Don't worry, we'll handle it all."

"How long will we stay?"

"Until you're okay."

"Do we have enough money?"

"We do, and if there are any problems, Ľubo's friends will help us." Marika just nodded silently. "Tomáš' silence unsettles me a little. He hasn't replied to my emails since we came back from Israel. He doesn't even answer the phone or Skype calls."

"He did seem a bit nervous," Marika observed.

"I hope he's alright," Michal pondered. "It's odd."

43 Burning at the Stake

Rav Anna bade Jesus and Lammas a friendly goodbye. The prince didn't protest very much against him leaving, in fact he even offered him horses, money, clothing and two servants. Jesus refused his offer politely – he wished to travel through the land like domestic travelers did. They would live on alms and the compassion of good people. What he did take from Rav Anna, though, was his letter to his father, King Gondophares, to give to him when they arrived in Takshashila. The young men parted dispassionately, both feeling that not only their status difference, but their manner of thinking divided them so deeply that a common understanding would not be possible between them.

Jesus and Lammas went north to Cuttack, where they spent several months; from there they continued via Rajgir and Nalanda to Banaras, the holy Hindu city on the river Ganges. There, Jesus became a pupil of Lammas' teacher, the famous healer Udraka. He found lodgings in his ashram, where the students grew their own crops, kept domestic animals, did their laundry, cooked and made their food. He started wearing their traditional garment, the dhoti – several meters of cloth which he wrapped around his legs and tied up on his belly. He wore white leather sandals and a holy dot – the tilak – at the center of his forehead. He was acquiring the Ayurveda, the Hindu art of healing. Udraka taught him to use water, earth, herbs, warmth, cold, light and dark.

"Laws of nature and laws of health are identical. He who obeys the laws of nature will retain an equilibrium and never fall ill. Everything that one needs to be healthy is in the mind, which is part of the universe. In the Ayurveda we learn how to treat health and life, this is the teaching about the proper way of life. Prevention is its foundation – we concentrate on health, not disease. That is why we speak of healing, not treating a disease. We see a person as a whole, and when we speak of the body, we mean the soul as well. A body, a spirit and a soul together constitute a human being. The soul in turn is connected with the universal world spirit, a cosmic energy. For us, no physical or chemical agent is enough to tackle a disease. Health is the harmony in a human being and his harmony with the environment. Only a holistic way of life guarantees health. Any disease is a disruption to the equilibrium, a failure to respect the cosmic rhythm. A human body is like a harp. It will play neither with strings too tight nor too relaxed.

Everything – thus our life too – is connected with the universe. Our soul is part of the universal world soul and goes through a cycle from birth to death. This cycle is called the samsara. Your karma in one life decides about your next life. We will reap the sowing of our previous lives in this one."

"Does that mean that after sowing in this life, we will reap in the next one?" Jesus asked.

"We may, and we may not. We will reap when the time comes. A lemon tree or a pomegranate will bear fruit in two years' time, while a mango tree only does in the next generation. Karma too bears fruit when the time is ripe for it."

"Can another person's karma affect yours?"

"No, it can't. A mango tree will not bear oranges. But by living well we can eliminate bad deeds from our previous lives, and conversely, bad deeds will corrupt our previous good ones. Bad deeds create the setting for future suffering. Simply said, we must understand that we ourselves are the makers of our destinies. We will reap the sowing of this life in a future one. The ultimate goal is to break the samsara and become one with the universe."

"How do I know which herb cures what?"

"We observe nature and animals. They are God's messengers, mediators of eternal wisdom. Nobody teaches an animal which herb to chew when it's sick – and yet it knows it by itself. Nature has everything a human being needs. Except one thing: faith. The moment you attain absolute trust in the Lord, you will attain absolute trust in yourself. He who gives faith is truly God-sent. Only he who comes absolutely close to the ill person's soul can heal. Because only he can give the ill person hope.

But faith can only give hope to those who are willing to abandon the well-trodden paths of human preconception. When you have total faith in the power of nature – of God – you can heal by simply breathing or applying your hands. And you can only do that when you love the ill person. Love of one's neighbor is thus a precondition for successful healing."

"Am I supposed to love an evil neighbor as well?"

Udraka thought for a moment. "I'll tell you a story. A farmer once found a lot of broken and diseased ears of corn in his field before the harvest. He then ordered the reapers to only bring the good ears to the barn. When he came to the barn after the harvest, it was empty. 'Where's my rye?' he asked. 'Sir, we did as you ordered, we burned all the crooked and broken stalks. No good ones were left for the barn.'" Udraka turned to Jesus and added, "If God only saved the perfect, how many would be saved?"

Jesus stayed with the wise Udraka in Banaras for four years. He was only twenty, but rumors about him were spreading across North India, and wherever he went, crowds of people gathered and listened to him zealously.

Jesus went to pay homage to the memory of King Chandragupta, the founder of the Maurya Empire. When he was near the city of Gorakhpur, he found himself and Lammas passing alongside a crowd of people who were shouting loudly and pointing at a place where there was a pyre made of wooden logs, on which a body shrouded in a white sheet rested. They were being accompanied by Lammas' friend, the priest Nanda.

"What's going on here?" Lammas asked, disconcerted.

"They're going to make a sati ceremony. The widow is going to burn herself along with her dead husband."

"What?" Jesus nearly exclaimed. "For what reason?"

"It's an ancient tradition. It's to keep her virtue."

"And this applies when a woman dies, too?"

Lammas didn't understand his question at first. "Do you mean does the man burn himself when he becomes a widower?" Jesus nodded. "But that's absurd. The man will remarry."

"But then burning a widow is a murder."

"It's a tradition inherited from our ancestors, and it's the widow's duty to observe it."

"What if the woman refuses to?"

"It does happen sometimes. If she tries to run away from the pyre, the overseers get her and throw her in the flames."

"What if she manages to escape?"

"That's happened too. She's driven away from her village, she loses her children and possessions, nobody gives her food or drink, and so she dies of hunger. There's no worse deed in India than violation of tradition."

"But that's pure madness. That's against God!" Jesus cried in a disturbed voice. He was trembling with anger and found it hard to control himself. The crowd of excited people went silent; it was getting dark and a young woman was approaching the funeral pyre on the riverbank.

Lammas looked at her compassionately. "Poor thing Amrita. I knew her as a child. She didn't have much of a life. Two years ago, her parents married her to a rich widower, she was fifteen. She gave him two children. She's not even eighteen…" In astonishment, Jesus looked at the young woman, who seemed to be absent-minded. She stopped by the pyre, where a small table with some food was laid. "That's thioy, sweet meat. She has to eat it before departing for nirvana, otherwise she won't get to paradise," Nanda explained.

"Silly fools. They're all fools. How can they believe in such nonsense? Do you agree with this?" he looked sternly at Lammas, who said nothing. "Do you consent to murder?!" Jesus exclaimed at the top of his voice in Pali, a language that he'd learned almost perfectly over the six years he'd spent in India by then. The people turned to him.

Lammas answered quietly, "I don't."

"Do you?" he turned to Nanda.

"It's our ancient tradition."

"It's a deplorable murder!"

"Do you – a Jew – blame us? Have we not adopted the fire sacrifice from you? Was it not your Jewish God who compelled Abraham to bring his son Isaac to the pyre? Doesn't your Torah speak about Abraham coming to the sacrifice site with his son, tying him up and lying him atop the ready wood?"

"Yes, but then God ordered him not to kill the boy; it was just a test of his faith! So, you too then act as Abraham did," Jesus cried at those present.

A priest, or a local shaman, standing with a blazing torch by the pyre ready to start the fire, listened to Jesus and then shouted at him hatefully, "This is not a test of faith, it's a tradition that can't be violated. It's her own independent decision. You have no right to disrupt our holy ceremony, our traditions – all the more because you're a foreigner."

"You call a murder a holy ceremony? You ought to know that one doesn't become wise by sticking to traditions. What smothers you most and hampers your development is traditions." He noticed that all the women, as well as some of the men, cast their eyes down in shame.

"It's the happiest moment in her life. She'll be in nirvana in a while. If your faint heart cannot handle looking at God's fire, leave this place!" Nanda advised him.

Jesus walked over to the woman, caught her by the hand and asked her, "Is this your own decision?" With her eyes blazing from fever or perhaps an unknown drug, the woman nodded her head unconvincingly, meekly. "Amrita," he addressed her by name. The woman became attentive and stared him in the eyes. At that moment a strange chill ran down his spine. His palms began sweating, he couldn't tear himself from her piercing green eyes, which were gazing at him without a word as if shining the light of the evening star descending from the sky. Those eyes, those eyes... he thought about where he'd seen them. Yes, they were those eyes. The eyes of Mariam, the beautiful Berber princess. No, this woman must not die, even if it cost him his own life.

"Amrita, your name means immortal. I'm asking you again whether this is your own decision." The woman made no reply. The priest grabbed her and tore her out of Jesus' hands. He pushed him roughly. She started walking slowly around the pyre. Accompanied by the priest, she circled it three times in one direction, then she returned to the table with the sweet meat and ate it absent-mindedly. After she swallowed a few pieces, she set out in the other direction. On her last round, she failed to notice an obstacle and hit the table.

The meat fell on the ground. Hungry dogs plunged at it. The woman and the priest stopped by an improvised ladder, which she started climbing, steadied by the priest, to the top of the pyre. She stretched out her arms, which, by some coincidence, pointed exactly toward the horizon, behind which the sun was setting. The sky was gray with the mist rising from the heated ground. The woman began dancing the traditional preterminal dance to a monotonous rhythm played by pipes and drums. She stepped over the white cotton sheet on which her dead husband was lying.

Jesus was incapable of a single sound; he just watched the horrid spectacle with a lump in his throat. The woman stopped dancing and lay down slowly in her designated place next to the dead man. Her eyes met with Jesus' stare for a moment. He saw no devotion in them, and certainly no joy. What he saw was deadly fear and a request. The woman lay down and put one hand underneath her neck and the other on it. At that moment, two Shudras came to the pyre and started covering both the woman and her dead husband with dry palm leaves. When the bodies could no longer be seen, one of them poured molten ghee butter over them for the fire to catch more easily. The other Shudra put two bamboo poles over the pyre to prevent wind from blowing the pile aside. The drums went silent and the pipes made their last notes. Nature too seemed to become aware of the horror about to take place and went silent. A wailing howl of a dog, or maybe a wolf, was heard in the distance. The priest raised his torch and walked toward the pyre.

At that moment, Jesus lost control and ran toward him. Lammas tried to hold him back but failed. Jesus yanked the torch out of his hand. The shaman didn't manage a word. "Let me, I'll do it." Shocked, those present were looking at the young foreigner slowly, solemnly walking up the ladder to the pyre. He stopped at its highest point. It occurred to him that it was an almost perfect speaker's stand. He raised the torch high above his head. The sky seemed to lighten. Fascinated, the people were looking at the foreigner, whose name they knew from tales told by many who had met him before. *They said he could work miracles.*

"Listen, ben Joseph, if you perform a miracle, the woman will be released," a Brahmin who had walked forward cried at him. He was the high priest, and people regarded his words as God's words.

Jesus looked at him angrily. "It will be a miracle if you and those like you ever stop ruining other people's lives!" Then he knelt down, raised his eyes to the sky and exclaimed in a loud voice, "Brahma, our common father, God of law and justice. This woman has done nothing wrong, only she should die because the priests have made up a pointless ritual to be able to take her children and possessions! Her death will be of no help to Him, and her children will lose their mother. Father, they say it's an ancient custom in this land in which women bring sacrifice for their husbands to maintain the family virtue. But you know very well that killing is a violation of your law and not even priests are allowed to violate your law!"

"I told you to perform a miracle, not outrage people," the Brahmin threatened him from below.

But Jesus appeared not to hear him. "Father, I know you're watching this terrible spectacle. I know we have no right to meddle with your decisions, but this can't be your intention. Neither is it the intention of this woman. I'm begging you, Brahma, her life is in your hands, and the lives of all the future widows of this country. If this is to be your intention, please make a sign for us. If not..."

At that point, one of the Shudras climbed the pyre on the Brahmin's order and knocked Jesus down brutally. The shaman yanked the torch out of his hand and passed it to the Brahmin. Assisted by several other men, the Shudras held Jesus' hands from behind. He wanted to wriggle loose, but they beat him cruelly with a bamboo stick. Lammas tried to help him, but he too was beaten. They were both kneeling not far from the funeral pyre, panting and with bloodied faces. The Brahmin gestured at the shaman, who approached the pyre with a cynical smile and set fire to the bottom leaves. The fire was spreading rapidly, but suddenly Jesus felt something trickling down his cheek. He wanted to wipe the tear, but he couldn't. More and more followed. After a while, he realized they weren't teardrops but raindrops. Others could feel it now too. In the dramatic moments, nobody had noticed how the sky had become overcast with heavy clouds. It started raining. An intense downpour came from the sky a moment later. It was now late fall, long past the monsoon rain season.

"The monsoon's back. It's never happened at this time of year before. We're in the middle of the dry season," people whispered in fear. The fire struggled with the life-giving water for a while longer, but hard as it tried, it went out finally.

"Do as you promised, set her free now," Lammas walked over to the Brahmin.

"But that was no miracle! The rainy season just hasn't ended yet," Nanda butted in. But the Brahmin shouted him down.

"Shut up! Our guest is right. The place of encounter between God and man is in everyone's heart. But if we are to hear God, we must be quiet. And we... we were way too loud today. We couldn't hear God's voice. Only he listened to it quietly. He was the first of us to hear it."

The Brahmin turned to Jesus, came up to him and embraced him. "You convinced Brahma."

The Shudras wanted to climb the pyre, but Lammas halted them. "It was him who saved her. It was his faith that caused the miracle." He stepped aside. People made an aisle, down which Jesus walked to the ladder and ascended it slowly. He tossed off the leaves and helped the woman stand up. She knelt and wanted to kiss his feet. But his firm hands lifted her and hugged her tightly. Her body was hot and trembling – nobody knew whether it was because of the cold, the downpour or what she had just been through. He didn't know how, but suddenly he heard his own voice ringing out, people listening to it. It was indeed his voice, but it seemed to come from a distance. Yet he could hear it distinctly and the people were nodding in silent agreement.

"Brothers and sisters! You were going to judge without any right to judge. Only the one who gives life may decide about life and death. The one who gave us law. The only law and the most just law, the law of cause and effect. A human being is not a speckle of dust that flutters through this earthly life without reason only to get lost afterwards. A human being is part of a larger whole, and its life only makes sense together with others. We enter and leave this world in order to develop the divine inside us. Today you nearly killed an innocent human being. Maybe today, when this murder was prevented, the cycle of destruction in your hearts has been broken. You all feel the relief in you. You are happy along with Amrita and her children. This morning, Brahma found a great injustice in your hearts, but tonight he's going to sleep calmly and with gratitude toward you, because you've withstood the test that he put up before you."

"I'm not sure if we've withstood the test, if our ancestors will forgive us," the Brahmin objected with a feeling of shame. "Since times immemorial, we've practiced the ritual of burning widows, and today's the first time we didn't carry it through. I fear God may punish us for that."

"Is saving a life a good deed or a bad one?" Jesus asked "Today you saved a young mother's life. How could God punish you for that?! Such thinking is blasphemy." He could see, however, that their faces were pensive and their eyes filled with fear. "There's a time for everything. A time to be born and a time to die, a time to sow and a time to reap, a time to cry and a time to laugh, a time to love and a time to hate. Today, you've left the time of evil for the time of good. You've experienced the moment of turning hearts, the most precious moment in every human being's life. From today on, do not burn any more widows, because God has let you know he doesn't wish so."

"And what about the burnings we've made so far? Will we be punished for them?" the Brahmin asked.

"No, because there's a time for everything – and now is the time of your realization of the pointlessness of burning widows. Had God wanted to, he'd have done it before, but he knows why he's stopped you just here and now. Spread his will wherever you go, because it's your task from now on. If you continue looking at burning widows silently, God will no longer forgive you. Be vigilant, because He will constantly watch every step you take – whether you wish it or not – just as your hearts beat constantly without any credit on your part."

It was dark now and Jesus and the woman were barely visible. Someone handed him the torch, which had lain in the mud. Wet and dirty, he took it in his hands. As soon as he lifted it above his head, the sky shone forth with bright moonlight. The crowd standing around the pyre only just realized that it had stopped raining. The sky cleared and glowed with an evening twilight just as it had done for ages before and would do for ages more until a new beginning.

The people were elated, only the shaman and a few priests were leaving with their teeth clenched in anger. "We must stop him, else he'll ruin everything we've been instilling in the people's heads for ages," the shaman hissed, and the others nodded gravely.

"We'll call him to the temple and tell him off," Nanda suggested.

When the temple messenger arrived in Jesus' abode with gifts and a request to present himself before the Priests' Council on the next day at noon, he told him, "Tell them the light is strong and shines for everyone. Those who search for the light shall come to it. Who wishes to hear my message shall come to me."

"But rabbi, sir, it's the priests summoning you. Nobody has ever dared to turn down their invitation," the messenger objected.

"If their varna pride hinders them in coming here, they aren't worthy of the light. We're all equal before God."

"But sir, they're priests…"

"Are you afraid of them?" Jesus looked at him sternly. The man nodded. "When one begins to be afraid of his creator and no longer sees his father as his friend, then he appoints men in vestments and calls them priests. He appoints them in the hope that they will forgive him in the name of the Father. But that's erroneous. Go therefore and tell him what I've told you. And take their gifts back."

The messenger bowed and was slowly leaving. He stopped in the doorway. "Sir, you don't know them. You've insulted them, and they won't forgive you for that."

44 Lotus Christ

"All right then, let's get to the point," Koggler said, uneager. He wanted to ask the archbishop many more unpleasant questions, but he realized he would make Falcone and Farabutto at least uneasy, if not enraged, and he didn't want to cause trouble for his colleague Hausser. It wasn't customary for the Congregation for the Doctrine of the Faith to send its representatives to meetings on cases handled by the intelligence service, but the heirs of the Holy Inquisition certainly suspected that there might be undesirable debates concerning the foundations of the Christian profession of faith in this case, so the prefect of the Congregation, Cardinal Levado, nominated the experienced Archbishop Falcone. He had the reputation of an ultraorthodox Church official, and his falconine last name alone made many a little uneasy. Since the Congregation was the authoritative institution of the Roman Catholic Church, the archbishop's decisive status in this case was clear to everyone. Hausser signaled Koggler with his eyes not to provoke the Congregation people anymore, but it was clear to him anyway that he'd have difficulty explaining why he'd invited the liberal American colonel. However, Hausser relied heavily on Koggler's abilities, which he had put to the test in the Code 9 case.

Koggler winked at Hausser and continued. "About two years ago, we intercepted information about the effort of a group composed of people from all around the world aiming at bringing the world's religions closer together, Christianity and Buddhism in particular. We have been monitoring these people for some time. We have no evidence, but we think a Michal Kráľ from Slovakia is one of the key figures in this operation. It came as a surprise to us; we didn't know there were people who could jeopardize the stability of our system in this country, of which we'd hardly heard before. Details are in the file, which we've called Code 9. We've denoted our current operation as Code 1."

"All we have had with these Slovaks is annoyance. Exactly a year ago, the Holy Father appointed a man called Bezák as the Archbishop of Trnava, and you know how many tumbles he's managed in a year. He's found some financial irregularities, he wanted to open up the archbishopric garden for the public, he's opened a restaurant for young people right inside the archbishopric building, he wears blue jeans and a pullover, he works out in a gym, and the worst thing is that the young love him. What we need is that church dignitaries are respected and esteemed, but not loved. They are supposed to love the ideal, not a living man. Slovak bishops have complained about him, we'll have to handle it," he meditated. "I apologize," he returned to the topic. "Why is this operation denoted Code 1?"

"While the Code 9 case consisted in a unification of religions based on the assembly of a code composed of nine religious symbols, this case deals with a single symbol, a symbol somehow expressing Unity, allegedly impersonated by Jesus Christ. That's the information from Dvoran, our man in Jerusalem whom Kráľ trusts."

"Thank you," the archbishop muttered contentedly.

Koggler smiled at him, and the atmosphere lit up a little. "Since, as pointed out by lieutenant colonel Hausser – that is, brother Max, I beg your pardon – details are in the dossiers, let me just recap the main points. As part of the previous counter-operation, prepared by the secret organization Global Power, we and our allied services unfortunately had to reach for some extreme measures. One of them was the physical destruction of our agent who had joined Kráľ; the other one was the detonation of Christ's alleged grave in the ghost city of Fatehpur Sikri in India. We thought we'd finally achieved some order with the destruction of the shrine, but we were wrong."

"How could you think you'd have order when you say in your dossier that you expected waves of opposition against al-Qaeda, on whom you put the blame for the whole operation?" Farabutto asked.

"Yes, I must say we can be proud of our media work in this case. Our assumption that both Muslim and Christian wrath would turn against al-Qaeda worked out perfectly. But we took great care to keep the tomb of the Muslim saint Salim Chishti intact."

"Who was Salim Chishti?" Toti asked.

"My dear colleague, it's all in the information dossier, your only excuse is that you've been on holiday. Chishti was the most important Sufi saint of the 16th century, highly esteemed by then King Akbar, in whose honor he had the new capital of the Mughal Empire built – Fatehpur Sikri. Sufi saints are considered to be God's friends and world overseers who can perform miracles. At first, the detonation caused panic, but when it turned out that Chishti's tomb was intact, the wrath of the Muslims focused on al-Qaeda. Christians hadn't paid the place much attention, because the claim that Fatehpur Sikri is Jesus' last resting place was more or less only a legend, according to which Jesus' body had been transported there from Srinagar by King Akbar, a very tolerant ruler. Incidentally, he strove for a unification of religions; one of his wives, Mariam Zamani Begum, was an Armenian Christian. But she was also a highly influential woman: she asked the king to have Christ's remains transferred to the congregation mosque in the capital. The reason she gave was her concern over the potential destruction of the Srinagar grave as a consequence of constant disputes between Hindus and Muslims."

"Is this the place with the two extant quotes from Christ on that famous gate?" Felix asked.

"It is. The first one is: Jesus said, 'The world is a bridge, cross it but do not stop on it.' The other one says, 'The world is a splendid house, take it as a warning but do not build on it.'"

"Why would the remains of the most important Christian be transferred to the Mughal capital?" Farabutto didn't understand.

"I beg your pardon, but Christ was not a Christian," Koggler objected.

"What was he then? Who founded Christianity?" The secretary jumped up.

"Begging your pardon, Saint Paul might be seriously offended by that. Christ is one of the main prophets in Islam and Muslims hold him in great reverence. His grave in Fatehpur Sikri would therefore be nothing unusual. But Akbar brought nothing to Fatehpur Sikri, and nobody was buried in the tomb that we blew up."

"Why then did you blow up this alleged tomb in Fatehpur Sikri if you knew Jesus wasn't in it?" Kruger asked.

"It was an intelligence game. The media had long written about Fatehpur Sikri being one of Jesus' possible final resting places. They wrote even more about Jesus' grave blowing up. Since then the numbers of visitors to that uncanny place has dropped sharply. Simply put, those who believed Jesus was buried there stopped going there."

"So why don't you blow up this Roza Bal as well?"

"What for? We're happy with the constant tension in Kashmir and Srinagar itself, a latent war in which Muslims and Hindus kill each other

–while we pretend that we are trying to prevent them from continuing. Since 1947, when Kashmir became part of India, not Pakistan, although it's almost entirely a Muslim territory, we've organized international congresses and meetings of key statesmen aiming at settling the conflict."

There was a long silence, interrupted by Falcone. "Well, we've been doing nothing but talk for almost an hour; you should finally inform us about how you're going to stop these fools' mad operation!"

"You are right, sir, although the information that has been given here is interesting from the factual and historical point of view, it will not help our operation very much." Hausser gave Koggler a reproachful look. He noticed the archbishop's thankful look. "Gentlemen, we're all in the same boat. We are living in a free society, which is why difference of opinion on secondary issues is quite natural. However, all of us in this room will quite certainly agree that the risk associated with a potential disclosure of the facts mentioned here is too great for the Holy See and also for us, its members. Let me therefore get to the next point of our debate today." He opened his leather briefcase and pulled out a paper with a *Top Secret* stamp. He paused for a while to lend more emphasis to his next words. "Measures to secure the interests of the Holy See in the Code 1 case. I command the operation.

Brother Carlo is in charge of intelligence matters, brother Felix of the operative ones." Toti and the trainee Kruger smiled contentedly. "Kashmir's police consist of several departments: public order, traffic, plain clothes, firefighters, jail wardens, railway, criminal, technical, and the most important one, which receives the least attention: the secret section. Given the irascible situation in the region, almost a borderland war, which grows into a larger conflict from time to time, this section is of a key importance. Its role is to monitor all the activities struggling to annex the federal state of Jammu and Kashmir to Pakistan, or efforts for the declaration of an independent state. I don't need to emphasize that since the partition of India in 1947, Kashmir has been one of the most dangerous areas in the world."

"Why?" Farabutto asked naïvely.

Hausser realized that the secretary hadn't read his dossier and that he'd have to explain the whole situation to him patiently. "Because in spite of the fact that Kashmir was majority Muslim, the then Indian maharaja decided to make it part of India in 1947. Since then we've had four direct war conflicts in the region, and the latent dispute is almost incessant. The demarcation line of Kashmir is crossed by militant Muslim guerillas, supported by Afghan mercenaries and, of course, the Pakistani government. In 1999 there was a risk of global conflict due to the tension, since both India and Pakistan are nuclear powers. China is on the side of Pakistan, Russians support India. America is on both sides, as usual. To this day, the conflict has claimed over seventy thousand victims. It is no rarity that Mujahideen sent from Pakistan abduct foreigners and then demand high ransoms or freedom for their prisoners in exchange. On the other hand, the Indian armed forces aren't idle. More than one half of the country's army of one and a half million is present in Kashmir. The central government in Delhi gives them a free hand. Kashmir is almost ruled by martial law."

"I wouldn't go to Srinagar if I was in Král's place," Falcone observed.

"My word," Hausser remarked. "As they are going, they must have a real serious reason!" Hausser sipped on some water. "Gentlemen, there's a supreme police commander in each of the federal states of India – a general director, who reports to both the state government and the federal ministry of the interior in Delhi. The secret service department of the police is in charge of security of special persons and structures. One such special structure is the Roza Bal tomb in Srinagar. Although we have a secret agreement about the tomb with the government of Kashmir, we cannot rely on it very much. Despite their commitment not to allow anyone inside, there have been numerous archeological surveys in it, and they've even let foreign nationals enter it. They have then produced heaps of papers on how Jesus is buried in the tomb and similar nonsense. Fortunately, the power of the Vatican media and money is sufficient for refuting such claims successfully. However, what we rely more on is the personal engagement of key people. One such person is the general director of Kashmiri Police, Surinder Kaur. Along with his wife, he's visited Europe several times at our invitation, he's our friend and I think he's reliable, even though you never know with an Indian policeman. The truth is, however, that no foreigner's been to the tomb since he became the general director. At least there's no information to the contrary."

"Why then are we so concerned about this Král' and his wife?" Felix asked.

Hausser spent a moment thinking. "Because those who have entered the tomb this far have only done so for scientific reasons. But this is the first time people are going there because it's apparently a life issue for them.

How would I put this… They're convinced that Christ is really buried there and when Mrs. Kráľová meditates by his tomb, it'll save her life…"

"Oh my God, what nonsense…" Farabutto smiled.

"That's why she's been to Jerusalem, but it didn't help much… After all, she might have known Christ was not buried there," Felix remarked.

Farabutto burst into laughter. "Ha, ha, ha… That's their version. But we know they're going for quite another reason!"

"People have gone to Lourdes or Medjugorie with similar desires," Koggler turned to Farabutto. "If they got inside the tomb and if Mrs. Kráľová was instantly cured, what does that prove? Do you know how many have been cured in Lourdes? And in Medjugorie?"

"Only these ones are allegedly informed that the tomb contains evidence of Christ being buried there."

"Stop this nonsense!" Falcone exploded. "It's not only blasphemy, it's pure foolishness!" He anxiously grabbed a glass of water and drank thirstily.

Hausser slowly took a sheet of paper from the binder and read out, "The rabbi says: According to legend Roza Bal is said to contain a statue of UNUM, symbolizing the original unity of humankind. It's meant to be Buddha sitting in the lotus position, but he looks more like Jesus. With his right-hand index and middle fingers, he is pointing upward symbolically, and with his ring and little fingers he is pointing downward, meaning both east and west. His left-hand gesture symbolizes cognition. He is sitting on a double lotus flower composed of seventeen flowers in the bottom row and sixteen in the top row…"

"Stop this bullshit!" Farabutto hissed and looked at the frowning archbishop imploringly. "What are you reading anyway?"

"A transcript of part of a message from Kráľ."

"From whom?" Farabutto goggled at Hausser.

"Dvoran has managed to replace his original glasses with ones made operatively in our laboratories, with all the latest microtechnologies installed. So, we can monitor every word he says. As long as he's wearing the glasses, of course." Hausser smiled and finished reading, "… and the right-hand side of Christ's, that is the Buddha's, chest shows a scar mark. Thomas the Apostle is said to have made the statue and put it in Christ's grave."

A silence settled in the room, interrupted by the archbishop a while later. He wiped some sweat off his forehead with a snow-white handkerchief.

"Where did he get this Christ… this Buddha thing from?" He tried to keep calm but was evidently failing.

45 Attempted Murder

Jesus was becoming a favorite of the oppressed and humiliated. Shudras loved him and even some Vaishyas followed him, but the Kshatriyas, priests and Brahmins hated him. Seeing the crowds attending his gatherings, priests were seized with panic. Their hearts trembled with fear and hatred whenever they heard his name. Jesus preached about brotherhood in life, demanded equal rights for everyone, declared that sacrificial rituals and priests were useless and hindered people from communicating with God.

"In my country, too, priests try to elevate themselves to a divine level and impose their rules on people that they hypocritically call divine," he enthused in a discussion with Barata, a young monk and a friend of Lammas', as they were debating for the umpteenth time in the small refectory of a Banaras temple consecrated to the Buddha. However, before they entered the temple and started a debate, a joint meditation or any prayer ritual, the youngest of the monks washed the other brethren's feet in a fired clay vessel.

"It's an ancient ritual symbolizing humility and respect to every one of God's creature," Barata explained. With their feet washed, they entered the temple and sat down on a camel-hair rug to continue one of their endless disputations.

"Nobody has the right to order others how to interpret God's words. Everyone has the right and duty to search for their meaning, but nobody has the right to force his own truth on others as the only truth. In my country, judges put the Book on the altar and force people to swear on it. But an oath to an altar is nothing. The Law which commands people not to lie is a gift. So only those who can be expected to tell lies need the oath. But I say: don't prevaricate, let your speech be a simple yes or a no."

"Brother," Barata addressed Jesus warmly, "we're beginning to be afraid for you."

"Who?"

"All the decent people. During your years in India, you've shaken the Brahmin system to its foundations; the walls of our caste system are crumbling under the force of your words; you've been ripping masks off idols, teaching that human and animal sacrifices are against God, and condemning altar construction. Priests are trembling with fear, and when you approach their temples, they say you've disappointed and betrayed them. There are rumors that your days are numbered."

"That's nonsense, I say nothing that would go against God," Jesus objected.

"Of course not! God favors your talk, but the priests don't. You should be more careful."

"You're panicking pointlessly. Instead, tell me, what does the Buddha say to the massive injustice caused by your caste system?" he asked, a little irritated. "None of the Brahmins will ever get in God's kingdom unless your country gets rid of the caste plague."

Ashamed, Barata sat in silence. "I'm not aware of the Buddha having dealt with the caste problem, but you're right. The castes are the plague of India, but it's so deeply rooted in tradition that I don't know if we can break free of them. And aren't your priests indeed the most privileged stratum of society just like our Brahmins?"

"They are. Just as your priests use God as a pretext, so do ours. They claim they were given their rights and mission by Moses, who in turn received them from God on Mount Sinai. Then he passed them on to the priests and, through them, to all the people," Jesus replied in deep thought. "They're the perfect rules for living, only the priests require everyone except themselves to adhere to them…"

"How did God give Moses the rules?"

"On two tablets of stone, they say."

"Wow, no one else has managed that, that makes you Jews truly unique. Getting a material gift directly from God… congratulations," Barata laughed. "Who was this Moses anyway?"

"A wise man who wished to help people escape from ignorance. He gave them the word of God, but instead of disseminating it, they proudly locked it in their Torah, and since Moses was a Jew, they declared that God has chosen them among all the peoples. He was the prophet who led my ancestors out of captivity in Egypt. For forty years they wandered the desert under his leadership until they came to the Promised Land."

"Forty years? Does Israel have such a huge desert?"

"That's one thing I don't understand clearly myself," Jesus pondered. "It would make sense that they would have wanted to return home as soon as possible. Compared to your desert here, ours is quite small; you can cross it in a few weeks."

"Perhaps they liked plodding around in circles. Or Moses had a poor sense of direction, maybe he didn't know the night sky," Barata smiled.

Jesus said nothing for a long while. Then he gave Barata a long look filled with trust. "Maybe the reason I'm here is that I could bring back home a better, more beautiful, more human doctrine with the help of people like yourself and our brother Lammas."

Barata frowned. "What's taking our brother so long? He just went to the market to get some flatbreads and fruit." Just then, the door opened and Lammas staggered in. He was bloodied, his clothes torn, bruises and swellings were visible on both his face and body, an ankle was sprained. The pain was vexing him, and he found it hard to breathe. "Water... please..."

"What happened?" Jesus and Barata hurried over to him.

"They swooped on me in the market. They wanted to know where you were," he gasped. "They kicked me, beat me with sticks, and even an iron bar."

"Who?"

"Priests and soldiers. Fortunately, one of them, my old friend, helped me hide and revealed to me that they're planning to kill you tonight."

"But you didn't tell them where I was," Jesus objected.

"They've got spies everywhere, and I'm afraid they followed me. You must leave this place as soon as possible. Right now would be best."

"But you can't go anywhere like this," Jesus said as he was bandaging his wounded leg. "That's alright, I'm not going anywhere. Brother Barata will accompany you."

"Where should we go?" Jesus asked.

"Barata knows," Lammas looked at the monk with trust.

"We'll go to the mountains. To the Himalayan foothills, to see our brethren. To the land of the Shakyas."

"The city of the awakened Gautama?"

"Yes, Lumbini, the Buddha's birthplace."

"But only with Lammas," Jesus said resolutely. At that very moment, the stomping of military boots and clangor of sabers and chains was heard from the wooden steps outside.

"Go, run. It's night; you'll be out of the city gates by morning."

"We're not leaving without you."

"Brother Lammas, I'll carry you on my shoulders. They'll kill you if you stay…" Barata didn't have the time to finish, as the door flew open and enraged soldiers, priests and monks swooped on the three shocked men. Barata pushed Jesus aside toward an open cedar wardrobe. In the fraction of a second before he slammed shut the heavy metal door, they saw one of the soldiers pierce the sitting Lammas with a sword. Blood spurted out of his mouth and he slowly sank to the floor.

"We can't leave him here!" Jesus called.

"We can't help him now. This way," Barata dragged Jesus to a staircase that ran into a cellar. "There's a secret passage from our temple to the river. There's a boat ready there. We'll be there in a minute. The Ganges is huge, full of boats, we won't be noticed. We'll be in Adampur by morning, and from there we'll set out north to the Himalayas."

As he boarded the boat, he stood for a long while and looked back at the receding temple in the oldest city in the world. Jesus stared at the distant lights of the city in which he'd spent three beautiful years. It occurred to him that he'd acted like a coward. I'll never flee from anyone like this again, he said to himself.

46   The Devil

The monotonous hum of the airplane put most of the passengers on the Air India Boeing 737 to sleep. It was dark outside the windows; the departure from Dubai was delayed for three hours due to technical reasons. There were whispered rumors among the passengers that the security situation at Srinagar airport was the real reason. Unknown terrorists had allegedly threatened hijacking one of the aircrafts ready for departure. Marika and Michal were among those few not asleep. They were thinking about the journey they had set out on. They were sorry about not being able to contact Tomáš before the trip; he had broken off all communication inexplicably. Marika was not leaving home in the best condition, but she seemed to be regaining energy as she was drawing closer to Kashmir. She had nothing to lose. She would be saved, or her worst expectations would come true; Tomáš had already put it in such stark terms. Since the doctor informed her that her cancer had returned, she was getting ready to die. She was surprised at the relief she felt since she began imposing on herself a humbleness before the great overseer of our fates. She reconciled herself to the fact she might not return from Kashmir: that she may die there, but she begged God to restore her strength so that she could remain in this world for as long as possible. She wanted so badly to live to see a grandchild. She glanced at Michal and realized that, despite all the crises that they had been through, he was the man of her life and she shouldn't leave him prematurely. As if sensing her thoughts, Michal put his book down on his lap, smiled at her and gripped her hand firmly.

"What are you reading this intensely?"

He pushed his glasses back up the ridge of his nose. "I don't know what's with these glasses. They've been slipping for a while now, as if they were heavier or something... I'm reading an interesting book about Christ in Kashmir written by an American, a woman by the name of Olsson. It says unbelievable things. Jews and Indians apparently have more in common than we think. The six-pointed star, for example, known to the whole world as the Star of David and a symbol of Jews, in fact originates from India. There it's called the Satkona, the Star of Goloka, and represents the heavenly abode of the god Krishna. The symbol was used in the ancient Vedas four thousand years ago, before Jewish legends even mentioned Moses. It's the central symbol of Indian spirituality. Many Indian students wear a six-pointed star around their neck during exams, as it's said to bring luck. The typological similarity of written Hebrew and Indian languages is interesting at first sight. Jewish rabbis today wear garments almost identical to those worn by Indian priests in the past: a white linen vestment over which they cast a seamless tunic with a belt with knotted tassels."

"Please stop saying that. I'm not feeling my best, and when you put such surreal stuff in my head, I'm beginning to feel like we're going on an expedition to reveal the greatest secret of humankind."

"I feel the same," Michal thought.

The stewardess brought them the cold water they'd ordered some time before but had completely forgotten about. Michal hesitated whether to reveal more of such unbelievable information to her, eventually he said, "I bought myself tarot cards while you were in hospital. I don't even know why. Maybe I've become superstitious, maybe I wanted to know how all this will end, or perhaps I was trying to find some invigoration. You know, this is all becoming a bit too much even for me..."

"And did you find what you were looking for?"

"I think I did. I pulled this one out. A fifteen."

Marika screamed and almost threw the card away. "The devil?!"

Michal nodded. "Take a good look at it."

Her face a frown, Marika gave the strange card a fixed look. "It shows a devil being devoured by flames, holding chains in his outstretched hands. A cage is fastened to the chains, in which there's a crouching naked person, as if afraid of something."

"The devil has an upside-down pentagram on his forehead, and there's another pentagram in the fire," Michal continued describing the card.

"Besides, there are upside-down pentagrams at the bottom of the cage holding the naked person... it's kind of rolled up in a knot, it's hard to tell whether it's a man or a woman."

"The five points of this star are explained as the five senses, or the four elements to which the spirit is added as the fifth one. But an upside-down pentagram symbolizes the victory of the basest instincts, with the top point, representing the spirit, turned down. The basic meaning of the card is primitive, uncultured inner energy. Hidden desires and aggression. Dependency. Obsession. Anger. Consequences of a suppressed desire that devours one internally. The person in the cage is crouching in fear and powerlessness, they're controlled by their own desires and hidden aggressions."

Marika gave him a questioning look. "Do you think it's referring to me?"

Michal continued quietly, "Take a closer look at the image. It's interesting that the cage is open. The person, gripped by fear, can't see it though, because they're covering their face."

Marika scrutinized the card. "Notice how oddly the devil is holding the chains in his hands. They're actually just resting on his palms loosely; he's not holding them tightly... And here, look... a correct pentagram is outlined in the background, with its spirit point turned upwards, the way it should be... As if the person had given up their life and put the reins in the devil's hands," Michal smiled.

"Are you suggesting I shouldn't rely on doctors and instead take my destiny in my own hands?"

Michal said nothing; Marika was studying the card carefully, and then she started commenting on it as if for herself only. "The flames are a symbol of eternal energy, which may be either good or evil. Fire is one of the four fundamental elements, and there would be no life without the light and warmth that it gives."

Michal observed her with a feeling of satisfaction. "But if there's too much of it, it burns and destroys. Too much desire burns one. The devil is a disruption of the equilibrium, the golden middle way. If something's too hot, it burns; if it's too cold, it freezes. The cage in which the fearful person is held symbolizes our concerns, bad habits, dependencies, dogmas, that we're afraid to abandon. We're afraid to step out of the cage, although the door is open. But we don't know that because we cover up our face. It's the effect of the hen that lived in a cage all her life and was afraid to go out when they opened the door."

"Right, the devil can burn both your courage and your fear. Like God, the devil is neutral. Everybody condemns him, loathes him, fears him, and yet judges him unfairly. He's an inseparable part of good, without which we couldn't recognize evil. Only thanks to his wrath do people know what's good, thanks to his ugliness do we know what's beauty, and thanks to his hatred do we know what's love…"

Marika caught Michal by the hand and went on, "He's the sunset that conditions and constitutes the sunrise; he's the exhalation that precedes every inhalation; he's the breakup without which there's no reunion; he's the disease, without which we wouldn't know what health is; he's the death without which there's no birth; he's both the west and the east, the shade, which can only be made by one who is lit; it's always the same light, the same devil, the same God."

"Ladies and gentlemen, please fasten your seatbelts, in fifteen minutes we'll be landing at the airport of the capital of India's federal state of Jammu and Kashmir, the city of Srinagar. It is Friday, May 7, 2010. The local time in Srinagar is five twenty in the morning, the air temperature…"

Marika and Michal clasped each other's hands firmly. They weren't aware that exactly one week earlier some Indian army soldiers had killed three Pakistani soldiers who'd crossed the Line of Control in the Machil sector of the Kupwara district. The killing of the Pakistani soldiers had provoked riotous protests among the majority Muslim population in Kashmir. There'd been shootings in the capital Srinagar. They were also unaware that the secret military section of the Kashmiri resistance movement was preparing for a hard retaliation that would start very soon. It would be aimed at the Indian government administration buildings in Srinagar. Based on information from its military intelligence, the Indian army in Srinagar was preparing for heavy fighting.

47   To Live Love

After almost a month's journey, they reached Lumbini, the birthplace of Siddhartha Gautama the Buddha and the holiest place for Buddhists. Almost ecstatically, Jesus and Barata were strolling down the lawn of the sacred grove in which the Buddha had played as a boy.

"That's King Ashoka's pillar, built in honor of his visit," Barata explained. "The Buddha lived here until his twenty-ninth year, then he left the royal palace and headed for the mountains in the north of India to seek a way to escape the cycle of suffering. He practiced asceticism at first, but he nearly starved himself to death. Four years later, on his birthday, he attained enlightenment after deep meditation and realized happiness consisted not in satisfying one's own needs but in satisfying other people's needs: in giving, not taking."

They sat down under the tree where the Buddha too had sat. Jesus realized he was nearly the same age as the Buddha when he had left home.

"As a keepsake of your arrival here I'd like to give you a pouch with a lump of earth from Lumbini. If you don't mind, I'll also put a note in it with the date, so that you will always remember the day you came to the Buddha's birthplace. It's associated with a great secret."

"What secret?"

"You'll know before long," Barata smiled. "Do you want to hear the Buddha's story?"

"I heard it from the Buddhist monks at Dositheos' monastery, but I'll be happy to hear it again."

"A long-awaited son was born to King Suddhodana of the Shakya people in Lumbini, in the Himalayan foothills, at the Vesak May full moon 638 years ago. The prince was given the name Siddhartha, meaning *he who has achieved his goal*. The king was looking forward to the birth of his son tremendously, and he only wanted one thing: for the boy to be happy. Siddhartha grew, and the king issued an order that everything that might make him sad should be hidden from him. Until his wedding day, the young prince never left this vast royal garden. A year after the wedding, he asked his charioteer Channa to take him out of the palace secretly. For the first time in his life he saw sick people, old people and he even saw a dead person in the city streets. Upon returning he thought only about one thing: that there was a need to find a way how to rid people of sickness, old age, death, and suffering. To find this he decided to leave his wife, son and parents, and he left the palace in secret. He travelled around the country for a long time and asked wise men and pilgrims how to discover the path of salvation. Only after many years of meditation was the path of salvation revealed to him in the four truths. The first one is that all people are exposed to suffering. The second one is that desire is the cause of the suffering. The third one is that if people wish to rid themselves of suffering, they have to defeat desire, and the fourth one is the four things you have to do in order to defeat desire. They are the awakening of the heart, cleansing of the mind, liberation from envy and jealousy, and the fourth one – awakening in oneself a love of all people and all living beings. Siddhartha spread the truth he discovered in his doctrine, which he formulated in the Ten Commandments, or rules for avoiding evil deeds committed through the body, the word and the mind. Do you want to hear what these evil deeds are according to the Buddha?" he looked at the pensive Jesus.

"Yes, although your monks have told me about them, I'll be happy to hear them again in this holy place."

Barata smiled. "Three of them are bodily, namely killing another living being, the taking of other people's things, and bad sexual conduct."

"I understand," Jesus replied. "It's what we call, Thou shalt not kill! Thou shalt not steal! Thou shalt not commit adultery! Unlike Moses, the Buddha commands us to protect all that lives, not only human beings."

"Human beings don't give life; therefore, they have no right to take it. They wouldn't have the right to take it even if they gave it. Killing any living creature is a violation of the Lord's will as he was the one who had brought the soul into being. Only he has the right to decide when to withdraw a soul from earthly existence. Every life is a part of the life force, on which all living beings depend. The Sanskrit term prana means "all that breathes", and thus it refers to all living beings," Barata explained.

"Plants too?"

"No, because they don't have a mind. There are five conditions that make the evil of killing complete: a living being, an awareness of being a living being, an intention to kill, an effort to kill, and the ensuing death."

"And what about killing a killer, an evil person or an animal in self-defense?" Jesus asked.

"The gravity of the evil depends on the goodness and generosity of the being in question. Killing a virtuous person is considered more evil than killing an evil person."

"What is the punishment for killing?"

"The Buddha says that the act of killing itself is the punishment. You move yourself to the level below, the level of evil people, the level of their suffering. You exclude yourself from the society of virtuous people, even if nobody knows what you've done. Awareness of the act is important not for others but for the one who committed it. He will live all his life with the consciousness of guilt, which will result in poor health, disease in himself or someone close to him, or a short and unworthy life. He will live all his life in fear of being exposed, which will devour him inside, until it causes disease and then death. That's the worst punishment: fear. It's the same with the other evil deeds, such as theft or inappropriate sexual conduct. The common denominators of theft and bad sexual conduct are the desire to enjoy property or unpermitted pleasure."

"Why are people willing to commit crimes for property or sex?"

"It may sound odd, but it's man's unconscious effort to put things in balance. That's the fundamental law of existence. If there were no balance, the world couldn't exist. A natural theft is when a poor person steals from a rich one: a decrease in imbalance. An unnatural theft is one where a rich person steals from a poor one: an increase in imbalance. Inequality is an unnatural condition that comes not from God but from people. God makes all people equal, because he knows that balance is unity. It is similar when applied to sex, which is in fact again turning imbalance into balance. A man and a woman are two poles that make up the fundamental unity of existence. Imbalance begins when a man or a woman has superiority. Violating any balance takes the two poles apart from one another and a tension develops. However, both the poles long for what is most natural for people, the greatest good: unity. Because unity is balance. People are capable of committing evil in the name of good."

"*Interesting*," Jesus thought. "Dositheos' monks didn't tell me that. I didn't know sexuality too was a theme in Buddhism."

"Buddhism deals with all aspects of life, and sexuality is one of the most important aspects."

"Is sexuality evil?" Jesus asked inquisitively.

"It is for those that only perceive it physically. They will lose their energy piece by piece. Conversely, those who perceive it as a conjunction between spirit and matter will multiply it. When a man and a woman unite only for physical pleasure, their joy and happiness aren't limitless, because they don't make a unity. Unity only occurs when the spiritual and physical union is in balance. It's good when the purpose is unity. People perceive sexuality as a relationship between two bodies and forget completely about the spiritual essence, which is unity. An unawakened person only seeks physical pleasure, thus only seeking one half; an awakened, conscious spiritual person seeks the whole. He doesn't seek the ephemeral physical, but the eternal divine. People have become separated from perfection – from paradise, if you will. We call it nirvana. The sexual force is the greatest force in the world, the driver of everything. Sexuality is only the base for sensual pleasures, but its deepest sense is the control of all aspects of life."

"How can you achieve that?"

"By controlling your instincts. When you master that, the world will be yours. Your energy will reach an unprecedented, invincible level. You will heal, fly, levitate, communicate over hundreds and thousands of miles, learn new languages, banish demons, put hands on the sick and heal them, hold snakes in your hands and feel nothing if they bite you with deadly venoms. You will perform miracles!" Barata said and gave Jesus a long stare.

Jesus said nothing and watched a tiny ant dragging a beetle at least ten times its own size into its anthill.

"I'm just watching this kind of miracle," he smiled. "What's your other evils?"

"Killing, the taking of unpermitted things and bad sexual conduct are the three bodily evils. Four others are committed through words: lying, slandering, insulting and idle talk. The consequence is that he who lies, slanders, insults and talks idly himself becomes untrustworthy, ridicules himself, loses friends, makes enemies, spreads evil energy and evil thoughts; his voice becomes coarse and his breath becomes foul. Ultimately, he himself becomes evil and lonely."

"How many lonely and evil people live in my country! We literally learn to slander and talk idly because we try not to fulfill Moses' laws but rather circumvent them in a way to feel we haven't breached them. We make up sophisticated excuses and rules that are nothing but deceptions of the law. And yet we delude ourselves that God has chosen us," Jesus sighed.

"Contrary to Jews, no Indians, Buddhists, or any other Asian people believe they're the chosen ones, the center of the world. Unless the Jews come to their senses, they'll pay for their pride one day. The world wasn't created for perfect beings, but it serves as a perfecting workshop for humans."

After a moment of silence, Jesus said ashamedly, "Yes, I'm too convinced that there's no chosen people. What are the three remaining evils?"

"Those done by the mind. Greed, evil will and evil opinion."

"Meaning that you in fact commit a sin even by thinking about a bad deed?"

"Why do you keep saying sin?" Barata asked with a rebuke in his voice. "It's an evil word. We don't use it; we use the word mistake. If you say to someone who's failed that he's committed a sin, you plant in him a sense of guilt and bitterness. But if you tell him he's made a mistake, you're giving him a chance of remedy, betterment. As for your question, yes, even an evil thought is regarded as an evil deed. Not against others, but against the evil-thinker himself. Under the influence of evil thoughts, you become evil, you push good out of your heart, you reduce the room for fulfilling your virtuous wishes. Your disposition becomes intolerant, evil and sick. He who becomes evil then sees things in an evil light. Having an evil opinion means seeing things as evil. As they say, everything's unclean to the unclean."

"How do you interpret evil will?"

"The inevitable consequences of an evil will are hatred, envy and ingratitude, which return to the one who radiates them."

"But people in my country aren't very grateful," Jesus interrupted him.

Barata looked at him in surprise, and Jesus went on, "In my country, when I give somebody alms, I expect him to be grateful, but the beggar takes the alms and looks at you with ingratitude."

"That's the basic difference between your understanding of compassion and ours," Barata laughed. "I can explain that very easily. The life of a Buddhist consists in committing good deeds, you could nearly say in collecting them. The core of our philosophy is compassion as the incessant commitment to good deeds. Each such deed gives you one good point, so to say. So, if you do a good deed for someone, it's you who ought to be grateful to them for having been allowed to do it. You understand?"

"I do. That's perfect compassion," Jesus nodded.

"You can only be compassionate based on your own experience. The full won't understand the hungry, the clean the dirty, the rich the poor. The Buddha attained awakening via a path that was his goal by itself. I think there's a fundamental difference between your concept of attaining knowledge and ours. God gives experience to you; man does to us. Which experience is more meaningful to you? Your own, or that experienced by someone else, even though he is God? Which is easier to remember? Your own falls and resurrections, or someone else's?" Barata looked at Jesus.

"Yes, I think I've understood the greatest problem with our faith. By not attaining it based on our own experience but having been given it from God via Moses according to our legend, we aren't truly convinced of it, we only delude ourselves of it. If we want Jews to become true believers, we have to bring faith closer to them, take it off the godly pedestal, so to say, and put it on the peasant's kitchen table. The Buddha has become a model for you through his life. We don't have such a model," Jesus sighed.

"Do you want to be that model?"

Jesus said nothing. Barata repeated his question. "What do you say? Do you want to follow in his footsteps?"

Jesus stared in the distance. "I'd like to assist in a reunion of the Jews. In bringing them back to the Father's house."

"There isn't such a thing as the Buddha's house or Moses' house, there's only one house: the house of love," Barata objected. Jesus made no reply.

"Do you want to preach love then?"

"I want to live it."

48   Operation Roza Bal

The atmosphere at the SIV headquarters was so tense it could be cut with a knife. Hausser's worst expectations were coming true. Instead of a pragmatic discussion of the situation report on operation Roza Bal, they were continuously opening theoretical and theological issues that dragged strong emotions into the debate.

"Come on, don't make up such nonsense. Christ in the lotus position… Don't make me laugh." Falcone tried to keep his peaceful expression.

"We would never dare make things up," Hausser responded in a raised voice. "We are police officers. I can replay what Kráľ said if you want to hear it. Since Dvoran replaced his glasses, we've recorded every word that comes out of his mouth or the mouths of those talking to him up to a distance of ten meters."

"Dvoran is that rebellious priest worshippers constantly complain about, saying that he spreads provocative words against the Holy Father and the Holy See. He's apparently even said derisively that Christ couldn't swim!" Farabutto remarked.

"So you see what a brilliant agent he is, having even this kind of information," Koggler smiled.

"What kind of information?" Farabutto turned to him in anger.

"That Christ was a non-swimmer…"

"Colleague, please…" Hausser reprimanded him, but couldn't resist a smile himself. He turned serious instantly, though, and informed Farabutto dryly, "I don't know about the complaints you get from worshippers, but we get quality information from Dvoran."

"How did you get him?" Falcone asked more quietly.

"I'm sorry, father, but there are some things that I'm not allowed to tell even the Congregation…"

"I bet he had a girlfriend and you put the screws on him!" he snapped.

"Maybe you're not far from the truth... Hm... But allow me to continue," he made a dramatic gesture, and put the paper back in his folder ceremonially. "Kráľ and his wife are going to Kashmir based on some kind of talisman. According to our source, Kráľová has given Israel a precious talisman, allegedly dating from Christ's time. Jerusalem rabbi Simonides has confirmed it."

"And do you believe such tales? Everyone has a talisman. I have as many as you can ask for. And I make up the legends for them," Falcone grinned.

"Only the authenticity of this one is beyond doubt. We have information from our friends in Israel. They've confirmed that the Tower of David Museum laboratories have proved that the locket really dates from the times of King Herod, who used to give such lockets to outstanding personalities. It's not out of the question that Jesus' father may have been given it..."

"The father of God receiving a medal from Herod?! That's a good one," Koggler laughed.

"It's a known fact that Joseph worked on both the construction of the Jerusalem temple and the renovation of Sepphoris," Hausser wouldn't be disconcerted. Farabutto and Falcone said nothing. "The locket looks like this." He produced a photocopy of a blow-up of both the obverse and the reverse of the locket and put it on the table.

The men clustered over the two pictures curiously. "What does *Templum Hierosolym* mean?" Koggler asked.

"Jerusalem Temple," Falcone replied.

Hausser nodded. "And as for the etymology of the word, there are speculations galore. Among others, it's said to be Solomon's temple, and some experts have even speculated the Throne of Solomon."

"What's the difference?" Falcone asked.

"The Throne of Solomon used to stand next to Solomon's temple and was Solomon's dwelling place."

"Don't give us this nonsense. I've never heard about a Throne of Solomon," the archbishop snapped angrily.

"You've got to read a Bible dictionary carefully, sir. They mention it."

"I'm happy enough knowing the Old Testament."

"And an accurate replica of Solomon's Jerusalem throne is in Srinagar, the capital of Kashmir..."

"Nonsense again, lieutenant colonel. You claim you're a soldier, then stick to facts," the archbishop rebuked him.

"I am sticking to facts. This is the Throne of Solomon in Srinagar. It's called the Takht-i-Suleiman." Placidly, he put a photograph of an odd building on the table.

The archbishop picked it up and stared at it for a long time. Then he asked in a perturbed manner, "What are your security arrangements there?"

With a sense of a little victory, Hausser continued, "Rest assured, your eminence, they're total. Nobody can get in the tomb."

"Are you sure of that?"

"We have our Afghan boys there."

"Is that it?" Falcone looked at him skeptically.

"Dvoran's going too," Hausser smiled self-confidently.

"Dvoran? Why have you put a double supervision on him then?"

Hausser couldn't hold back his surprise. "How do you know that?"

"Even the Holy Congregation has secrets that it cannot disclose. We call it double protection," Falcone laughed, seconded by Farabutto's noisy laughter.

"They'll be watched by two more of your people throughout their stay… Despite your claims of the reliability of this Dvoran…" the archbishop sneered.

"Do I understand it right that your people are supervising ours, who are supervising Dvoran?" Felix Kruger, shocked, turned to the Congregation men.

"Do you have a problem with that?" Farabutto replied cynically.

"Dirty tricks," Felix ground out.

"Did you say something?" the secretary leaned toward him ominously. Felix was silent, but his jawbone twitched nervously.

Hausser quickly steered away from his younger fellow's indelicate question. "Double protection is our normal working method."

The archbishop gestured for Farabutto to let the matter be. He picked up the photograph of the Throne of Solomon and gave it a long examining look. His hand was shaking visibly.

"Are you sure of what you're saying?" Hausser made no reply. "Because I'm afraid you aren't too sure. You're well aware yourself that Dvoran hasn't reported to you for a week." He tapped his fingers on the table nervously. "I want to ask a pretty clear question: If all your measures failed, all your people failed, and there was a real risk of these maniacs actually opening Jesus'... I mean the grave in Kashmir, do you have a back-up plan?"

"If there was no other chance of preventing the opening of Jesus' grave... we'll use the same method as in Fatehpur Sikri. Another plus for us is that, according to our intelligence information, the Indian army is preparing a massive offensive against Kashmiri rebels concentrated in Srinagar just when they'll be there. The rebels are supported by the fighters of the Lashkar-e-Taiba, the Army of the Rightful, based in the Pakistani part of Kashmir and focused on liberating the Muslims living in India. They even use ground-to-ground missiles, so it won't be suspicious if a building is hit by one extra bomb. We have accurate information about their movements; we'll try to do it when the two are inside the tomb."

"So you're assuming they will actually enter the tomb?" Koggler asked.

Hausser thought for a moment. "It seems this Doctor Bashrat is more cunning than we thought."

A deadly silence descended on the room. A barely visible vein was throbbing on Felix Kruger's left temple.

49 The Price of Death

The sun over Lumbini was slowly setting. The ground was warmed with its life-giving rays, so Jesus along with Barata and other pilgrims made their beds under the tree where the Buddha used to sit and meditate about life. None of them could fall asleep, as the air was replete with the cosmic energy of that magical place. Barata stared at Jesus for a long time. His deep eyes shone with a peculiar light that he couldn't fail to notice. He smiled happily. He knew that the young man who had travelled this far from Palestine was experiencing a state of enlightenment in this holy place, which only came to those whose hearts and minds were ready to set out on the path defined by the Buddha five centuries before. He felt good about having accurately touched his friend's deepest emotions, thoughts and reasoning. He knew that Jesus had made his decision while in Lumbini.

"I'm thinking about how incredibly close Moses' and the Buddha's teachings are," Jesus contemplated quietly.

"What's the Jewish teaching based on?"

"The Decalogue, or the Ten Commandments as the people call it."

"What are they about?"

"They're listed in the Torah. The first one is that you mustn't have any other gods beside the one God."

"The Buddha says all suffering comes from desire: longing for wealth, power, glory, sex… Those are our gods. They're often very evil."

"Can a god be evil?" Jesus asked in surprise.

"Gods are neutral, because each of us is his own god. More precisely, you have a potential to become divine, that is, perfect. When you're born, you're given this potential as a gift, and it's only up to you what you do with it." He stared into Jesus' eyes attentively. "It's up to you whether you continue from zero into positive or negative numbers. You decide how and to what end you use your free will, the intellect that God gave us all. The Buddha teaches that the only way to worship God is to live according to his commandments. Not memorize them, but live according to them," Barata said emphatically. "That's real faith. Actions, not words! God is in each of us, he can't be pictured or carved out of wood, he needs no altars on which you put sacrifices; he doesn't need enforcement of indulgence by spilling the blood of the innocent, or any sumptuous temples filled with riches: the only thing he acknowledges is a courageous life. What are your other tenets?"

"Commandments," Jesus corrected him with a smile. "You must not abuse the name of the Lord, your God."

"I guess many interpret that as not swearing," Barata smiled.

Jesus reciprocated his smile. "Unfortunately, you're right. They don't know, or don't want to know, that abusing God's name – uttering his name in vain – is not only by swearing but mainly in hypocrisy, when you refer to God, preach God, but act differently from what you say."

"You also abuse God's name when you go to church only to be seen because that does you good; you abuse it when you perform good deeds ostentatiously in public. But the worst abuse of God's name is when you invent dogmas in his name, and even insist, in his name, on people following them and believing in them. You then even punish them for not liking the practice. Power and punishment are not God's attributes," Barata added.

"Many are convinced that when they commit an evil deed and then say a prayer, God will forgive them," Jesus smiled.

"Buddhism condemns prayers connected with requests. The only thing we accept is meditation aimed at self-improvement and enlightenment."

"You don't make requests to God?" Jesus looked at him in surprise.

"Making a request to God is insulting him. God knows very well what each of us needs. And a person who sows evil may request God as much as he can, he will only reap evil. That's the law! That's why we meditate; we don't pray, don't make requests. We meditate to improve ourselves. We promise to try our best, day after day, to become better than we were yesterday. That's the right path to perfection."

"So, you don't need God for self-improvement?"

"We do. God is crucial in our self-improvement. It's God that holds the mirror for us and brings us as close to it as possible so we can get a good picture of ourselves. Often it isn't pleasant at all, but we're grateful to God for persistently bringing us to the mirror. According to the Buddha, no liberation – or salvation as you say – can be achieved other than by one's own effort, working on one's self-improvement. Those who don't do that and only declare their efforts verbally, are abusing the name of God. Contrary to Moses' teaching, where God is at the center, the human being is at the center of Buddhism."

Jesus said nothing for a long while. Barata patted him on the shoulder amicably. "What are your other commandments?"

"Remember the day of festive rest. We say that after six days of work, you need to concentrate on your soul, and stop to think."

"But not everyone works for six days, so even those who don't work have to rest?" Barata asked.

"They don't if they worked with their soul during the week, but if they do work, they have to do so in a way that doesn't disturb others. Only working publicly on a Saturday disturbs the peaceful energy of that day. We mustn't forget that people generate energies by working together. You do feel the general peace and quiet on a Saturday."

Barata thought for a while. "The next one?"

"Honor your mother and your father given to you by God so you can live a long life on earth."

"Yes, that's essentially an iteration of the principle 'You get back what you give'. If you don't take care of your parents, your children will treat you the same when you grow old. It's unthinkable here that children wouldn't take care of their old parents."

"It's the same with Jews," Jesus confirmed. "Our customs are identical in this respect then. The fifth commandment is also similar. It says you mustn't kill. Unfortunately, our cruel God prescribes animal sacrifices in the Torah. The popular interpretation is that only human beings mustn't be killed."

"We too have the commandment not to kill. Our hypocrisy is most manifested in the protection of cows, which we've even declared holy."

"But that's great! To me, protecting cows means that humans have risen above the level of their species. To me, the cow is a symbol of the world below the human level, and I see its protection as an embodiment of compassion," Jesus enthused.

"It would be great if we protected all animals the same way. But every Hindu or Buddhist festival is accompanied with the spilling of blood of innocent sacrificial animals. People fail to realize that whoever kills animals kills himself, draws food from the body of death, the animal's flesh slowly turns to rot, and the death of the animal that he's eaten will turn into his own death."

"People as well interpret the killing of neighbors only literally. You mustn't draw a sword against your sister or brother, but you're allowed to kill them by turning their life into hell. How many men maltreat their wives or children in the privacy of their homes; women destroy their husbands' lives with their shrewishness. And nobody minds that!" Jesus raised his voice so much that the monks sleeping around him grumbled at him to hush.

"We've got to talk more softly," Barata rebuked him. "You see how much we still have to go through? I think we're only at the fifth commandment."

"The sixth one says you mustn't commit adultery."

"There you go! Desire, lust. All suffering comes from desire."

"But this refers to marriage," Jesus protested.

"The Buddha conceives desire much more widely. Your bed is virtue, and any desire that takes you away from virtue is adultery, perfidy of the truth bed. It may be a desire for money, fame, power, wealth and, of course, another woman or man."

"Anyone may fall into the dust, only they mustn't linger in it too long," Jesus smiled.

"If a woman forgives her husband's failure, or a man his wife's, they may be cleansed and continue," Barata explained.

"And what about God? What if he doesn't forgive them?"

"There's your Jewish thinking again: punishment, punishment. Why should God punish if the partner has forgiven?" Barata broke off for a moment and then continued, "People are easiest to control when they fear, when they feel constant remorse. Maybe that's why many people here retreat into celibacy, to have as little enticement and temptation as possible, to minimize the remorse."

"Celibacy isn't in accordance with God's will. Even the prophet Ezekiel says clearly, *a priest may not marry a widow or a repelled woman, only a virgin from the progeny of the house of Israel or a priest's widow*. God wishes people, even priests, to live together, to give each other strength by overcoming their own weaknesses. No human being is perfect, a true believer struggles for perfection every day. The greater the temptations he overcomes, the stronger he is. So, monks who have fled into celibacy are weak and, I'm not afraid to say, cowards," Jesus raised his voice again.

"You're quite right, but I must warn you. You'll have a hard life with such opinions. Very hard," Barata sighed. "But yes, someone has to say it out loud. The Buddha started it, and you'll be his continuator."

"I don't have the ambition to be anyone's continuator. I have the ambition to seek truth."

Barata broke the silence after a moment's pause. "Do you have any other rules?"

"The eighth one is not to steal." Then he turned to Barata questioningly. "Sorry, a silly question: do you have thieves here?"

Barata pondered. "I'll tell you a story about a general and a pilgrim. The pilgrim was sitting in the lotus position on a forest path and meditating, and an army approached him, headed by a general on the horseback. The general asked him to move out of the way. But the monk continued his meditation peacefully. The general repeated his demand several times, but the pilgrim didn't budge an inch. 'Don't you know I have the power to kill you anytime I want?' He drew his sword. 'Don't you know I have the power to die anytime I want?' the pilgrim said calmly and continued meditating. The general was a fair-minded man, he walked around the pilgrim and his army with him."

"A nice story," Jesus laughed.

"The only belonging the pilgrim had was his life. If you aren't afraid for it, no one can steal it from you, because if you know it's ultimately just lent to you, you're free. Because fear is bondage. In the West, you think the wealthier you are the freer you are. It's the other way around here. If you have something to give, you have some power; if you have something to take, you have more power; but the one with nothing to take has the greatest power."

"Possessions are the god in Israel. All our Torah speaks of is numbers of cattle, herds, servants, houses, money, land," Jesus sighed.

Barata smiled. "The worst theft is the theft of time. Whoever allows others to command him, although he knows that it is not his way, walks outside the destined path towards a wrong destination. He does not use the gift of time but agrees with the abuse by those who he obeys."

Jesus pondered – for a long while this time. "Thank you, dear Barata, I've never thought about theft in this way. In the West, we think we're blameless unless we touch a neighbor's property."

Barata continued, "And what about mother earth? Why, we've been only taking, plundering her forests, rivers and fields for millennia. Isn't this exploitation of nature theft?"

"How come animals live in harmony with nature?"

"Because every animal is perfect compared to a human. Nature – that is, God – thinks for it. Only in the human being has God taken the liberty of experimenting by giving it reason, that is, freedom of will. And you see for yourself where it's going when people think for themselves... Hm... What's the next rule that your Jewish God offers you?"

"You mustn't bear false witness against your neighbor."

"Slander, condemnation, judgment, making conclusions considered to be real. We have the same thing. People forget that everyone is the guarantor of truth before God. If your words and thoughts are only assumptions, you mustn't utter them out loud as true. At any given moment, you bear false witness against yourself by speaking and acting differently. A true witness is not words but actions."

"Don't judge lest you be judged," Jesus added.

"Do you have any other commandments?"

"It's a bit too long, but it can be summarized as, 'Don't long for anything that belongs to your neighbor.'"

"So, in conclusion, it's back to desire and lust. We forget that he who demands the least is the richest. It's easier for a camel to go through the eye of a needle than for a rich man to enter nirvana," Barata smiled.

"I'll remember that," Jesus replied, and asked, "Can you liberate yourself from desire?"

"By realizing life is the price of death."

50 Do Not Fear

Michal was leaning on Marika, who was watching the sunrise over Himalayan peaks in fascination along with the other passengers. The incredible spectacle, enabled by the beautiful weather and three-hour delay, would forever remain engraved in their memories. They watched glittery summits capped with perpetual snow, endless mountain crests and variegated meadows at the lower elevations.

"It's heaven on earth. From above, Kashmir really looks like a depression surrounded by mountain massifs. When you imagine the Indus, entering the Kashmir basin in the east and leaving it in the west, as the axis of the whole area, then I think a single minor earthquake that would bar the river outflow – or a torrential storm – and all of Kashmir would be inundated."

"A flood this high up?" Marika asked in surprise.

"They say the biblical flood took place here… A fascinating country, I can't even imagine anyone being ill here… You'll definitely get over it here. I know it, I feel it, I'm absolutely convinced about your healing." He hugged his wife tightly. He noticed she was paler than usual. "Are you feeling bad?"

"I'm just tired. I mean, we haven't slept all night…"

"You'll take a rest, and when you're okay, we'll take a look around the city."

* * * * *

"I'm Eli Ghulam Bashrat, Doctor Bashrat's son," a likeable forty-something introduced himself to them at the airport ten minutes later. He was lowering the sign with their names on it that he'd been holding over his head. "I'm happy to have you as guests. Our mutual friend, Mr. Ľubomír, turned to us with a request to take care of you. He's a respectable man who loves Kashmir, and we regard him highly for that. His friends are our friends too. My father is awaiting you in his study in Sonamarg, but first of all we'll go to our houseboat on Dal Lake, where you'll be accommodated. It's less than ten miles from here."

He turned to Marika and informed her confidentially, "Professor Vaidya is expecting you for testing the day after tomorrow. Enjoy some rest tomorrow before the procedure." He noticed the flicker of fear in her eyes. "Don't worry, everything will be alright," Eli smiled encouragingly and began loading the baggage on a cart.

"Is that all you have?" he looked in surprise at the two small suitcases. Michal and Marika shrugged. "No problem, you'll dress as us Muslims if need be."

"Do you think we'll stay longer?"

"I've no idea. My father and the professor will decide about that. My father's a physician recognized all over Kashmir, and I try to follow in his footsteps. I'm absolutely sure he'll heal you just as he's healed many before you, with your cooperation, naturally," he gave Marika a friendly smile.

Her eyes lit up with hope. Michal helped Eli load the baggage onto an elderly Toyota Land Cruiser Prado. Eli noticed the guests' confusion over the luxury car.

"As a recognized physician, my father is a relatively wealthy man. People from all around the world come to see him. My grandfather too was known for his incredible abilities. True, we aren't doing the best financially at the moment, you know, the tension here is almost constant – people are afraid to go to Kashmir. My granddad was a healer too," Eli added and started the engine. "You're about to see the most beautiful lake in the world. Only after you've spent some time on the Dal Lake, will you understand why Srinagar is dubbed the Venice of the East. Yes, Kashmir is heaven on earth," he smiled. "Or, it might be... We Muslims call it the Bagh-i-Suleiman: Solomon's Garden."

Michal listened on. "They say King Solomon himself visited the area during his reign. I love this country, full of snowy mountains with glaciers, which give rise to rivers filling Kashmir's lakes in the green valleys. Richly green meadows alternate with fruit orchards and rice and corn fields. The second chapter of the Book of Genesis says, 'The Lord planted a garden in Eden in the East... from which there flowed a river to irrigate the garden, and from there it split into four arms.' What was 'the East' for the author of the Book of Genesis? There are only two rivers in Mesopotamia, which is east of Egypt and Israel. The only area in the East that matches the biblical description is Punjab – Five Rivers – in Pakistan and partly in India. The river Indus flows out of our Kashmir, which receives four tributaries from the left side: the Sutlej, Ravi, Chenab and Jhelum. The last one flows through Srinagar, the capital of Kashmir," Eli enthused about his country. Suddenly he turned serious.

"The only thing that's spoiling this heaven on earth is the constant tension, the almost permanent underlying war, turning at times into actual warfare, between India and Pakistan. It's been like that since 1947, when British India was split into the Muslim Pakistan and Hindu India. The first war broke out then, and the United Nations delineated the demarcation line a year later and Kashmir split into two parts. There've been more wars since then: in '65, '71, and '99. Kashmir and Srinagar are places of constant military skirmishes. The Pakistanis want to make it part of their country, the Chinese too claim a part of it, and Afghan mercenaries, unofficially supported by the Pakistani government and purportedly even by al-Qaeda, have been increasingly infiltrating the country. Tens of thousands of civilians and soldiers have died in the fighting..."

"And what do the people want?"

"I think what the people want most is peace. Some want independence, others are attracted to Pakistan for religious motives, yet others wish to remain part of India because of its higher standard of living. Most of all, though, we want peace. The people have always lived in peace here, until politicians started meddling with them and instigating hatred in them."

Michal was observing the landscape curiously, and then he turned to Eli. "You're a Muslim, but you know the Old Testament?" he asked.

"I am a Muslim, but my ancestors were Jews. We still have the Hebrew Torah at home."

"How bizarre! How did you become Muslims?" Michal inquired.

"It's a longer story, you'll learn it all over time."

Listening to Eli's calm, mellifluous voice and perfect English, Marika closed her eyes. Michal put her head on his lap and folded his anorak jacket under it. Eli gestured to him to take a blanket from the trunk. Michal covered his wife with it, and she fell into a deep sleep. Michal turned to Eli quietly.

"Mr. Eli, you and your father are our last hope. Please, do what you can to save her. We need her. Our daughter needs her too... She's the most amazing being in the world... I can't imagine living without her." He fell silent, and tears welled in his eyes.

"You know, your problem in Europe is that you're too well off. You're too far from death, which makes you not think about it. In Kashmir, we stare death in the eyes on a daily basis, so we're not afraid of it."

"You're not afraid of death?"

Eli smiled gently. "Death is just an exchange of energy, it brings you back to the divine cosmic flow of love and universal unity, from which humans have disengaged themselves and become dependent. They've forgotten they come from eternity, where nothing's dead. There's only energy, identical in the earthly and the celestial life, only vibrating at different frequencies. Our souls are cosmic creatures that only inhabit an earthly physical envelope conditionally for a limited time. People struggle with death, defy it, don't want to die, and yet it's the most natural thing we have in our lives. A human being doesn't die upon death, it only changes. Nature knows no demise, only transformation. If you want to stop being afraid of death, you have to make friends with it."

"Can you prepare for death?"

"Each of us survives a little death every day. It's called sleep. I'm sure you'll agree that the place our soul goes while we're asleep is not a bad place, seeing as we never feel like getting up in the morning," he laughed. "After your last breath, your soul keeps on breathing, only in a different rhythm. Natural realms breathe in long cycles, human beings in a short one. The last breath on this earth is followed by the first breath in a different rhythm. It's the birth to your initial state, a return."

"So why are people afraid of death?"

"Because they've broken the unity. They don't perceive a life as a part of a whole. It's like your Western medicine, in which doctors don't treat the whole but only its parts. They never heal anyone like that. Life and death belong together like day and night, like exhaling and inhaling. But everyone who devotes their life to God will find the meaning."

"How can you devote your life to God?"

"By giving your neighbors and yourself the best that's in you. Our only purpose is to give and accept love. Love heals everything. Even your wife. If her faith and that of those who love her is complete, everything will be alright," Eli smiled at Michal and clutched his hand encouragingly. "Does your wife believe?"

"Very much."

"Then she will be healed. Do not fear!"

51   False Prophets

After a brief stay in Lumbini, Jesus and Barata set out west up the Rapti river valley, on through the Himalayan foothills and the Shakya kingdom to Alamgirpur between the upper reaches of the Ganges and the Yamuna, and then to the town of Ropar on the Sutlej river, which rises underneath holy Mount Kailash. The river spills over the Punjab plain at Ropar. The two men traversed the plain down to its bend downstream of Lavapuri. In this city, the biggest in Punjab, they rested for nearly a month before they continued travelling the country. The people welcomed them with flower garlands and didn't want them to leave. Jesus stayed at many places, learned from simple peasants as well as from wise Brahmins. After another trip of almost six months through upper Punjab, they arrived at the gates of Takshashila, the capital of the Gandhara kingdom, which lay in the Himalayan foothills at the crossroads of three major trade routes. The route known as the Utarapata linked the western kingdom of Gandhara with Magadha in the east; the northwestern route via the Khunjerab Pass linked Punjab with Bactria, where it joined the main Silk Road from China to Europe, and the north-south route linked Kashmir with the Indus valley.

Moved, Barata was looking at the tall peaks looming to the east of the city. "When the Buddha was born, Takshashila went into the hands of King Darius of Persia, after whom Alexander the Great won it. After the conquest of Bactria in the year 331 before our era, his armies advanced over the Kabul river valley all the way to the Indus. Omphis, then ruler of Takshashila, didn't fight Alexander, but instead welcomed him with all due honors. Alexander was fascinated by the excellent quality of science and education in Takshashila. I have no doubt that the city's wisdom will fascinate you, too," Barata smiled.

"For more than seven hundred years – since the university was founded – the city has received teachers, philosophers and scientists from the most advanced cultures of China, India, Persia, Bactria, Greece and the Roman Empire. This has made the university the most important known center of scholarship. Since Alexander's time, Greek has been one of the teaching languages at the university.

Pythagoras studied here with the disciples of the Rishis, and he's been remembered as a great thaumaturge called Yaivancharya. It was at this university that the scholar Panini wrote the first grammar of Sanskrit five hundred years ago; a hundred years later Chanakya wrote the first textbook on state administration, economics, management and financial operations entitled the *Arthashastra: Science of Material Gain*. His work *Neetishastra: The Ideal Lifestyle*, has been a source for Indian hygiene to this day. King Gondophares I, whom we're about to see, has purportedly invited the young Greek philosopher Apollonius of Tyana to his court."

They arrived in the city in the summer of the year in which Jesus turned thirty-two years of age. The fair-haired Nazarene with deep blue eyes and a long, straight nose, which distinguished him noticeably from locals, was welcomed by the sixty-five-year-old King Gondophares with honors that were only given to the most outstanding persons visiting his court. Barata said goodbye to his loyal friend outside the city gates.

"You no longer need a guide. The hands of King Gondophares are the best in which you could have gotten. God bless you." The friends hugged each other tightly. They would never meet again.

Jesus handed the letter from the prince to his father, and Gondophares was very pleased by it. The visitor politely refused the king's offer to stay at his palace, and instead stayed along with the other students in a compound that housed nearly eleven thousand students from all around the world. He was free to choose any of the sixty-four study specializations. He studied the Vedas, philosophy, Ayurveda, hygiene, surgery and astronomy. His name and the king's protection opened doors for him to each of the university's teachers. He became the favorite student of the excellent philosopher, physician and healer Kanaka, who introduced the young Nazarene to various healing methods and interventions and taught him which medicinal plants to use for which disease. From textbooks written five centuries earlier by one of the most prominent students at the medical faculty – the Buddha's private physician Jivaka – Jesus learned lots of recipes for healing herbal blends. His studies built on the foundations of the medical education which he'd received from Udraka in Banaras. In his yoga classes, he learned how to harmonize opposites; he meditated and learned how to devote his life to selfless action. Kanaka introduced him to the incredible abilities of a man with a concentrated mind, taught him self-discipline, breath control, liberation of the senses, cultivation of physical strength and vitality, how to attain perfect inner peace and how to focus the prana. Jesus learned to work with chakras and meridians, acquired the art of concentration, cleansing techniques, the shankhaprakshalana, proper use of urine and saliva; he understood the power of positive thinking, acquired the art of anaesthetizing parts of the body, learned to develop higher levels of consciousness, control emotions and many more capabilities. He understood the mystery of a flock of birds in the sky or a school of fish in the water changing its direction collectively in a single instant.

He understood that basic life processes exist independently of our consciousness. Digestion, sleep, breathing, heartbeat and growth all appeared to be controlled from without. He learned that the brain is the most complex, most acute and most intriguing physical object in the known universe; he knew how to estimate people's dispositions from their breath; he learned to control his pulse, breathing and blood pressure, which enabled him to attain astonishing physical performances, which meddled with the world of gods in the minds of untrained and uneducated people. He realized that from the perspective of eternity, our earthly life is but an inhalation that will be exhaled one day. He observed nature, with which humans are tightly linked and even find their own reflection in its formations. He understood that there's nothing inside a human being that would not correspond to something in nature. The intestine is the shape of a worm that processes nutrients just like the intestine does. The lungs, which help us move around, are in the shape of bird's wings. His teachers of mysteries taught him that looking at the internal organs of a human body from above, as if from the sky, they arrange themselves similarly to the solar system. He found out that the complex, symmetrical shapes of plants are accurate matches to the routes along which stars and planets orbit. He found out that even the shape of the human body correlates with routes of stars to a certain extent. He learned that nature's rhythm is identical to the rhythm of processes happening inside the human body. A human being inhales 25,920 times a day on average, which is exactly the number of years in the Great Platonic Year. He understood that all things are ideas, that life is an idea in action, and that all beings are forms of manifestation of the original idea.

Jesus' enthusiasm for new findings and knowledge was not ceasing, but he felt an increasing urge to apply his knowledge to real life. The university was a great place for self-improvement, but he felt he could only elevate his body and spirit among the people. That was why he often walked out to villages, fields and forests, searching for people who searched for him. They dubbed him Isa, and crowds gathered wherever he turned up. At one such gathering, which formed spontaneously in a marketplace in Takshashila, he criticized Brahma's priests for collecting contributions for absolution of sins from paupers who had nothing to eat. There were even rumors of spending part of the money for pleasure with prostitutes.

"You've rejected God, and He will reject you for that. You live off the sins of people, you long for their wrongdoing, you cast them in it, you keep people in guilt, so that you can then decide on whom to forgive and for what reward." He nearly shouted at the priests. "But has anyone asked you for such a service? Does God want you to do it? What gives you the right to stand between Him and people? You ask God to punish your daughters for committing adultery with you!

They do it not for love, but for want, because you tell them that if they have nothing to redeem themselves with, they can pay with their own bodies. You yourselves commit the disgrace for which you then judge others. You preach Scriptures but you defy them with your own deeds. You are false prophets, for whom only the vaults of tombs will remain! Be ashamed and get out of people's sight!"

In exchange for these words, the priests placed Jesus-Isa under an interdict and started devising a plan to take his life.

52 The Heart

Michal and Marika were sitting on the nocturnal deck of Bashrat's houseboat and sipping masala chai. A huge full moon was floating serenely on its path over the lake. It was completely quiet, only the distant singing of a waking nightingale could be heard. When the singing subsided, they could hear the soft, almost inaudible lapping of the water. A boat was passing very close to them. They looked at each other in surprise. They'd been watching the lake all the time but hadn't seen any boats anywhere. However, this one was floating by calmly in the fading rays of the moonlight. On the unusually long and narrow boat there stood a woman wearing a long dark blue cloak with a hood that covered her hair. The boat was floating toward the eastern shore of the lake, surrounded by tall snow-covered mountains; the woman was holding a long oar of a strange shape, reminiscent of a heart. The peaceful lake surface conveyed the impression of infinity; a vast space with the stars and the moon extended over the boat, full of fresh, invigorating air, which the woman was inhaling deeply. In the background beyond the boat, they could see the shore with little cottages, vanishing into the distance. The boat was protected with three swords at the front and the rear. Its prow showed a picture of a feminine face in the center of a circle, emanating what looked like sun's rays. A lamp shone over it. As the boat was passing its closest point to them, the woman turned to face them and waved her hand at them. They did likewise. Then she turned her face back toward the east and floated on. Marika and Michal were completely speechless.

"Our friend, Professor Vaidya, will admit you the day after tomorrow," said Eli, who suddenly turned up aboard. They turned toward him and shook hands with him heartily. Eli took a seat. Marika and Michal turned their eyes back to the boat, but there was no boat. The peaceful lake surface was only covered with endless lily and lotus pads. Marika's face was suddenly distorted with pain. She put down her teacup so swiftly that some of the chai splashed out. She gripped her left foot.

"What is it? What's going on?" Michal said to her.

The pain made her speechless for a while.

"Does it hurt…?" Eli asked. She nodded.

"Where?" She pointed at the sole of her foot. He knelt down by her and compressed a point on the sole. She yelled out with pain.

"You're totally hyperacidic. I'll call the professor immediately. I'll ask him to admit you tomorrow."

Marika usually protested in such situations, not wanting to trouble doctors pointlessly, but she said nothing this time.

It turned out that they'd see Eli's father, healer Ghulam Bashrat in Sonamarg no sooner than in a week's time. Professor Vaidya ran some blood tests on Marika, which showed ten times the white blood cell count than is the norm. To make sure, he ran one more test, which confirmed the increased white blood cell count. The professor didn't want to tire Marika with another trip to the clinic just to confirm the results, so he came to see her on the boat. They were sitting in the beautiful onboard living room made of carved cedar wood, evidently the work of old masters. There were pictures of Kashmir landscapes on the walls. The professor examined the results meticulously, while Marika and Michal were awaiting his words with tension.

"It's not good. I mean… it's bad. You've got AML."

"What's that?" Michal asked.

"Acute myeloid leukemia. The worst type of cancer in the blood, in which the bone marrow produces excessive numbers of immature white blood cells, which travel the blood stream and enter the brain, skin, ovaries, in fact they invade every organ." Marika and Michal listened to the physician with pale faces.

"That means it's serious?"

"We'll struggle…" the doctor avoided an answer.

Marika could hardly swallow, and her mouth was running dry.

"What hope is there?" Michal asked.

"The success of the treatment largely depends on the patient's cooperation, who must be informed about their condition… If only thirty percent of your wife's cells were invaded, it would be hopeful. But she already has sixty-seven percent…" Marika's eyes welled up. "Calm down, please, I didn't say there was no hope… I'd like to ask you… When you had the breast carcinoma, were you treated with chemotherapy?"

Marika sat silent for a long while, then she said softly, "I was."

"But you told me you cured yourself with fasting and juices!" Michal nearly jumped up.

"Yes, I cured myself with fasting and juices. Long before you went to Nepal. It was ineffective, so I…"

"It's manifesting itself now. This is exactly the outcome of Western allopathic medicine. They treat a tumor, not cancer. A tumor is not cancer, but a symptom, a signal that there's something wrong with the body. They remove the tumor and claim the body's been cured. But that's deception. They don't treat the cause of the cancer. So you can have yourself cut up, irradiated, have chemotherapy, but your cancer won't be removed. It may be effective if it's intercepted at an early stage. They stabilize your body, but you must change your mental and dietary habits immediately. Irradiation and chemotherapy significantly reduce your immunity, thus encouraging the disease further. Chemotherapy is literally an attack on the immune system," the professor tried to remain calm.

"And irradiation?" Marika asked.

"Dear Mary, you know every nurse that works by the X-ray machine shields herself from the radiation. And they treat cancer with irradiation! That's madness!"

"But some tumors have been demonstrably reduced by irradiation," she objected.

"That's the worst deceit. A tumor consists of about twenty percent of diseased cells and eighty percent of healthy ones. So, if you irradiate it, you kill a quarter of the diseased ones, but also a quarter of the healthy ones, of which there's four times as many, so the tumor really becomes smaller, but the loss is mainly incurred by the healthy cells."

"What you're saying is logical and clear. Don't people know this?" Michal asked.

"They don't, because the media, politicians and doctors are vassals to pharmaceutical companies. It's a much better business than weapons, oil, churches or opium. Don't forget the food and pharmaceutical industries are not geared toward your healthy diet or curing you but making money of you. The whole of Western medicine is fallacious. The doctors know nothing at all about diet. The consumption of meat, sweets, coffee and milk is normal in oncology hospitals. We're also sick because instead of seeking unity, we succumb to breaking it apart in every aspect. Western medicine has not only separated the body from the mind, but it doesn't even treat the body as a whole; it only treats its parts. The worst danger for an ill person is an expert physician with a narrow specialization. A physician ought to be an excellent and comprehensive expert in the human soul and body. A specialist is like a ship being mastered not by a captain but by a radio operator, who knows nothing about the ship except how to control his wireless gadgets."

"It's just as you say. When I was in hospital with my kidney, I wasn't Michal Kráľ but the kidney in room eighteen."

"Yes, another was the heart in room twelve, yet another the liver in room five," the professor laughed. Then he added more gravely, "But a human being's a human being only if it represents a unity of the body and the spirit. Otherwise the healing energies don't flow. Western physicians don't treat causes but instead remove consequences: pain, rashes, fevers. And the outcome is here," he complained.

"Mister Kráľ, may I ask you something? Could you wait outside, please? Have some tea on the upper deck, we'll then join you." Michal walked out and left Marika with the professor, who talked to her for almost two hours.

"Do your elbows hurt sometimes?" She nodded. "And do you feel pangs in your palms?" A nod again. "There, it's obvious. It would all be clear to an Ayurvedic doctor."

"I was given sedatives, they said I was overworked."

"Excuse me, is your marriage peaceful and harmonious?"

"Like every other marriage..."

"Have you experienced a lot of stress? Do you have a lifelong trauma troubling you?" Marika made no reply. "What kind of family did you grow up in?"

"I never met my father."

"Does it bother you?" No reply. "Does your husband travel a lot?"

"He does."

"And do you?"

"I don't."

"And did you want to?" She said nothing again. "Why didn't you travel with him?"

"I preferred saving the money for furnishings. Our apartment is really exquisitely furnished," she smiled contentedly.

"And are you happy in your beautifully furnished apartment?"

"Well, I think… I think I am…"

"You're not totally sure of it." He examined her pupils. "Do you envy your husband's travels a little?"

Marika felt something breaking inside her, as if a dam was being opened and dirty, reeking water was beginning to flow out of her. "A little, yes."

"Do you have children?"

"A daughter."

"Does she live with you?"

"No, she's in Africa. She went there with her boyfriend. Helping the poor in Sudan."

"Do you miss her?" She nodded. "Do you feel lonely at home?" She made no reply. "Okay, I'm not going to interrogate you. Instead let's talk about how you can get over your disease… You have a very delicate vata-pitta constitution. Poor alimentation of the bone marrow. Have you done any sports?"

"I used to swim, do athletics, five-kilometer runs…"

He examined her pupils thoroughly and then he measured her pulse with three fingers. "Did you feel dizzy in increased strain?"

"Yes, I even lost consciousness out of exhaustion once."

"Your hemoglobin level is lower than one half of the normal rate. When vata penetrates the bone marrow, it results in a strong pain in the bones, joints and then muscles… Do you know what cancer is?"

"Well… erm…"

"A rebellion of cells against their body. The rebellious cells not only get out of control of the immune system, but in fact attack it."

"Why do they rebel?"

"Long-term stress, bad diet, meat eating, alcohol… Do you smoke?"

"I don't. That is, no longer…"

"When did you quit?"

"When I was first diagnosed."

"Your parents?"

"My mother died of cancer. She was a heavy smoker."

"How's your sleep?"

"Not excellent."

"Have you ever held in stool or urination?"

"Since I was a child. When I came in to pee, my mother wouldn't let me out in the yard again, so I held it instead."

"Then I don't need to ask if you suffer from constipation. Are you often tired or suffer from cold?" Marika nodded.

The professor observed her pulse and examined her tongue at length. "The prognosis isn't good, the ahamkara might cause problems. But we'll get down to work. You need to change completely."

"Change how?"

"Mentally. You need to get a positive setup. But you can do it," he stood up. "Well then. It was my task to run the tests and provide Doctor Bashrat with the results. The homeopathics I gave you have improved your blood count somewhat; you can go to Sonamarg without difficulty. It's about fifty miles from Srinagar. You have nothing to fear after my friend Ghulam Bashrat takes care of you. He's a miraculous healer, you won't find a better one in all of Kashmir. Nowhere in the world maybe. He really performs miracles. I've seen them with my own eyes. He's got people who were paralyzed their whole life walking again, he's cured lepers, and he's even restored blind men's eyesight. Have no fear, you'll win with him," he shook her hand encouragingly. "Let's get some sun on the terrace."

As soon as they reached the deck, Marika stared at the trader who'd arrived on his narrow boat fully laden with Kashmiri fabrics, rugs, spices, flowers, fruits, vegetables and souvenirs. The trader tied his boat to the deck and started unloading his wares. Others arrived in the meantime. They immediately offered their wares to Marika as well as the professor and Michal, who had come down. Marika stared at the boat in fascination. "Excellent quality, great price, madam, this rug is hand-woven…"

He pushed the rug in her face, but she was looking at something else.

"The oar," she said.

"The oar?" the trader was perplexed. "I can't sell you that. How would I get back home?"

"Can you pass it to me?" The trader put the oar in her hand. Michal took it from her, examined it and stroked it. He looked around the other traders: they all had the same oars.

"May I ask you what's so interesting about these oars?" Eli asked.

"The hearts," Marika burst out. "They're all heart-shaped."

53 You Shall Become God

The teacher Kanaka remained in endless conversation with Jesus. It was difficult to tell which one of them enjoyed them more.

"The most important thing in a human life is detachment. Only if you are fully detached will you release yourself from the cycle of suffering."

"Full detachment?" Kanaka nodded. "How can it be achieved?"

"Through patient exercise. But if you're in a bad psychic condition, you'll be helped by... erm... it's a secret recipe, it can be dangerous, and I only teach it to those who've stepped out on the path. You're on it already, so I'll tell you how to get into the state between heaven and earth, a state of total detachment. But you should only use it in exceptional circumstances, when you can't detach yourself by meditating. When you get used to it, it can be dangerous. Make a decoction in which you blend hemlock, henbane, saffron, aloe, opium, mandrake, salorum, poppy seed, asafetida, kykeon, blue water lily, and parsley."

"How much of each herb?"

"I won't tell you that: you must find out for yourself."

"How?"

"I said, through patience."

Jesus smiled for the first time in a long time. "That's a good one. Is the patience of one human life enough?"

"It is for the best ones. It suffices to turn you from an active participant into a spectator. You will patiently disengage yourself from bonds but will remain linked to others with the bond of compassion. You must defeat the second strongest desire: the desire to persist. It's not that difficult once you realize nothing is permanent."

"And if I fail?"

"You'll succeed. You have no other option. God will send you down here again and again, until you succeed. He will make signs for you in the form of diseases and unrequited loves. The most frequent disease that results from unfulfilled desire is cancer. Desire for recognition, love, beauty, fame, power, wealth and pleasure can literally devour us from within."

"Is there a way to diagnose this?"

"In a cancer, the weak point of the body first shows a blotch, an unobtrusive dot that wasn't there before. In time, it starts sending out veins, like the claws of a crab…" Kanaka looked Jesus in the eyes for a long time. "Just in case, I'll give you a medicine. It's an almost miraculous cure for the disease. It's a secret formula of the Tibetan monk Tonzin Chodrak. So far it's helped everyone who's taken it."

"What good is it for me?"

"You never know."

"Thank you." Jesus put the bag of little gray balls in a leather pouch. Kanaka grabbed his palm in a friendly way. "You're the most brilliant student I've ever had in my life. Thank you for that. I wish you to understand every sign of God that you come across in your life."

"What if I don't?"

"You will."

"And the people?"

Kanaka thought for a while, ran his hand down his chin, and smiled kindly. "There was once a sower, whose grains fell on the edge of a road. Some birds came down and ate them. Other grains fell on a rock, and the sun rose and burned them. Others fell into some thorn bushes, which smothered them. But many fell on good soil and yielded a crop. Some a sixfold, some a hundredfold, others a thousandfold."

"I don't understand," Jesus objected.

"Let those who have ears listen," Kanaka smiled. He watched Jesus, whose mind was obviously wandering. "Do you want to know which is man's first and greatest attachment?"

"Love?"

"Indeed so." Kanaka nodded, put his arm amicably around his shoulders and led him over to his medicinal cabinet. He took out a white-orange alabaster cup, fondled it for a long time, then turned it toward the sun, whose rays reflected off the peculiar chalice-shaped vessel in a beautiful colorful spectrum. He removed the stopper and let Jesus smell it.

"Holy spikenard oil. It serves both life and death equally well. We used it for both embalming and healing. It's made from a precious plant that grows in high mountain regions. We call it jatamansi in Sanskrit, and it's known as valerian in the West. It's got marvelous healing effects; the Ayurveda regards it as the perfect medicine for vata-type people."

"That's those who worry needlessly," Jesus smiled.

"No, that's those who don't worry needlessly but love others more than they love themselves," the teacher corrected him. "It heals wounds, disinfects, and above all, it strengthens the mind."

"The scent is a little like roses and lavender," Jesus smelled it again. "I think we call it nard in Hebrew."

"Yes. It's nardos in Greek. We also call it oil of the infatuated. The scent of the oil is capable of evoking an illusion that you're with the one you love."

"I would need gallons of that," Jesus smiled bitterly.

Kanaka caught his hand. "Are you attracted to the girl you once told me about?" Jesus said nothing. "I too used to suffer like this, when I was unlucky in love..." Kanaka tried to console him.

"I can't drive her image from before my eyes. She's not only in my eyes, she's in my heart. I thought I'd forget her with distance and concentration on my studies, but I can't..."

"Birth is suffering, death is suffering, disease is suffering, union with an unloved person is suffering, and separation from a loved one is suffering. The cause of suffering is desire. The end of suffering cannot be achieved by fulfilling desire, but – as I've told you – by detaching from it. You will attain this state through austerity, which is the basis for self-discipline, the only path to victory without a fight. We all fight others, yet the winner is the one who doesn't need a loser."

"I had enough austerity at Dositheos' monastery. I don't think it made much sense."

Kanaka gave him a roguish smile. "I too was in a monastery, but not one like you have in your country. Yes, one is only strengthened by struggling with temptation, and that is indeed missing in your monasteries. In our monasteries, though, temptation is the important bit. It's the burden that God loads on you, and when you can lift it, you will detach yourself."

"How am I to understand that? What temptation?"

Kanaka looked at him secretively. "It would be best if you stayed in such a monastery yourself. Our students undertake stays compulsorily, but you're a guest here and so you may decide freely."

"My dear teacher, you know your words and recommendations are holy to me. I'd love to go to such a monastery."

"Then I recommend the one I've been to. It's a week's horse ride from here. It's in Kashmir. Kashmir, Nepal, Tibet and areas high up in the Himalayan valleys became the retreat for the Buddha and the center of his teachings when he fled the aggressive persecution of the Hindu Brahmin priests."

"Where is your monastery?" Jesus asked impatiently.

"Beyond the mountain ridge of Panjal is Srinagar, which King Ashoka transformed into a center of Buddhism. That's where the Dajendra Vihara monastery is, where you will learn to detach yourself. If you can do that, you'll reach out for nirvana."

54 Afraid to Tell You

"It's an excellent idea, we'll set out tomorrow morning. We'll arrive there when the spring meadows are lit most beautifully. Father has called a few times to ask what was taking us so long," Eli said merrily. Breakfasts together on the houseboat energized them all incredibly. They would sit in the morning air every morning shortly after daybreak and meditate together to the sounds of the muezzin summoning Muslims for morning prayers. His clear voice flowed over the lake and created a magical atmosphere.

Marika and Michal had spent a week in Srinagar and the only places they'd seen so far were the boat deck and the laboratories of the professor's clinic. Due to the total weakness of Marika's body, she was strictly forbidden from leaving the boat. Today they'd finally go to Sonamarg, where she'd place herself into Doctor Bashrat's hands, her last hope. They loaded everything they needed on an off-road car after breakfast; Marika and Michal's baggage had grown with some warm clothes, several pairs of hiking boots and, above all, herbal blends prepared by Professor Vaidya in his lab based on Ghulam Bashrat's instructions. Then they set off.

They reached the arterial road for Sonamarg about an hour later. Eli was in a good mood, the sun shining off the limpid Kashmiri sky made their faces smile. The sun's rays were also warming Marika's hopes and brought a cautious smile to her face.

"We're driving toward Leh. The weather's fine, we should reach Sonamarg in two hours at the latest. It's heaven on earth, you'll see. That's why father has opened his summer consulting room there. He has a winter one in Srinagar too. He's like the government of Kashmir: it sits in Jammu in winter and in Srinagar in summer," Eli laughed.

Michal and Marika were sitting in the back seat, observing the countryside curiously and listening to Eli's presentation.

"Sonamarg is located at eight thousand nine hundred feet. Past it, the road climbs to the Zoji Pass, beyond which lies Ladakh, the Buddhist part of Kashmir, dubbed Little Tibet. The first town on the other side of the pass is Dras, the second coldest place in Asia, where minus 47 degrees Fahrenheit has been measured. In Sonamarg, drivers of various religions pray to their gods to protect them from the dangers that lie on the road ahead. The roads climbing to the Zoji Pass are more than eleven thousand feet above sea level and are extremely dangerous."

They didn't even notice how quickly the time passed. When the car entered the widening Sonamarg valley before nine o'clock, they all understood why the marvelous valley was given the name Meadow of Gold. It was not only because gold used to be mined from the Sindh river flowing through it, but mainly due to the meadows strewn with primroses, pheasant's eyes, garlic, dandelions, milk thistles, buttercups and other golden yellow flowers that had begun to push their sun-longing heads from the melting snow.

"This really is heaven," said Marika, watching the beautiful country with her breath held.

"Only there are a few too many military convoys here," Michal remarked.

"Sonamarg Indian Army welcomes you. Headquarter Alpha sector," he read out loud the large banner spread across the road as they were entering the town. To his right he noticed a sprawling military camp with combat vehicles, tanks, helicopters and barracks for soldiers. "There's a garrison here too?"

"There are military garrisons almost everywhere in Kashmir. The Indian army has more than one and a half million soldiers, and over one half of those are in Kashmir," Eli explained. The engine rumbled, and houses spread along the road appeared soon.

"Here we are then." Eli stopped on the main road, composed on the left side of a long row of two-story houses with little shops and restaurants on the ground floor. Many were adorned with the proud name Hotel, even if they were just plain rooming houses for truck drivers. On the hillside on the opposite side, there were a few modern hotels for the wealthier clientele. Eli started to unload the baggage.

Suddenly, everything was deafened by music pouring out of loudspeakers on the lamp posts.

"So this is typical, listen to this," he laughed. Sonamarg was resounding with Muslim songs mixed with the sound of Indian melodies. "This is Kashmir in a nutshell. They play Hindu songs at the lower end and Muslim ones at the upper end. They mix up in the middle, which is where we are. Nobody minds it."

He thought for a while and then said, "It's not Muslims, Hindus or Christians that are dangerous to the world. It's fanatic Muslims, fanatic Hindus and fanatic Christians... So, this is my father's consulting room. And he's even coming to welcome us."

In the entrance to a newly built two-story house there stood a grayish, sun-tanned gentleman in his seventies with a thick mane of hair, gilt eyeglasses and a good-natured, cordial smile. His welcome was so spontaneous they felt they were old friends with Ghulam Bashrat.

"Welcome, dear Marika, dear Michal. Please, make yourselves at home." He hugged his son equally warmly and offered to help them with their baggage. But Michal and Eli carried up the stuff themselves. "Eli will show you to your room and then I'm expecting you in my parlor. How much time do you need for refreshment?"

"Not much. Maybe fifteen or twenty minutes."

The doctor smiled. "Do you prefer green tea from Assam or Darjeeling?"

"We'll leave that up to you." Marika reciprocated his smile.

She and Michal entered their simply furnished but clean room facing the river, whose torrential stream was playing its swift symphony. Marika went out onto the balcony and took a deep breath. "It's not air, it's literally prana, divine nectar."

Michal put an arm around her shoulders. "I feel everything's going to be alright."

"I think so too. Michal. I wasn't asleep in the car as we were coming from the airport. I heard everything you and Eli talked about. I'm sorry. I love you very much. I understood more from what he said about life and death during that short drive than from a heap of wise books." She ran a little out of breath. "This Doctor Bashrat and his son make an excellent impression on me. And everyone in general is extremely kind here."

Michal thought for a while about how to break it to her. "Do you know who the Bashrat family are?"

"No."

"In fact, I'm almost… afraid to tell you. Ľubo told me once, and Eli mentioned it to me only yesterday, when you were asleep. By all appearances, Doctor Ghulam Bashrat and his son are descendants of Jesus Christ."

"Of whom?" Marika nearly choked.

Michal gave her an enigmatic smile. "I guess he'll tell you everything himself. Let's join them."

55 An Unpermitted Wedding

Following the death of King Ashoka, the Buddhist monks slowly left from their positions in India and retreated into inaccessible monasteries in Tibet and Kashmir to escape persecution from the Brahman priests, who hated them for their doctrine of equality among people. The Dajendra Vihara monastery looked like a hideaway more than a place of meditation and an inspiration to solitude. Jesus was spending his fifth month here; he was not allowed to leave the walls of the monastery without permission from the superior or the king. In his solitude, he preferred to sit by the tiny window of his cell, which had a view of the peculiar structure on the opposite hill. It was the Throne of Solomon.

How much he'd heard about it! He asked the monks, but they knew little about the origin of the building. The superior Son told him that the building was purportedly founded by the Jewish King Solomon, who had arrived in Kashmir a thousand years ago along with King Hiram of Phoenicia to build a drainage canal for his Jewish ancestors so that they gained some arable land.

Jesus could only hope to visit the Throne of Solomon after completing the three-month white path, on which he'd set out after the initial meditations. After its completion, the superior would judge whether he had enough internal strength to withstand external temptations. During the three months, he was tempted by the devil daily in the form of a beautiful maiden with whom he would spend every night. He wouldn't wish this traditional method of reinforcing self-control on any normal, healthy man. For many years after passing this test, whenever asked what hell was, he answered that it was this. He experienced it from the first moment she entered his cell. He could hardly believe his eyes, but she was the spitting image of the Berber princess Mariam. The same dark skin, the same piercing dark-green eyes, the aquiline nose, the black birthmark on her left cheek, all crowned with her beautiful smile with dimples on her cheeks. He felt he was back on the prince's ship in the middle of the Red Sea. Mariam of Barbary, Miriam of Kashmir…

He fell in love with her after their first night together, which they spent lying naked next to each other in silence. It was the traditional acid test, as the monks referred to it. With her bare presence, the beautiful young woman seduced the young monk, who was undergoing a heroic battle with his desire. Jesus knew he'd lose control of himself once he started a conversation with her. He was very grateful to her for her silence. The more experienced monks shared with him the news that the attentive eye of the monastery's superior could be watching them through an inconspicuous hole in the ceiling, and that he'd be expelled from the monastery the moment he was found to have any physical contact with the woman. He begged God to give him strength to withstand the most powerful human instinct. From time to time he caught himself looking at, or in fact sensing her naked female body, which radiated a pleasant warmth and fragrance. The temptation was unbearable; he'd never had a woman although he was more than thirty. He felt her calm breathing, and his breathing merged with its rhythm. Each evening as she came to him, he was aware of her incredible likeness to the Berber Mariam. She even had identical gestures and movements.

Tonight, he'd meet the nameless woman for the last time in his nicely warmed cell with a comfortable wide mat for two. He couldn't wait for the evening. He was persuading himself that he could control himself, but his heart made every effort to break free of the influence of his cold reason, which told it to keep calm as it was the only way to reach the longed-for light. In the last hours spent with her, he'd withstand the voice of reason and not let his feelings take their natural course. In the course of those three months, he never stopped telling himself that it was not his Mariam lying next to him but a strange woman. But the one lying next to him was as magical, kindly, enchanting, wise and beautiful as his memory of the Berber princess.

She entered, took off her white robe and lay down beside him silently as she had done every day before. The monastery bell stroke midnight.

Jesus breathed heavily. Suddenly, his hand moved, as if by itself, closer to the woman's hand and clutched it.

Her hand lay motionless. "Don't spoil it," were the first words he heard from her. She had a beautiful and tranquilizing, velvety voice. He closed his eyes. It was the voice of his Berber Mariam. *Oh Lord, what are you playing at? Is it her? How did she get here? Did she die and is she reborn in this one? Why have you sent her to me and not any other? What have I done to deserve this test exactly?*

"You've endured for three months, more than ninety days, do endure the last day of your test."

Jesus suddenly broke out in a healthy laughter. He had to control himself to not make his unprompted laughter heard in the other cells. "You're wrong. The superior's wrong too. I'm a Jew, and for Jews a new day begins on the sunset, not the sunrise. So, this is not the last day of the third month for me, but the first day of the fourth."

She sat up and gave him a short uncomprehending look. Then she lay down again. He felt her hand grasp his firmly. The stream of her words broke the three months of silence. "Five years ago, when I turned eleven, my father brought me to this monastery. I'm from a poor family, you see, so my parents decided there was only one choice for me: to become a devadasi." She broke off, it was hard for her to speak. "When I was three, I was given a necklace of red and white beads and my fate was sealed. I wanted to kill myself at first, but I got used to it after some time. You can even get used to hell…"

"I still don't understand." Jesus looked her straight in the eyes. She was breathing rapidly, her white breasts were rising in a wild rhythm, which Jesus watched sideways, excited. Suddenly he regretted there was only one flickering torch in the cell. She seemed more excited by him than her ancestors' silly customs.

"According to tradition, being a devadasi is a woman's most sacred task. I'll never forget the day when they gathered us, ten girls, in guru Champa's large shrine and wed us symbolically to some god before the gluttonous looks of priests. As soon as the ceremony was over, they came to get us…"

"What followed after the wedding?"

"They would rape us. They turned us into monastic prostitutes. They say the Buddha himself used to do that, but I don't believe that."

Jesus clenched his teeth in anger. "The worst atrocities are most easily committed in the name of saints."

"Young girls who embody temptation have been in Hindu and Buddhist monasteries since time immemorial. They learn to play the bansuri, dance and sing... I serve the pleasure of priests and tempt monks and novices. They say the sexual force is the strongest force in the universe. He who masters it will discover the philosophers' stone and become a white magus. I don't know..."

"I too was told that a person isn't the master of the sexual force if they're at a low level of consciousness, but it controls them, and they aren't aware that the sexual force is so empowering that it can open the door to the power of the spirit, control over matter, nature, find the key to the philosophers' stone, and become a white magus. Hm," he ruminated. He felt the girl clasping his hand more firmly.

"It's terrible!" he burst out. "How many were those priests?" She made no reply. "And the monks you've tempted like this?"

"I don't know, I haven't counted them. About twenty in those five years..." her voice faltered.

"And how many managed to withstand the temptation?"

She laughed bitterly. "Those who didn't lust for a woman or preferred unclean intercourse. Out of the normal ones, you're the only one."

"You say it as if you felt sorry about it."

"I didn't want any of those who had me. The only one I really wanted... is you. But you've become a white magus. You've controlled your sexual force; you've discovered the source of life. I've had lots of men, but I loved none of them. Only... now..." They lay side by side, and Jesus observed the flickering shadows of the torch on the ceiling. He turned to her and looked her straight in the eyes.

They were exactly like princess Mariam's eyes. She was weeping. He wiped her tears. "You've made it too. All these three months we spent lying next to each other every night, I felt your longing for me..."

"... I can still feel your longing for me now..."

In her eyes, he could see the entire universe with its corners beyond sight, and she was in each of them. He knew she wasn't the Berber Mariam, but he felt this woman was destined for him. He was reflected in those pitch-black eyes like in a mirror. Heated by desire, he leaned to her. She started circling on his lips slowly with her index finger. It was their first physical contact. It electrified him. No woman had ever touched him like that. She seemed to chant something monotonously, mysteriously. He wasn't even realizing it, but his mouth was making identical sounds. He lifted himself a little and wanted to embrace her, but she halted him with a movement as light as a feather.

"We always had women teachers of union, not men."

They watched their naked bodies for a long time. Her finger slowly ran down to his chin and then to his chest. The lower down it went, the faster his breathing became, his heart was beating at a faster rate, and blood was rushing to his head. He felt as if it was going to burst with excitement, that it would spill across the room charged with the force of love transformed into sexual energy. He felt he could smell the strange fragrance of myrrh and spikenard, see an infinite blue light, and hear the sound of zithers. Her mouth came close to his. He could feel her pleasant warmth, their bodies both trembled, her hand continued downward and then it returned. He too dared to touch her body. She didn't resist. Time ceased to exist. It was beginning to dawn and their bodies, charged with the energy ready to explode at any instant, were trembling with escalating desire. They were trying to control their excitement, but they were increasingly failing, as the pleasure of the anticipation was flooding their bodies and souls. She had her hands resting on his abdomen, her eyes closed, and so did he. When she felt his excitement reaching its high point, she gently caught his hand and stopped him. The first wave of desire subsided. She allowed him to develop another, but then she stopped that as well. Then they continued like that until the climax. At the highest peak of trance, their bodies tingled in absolute trust. They entered the highest level of essence in the rhythm of the universe, the eternal vibration of life and death. They had reached the perfect universal union. They created Oneness. Their souls' three-month individual journeys amalgamated. Unum prevailed. The sun entered the cell. Her mouth was whispering in a tongue that Jesus hadn't heard in a long time. It seemed to emanate from a great distance, a place where only echoes dwell. He realized the girl was speaking in Hebrew.

"I love you," she said.

"And I love you."

"I've got to go now."

"What's your name?"

"Mariam."

"What?" he stared at her in a state of shock.

"Mariam."

"Are you a Jew?"

"Why?"

"Sorry, but you whispered the Hebrew words *lay me on your heart because love is as powerful as death*... those are words of Solomon's Song of Songs."

"I am a Jew. I heard my ancestors came here with Alexander the Great from the kingdom of Siwa in western Egypt. The king was there to hunt for lions in the desert."

Jesus stared at her inquisitively. "How can you get out of here?"

She thought for a while, then said quietly, "Only if I get married."

* * * * *

The monastery's superior, Son, invited him to his cell on the next day. There was a man wearing riding clothes waiting for him as well.

"A messenger from King Gondophares."

"Sir," the man bowed and handed a document with a royal seal to Jesus. He gathered from the man's grave expression that the news wasn't good. He removed the royal seal and opened the envelope. There were two letters in it. In the first one, the king informed him that after reading a letter from his mother, he asked the reputable merchant Al Rawahi, whose caravan would soon leave the city of Pattala on the Indus for Palestine, to take him along. The esteemed Al Rawahi was offering the honorable son of Joseph a prominent place in the caravan. The other letter was from Jesus' mother. It had been brought by the merchant Evyatar of Nazareth, continuing to Sian in China. His mother informed him that his father had died and asked him to come back and mourn together with the family. It would be his honorary role to collect his father's dry bones a year later and store them in the ossuary for good. Jesus finished reading.

"Sir, your horse is ready," the king's messenger bowed again.

Jesus paced up and down Son's room nervously, then he looked at the abbot. "Brother Son, I'm going to Palestine. But before I do so, I must fulfill a promise. Only you can help me with it."

"My brother, white magus, I'll be happy to oblige as much as I can."

"I want to get married."

"I thought you came here for our wisdom, which is like clear spring water and is best drunk in meditation…"

"Yes, that's why I came here."

"But… but… how are you going to accept the wisdom of the Vedas and the Buddha if you have a wife?"

"Wasn't the great Siddhartha married as well? Brother Son, I revere and love you greatly, but my love to the woman is greater."

Son sized him up for a long while. He'd enjoyed watching Jesus' union with Mariam through the ceiling hole the night before.

"Is she the prostitute?"

Jesus nodded. "And please stop calling her that. She's my wife. I got to know her last night. I'd like you to confirm our union with an official wedding ceremony."

"A wedding? That's out of the question altogether. She's forever devoted to gods," the superior raised his voice. "She's our best singer and dancer, our puja ceremonies would be no good without her!"

"Your intercourse would be no good. I know what you have these girls for. I'm asking you to marry us!" Jesus raised his voice too.

Son clenched his jaws. "It's not as easy as that here. Things have to be examined with a horoscope first to see what prospects your relationship has."

"Good prospects I'm sure, we love each other," Jesus interrupted him coldly.

"That doesn't matter the least!" The abbot was losing control of himself.

Jesus didn't want to abuse his good relationship with the king, but when he saw that Son was readying to leave, he said firmly, "I'm asking you in the name of Gondophares. I think you care for good relationships with the king!"

Son stopped, veins on his temples slightly throbbing. He paced up and down for a while in silence, then gave Jesus a kindly look. "You don't know her family, her family doesn't know your family; according to our tradition parents choose partners for marriage, not themselves. Few people here know who you are, and as far as I know, Mariam's family is very poor. They come from the herdsmen's valley of Pahalgam, where traditions are observed very consistently."

"Brother Son, with due respect to your traditions, now isn't the right time to adhere to them," Jesus replied more calmly.

"But you should at least see her father and inform him. The bride's father sets the wedding date in these parts. If you fail to do so, you'll insult her family and her brothers won't forgive you for that… you see what I mean?!"

"The trip to Pahalgam would take me at least two days and two more to come back. I can't afford that; the caravan isn't going to wait for me. And after all, as far as I know, Mariam's father disposed of his daughter."

"What do you mean, disposed?"

"He simply sold her to you. He made her become a monastic prostitute."

"Being a devadasi – a monastery servant – is an honor and recognition for young women."

"Do you think they're convinced of it too?"

The superior said nothing. A horse neighed outside.

"Brother Son, please, marry us."

"I can't do that. I'm not taking her family's wrath on me."

"Are you taking her slow death in here on you? Her only way out of the monastery is through marriage."

"We've never had anything like this before," he protested.

"You've got to start one day."

The abbot smiled at him affirmatively. "But it will be an unpermitted wedding according to our tradition."

After the wedding ceremony, which took under an hour, they made an entry in the monastery chronicle, signed by the abbot and two monks as witnesses. The young people's faces were aglow with happiness. Mariam sat on the horse in front of Jesus and they set out toward Srinagar, followed by the king's messenger.

56 A Murderous Conflict

Doctor Bashrat's living room doubled up as his consulting room. They wouldn't have noticed if he hadn't told them. The space made the impression of a homely room, furnished with typical Indian mahogany furniture, the floor covered with a large cashmere carpet, a tapestry with varicolored flowers on one wall and a large painting on another, showing a minaret next to a female figure with an elephantine nose next to Christ. There was a crescent over the minaret, a Buddhist and Hindu Om symbol next to it, and a Christian cross over Christ. Marika and Michal examined the unusual painting for a long time. The doctor poured tea for everyone.

"That's a painting of tolerance and understanding. Muslims, Hindus, Buddhists, Christians, everyone has lived in peace here since time immemorial."

"Are you Christians?" Michal asked.

"We're Muslims, but to me being a good Muslim means also being a good Christian, a good Hindu, and a good Jew," Bashrat replied calmly.

"Do you believe in God?" Marika asked.

"Do you know of anyone who doesn't believe in God? Everyone who believes in good, love, justice, that everything on this earth has a meaning and purpose, believes in God." He sized Marika up. "Do you believe?"

"I'm trying…"

"You must believe. Else you won't be cured. Do you have anything or anyone that you trust absolutely? God, the Buddha, Jesus, a locket…"

Marika thought for a while. "My husband."

They all laughed heartily. "Well, congratulations, that's wonderful, but I meant a sort of splendid idea, a universal moral personality or a special place…"

"I believe the energy of Jesus will help me."

"That's why you came to Srinagar?" She nodded.

"Do you believe he's buried here?" She agreed silently.

"You've come to the right place. I assure you this belief will help you."

"Do you believe his bones are buried in Roza Bal?" Michal turned to ask the doctor.

The doctor analyzed him momentarily. His eyes emanated a strange glow that Michal and Marika had never seen before.

"I know it." He stared Michal straight in the eyes with a special, mesmerizing look, his thick white hair falling gently over his forehead. He turned to Marika. "Jesus is one part of your belief. I'm the other one. Do you believe I will help you?"

"I do."

"I've been a healer all my life. I've helped get rid of cancer even in those in whom chemotherapy, surgery and irradiation had failed. True, I haven't had a case as serious as yours. I've carefully gone through the results of all the test carried out by my venerable colleague Professor Vaidya. Hm... I'm taking you as a challenge."

"I beg your pardon, are you a professor as well?" Marika asked flippantly.

"Yes, of finance. I studied at the University of Lahore and when it split, I worked as the head of the financial department of the government of Kashmir."

"So, you..."

"No, I have no medical education. I've learned everything by myself. Or better said... somebody's taught me well; it's kind of always been in me... Just like in Eli here."

"Is it true you're descendants of Christ?" Marika burst out suddenly.

The doctor smiled, took her pulse calmly with three fingers and gestured for her not to disturb him. A moment later, he said, "We need to cool down the vata. And cleanse the blood. Are you ready for a forty-day fast?"

"I've been expecting it."

"Have you ever done a longer fast?"

"I have."

"How long?"

"Forty days."

He looked at her in surprise. "Did you do it under medical supervision?"

"No, only under a friend's supervision; she had experience with it."

"Did it help her?"

"It seemed to at first, but then… her cancer returned."

"Is she alive?"

She nodded. "But they took her breast."

The doctor broke off for a while. Then he stood up and took a vial with some little gray balls out of a drawer. "This is a medicine made by the Tibetan monk Tonzin Chodrak. He made it according to the Kalachakra Tantra."

"What is the Kalachakra?"

"An ancient Tibetan prophecy. It speaks of new diseases that people of the future will suffer the most. Cancer is one of these diseases. Chodrak also made a prescription against cancer."

"When?" Marika asked.

"Before Christ. It contains gold, silver, copper, iron, tourmaline, a pearl extract, a powder from emerald, turquoise, diamonds, sapphire, and ruby, all in a detoxified form. That's complemented by herbs such as saffron, bamboo essence, nutmeg tree, pokeweed, clove, crazyweed, barberry, and nearly a hundred more ingredients. This medicine is a hundred times more effective than all chemotherapy and irradiation combined and it has no side effects."

Marika's eyes lit up with hope, which she'd been hiding deep inside so far.

"Is this the famous medicine that saved the lives of many in Chernobyl?" Michal asked.

"It is."

"I'd believe you even without it," Marika said.

"Nobody knows the secret formula except he."

"Why didn't he release it for others?"

"He feared that if people knew an almost perfect medicine against cancer, they'd begin to act and live irresponsibly. Take two balls at a time every day at daybreak while praying, and two at dusk while praying. You will fast and drink only pure energized water. If possible, wear yellow, orange or red clothes. I'll also give you this stone. It's jasper. It's the best cleanser and harmonizer of chakras; it helps the healing, absorbs negative energies, reduces stress and tension, and most importantly, it removes from the body any electromagnetic and other contamination, chiefly radiation, of which you've received immense quantities during your treatment this far. That's the fundamental cause of your energy depletion: chemotherapy and irradiation. In addition, you will put on the Bala Narayana oil every morning, noon and evening. You'll leave it to take effect for ninety minutes. Then you'll drink warm energized water again for fifteen minutes. It's important to start a gentle sweating. The oil and the warmth are important for vata control."

"What's this vata?"

"How would I explain simply? All the physical and mental processes in the body are governed by three humors: the vata, pitta and kapha. However, these three humors put every person in a certain place in the universe, of which they are a part. In modern, allopathic medicine, a disease is essentially suppressed by identifying its symptoms. We remove a headache, a toothache, a fever, but we don't investigate into why the teeth or the headache. But Ayurveda is a holistic medicine. According to Ayurveda, an imbalance among the three humors is the cause of health defects. Vata originates from the ether and the air and is responsible for everything that is associated with fast movements. The brain, peripheral nerves, excretion, bodily movements, breathing, fear, pain..." He took a half-quart bottle of oil from a drawer; its scent seemed familiar to her. "Eli will apply this oil to you every day. The application will be painful at first, but the pain will subside over time as your condition improves."

"Doctor, why do they have to take so many women's breasts away?"

"I don't mean to be sarcastic, but your physicians remove women's breasts, not cancer. As a rule, when you remove one node, the diseased cells shift elsewhere. They don't treat the diseased cell but instead kill them. But we use love even in our medical treatment. A cell is a living organism, and we want it to have trust in us. We don't kill it, we heal it. It's like an updated version of the commandment: thou shalt not kill a cell," he smiled. "Violence provokes fear, even in cells. But if you heal it, you achieve trust. The cell nucleus contains chromosomes, which are the carriers of genetic information: heredity. The cell nucleus controls all the life functions of the cell, including breathing. But the cell also contains other components, invisible to the human eye. These include spiritual particles, flowing from spiritual centers to our world of perception, where they initiate the formation of elementary particles and atoms. They are linked with the spiritual emanation of the human spirit, incarnated in the earthly body. Unfortunately, the emanation of the human spirit is significantly weakened nowadays because a person grounded in the world is mainly concerned with the material.

"Their emanation is therefore unable to fully animate the function of cells and organs to produce a radiant healthy condition. In a situation where the spiritual emanation is weakened, the bodily damage factor due to long-term irritation of cells with toxic substances becomes most prominent. Oxygen supply to cells is impaired, fermentation occurs in them and it produces a swelling: a tumor, which starts invading adjacent healthy cells, just as a bad apple in a basket slowly spoils the good ones as well. Diseased cells also enter other parts of the body via the blood circulation. If you want to understand a disease, any disease, not just cancer, you have to understand the cell and the soul. No disease is curable if you treat it only at the physical level, ignoring the spiritual one."

"So then the whole so-called Western medicine, based exclusively on material treatment, is good for nothing?"

"Such treatment is good for nothing if you don't include your soul in the healing process. Not only the human being, but also its cells require love…

"Lest I forget the most important thing: Every day, every possible moment, any time you remember to, you tell yourself the mantra: I'm healthy, Jesus has healed me."

She gave him a surprised look. "You're a Muslim and you believe in Jesus?"

"You believe in him, and your faith will heal you. Nobody has ever been cured without faith. But only if the faith is based in God's laws. If it's based on material laws, such a faith is destructive for humans. One of the cardinal factors of Catholic religion is sin. From infancy, a Catholic child is indoctrinated with a sense of guilt. A Catholic Christian lives his whole life in remorse. And what is remorse?"

"Stress," Marika replied dryly.

"Exactly. As far as I know, Christ never mentions sin. I've studied the gospels very carefully. Jesus doesn't know sin or punishment, only human failure and forgiveness. Did you have a strict Catholic upbringing?"

Marika nodded. "It's a kind of tradition where I come from."

"Nothing's more harmful than bad traditions. This is the worst one. Liberate yourself from its slavery and walk freely down the path of Jesus and the Buddha. Your cells are literally begging you to do so. They aren't set up for long-term stress caused by a sense of permanent guilt."

They sat silent together for a while, and then Doctor Bashrat stood up, poured everyone some green tea and gave them an encouraging smile. "So then, let's get down to work. First, we must cleanse you perfectly. You'll fast and take special medication according to my instructions. It won't be pleasant, things are going to come out of all your orifices," the physician nodded his head warningly. "But you'll feel a great relief in three or four days."

Marika's face screwed up in pain momentarily.

"The foot?" the doctor asked. She nodded. "Come on, show me."

He took her left foot gently, put it on his leg, and held her sore sole in his hands for a long while. She could sense a pleasant, relieving warmth penetrating her leg through the sole of her foot and continuing onward into her whole body. The pain disappeared after some time. "Alright?" he asked.

"Alright. What happened?"

"Nothing, you just trusted me," he smiled. "Remember this day. It's the day of impregnation of your mind with faith, which will result in the birth of a new, healthy Marika."

Doctor Bashrat indicated that their first consultation was over. Marika stood up, thinking of how to ask him about what she cared about the most. "Excuse me, you asked me if I had something that I'm convinced would help me... Doctor, I have a great request to make to you. I'd like to go pray in Jesus' tomb."

"I understand you absolutely, I too care about you getting there, only it's not as easy these days. It's almost impossible. The only person who could help me... hm..." he paused dramatically for a moment, "... is me. My family are the guardians of the tomb. My cousin Sahib has the keys. He can only give them out to me and the general director of Kashmiri police."

"When could we go?" she asked impatiently.

"It's impossible during the day, something's hanging in the air. We must go early in the morning, while our Muslim brethren are praying in the mosque, because Roza Bal is also the resting place of a Muslim saint and unbelievers are forbidden from entering it. Surely you understand it would be a risk for me as well. All the more that the government of Kashmir has strictly forbidden all entry into the shrine without the consent of the police chief. Besides, we can't interrupt your fast. No way."

"I... I'd like to, if at all possible, to visit the tomb before I start my fast. It's very, very important for me... Do you see..."

The doctor gave her a long look. "The situation in the city is very tense. The declaration of a state of emergency is expected. You know, this murderous conflict has cost more than seventy thousand human lives. They say that the number of divisions of the Central Reserve Police Force has increased from the normal twenty-eight to thirty-five. That's thirty-five thousand elite police officers armed to the teeth in Srinagar alone, five thousand state police on alert, countless secret agents, plus one detail: six hundred thousand soldiers of the regular army. Three unsuspecting people were killed in the city yesterday. An eleven-year-old girl was badly injured helping her father collect old cartons in the streets to make their two dollars a day..."

"Sorry, father, how do you know that?" Eli asked.

"Her father, Mohammed, has been collecting cartons in our street for twenty years. He called me yesterday if I could lend him some money for an operation for his daughter, otherwise she'd die."

"How much was it?"

"Fifty thousand rupees."

"Where did you get them?"

"I sold our motorbike."

"Did it help?"

"She's saved."

"Alright, father. Thank you."

Doctor Bashrat turned to Marika. "The Roza Bal shrine is situated in the Khanyaar neighborhood, the most dangerous part of the city. It's in the middle of the old city." He paused. "Oh my God... oh my God... We have a state of emergency perpetually in fact. Kashmiri police have no scruples... The biggest problem is there's also an important Sufi saint buried in the tomb, and the Muslim adamantly refuse any attempt of so-called unbelievers – non-Muslims – to enter the tomb, as they purportedly desecrate it... But I understand how much it means to you.

I'll try to do something about it. I'll let you know. Tonight. For the time being, don't take the medicaments I've prescribed for you. Don't start the fasting either. You'll go for walks and, most importantly, spend as much time as you can in our Kashmiri sun and air; you'll take Chodrak's medicine, Eli will massage you with the oil, you can drink energized water, of course you won't eat any meat, just fruit and vegetables, and you'll apply jasper."

"Why jasper of all stones?"

"Read the Book of Revelation. In the chapter *Heavenly Jerusalem*, which symbolizes rebirth, you'll read that the brilliance of New Jerusalem is like that of jasper. It's the first and founding stone of its walls. But maybe it's just a legend," the doctor smiled.

"I also wanted to ask you if you really are…"

"Now excuse me please. I've got to go to Srinagar in the morning to see the professor, but I'll be back in the afternoon."

57 A Perfect Prophecy

King Gondophares clutched Jesus' hand. "My dear son, please accept my heartfelt condolences. I didn't know your father closely. I know he wasn't your blood father, but he must have been a good man to raise such a son. I cannot judge how much your faith commands you to go home…"

"Yes, my father Joseph was a good man. I will go home, bow to him and comfort my mother. Although…" he thought for a moment, "… my heart tells me to stay here."

"Yes, the rumor of your unusual wedding with Mariam, the daughter of a Pahalgam shepherd, has reached my ears. I must give you a fatherly admonition: we're not accustomed to this sort of thing in these parts. She has escaped the monastery thanks to your big-hearted deed, I admit that, but I'm afraid she won't receive a warm welcome at home…"

"It was no big-hearted deed. I honestly love her," Jesus replied nervously, "and I can't go to Pahalgam because the caravan sets out tomorrow…" Then he paused in embarrassment.

As if reading Jesus' thoughts, the king said, "Of course my palace will be your wife's abode until you come back."

Jesus noticed the rancorous looks of the king's courtiers, obviously not too excited about the monarch's offer to the foreigner. It was to them more than to the king that he addressed the pleading words, "Your highness, Mariam is modest and will be useful to your court. She masters the bansuri, sings and dances beautifully…"

"You don't have to persuade me, the sojourn of Isu Asaf's wife will be an honor for my house. You have my word." The king took him by the shoulders amicably. "At least you have one more reason to return." Then he thought for a moment. "Things are not good back at your place.

A certain Pontius Pilate has superseded prefect Valerius Gratus in Judea. The Emperor Tiberius has purportedly appointed him according to recommendation by Sejanus, the chief commander of the Praetorian Guard, in which he was known as an elite and feared equestrian. Sejanus is notorious for his hatred toward Jews. I fear bad times are ahead in your country. Upon examining your horoscope, our astrologers have predicted the worst for you during your stay at home," the king tried to convince him.

"What do you mean 'the worst'?"

"Death."

"Let it be so if it's God's will…"

"Isa, please, come back as soon as you can. It's your mission. I know Brahmin priests hate you, but they have no influence in my kingdom or in Kashmir. Dear Isa," Gondophares walked up to Jesus and embraced him, "I love you as my own son. Maybe even more. I'm not the youngest…"

"But Rav Anna is your son."

"Of course, he's my only son, only," the king hesitated and ran his hand down his chin, "only he's falling to the influence of the Brahmins a bit more than his father would like him to. To be precise, our opinions on religion are very different. He accepts the priests' doctrine uncritically although, I admit, sometimes I feel he might be ready to think, but…"

"You're a king, and you have to respect the priests according to your caste system."

"I have respected them all my life, but the older I become, the more aware I am of how such faith is harmful to one. And I'm increasingly aware of the beneficial effect of the teachings of our great enlightened Gautama the Buddha."

"Are you refusing the primacy of Brahmins?" Jesus asked in surprise.

"It's my duty to be happy. And the Brahmins' doctrine is not from God but from themselves. It's been falling into formalism, opened its gates wide to hypocrisy and superstition. Voices against this doctrine dividing people into castes had been heard for ages, but none has managed to undermine and reveal the fraudulence of this system more than the Buddha has. He was the first in history to preach the principle of humanity, meaning that all people are equal in his teachings. You can imagine that this wasn't just a new doctrine but a revolution in a land of castes."

"He was indeed driven away from India to the Himalayas," Jesus remarked sadly.

"But nobody has managed to stop his doctrine from spreading even from up there. It's been disseminated around the world. People love him. Only the Buddha's teaching is suffering what's typical of any noble doctrine. When the powerful don't have enough power to crush it, they appropriate it, subjugate it and begin to adjust it to their needs. Even our Greek father of wisdom, the famous Socrates, was turned upside down by the powerful. He bravely taught the youth about morality and was then condemned for leading them astray!"

"Sorry, you said 'our Socrates': Do you have anything in common with the Greeks?"

"I do, but now isn't the time to explain the lengthy history," the king smiled and got back to his point. "Even our teaching has been adopting such terms as sin, guilt, punishment, humiliation of people. The worst thing is, though, that the man who preached that man is the center of everything is himself beginning to turn into God. Along with people of political power, priests are trying to install the Buddha on God's pedestal, and have even declared him to be God, although he never said in his lifetime that he was a son of God."

Why are you telling me all this?" Jesus asked.

"My son, I know your ambition is to unite the Jews." Jesus nodded. "But that's too little. You ought to have the ambition to unite all people of good will. Indians, Jews, Persians, Romans, Greeks, Armenians, Egyptians, Phoenicians, Chinese, all these marvelous peoples wish but one thing: peace and love. Only they're hindered by the leaders of their countries and religions."

Jesus thought about that. "It's funny that a king should be telling me this."

"I'm not going to be king for long. Rav Anna is going to take over my royal scepter. I'm afraid that the Buddha's teaching of loving one's neighbor will be lost. Every king and emperor since Nebuchadnezzar and Darius to Cyrus and Alexander fought for material values. A time is coming for a king who will fight for spiritual values. Your time's coming."

"My time?"

"Yours. You're not an ordinary Jew. You're from the lineage of the kings David and Solomon. You're the one who's destined to bring not only Jews, but everyone back home."

"Why do you think so?"

"And why do you think I brought you gold, incense and myrrh to Bethlehem back then, together with Balthazar and Melchior, my noble friends? Our astrologers, astronomers, occultists, philosophers and magi accurately recognize signs that herald a new Buddha. It was me who brought you myrrh: the symbol of the spirit and the healing power. All the circumstantial evidence of our great master Hillel matched ours. What do you think, why did I send my son to Jerusalem? Why did rabbi Hillel let his best student travel to the far east without a grumble?"

"Rav Anna was there for the sake of business."

"Of course he was in Palestine to do business, and not for the first time, but that one mission was different. The most precious article on the *Orissa* was not bitumen or gold, but you."

"Me?"

"Don't your miracles attest to your exceptionality? You've healed many by applying your hands even before you studied at our university; you sent a storm down on rabbis in Cochin, you sent rain down on the widow's funeral pyre..."

"That was all coincidence, I wasn't that educated about those matters yet. And I'd learned much from Udraka before I arrived at the university."

"That was no coincidence," the king mused. "How would I tell you... Palestine doesn't want you; it doesn't deserve you. According to the signs, you belong here, to this country. Dear Isa," he walked up to Jesus and embraced him in a fatherly way, "we're of the same lineage. I've forgotten our fathers' language, but I've kept their faith. The prophecy says, *'The world shall belong to the east, and men of Judea will rule it.'*" Then he paused for a while. "Palestine is ruled by money. Alexander's incursions have brought that custom here too, but if we fail to stop the power of money, it will ruin our ancient civilization, whose pivots are fleeing to the mountains. I wish the spirit of love and compassion continued to rule here. You're the son of the Buddha, not Moses. Moses invented guilt. It was the worst gift that the humankind could've been given. You haven't come to the world to abolish the law but to fulfill it. That's your attitude too, isn't it?"

Jesus pondered. "There's only one way to fulfill the old law: drawing up a new one. The old law is about punishment: the new one has to be about forgiveness. The old one's about hatred: the new has to be about love..."

"Precisely. The Buddha was the propagator of the new law. The power of his words has been vanishing since his death, because priests have been increasingly distorting it. But hope has come to us now. You've come to the world."

"What have I got to do with the Buddha?"

"More than you think. But before I tell you, promise me you will come back. You must come back, because your place is here, and your mission here has not ended by far. You must return to Kashmir; it's your true home. Kashmir is the Eden that Moses' Book mentions. He too is buried in our mountains," Gondophares smiled secretively.

"I'm sorry but Moses is buried under Mount Nebo in Transjordan Palestine."

"Has anyone ever found his remains there?" Jesus made no reply. "One part of the Torah says, *'Then Moses ascended Mount Nebo – Mount Pisgah.'*" The king watched the silent Jesus. "Then it says, *'Then Moses died in Moab and the Lord interred him opposite Bet Peor...'* Now Bet Peor refers to a place where a river spreads wide. There's a town of Bandipur where the Jhelum river leaves the mountains and spreads across the Kashmir Plains. It's located about a days' trip north of Srinagar. It was previously called Behat-pur and Bet Peor before that. North of Bandipur, above the Moab wasteland, is the Pisgah range, and the real Mount Nebo is two hours away from Bandipur."

"Impossible," Jesus shook his head in disbelief.

But Gondophares continued calmly. "At the foot of the mountain is a yard-tall stone in the shape of a column, and Rishis have taken care of it for almost a thousand years. North of Mount Nebo, as the locals call it, is the village of Hazbal, previously known as Heshbon..."

"The Book is coming true..." Jesus reacted in astonishment.

"Moses' tomb is waiting for you."

"If all of this is true, then it explains where Moses and his Jews wandered for forty years after leaving Egypt..." Jesus started pacing up and down the hall nervously. "What evidence have you got that I've anything to do with the Buddha?" he turned to the king sharply. The king stood up and walked over to Jesus with a smile on his face.

"Hand me the pouch you have on your neck, please." He pointed to the cloth sachet that Barata had given him. "Did your friend Barata give it to you when you arrived in Lumbini?"

"Yes," Jesus replied in a low voice.

"Do you remember the day you reached the Buddha's birthplace?"

"I do, exactly. It was twenty days after the spring equinox."

The king smiled and opened the pouch. "It contains soil from the place he was born. There's also a note indicating the day." The king spread out the tiny slip of paper before the surprised Jesus. "It states the exact date of your arrival to Lumbini." Then he smiled impishly. "Do you know why this day is significant?" Jesus shook his head. "In the Buddhist scripture *Laggawatti Sutatta*, Gautama Buddha speaks about the advent of a second Buddha five hundred years after himself, who will be of a white complexion and named the *Bagwa Metteia*. *Bagwa* means white in Sanskrit, and *metteia* is messiah."

"Interesting," Jesus shook his head again. "The Hebrew for a messiah is masiha."

The king wouldn't be interrupted, and he continued, "The Buddha says, 'There will come from the West a messiah who will be followed by thousands.'"

"I still can't see what I have to do with this prophecy," Jesus objected.

"You arrived in the Buddha's birthplace in Lumbini five hundred years after his death, precisely to the day. His prophecy has come true."

Jesus swallowed his saliva and gave the pouch in his sweating hand a long stare. He walked around the hall nervously, then he walked to the king and looked him firmly in the eyes.

"Thank you for your promise to take care of Mariam. I'll definitely come back!"

58 Jews in Kashmir

Doctor Bashrat's car left early in the morning. Eli massaged Marika's weary body with a refreshing oil, gave her the medicines as his father had ordered, and made tea for everyone. They were sitting on a terrace facing the river and relishing the beautiful morning.

"Excuse me," Michal asked, "are you a Muslim?"

"Yes, we're Sunni Muslims. Our ancestors converted to Islam from Christianity and Buddhism in the first half of the 14th century, when it arrived in Kashmir. My granddad used to have our complete genealogy in Hebrew, I saw it with my own eyes. The documents were lost mysteriously a few days before he was going to give them to my father. They were three large volumes."

"How do you know it was a genealogy? Do you read Hebrew?"

"There was a Sanskrit and Persian translation there too. It also included an accurate description of when and how the founder of our lineage arrived here; he was Isa, or Yuz Asaf, that is Joseph's son, as Jesus has been called in Kashmir."

"It's all just oral interpretations, legends," Michal pondered.

"I have something interesting here. An official document issued in 1766 for the guardian of the tomb, Rahman Mir. It's in fact a law concerning Roza Bal. Look, there's an English translation as well."

Michal took the photocopy of a text written in a script unknown to him and started to read out the English translation. *"In this kingdom, in the section dealing with doctrines and religions and in the Court of Justice, Rahman Mir, the son of Badahur Mir, states that aristocrats, ministers, kings, dignitaries and other venerable persons from all corners of the world come to the holy grave of Yuz Asaf (May God have mercy* on him), to commemorate him and bring him offerings. He testifies that he is doubtlessly authorized to accept and use these donations, that none but him have this right, and that he will prevent anyone who tries to encroach on his rights. Having examined the facts, it is stated that the man known as Yuz Asaf, who repaired the temple on Solomon's hill and built many more temples during the reign of King Gondophares, came to this country. He was a real and genuine prince; he turned away from earthly matters and fought for justice. He devoted himself to prayers to God day and night and spent much time in meditation. This happened after the first big flood in Kashmir, when people bowed to idols. The prophet Yuz Asaf was sent to preach to the people of Kashmir. He invoked the oneness of God until his dying day. He was buried in Mohalla Khanyaar on a riverbank, in a place known as Roza Bal. In 1451, Syed Nasri ud Din Rizvi, the son of imam Mosa Ali Reza was buried next to Yuz Asaf. As the place is regularly and equally visited by many outstanding as well as ordinary people, and since said Rahman Mir is the hereditary guardian of the place, he is hereby authorized to accept the sacrificial gifts that will be handed in there. Nobody has the right to said gifts and must not handle them. This is certified on the 11th of Jumada-al-Thani, 1184 AH. Undersigned Mullah Fazal, Mufti Azam, Abdul Shakur, Ahmadullah, and six more dignitaries."

"This Hijri year translates as the year 1766," Eli added and sipped some tea.

"It's interesting, but it doesn't prove anything," Michal said.

"The gospels don't contain any evidence of Jesus' being resurrected either; it's only mentioned that an empty tomb was found. That proves no more and no less than the fact he disappeared from the grave," Eli smiled.

"This may interest you too." He produced a pile of books in old bindings. "This is our real family treasure. When I have the time one day, I'll translate it all into English so that the world learns that the ten lost tribes of Israel came to India, Tibet and Kashmir via Afghanistan. They're works by numerous respected authors. *The History of the Afghans* by Niamatullah, as well as the famous work *Tarik-i-Hafiz Rahnmatkhani* by Hafiz Muhammad Zadek, in which he proves that Afghans are descendants of the Bani Israel, the tribes of Israel. There's also *The Lost Tribes,* written by George Moore in 1861, works of Sir

William Jones, Sir John Malcolm, Kashmiri historians Mullah Nadiri and Mullah Ahmad, which bring a lot of evidence on the Israeli origin of the Kashmiri."

"Can you name at least a few?" Michal asked curiously.

"For example, this book by Nazir Ahmad presents a list of more than three hundred Kashmiri tribal, family, caste and geographical references and female and male names that are completely or nearly identical to names in the Old Testament."

"Are you serious?"

Eli smiled. "Wait," he stood up and pulled a large edition of the English Bible out of a drawer. "Let's see. The Kashmiri tribe of Gaddi is mentioned in the Fourth Book of Moses 13:11, the Kashmiri tribe of Gomer is mentioned in the First Book of Moses 10:2, the Kashmiri tribe of Raphu is mentioned in the Fourth Book of Moses 13:9, the local name Babel in the Anantnag area of Kashmir is mentioned in Genesis 9:9, the name of Harran Lake in Srinagar is mentioned in the Book of Kings 19:12, the part of Srinagar known as Mamre is mentioned in Genesis 14:13, the place of Taharan in Kulgam is mentioned in the Fourth Book of Kings 26:35, the place of Suru near Bhawan..."

"Enough, enough, you don't need to name all three hundred!" Michal was shaking his head. "It's odd. May I?"

He took Eli's book in surprise and compared the names with those in the Old Testament. Marika joined him.

"Unbelievable. They all match."

Eli poured more tea and continued. "It really is odd. It can't be a coincidence that the name Israel is so popular among the people of Kashmir despite the fact they're Muslims, while it's not common in other Muslim countries. It's odd that the Kashmiri have customs and traditions identical to those of Jews: they light candles on Saturdays and wear the Star of David as a symbol. Like Jews, the Kashmiri only use oil for baking, never animal fat; the most popular dish in Kashmir is a boiled fish just like in Israel, and believe it or not, the fish is called the fari – the same as Jews call it. Young Kashmiri women practice a traditional dance: they stand in two opposing rows, join their hands over their heads and sway together. This dance is called *rof* and is known in Israel too. When a baby is born, Kashmiri women only bathe after forty days, which is an old Jewish custom. Many old graves in Kashmir are oriented east-west, which is the way the Jews bury their dead, while Muslims have north-south graves. There's a grave with a Hebrew inscription in an old cemetery in Bijibar. Kashmiri butchers use the same semi-circular meat cleaver as is used in Israel for preparing kosher dishes. And you saw on Dal Lake for yourselves that the fishermen's oars are heart-shaped: the same shape as oars on Lake Tiberias in Christ's time. Old Kashmiri and Jewish women wear almost identical clothes…"

"Wait, wait," Michal shook his head. "This is all amazing, but how does it prove Christ's presence in Kashmir?"

"There's a large winter hill station some thirty miles south of Srinagar, built on a vast meadow that's been called Yusmarg – Jesus' Meadow – since time immemorial. The people of the Yusmarg valley refer to themselves as Jadu and derive their origins from the Jewish tribe of Judah. Do you think it's a coincidence that the temple we're going to visit is named after Solomon? The temple is totally architecturally different from Hindu temples, which traditionally have a roof in the shape of a shikara boat, symbolizing the mountains in which gods reside. Indian temples used to be built under the supervision of Brahmins, who took strict care that Hindu temples had identical architecture. But this one is totally different.

"While we're there, notice the outer vault of the Throne of Solomon. Doesn't it remind you of something? Look," he picked up a photograph showing a kind of box, likely made of marble. On top of it, there were two opposing upper halves of two male bodies with raised arms leaning against each other. Marika and Michal stared at the picture in bewilderment.

"Who are these guys?" Michal asked.

"They are no guys, but cherubs, angels guarding the case of the old Jewish Ark of Covenant, which contains the Ten Commandments that Moses was given by God as he was leading the Jews out of Egypt. It's made entirely of pure gold. It's the tabernacle, containing the most precious item that's owned by the Jews. Or should be owned, to put it correctly. And it's not their hands that are joined, but their wings. This Ark used to be treasured in Jerusalem Temple from the time of King David. It was in fact the reason for building it. But six hundred years before Jesus, at the time of the Temple being destroyed by Nebuchadnezzar, the Ark was lost, and nobody has seen it since. Some say it's hidden in an underground passage under the Temple, others think it's by the Dead Sea, but there are also some who're convinced it's hidden right here, in Srinagar, in the secret interior of the Throne of Solomon.

Look," he showed them a photograph of the Throne of Solomon. "Can you see the clear analogy? The outer vault of the temple shows evident features of raised, protective angels' arms. What if the temple builder wanted to suggest something? And why is the temple named after a Jewish king? Notice, it's on an octagonal footprint, like many original buildings of old Israel. In 1869, the then superintendent of Indian archeological survey, Henry Hardy Cole, photographed the inscriptions on two interior columns of the temple, which were ultimately destroyed during a later renovation. Here they are."

Eli put on the table four photographs with some indecipherable signs. "They're in Persian."

"What do they say?" Michal asked eagerly.

"The first one says, 'Yuz Asaf started his mission at this time. It was in the year 54.' Another says, 'Yuz Asaf was a prophet of the children of Israel.' The third one, 'This column was erected by Raji Hashti Zarko in the year 54.' And the last one, 'This column was erected in the honor of Eli Kim, the son of Mariam.'"

Marika looked at him in surprise. "That's the same name as you have, and Mariam was..."

"Jesus' wife by all appearances."

"But why are the inscriptions in Persian?"

"The temple was rebuilt several times, and the inscriptions were always rewritten in the language of the ruler who renovated it. The first renovation was during the reign of Sultan Zain al Abidin in the 15th century. It's been proven that Thomas the Apostle was in India in the years 52 to 72. Even the Vatican doesn't deny that."

"Thomas in India?" Michal stared at him in disbelief.

"He's one of India's saints. He even appeared on an Indian postal stamp in 1972. In the year 394, his remains were transferred from Mailapur, where he'd been buried, to Edessa, present-day Uru in Turkey. These are documented facts. According to available information, he arrived at the court of King Gondophares in the year 49, and very probably Jesus arrived with him to manage the renovation works together."

"But why should foreigners repair the Throne of Solomon?"

"Maybe because it was used as a genizah, a place for hiding of holy Jewish relics."

"You have an amazing relationship to everything that's connected to the Old Testament," Michal remarked.

"You know, you do take interest if you're of Jewish origin. I know the New Testament decently as well. In chapter 15 of the Gospel of Matthew, Jesus says, *'I've been sent to the lost sheep of the house of Israel only.'*"

"Your name, Eli, is actually biblical as well. It's mentioned in the First Book of Samuel," Michal boasted.

"It's interesting that both you and your ancestors have unusual healing abilities," Marika nodded.

Eli wanted to show them some more documents, but the engine of the doctor's car whirred outside the house. Eli glanced at his watch, "Why would father be returning now?"

As soon as he finished saying that the annoyed Doctor Bashrat came up to the terrace. "They halted all traffic past Sonamarg and wouldn't let us go on. They're moving an endless military convoy toward Srinagar. They said the road would be opened in three hours if things went well. There we go, trouble is beginning," he sighed. "May I have some tea?"

An ominous silence descended on the terrace.

59 God Won't Help Us

Jesus said goodbye to Mariam outside the city gate, where she saw him off together with the king's retinue. He was leaving content. The king himself had shown him around the rooms that she would use as her apartment until his return. He had even been introduced to the servants made available to her for the whole time. Jesus embraced his wife firmly. At that moment, neither was aware that a new life was growing inside her body.

King Gondophares provided Jesus with a horse with a complete harness, on which he rode to Ashgar on the Indus river, less than a day's ride from Takshashila. There, the Nazarene was awaited by a royal twenty-oar rowboat, an unusually fast vessel, which transported him to the port of Pattala on the lower Indus in less than a week. There he joined the caravan of the Babylonian merchant Al Rawahi, which set out to the west via the Sindh province, following a similar route to Alexander the Great's army's return more than three centuries earlier. The caravan took a rest in the city of Rhambaxia, continued via the land of Geodrosia to the city of Pura, via Alexandria in Carmania to Pasargadae, where Jesus bowed to the tomb of King Cyrus the Great, who had released Jews from Babylonian captivity. They spent a longer time in the former capital of the Persian Empire, Persepolis, where there were still noticeable remains of destroyed palaces and burned-down buildings, set on fire by Alexander in person as an act of vengeance for the destruction of Athens by the Persian King Xerxes. In Persepolis, Jesus met with the sages Horus, Lunus and Merus, who invited him to the headquarters of the Silent Brotherhood association. During the week-long break, while the merchants were unloading and loading their wares, he debated with the sages about the legacy of Zarathustra, the founder of the oldest monotheistic religion and a philosopher of good and evil.

From Persepolis, the caravan continued to Susa, a former winter residence of Persian kings. Several days later they crossed the Tigris, reaching the caravan's destination in Babylon. From there, Jesus continued toward Damascus on his own, until he reached Nazareth three months later.

He was thirty-three years old. He was back in Galilee again after eighteen years. There were rumors that the emperor had withdrawn from Rome, but it was of no consequence for the conditions in the province. Jesus greeted his mother, who had hardly changed during his absence. Since she became a widow, his father's stepbrother Joseph of Arimathea was spending a lot of time in Nazareth, helping Mary secure a living for the family, getting seeds and fodder for the animals. The long absence had registered in the family's relationship to Jesus. When the rumor of his return spread, his brothers and sisters came to the house on Marmion Road, heard a few of his tales and then went back to their homes, which they'd established during his absence. His mother was staying alone in the house.

He was considering what to do next. His father's workshop was left in almost the same condition as when he'd left it years before. He mended the furniture, tools and the roof, but he didn't have the intention of staying at home. A year after the father's death, the whole family met again in Nazareth and went to his grave together. They opened the wooden sarcophagus, collected the bones as tradition commanded, and stored them in a small stone coffer. They carved their father's name on the coffer along with a warning for potential thieves. The family headed back home after the commemorative ceremony.

At the end of the funeral banquet, Jesus announced he had decided to go back to Dositheos' monastery. He was asking himself whether he really wished to go there, but it was the only place where he could retreat. None of his siblings protested, none tried to talk him out of it. On the contrary, they seemed to be relieved. He was sorry for his mother, who was in a difficult situation. She lived on her own; Jesus' older brothers Jacob, Joseph, Simon and Judah and sisters Rut and Lydia had their own families and there was no bond between them and their stepmother after their father's death. Mary knew it was pointless to try to change Jesus' mind and that his place in the house would remain vacant forever.

"Mother, don't you worry, I promise I'll take proper care of you."

He kissed his mother's hands and left the house on Marmion Road forever.

Jesus didn't receive a warm welcome in Dositheos' monastery either, although nobody had appropriated his mat. The atmosphere had changed radically compared to Jesus' first time in the monastery. It was now controlled by people who were fawning and bringing presents to the great master. Those who'd come with the objective to fortify themselves spiritually were overshadowed. Many of Dositheos' monks came from wealthy Sadducee families and it was obvious that their objective was not to prepare themselves for a path of humility but rather a priestly one. Dositheos had grown old, was spending ever more time in bed and was increasingly bad-tempered as his age progressed. Many of the Buddhist monks had gone back home or continued their mission in Egypt.

Jesus' only joy was his cousin John, with whom he became very close. He was the only one who listened attentively to his talks of distant India, and he himself told him about the Essene sect who lived in harmony with the Torah law. John had spent several years with them and recommended his cousin cordially to see them in Qumran for at least a short time. Three months later, Jesus and John decided to leave Dositheos' monastery. They set out to the south and parted after two days of travelling together. John aimed eastward for the desert toward Gerasa. Just in case, he gave Jesus a letter of recommendation for the Qumran monastery, situated in the inhospitable desert on the northwestern shore of the Dead Sea. For nearly two hundred years, it was inhabited by descendants of radical Hasidim, monks of the Essene sect who had left Jerusalem Temple in protest against the growing influence of the Sadducees, who they believed had desecrated the temple because their object was not to elevate the spirit of the Jewish nation but exclusively to attain power and positions in the temple hierarchy. The sprawling Qumran monastery compound contained lodgings, chapels, storerooms, purification rooms, classrooms, outhouses, baths, and huge stores of water carved in rocks to which water was brought from a well or from a mountains spring via an aqueduct. The monks stayed together, shared their property, drank no wine or other alcohol, and used their own workforce instead of slaves. Every morning, just after the sunrise, they gathered in the common bath to take a purification bath wearing loincloths. The central courtyard in the middle of the monastery compound was dominated by a two-story tower, surrounded by workshops for the manufacturing of daily use items, with a long hall in which the community members met, debated and dined. Next to the hall was a scripture room, where they copied holy texts. The most important ones included *The Handbook of Self-Control* and *The Community Law*. The monastery inhabitants referred to themselves as the sons of light and, like other Jews, they believed that the advent of the long-awaited Messiah would end the influence of the Romans and the Kingdom of Israel would be restored. The monastery walls were broken in places as a consequence of an earthquake fifty years before. Many of the monks retreated to the solitude of surrounding caves, where they meditated and fasted for months. Jesus made friends with Adam, the unusually young abbot of the monastery. He was a well-read man from Jerusalem, who'd arrived ten years earlier as a boy and earned great respect among the others with his conduct. In endless talks with Adam, Jesus got the impression that many things were unclear to him and that he himself wasn't convinced of many of the things he preached about to his brethren. However hard Jesus tried to behave like the other members and adhere to the Unity Order of Qumran in his first year, thoughts from India whirled through his mind. He had a growing impression that monks and priests were the same everywhere and only differed in their rituals, whereas the crucial thing – the right way – eluded them. Jesus expressed his discontent openly and clearly, and even Adam began to shun him over time. "Retreat to monasteries to avoid temptation. But remaining in a monastery is a manifestation of weakness, not strength. You act in quite the opposite way to how you ought to. The strong and brave ones will go out among the people, expose themselves to temptation and fight it."

"But when you don't need to worry about a wife and children, you don't have to fill the table with food every day, don't need to make money to pay taxes to Romans, Herod and the Temple, your hands and mind are liberated, so that you can serve God better and more effectively," Adam objected to the others' approving nods during one of the many common dinners.

"Your doctrine is alright, but every doctrine is like sourdough. It consists of many useful tenets that lead to a proper life. But for sourdough to have any beneficial effect, it has to rise. And it only rises when mixed with dough. Do you understand?"

"I don't," Adam shook his head.

"The sourdough in itself contains everything that's needed for bread to arise from dough. If you don't mix it into the dough, neither the sourdough nor the dough makes any sense. It goes bad in spite of its purity. Priests' wisdom and love are the sourdough, and people are the dough. They only make sense if they're together."

"But celibacy is the shortest way to God," one of the brethren objected.

"The shortest is the way of modesty and mercy. Blessed are the poor in spirit."

"What do you mean by poor in spirit? Do you mean fools?"

Jesus laughed heartily. "Almost everywhere I've said these words I've been asked this question. I mean poor for the sake of the spirit. It's those who are interested in spiritual matters and don't strive for possessions. They don't think about earthly matters and don't strive for them. Their purpose is the Kingdom of God inside them, not outside. The Kingdom of God is a state, not a place. Heaven and hell are not places outside us, but right inside each of us. Therefore, practice positive living and thinking, give and don't take, for only thus can you become just. And think about the purpose of celibacy. They preach it to you to prevent splitting of monastery property. That's the purpose of celibacy. That's why you ought to follow the married members of the brotherhood. They disseminate your advice and their descendants will be vectors of their ideas. Or do you want Essenes to die out?"

"All of that is clear to us," Adam objected, sounding irritated, when he saw some of monks nodding to Jesus' words. "You're not talking to some simpletons from the street who don't understand Moses' laws. Men in this monastery are well-educated and have their own reason. You don't need to preach to us about what's self-evident."

Jesus inhaled lightly and replied calmly, "For myself, I feel I'm needed more outside the monastery than within its walls. I'm sorry, brethren, I've never desired to be a monk, and I don't have the right mindset for the vocation. I think one best serves God when he serves amidst people. Your rigorous monastic order restricts one too much. One should take pleasure in life, not deliberately and willingly repudiate the joys offered by God."

"Life is a suffering, and it's the destiny of man to suffer."

Jesus thought for a moment. "And one more thing, brother Adam, I dislike the practice of your Essenes not admitting anyone with a physical defect; aren't the blind, the lame, the deaf or the stuttering identical children of God?"

"They hold the brotherhood back on its path, just like those with inclinations to impure intercourse!"

"That's ludicrous. The opposite is true: if you helped such people – because they need your help more than others – your path to heaven would become better. And as for men with unnatural conduct, you have no right to exclude them as long as they do nobody harm. The less so because the whole order of your brethren is just like that. They've retired to the monastery so that the world, their families and friends wouldn't discover their inclinations. They suffer here immensely due to your hypocrisy."

The abbot was pouring himself tea; his hand was shaking nervously. Jesus knew about his problematic orientation, and it was clear to him that he had parted with him completely after these words. However, he continued in a conciliatory tone to calm him down. "I want to go out to meet people. To Judea, Galilee, Samaria, Persia, India."

"What do you want to do among non-Jews? Aren't you going to preach the word of God to those unbelievers!" Adam nearly shouted.

"That's another thing I find hampering in Qumran. God doesn't distinguish between Jews and non-Jews. He only knows good and bad people."

"Are you saying God will redeem the uncircumcised too?"

"God won't help us, each of us has to redeem himself. God only opens the doors."

"Do you think God prefers the uncircumcised?!" Adam repeated his rhetorical question emphatically.

Jesus smiled. "Answer me then. Is it the effort of the Essenes to help one on his path to virtue?"

"That's self-evident."

"So, you prefer the virtuous ones from the vicious ones…"

"Why are you asking that? Well, that's clear."

"So why would God prefer the vicious ones?"

"I don't understand what you're on about."

"I'm asking you if God prefers a virtuous circumcised person or a vicious circumcised one?"

"Well... erm... God must clearly prefer Jews circumcised..."

"Even if they're bad? Does the fact a person has had a circumcision guarantee that they're good? And is there a guarantee that uncircumcised people are bad?"

The abbot lost his temper like every time he ran out of arguments. Jesus' unanswered questions disconcerted him and reduced his authority. He began spreading a rumor among the monks that Jesus was a heretic, denied the Torah and refused the prophets. Therefore, when the Nazarene informed him he was leaving the monastery half a year later, he accepted his decision with relief.

Jesus packed his stuff and spent his last night in the monastery in pensive prayer. When he entered the purifying bath for the last time in the morning, he noticed with unease that the strange little dot in his armpit had grown bigger and now clearly showed reddish veins radiating from it. He dried in the sun and stepped out into the desert toward the north-east, where he surmised to meet John.

60 The Countdown

Tomáš switched off his cell phone and stared ahead for a long time, motionless and uncomprehending. He was shaken by what his college classmate Felix Kruger had just told him on his secret line. By orders of General Parera, known as brother Giordano, the SIV had decided to blow up the alleged final resting place of Jesus Christ – the Roza Bal tomb in Srinagar. It was supposed to take place at a time when severe fighting between the government forces and rebels was expected around it. According to Felix's information, some Afghan mercenaries were going to carry out the explosion.

Tomáš was sitting with his head in his hands. *Oh my God, and it's all my fault. It was me who gave Michal those awful glasses, thanks to which they know everything about them. They know their place of stay and every word that they say. Not only the tomb but their lives as well are threatened. Thank God Felix is there.* Tomáš thought about what to do. His hands were shaking lightly. Thoughts were flitting around in his mind like a wild hog. Remorse gave way to pity; ideas to end it all were replaced with a resolution to correct his failure somehow. *I'll meet them. I'm fed up with all of this anyway. I find it repulsive to defend, or even explain what's untenable and inexplicable. I'm ashamed of being a part of a totalitarian, intolerant and power-striving organization that's turned Jesus' teachings upside down. I no longer want to be a part of this mendacious machinery. As long as Michal is wearing those darned glasses, they'll know everything. I can't give him a call: his phone is wiretapped. Hm… I wanted to go to Ladakh long ago anyway. I'll go to a monastery there. But before, I'll try to mend what I've messed up!*

His eyes now gleamed with hope and he smiled a little. He dialed the airline. "Hello, I need to get to Srinagar, Kashmir, as soon as possible. Can you help me, please?"

"Wait a second, I'll look on the computer," a pleasant female voice replied. "How soon do you mean?"

"As soon as possible."

"Then you're in luck, sir. Flight LY 312 of El Al departs from Ben Gurion Airport in Tel Aviv tomorrow at 22:00. The arrival in Srinagar is at 03:20 on May 21. There's one vacant seat."

"Nothing sooner?"

"No, sir, I'm sorry."

"Can you tell me, please, how long is the trip from the airport to the center of Srinagar?"

"Just a second… the airport is… eight miles from the airport."

"That's nice. How much is the ticket?"

"Do you want it in shekels, dollars or euros?"

"Euros."

"It's three hundred and fourteen euros."

"Book the ticket for me, Tomáš Dvoran, please."

"And the return too, sir?"

Tomáš hesitated for a second, but then he said in a resolute voice, "No!"

I hope I can make it before the explosion. It's been scheduled for five thirty in the morning on May 21, 2010.

At five that morning, Marika, Michal, Eli and Doctor Bashrat had decided to enter the Roza Bal shrine according to the information gathered from the transmitter in Michal's glasses.

61   The Time Has Come

He was sitting at the foot of the Jebel Kuruntul hill, northwest of Jericho. The desert heat was clanging through the void. He was holding his right arm, which was raised, and observing in discomfort the odd shape of the mark, like a crab. For a long time, he had refused to admit that it might be cancer. What was devouring him internally? The disappointment over Dositheos' people? Or the disappointment over the Essenes? The ignorance of people he met, who were driving themselves into perdition, willingly and knowingly? The powerlessness and disillusionment over the fact that in spite of all his efforts, he was incapable of getting people to follow the right way? Or was it just his pride and self-conceit telling him he ought to be a savior? The fact he didn't know who his father was? His exceptional, unfulfilled abilities?

Or Mariam in faraway Kashmir? He was asking himself whether he'd done the right thing when he married her. He reproached himself for the imprudence of youth and the momentary gust of love on the one hand, but he took comfort from having liberated Mariam from monastic captivity. He was relying on the king's promise to take care of her. He was intending to go to Jerusalem and seek out a merchant from a caravan, which arrived from the east from time to time, and ask around to see if anyone had brought news from the royal court of Takshashila, but some kind of inner voice seemed to keep him away from people. It occurred to him that the strange mark might be a consequence of his internal conflict. He rebuked himself for leaving Mariam alone in faraway Kashmir.

He was alone in an endless desert, two days away from the nearest dwellings. He was beginning to feel afraid. He couldn't accurately define why; he just felt an infinite loneliness and despair. He tried to drive away his dismal thoughts, but the more he tried, the stronger they were. His father's remains had been put in an ossuary, and in a depressed mood he started thinking about returning to India.

A spider ran in between his bare feet. He studied the tiny creature and realized its shape was nearly identical to that of the mark in his armpit. Was it suggesting something? He took it in his hand. The spider made no effort to escape; it nestled comfortably in his palm and cuddled up in a ball, as if it felt secure and safe in Jesus' hand. *You have to go back to the safety of your home. Your home is your inner being, peaceful, happy, free of prejudice and hatred. You're being devoured by hatred, you hate – not love – yourself for abandoning Mariam, you hate your fate because you can't pass on any of the wisdom you learned in India. You advise others to go out and meet people, yet you yourself are hiding in the desert. But if you find your way home, everything will change as if with a wave of a magic wand. Begin! Begin now and don't wait for more signs! Don't shy away and concentrate! Cleanse your soul! But first of all, cleanse your body!*

He smiled, entered the cave and came out again with a large, slender gourd with a runner about a yard long, which he'd found, along with other gourds, at the end of a field before he entered the desert. He'd cut off its top, cleaned it and let it dry. He'd done the same with several more. Then he'd taken some more, cut off their runners along with a bit of the top, and removed the flesh. Thus he'd produced containers. He'd stored the gourds in his rucksack. When he came to the desert cave the next day, he brought water from a spring in one of the gourds, laid it in the sun and let it warm up to body temperature. To the water he added his urine, which he'd been collecting in another gourd.

Then he filled the gourd with the runner with the mixture of warmed water and urine and hung it on a branch of a dry tree, knelt down and inserted the runner into his rectum. The water ran through all his entrails as he was taught by Kanaka in India. He knelt and prayed. After all the water and urine from the gourd had entered his body, he remained kneeling for as long as he could endure, then he strolled until he felt the urge to defecate. A turbid, stinking compound ran out of him. He repeated this ancient purifying procedure using water and his own urine for a full forty-two days on the dawn of every day. On the last few days, he purified himself using only clear water, which left his body as clean as it entered. He alternated the water purification with solar energy, letting the sun's rays embrace his whole body, naked and with sandals removed. He ate no food, only drank pure water from the gourd at body temperature, and took the mysterious medicine made by the Tibetan monk that his teacher Kanaka had given him. He watched as the mark in his right armpit was disappearing.

With his body weight diminishing, he began to discover his soul; the best that was within him was getting to the surface. He immersed ever deeper inside himself.

His fast was now over; slowly and carefully, he started to eat grasshoppers and plants that he found in the desert. He grew stronger and realized that separation from people, retreating to solitude only made sense for some time, to calm down one's soul, but that remaining alone in the long run was a wasted opportunity.

He picked up his rucksack, gourds and stick. He was standing outside the cave, and tears were rolling down his face. A spider was basking in the sun on the rock. He raised his arm and looked at his armpit. There was no sign of the crab-shaped mark. It was now eight weeks from his arrival in the desert.

He set out. He had a splendid, all-embracing feeling in his heart. He'd forgiven his mother for never having told him who his father was; he'd forgiven his friends from Marmion Road for mocking him for it all his childhood; he'd forgiven the priests and tried to understand why they attempted to squeeze the Creator's great work into a cast-iron dogma fettering the human spirit. A peace never experienced before had entered his heart. *Your mind is like the water's surface. You will only see your reflection when the surface is completely still.*

Jesus had died in the desert, and Christ was born. He headed for the Jordan to wash away the desert sweat and dust. He walked at a slow, uncertain pace down to Bethabara, the place where the Jordan discharges into the Dead Sea. It was there somewhere that his cousin John was going to baptize those who'd decided to walk the path of seeking the truth.

It was shortly after the spring equinox of the fourteenth year of the rule of Emperor Tiberius. Jesus had completed his thirty-fifth year. His heart filled with joy when he saw his cousin. Surrounded by friends, he was standing waist-deep in the waters of the Jordan, naked, with only a strip of leather wrapped around his loins. Jesus was unsettled at the sight of his weakly body.

"You should start to eat properly," he smiled and hugged his cousin after a long time. "I hear your only food is grasshoppers and wild bees' honey."

"Well, you're not looking any better," John retorted with a smile. "Have you come to accept baptism?" he changed the topic. Jesus nodded. "Come closer then."

Without a hesitation, Jesus took off his sandals and went into the water in his white tunic.

"Do you confirm you've come to us freely and without anyone else's coercion?" John asked.

"Nobody has coerced me to do this, I'm undertaking it based on my own free will."

"Do you confirm you're not under the influence of mandrake, opium, extract of hemp, henbane, stinkweed, or another drug?"

"I do."

"Are you aware of the fact that there is no coercion in the eternal law, that your free will is the most precious gift from God?"

"I am."

"Are you aware of the fact that baptizing the unwitting, whether they be old people who are losing their wits, or infants who haven't acquired them yet, is not a real baptism and is against God, and that baptism accepted without conscious and free approval is worthless?"

"I'm aware of that."

"Are you aware of the fact that everyone who forces another to accept rituals through baptism, is himself destined to fall?"

"I am."

After these words, John dipped Jesus in the calmly flowing Jordan, and held his head under the water for a while. When he came back up, he embraced him.

"My brother, from now on you'll do unto others what you want them to do to you. Welcome among the sisters and brothers who've prepared the path for you." Men and women he didn't know approached him one after another and embraced him.

"Go now and preach the word of God," John said as a goodbye. "The time has come."

* * * * *

After accepting the baptism, he set out north, up the Jordan valley, to Galilee. He travelled via Gilgal, Sukkot, by Skythopolis, and even came to his native Nazareth to say goodbye to his mother, and then he headed back east. But when he saw the incredible poverty of the ordinary people, he could not but start to help them. He healed them, using the education and experience that he'd acquired from his Indian teachers. He instructed people on how to nourish themselves and what habits they ought to acquire for a good life. Many were displeased by his words, because what they ate, what they wore and how they acted had come to them from their ancestors, and tradition was inviolable for the Jews.

"The best thing there can be for you is adhering to your ancestors' customs. But only follow the good ones. Adhering to bad customs destroys you," he persuaded the Nazarenes. "You suffer because Satan and his diseases are ruining your bodies. You kill animals, and your bodies become their graves in which they decompose. Whoever can kill an animal can kill a human being as well."

"What are you talking about?" chazzan Machir, recognized as an expert on the Scripture, halted him. "Moses, the greatest in Israel, permitted our fathers to eat the meat of clean animals, and only forbade the meat of unclean ones!"

"Because our fathers couldn't adhere to the commandments, Moses broke the two stone tablets with the Ten Commandments given to him by God and passed down ten easier commandments to his people. One of them was the permission to eat meat of clean animals. But your fathers' hearts hardened, and they began killing people as much as killing animals. I tell you therefore, if you want to stay in good health, don't eat what fire, frost or water have corrupted, because burnt, frozen or rotting food will burn, freeze and rot your body. Don't make food using fire, which kills your bodies. Always eat off God's table: the fruit of trees and gifts of soil, grains and grasses of the field. Eat everything as it is found on mother earth's table, that is, raw. Don't cook and mix things, else your intestines will become a stinking swamp. Be content with two, no less than three types of food; eat fruit first and in no case should you ever mix it with vegetables. And when you do eat, never eat to the bellyful, because that's Satan and his power tempting you to eat more. Therefore, observe how much you've eaten to get fully sated, and then eat a third less each time. Your body benefits from neither too much heat nor too much cold. Don't drink the milk of mammals, because it's meant for animal young and harms people.

At the start of the month of Iyar eat barley, starting from the month of Sivan eat wheat – the most accomplished of all plants bearing grain; starting from Tammuz eat sour grapes to make your body lean, in Elul gather ripe grapes to cleanse yourselves with their juices, in Cheshvan gather sweet grapes dried in the sun to fortify your bodies. Eat the herbs that rise after the rains of Tevet to cleanse your blood. Don't eat any unclean food brought from faraway lands, only eat what our trees and our soil give. And while you're eating, have the angel of air above you, chew to make the food liquid, and eat slowly as if it's a prayer that you dedicate to the Lord. And don't forget that if you eat mother earth's gifts for six days, you shall consecrate the seventh day to the Father. You shall eat no food and you shall fortify your spirit. God will send you a sunshine angel every morning to wake you up from sleep along with heavenly birds. Don't remain in bed after you wake up, because the water and air angels are already waiting for you outside. To wake up merrily, don't stay awake at night and don't sleep during the day. Don't find any pleasure in drinking alcohol or otherwise intoxicating your bodies. Don't have intercourse at inappropriate times, because a dissipated sexual life is like a tree from whose trunk resin flows out."

Some tried to live according to Jesus' words, but because most of them were unable to put his teachings into practice they started to desire his banishment from Nazareth to avoid a pricking of conscience. They even tried to throw him off a rock into an abyss. He therefore took his rucksack and went north to Capernaum, where he was gradually joined by Peter, Simon, his brother Andrew, Zebedee's sons James and John, Philip, Bartholomew, Matthew, Thomas, James the Younger, Simon the Zealot, James' son Judah, and Judas Iscariot, the only one not born in Galilee. Together they traveled Galilee, Samaria, Perea, Decapolis, Judea, and their numbers grew constantly. At times, the numbers of women and men who accompanied him went up to seventy.

After a daylong travel through the inhospitable country, Jesus and his disciples were often invited by their wealthy sympathizers to their homes, where they gave them food and lodgings. It wasn't considered proper conduct to welcome honorable guests with water; they always offered them wine. They never refused to drink it, but would mix it with water, thus symbolically expressing the golden middle way preached by their Master. The rumor of his miraculous healing abilities was spreading across Palestine; people showed immense faith in him, developed a liking for him for his friendly and kind disposition, and he never refused to help and encourage. He traveled around cities and villages, helping wherever he could. He remembered Mariam less and less often.

One day – two years after his baptism in early fall – Jesus and his friends arrived in Korazim in northern Galilee. His secret sympathizer Nicodemus, a member of the Jewish Council and teacher, invited him with his friends and wives to his home to entertain them with a banquet. The three-story villa rose majestically in an elevated place at the end of the town. Behind the house were vineyards, olive groves and pastures. Nicodemus was among the richest people in Galilee. Other wealthy citizens gathered in his house as well. They loudly criticized the Roman military administration, which had again risen their taxes. In addition to Rome, they also had to pay taxes to the hated Herod Antipas, and a tithe to the temple in Jerusalem.

"I wanted to put a new mosaic in the bath this year, but I can't afford it. Plus, the drought, poor harvest, and these taxes are ruining me," the wine trader Amiel groused.

"True, my wife too has had to put a stop to leg bracelets and toe rings, and if things continue this way, she won't even wear them on her hands," the rich man Matheno complained.

"Soon there won't be enough left to make a living," another joined in.

"Too little for living, too much for dying," the discontented Nicodemus grumbled and merrily sank his teeth in a crunchy leg of goat. Jesus and his friends sat by the table timidly and were quiet.

Nicodemus, who lay on a massive ebony sofa, gestured to the servants to offer the guests bowls of water in which to wash their hands ritually before the meal and during the courses. The servants also offered the bowls to Jesus, and began the wait on him and his friends with a green salad seasoned with red onions, parsley, thyme, dandelion, celery and coriander, followed by the main course – roast goat with mint sauce, various types of fish, ostrich brains, seafood, accompanied with artichokes, chard in a lentil and bean sauce, followed still by pomegranates, apples both fresh and dried with roasted sesame and, of course, wine.

"There wasn't much sun this year, so I recommend last year's wines," the host excused himself. "The cultivated ones are flawless," he flattered an honorable guest.

However, Jesus only tore bits of bread and ate it along with pieces of fish. His friends didn't touch any of the more extravagant dishes either. Nicodemus urged them again and again, and Jesus spoke after a while of his insistency. "There's a custom in Galilee according to which local paupers are invited to every feast held for a stranger." The diners fell silent, and the men on the chaise longues stared at the host sheepishly. "Where are the paupers?" Jesus asked more emphatically. "Don't they too have the right to eat these God's gifts with us?"

"But, Master, we haven't observed this custom since long ago," Nicodemus replied, ashamed.

"When we're guests in poor homes, even poorer people are invited everywhere. Maybe this custom isn't observed in wealthy homes," Jesus replied.

"Or maybe there aren't any hungry people in Korazim," one of the local aristocrats laughed.

Jesus gave him an angered look. "You complain you don't have the money for a new mosaic and for jewels for your wives' feet. You widen your prayer belts when you pay a tithe of mint, dill and caraway; you boast about it everywhere, but you forget what's the most important in the Law. You boast about its letters and know nothing about its spirit: rights, mercy and love."

"I beg your pardon, teacher," Matheno said sharply, "but your words are unjust. We donate a proportionate part to the temple, and the temple divides our contributions among the poor."

"Has any of you seen a priest or a Levite giving something to the poor?" Jesus asked sternly. "Do you want to go to the Kingdom of Heaven?" The men agreed silently. "Do you think God is a merchant and the more you pay to the temple the easier your way to salvation? You're rich in earthly possessions. But you only got that gift from God to be able to bring welfare to everyone in the larger whole. Only thus can you fulfill God's law, only thus can you fulfill the spirit of the Ten Commandments. You can prove your compassion right on the spot if you wish to." He turned to the host. "Do you agree, please, with our honorable host inviting the hungry to the table?" The men and women looked at each other, ashamed, and nodded one by one.

Nicodemus gestured to the servants. A while later, dirty, ragged, sick and hungry people started to come into the large dining room. Some smelled of sweat, others of dung. Their feet were dusty. They all looked at Jesus, who was watching Nicodemus, who suddenly walked over to the first brave man who took off his hat and bowed to the master of the house obligingly. Nicodemus embraced him and said, "Brothers, these foods are from our Father and belong to everyone. Please, take your seats at the table." The man stood at the middle of the room sheepishly and didn't dare to go to the table. Then Jesus stood up, sat him down and asked a servant to bring him a ceramic bowl of water for the man.

The man put his dusty and cracked feet in it. Jesus knelt in front of him, took some fragrant oil, poured it into the bowl and started washing the man's feet. Then he wiped them dry, changed the water and invited the next one. His disciples followed him. When Nicodemus joined them, even Amiel, Matheno and the others knelt before the crumpled men and washed the visitors' feet. Progressively, they smiled at each other, talked, and a hubbub and merry shouting ran across the room.

"These people's souls have needed feeding more than their stomachs. And we have provided them with that today," Jesus said and hugged Nicodemus cheerfully.

The news of Jesus bringing the wealthy to humility spread across Galilee, Perea, Samaria and Decapolis. Poor people began to raise their heads. Maybe that was the reason why Herod Antipas had John the Baptist imprisoned in Fort Machaerus east of the Dead Sea. He ordered him beheaded ten months later.

62 God Bless You

Marika's condition was now stable; at least she looked that way, and her temperatures and aches had subsided. Doctor Bashrat, along with Eli, spent long hours with her. Eli regularly smeared and massaged her with the special oil; she used Chodrak's medicine, applied jasper, only drank energized water, and only ate raw vegetables and fruit. Her encouraging talks with the doctor and his son injected new vigor into her weary body. The beautiful country, magnificent weather, fragrant spring meadows, clean mountain air and strolls to the Sindh river encouraged positive energies in Marika, and her cells rejoiced along with her. However, Michal knew her too well and her eyes convinced him that she still wasn't on the right path. He knew what his beloved wife's heart longed for. That was why he jumped up with joy when Doctor Bashrat told her that they would soon be going to Professor Vaidya's Srinagar clinic for a few days, for blood control sampling, and that they'd visit the Throne of Solomon as well on the occasion.

"Doctor, I wanted to ask you if we could also manage Roza Bal..." Marika asked carefully yet urgently, a question that had been on her mind since arriving in Kashmir. "You know how much it matters to me..."

"I understand. I have good news for you. The tomb guardian, my cousin Sahib, is ready to take us in, although he wasn't very happy about it... You see, there has been severe fighting in the past near the shrine, in fact directly in the Muslim cemetery that surrounds it. Fights have broken out again in Srinagar today, but it's all the more reason for me to fulfill your wish. Before it erupts..."

"What should erupt?" Michal asked anxiously.

"When are we going?" Marika stood up in front of her husband resolutely.

"If praying by Jesus' grave is so important to you, it makes no sense to start with the fasting, even though it's so significant for your curing. We'll spend a few days on our houseboat, so that I can consult with the professor, and then we'll return here to Sonamarg, full of healing energy, and get on with it." He clutched her hand encouragingly.

On May 19, Marika and Michal couldn't fall asleep for excitement.

"Are you asleep?" he asked and listened to her uneasy breathing. He was sitting in an armchair, watching his wife lying in the bed in the dim light of the rising moon. The young night was giving the room a strange, magical atmosphere. The window was open, and the air carried sporadic whistles of lonely birds, screeches of monkeys, howls of wolves, and the neighing of scared horses into the room. The occasional noises of the indigenous inhabitants of this heaven on earth blended with the fascinating melody of the crystal-clear Sindh river, coming from the endless distances of Himalayan valleys.

"I can't."

"How are you feeling?"

"Excellent. I'm full of energy. You?"

"I feel better too when I see you improving. I'm quite fresh. Do you mind if I take a stroll?"

"What time is it?"

"It's before ten."

"Isn't it dangerous going out alone after dark?"

"I don't think there's a place safer than Sonamarg. There's more soldiers here than civilians," he laughed bitterly. "I won't be long. Can you feel the air? Even Eli says it's unusually warm for May. I'll be back in a moment."

Michal went out of the building right onto the main road, whose opposite side was lined with rows of trucks. Their drivers were resting in modest little hotels and guesthouses, recharging before the difficult mountain climb on the following day. Michal headed south, downriver. Suddenly, he noticed a little red light in the distance, almost at the end of the village, where the military camp was. Something was drawing him toward the light magically. He walked toward it, past the banner "Indian army welcomes you", and read the identification sign on the single-story wooden building with a roof made of green tin: R Centre 5231. Now near the barrack, he noticed that it wasn't a chimney sticking out of the roof, as he had thought before, but the top of a Buddhist stupa. He realized he was indeed inside the fence of the military camp, which was still busy, unusually for the time of night. He looked around to see if anybody was coming to stop him, but then he entered the barrack with the lantern over the entrance and went on into a room lit with sharp light. He glanced inside, but there was nobody there. Suddenly somebody grasped his shoulder lightly. He twitched. A soldier was standing behind him, wearing a yellow scarf around his neck and a camouflage battledress.

"Please, do come in," he invited him. His honest smile freed Michal of any concern. He reciprocated the smile and went in. The room was dominated by a statue of the Buddha sitting in a meditating position, next to him a statue of the god Ganesha with an elephant's face, over him a statue of his father Shiva, the goddess Lakshmi, and some inscriptions in an unknown language.

"Excuse me, can you tell me what shrine this is?"

The soldier bowed, wet his fingers in a bowl of water, and ran it across the crown of Michal's head. "You're in an ecumenical chapel of the Indian Army. You see, our army consists of Hindus, Buddhists and Muslims, and we can't afford to have a separate shrine for each of the religions. But it works very well. Our gods tolerate each other quite well here," he smiled.

"And Christians?"

"Of course." With his eyes, the soldier indicated a picture that Michal hadn't noticed. He turned around and couldn't believe his eyes. On the wall was a portrait of Jesus with a naked heart – precisely as he remembered from children's prayer books, only with a third eye on his forehead – a Hindu tilak. "That's Isa, Jesus the Messiah."

"Do you know Jesus?"

"Of course I do. I did religious studies, but you know, I couldn't sustain my family on that, so I enlisted in the army."

Michal sized up the soldier in his battledress and combat boots, only worn during alert. "Excuse me, are you a paratrooper?"

The soldier avoided a direct answer, only smiled shyly, almost guiltily. "Our brigade is going to Srinagar tomorrow. I've just come here to pray."

"Are you afraid of being killed?" Michal burst out. "Oh, I'm sorry," he apologized immediately.

"I've come to pray so that I don't have to kill." The soldier fell silent and his eyes fell on the painting of Christ. "They say he was in Kashmir once," he smiled.

"May I take a photo?"

"Please yourself. Are you a Christian?" Michal nodded.

"Your god is nothing special."

"I don't understand."

"I'm sorry, I don't mean to hurt you, but this Jesus... wherever he went, ruin followed. There's war in Israel, war in Kashmir... Just looking at him makes you feel sad."

"Why?" Michal asked, uncomprehending.

"He's kind of, you know, sad. Look at our gods." He pointed at Ganesha and Shiva. "They dance. He must have been cheerful too, I'm sure he smiled like the Buddha. Nobody would have followed him if he hadn't smiled."

Michal examined the picture of Christ carefully. "Can I take a photo of it?"

"Of course, just be quick, please, because I'll have to go. We're leaving in the morning. Unfortunately, I'll have to fight against my Muslim brothers."

"Are you a Muslim?"

"An Indian." The soldier gave him a strange sad look.

"I wish you a lot of luck then."

"God bless you," the soldier said and took a bowl of purple pigment in his hand. He dipped his middle finger in it and made a dot in the middle of Michal's forehead. "So that God protects you."

"I think you'll need it more. May I?" Michal smiled timidly. The soldier nodded. Michal dipped a finger in the bowl and made a dot in the middle of the soldier's forehead.

"May God protect you." He extended his right arm toward the soldier. He shook it firmly.

63   A Surprise

After John's death, Jesus retreated to the land of Herod Philip near Caesarea Philippi for some time. He was accompanied by his disciples, who had nothing but sticks, tunics and sandals. It was difficult for many of them to accept Jesus' ways and teachings because he questioned truths which they had held their entire lives. Many also found it hard to be far from their families, and they made this known to him. Jesus himself doubted occasionally whether he'd succeed in convincing his disciples to stay with him. Deep within his heart there smoldered a tiny flame named Mariam; sometimes he remembered his Kashmiri wife and tried to drive away the urgent qualms over having left her. He knew that he was expected by some to try to establish an earthly kingdom and overturn Herod, the hated vassal of Rome. Likewise, the people expected him to rail against the heavy Roman oppression. Instead of fighting against Rome and its domestic minions, he preached them about some kingdom of heaven.

His authority was kept up by his miraculous healings of leprosy, malaria, cancer, paralysis, and even the resuscitation of the dead Lazarus, the brother of his zealous follower Mary of Magdala. In India, Jesus had frequently come across the practice of resuscitating the dead, whose hearts had not beaten for up to several days; reviving the seemingly dead Lazarus was therefore not a problem for him. When he arrived in Bethany near Jerusalem and rolled away the stone on Lazarus' tomb, Jesus asked Mary, Martha and, most importantly, Thomas, who was ready to lay down his life for him, to leave him alone with the dead man in the tomb. The dark cave used as the tomb was lit by the dim light of a torch. Jesus raised his eyes to the sky and begged God for help in Aramaic. He pulled the bandage off the dead man's ears and then put his own fingers in them. He thus tried to change the man's sensory perception as his spiritual body was still alive. It was a change from external perception to an internal one. Jesus had learned in Takshashila that one hears inside better than outside and that the physical consciousness reconnects to its source by means of hearing. He applied his hands to Lazarus' body around the heart, the place that he called the leba – the center of courage and feeling and started saying a mantra with which he attracted the exact same frequencies from the universe that Lazarus' disease had, only of the opposite polarity. *With a grinder made of the god Indra's stone, which will destroy all the krimi in this man's body, I am grinding all the krimi that have proliferated in his body, I will destroy all the visible and invisible krimi that have invaded his body. Father, let it be that they all die. I will finish them all off with the power of the mantra. With its power, I will destroy the krimi in his viscera that have come from the mountains, deserts, fields, plants and animals and entered him with food, water or through wounds. Oh, haridra, full of cosmic life energy, show your power! Father, please, hear me, because those who believe do not die. Please reconnect this man to your source, breathe the rhythm of your breath back into him.* Then he produced a tiny pouch of yellow powder from under his clothes and sprinkled it over Lazarus' body. Nobody noticed the powder as Lazarus' body was wrapped in bandages that had turned yellow with sweat and dust. The tomb, filled with a stale deadly odor, was pierced by the unfamiliar scent of turmeric, the main ingredient of the peculiar powder that Jesus had brought from India. About an hour later, he sensed that Lazarus' chest had reconnected to the vibrations of the universe and began breathing slowly. Only then did Jesus take his fingers out of the man's ears, spat on the floor and removed the bandage where Lazarus' mouth was. He gripped the tip of his tongue, thus leveling Lazarus' perception with his at the same wavelength. The echo of Jesus' breathing pulled Lazarus into the same rhythm; he responded to Jesus' healing touch and his consciousness was awakening.

Jesus was exhausted but smiled peacefully. He walked out and hugged Mary. "Unwrap him and let him go," he instructed the relatives waiting outside the tomb. When Lazarus finally stood up, the people fell to their knees in front of Jesus and praised him as a messiah. Later he healed the son of a royal official; he cured a blind man with mud made from his own saliva and earth. Lame and sick people came to see him all the way from Tyre and Sidon. He performed many more acts of healing, in which he put his excellent education to use. There was a rumor that even Pilate's wife Procula had invited him to heal her son who was suffering from epilepsy.

News of his art of healing and truthful speech spread irrepressibly across Palestine. Humiliated people started to raise their heads and quoted the modest preacher as a model for proud priests. Spies of the Temple and the acting high priest Caiaphas followed him at every turn. Each act of healing or public appearance by Jesus among ordinary people outraged the priests, who sensed deadly danger in him. They couldn't tolerate such deeds because uttering secret incantations in public was prohibited under the penalty of death.

Six days before Passover of the sixteenth year of Emperor Tiberius' rule, Jesus' group set out to Jerusalem. On their way, they stopped over in the hamlet of Bethphage on the Mount of Olives; from there they continued onto the capital. Jesus entered it riding a donkey through the Golden Gate, also known as the Gate of Mercy. A street led from it straight to the Temple. Jesus and his disciples were making their way through the crowd, who greeted them enthusiastically. To their surprise, however, he didn't say any of the expected words but entered the temple courtyard and dismounted from his donkey swiftly. The courtyard of the house of God looked like a marketplace with sprawling tables of vendors offering animals, trinkets and refreshments for those who were swarming into the city before the upcoming Feast of Unleavened Bread. Nothing had changed in the place since he used to come there with his parents.

Money changers had heaps of Tyrian and Hebrew shekels on their tables and exchanged money brought by pilgrims from abroad. They were all shouting over each other and haggling. The priests had even made an arrangement with the merchants, who now only sold the sacrificial animals for Syrian and Tyrian shekels. Foreigners were thus forced to exchange their currencies at an extortionate rate, which brought unprecedented profits to the traffickers and the priests alike. Jesus looked around for a moment, then he started trembling with wrath, bent down swiftly, removed the leather laces from his sandals and made a short whip with them. He raised it high above his head and with the words, "Is it not written that the Father's house shall be a house of prayer?" he lunged at the tables, turned them over in a fit of wrath, beat and whipped the shocked merchants, and tossed cages with animals and pigeons off some tables. Whistling and wailing, the pigeons flew up to the sky, and untied lambs ran through the crowd in the hustle. Money was rolling on the ground, and people jumped at it and took as much as they could manage. The temple guard, called by the priests and Levites supervising over order, arrived in the general commotion. They had long been looking for a pretense for arresting Jesus. What was happening now was very convenient for them.

"You've sold the house of God for your stinking money! You've turned the house of worship into a bandits' nest. You don't have the slightest right to call yourselves God's representatives if you tolerate such filth!"

"Get lost and stop this nuisance!" one of the priests confronted him and tore out his whip.

"You've torn down our Father's temple in your hearts, but I'll rebuild it in three days!" But he was now being pulled away by his own disciples, who saw the temple guard running in. Jesus and his disciples lost themselves amongst the crowd, thus preventing the soldiers from following them. Via the Golden Gate, they then returned to nearby Bethany, where they spent the night in the house of Bar Simon, whom Jesus had once cured of leprosy.

Although Passover was a holiday when Jews were supposed to commemorate their ancestors' exodus from Egypt, the commemorative event had turned into entertainment, impious eating and drinking. Music was playing in Jerusalem, and people were singing and dancing.

However, disquiet ruled in the palace of the formal high priest Annas, the father-in-law of the current high priest, installed in his position by the Roman administration. Furtively, his closest friends were gathering in the palace: tricksters, traders, corrupt Jewish judges, and members of the temple guard, of which Annas was the supreme commander. A decision was made to arrest Jesus in the garden known as Gethsemane, at the foot of the Mount of Olives, where he usually went to rest with his disciples.

Jesus and his disciples lay on the sun-warmed ground after dinner. He heard the hooves of a horse a while later. His heart started pounding. In the dusk, he could see a soldier dismounting from the horse and walking toward them. "Is the man from Galilee among you?"

"We're all from Galilee," Peter replied.

"I'm looking for Jesus, nicknamed Christ."

Jesus stood up and went over to the rider. He looked at him in surprise; he was expecting a group of soldiers, but this one was alone. Another saddled horse, without a rider, was standing next to him.

"Who are you?"

"I'm centurion Gaius Cassius Longinus." The soldier came up to Jesus and what he said surprised him.

64 The Crunch Is Coming

On the forenoon of May 20, Michal and Marika set out from Sonamarg to Srinagar, accompanied by Ghulam Bashrat and Eli, who was driving the Toyota. The trip was quite quick and would have been very pleasant if they hadn't been halted by the unusually frequent military checkpoints. Eli had his radio turned up. It rang out with Indian songs, to which Michal never got used to, even during his first stay in India. "Can you change it for some less irritating music?"

"I can't, unfortunately. No other stations have been working since this morning except the state broadcast and television."

"Why?" Marika asked, disconcerted.

"Something's going on. You see, we're used to this by now. I think it's another offensive preparation by the Indian Army. They said in the news that the head of the National Security Council and the head of the intelligence service have flown in from Delhi. That's not a good sign," Eli explained.

"Kashmir has a public security act in place that allows the police to lock up anyone for up to two years without a trial just because they're a suspect. Every other person here's a police informer... nobody trusts anyone... thousands are missing." Doctor Bashrat added.

"When the government of Kashmir allotted two and a half acres of land around the Hindu shrine of Amarnath Cave to the Hindus two years ago, a wave of Muslim protests arose in which twenty-one people were killed. Can you imagine anyone coming up now and proposing to open Roza Bal, a Muslim and Jewish, and partly Christian shrine?" he smiled bitterly.

A tense silence descended on the car. They were slowly approaching the Throne of Solomon area. Doctor Bashrat stared worriedly at Marika, who was noticeably pale.

"You'll take a rest after the visit. Luckily it's not far from here." Marika gave him a grateful smile.

"But if you want to go to your room now…"

"Oh no, I want to see the shrine."

"I've arranged with my cousin Sahib that we'd come to see him this evening. If we were found walking the empty streets to Roza Bal early in the morning, we would look suspect and I really don't know what we'd tell the military patrols that would be bound to check us."

"Is this an arrangement with the tomb guardian?" Michal asked.

"His house is perhaps ten yards away from it. We'll have a comfortable night's sleep at his place. We'll go to the shrine before five in the morning. The sun rises at half past five. Muslims will be going for their morning prayers in a nearby mosque before six. How much time do you wish to spend meditating in the shrine?" Bashrat turned to Marika.

"Well… I don't… I don't want to get you into a dangerous situation…"

"There are no safe situations there," Eli remarked.

"Are two hours enough? From five to seven, or half past seven at the latest? The religious services will be over then and visiting hours for Muslim pilgrims to Roza Bal start at eight."

"Yes, I'll be happy to spend any amount of time by his grave."

Michal asked cautiously, "It seems a bit strange to me that a Muslim saint was buried later in a shrine in which a Jew is buried."

"This Syed Naruddin Rizvi, buried there in the 16th century, was no real saint. He was just turned into one. I think they put him there just to give Muslims a reason to declare Roza Bal their shrine."

In the bend of the road past the exit from the city center, at the Swiss hotel, they made a right turn onto a minor road that zigzagged up the Gopa hill. They were checked by several military patrols along the way. They stopped in a large car park, as the onward road was only open to pedestrians. The first body search followed outside the car park. The Indian Army soldiers were nice to the foreigners, gesturing that they were only carrying out orders. They weren't as nice to the locals, though. The third check at the end of the climb was the strictest. Large blue signs contained a warning in national languages and English for everyone who would try to sneak a camera in the Shankaracharya or Takht-i-Suleiman compound.

"Why aren't we allowed to take pictures of the shrine?" Michal asked, disappointed.

"Because although it's a holy place, it's also one of the crucial mountain fortifications over Srinagar."

"What would happen if they found us with a camera?"

"You could be locked up for three years. I hope you left it in the car," Eli gave Michal a warning look.

"Sure I did."

"I've been here many times, but I've never seen this many soldiers," Eli muttered under his breath.

Michal excused himself and ran off to the toilet. There, with slightly shaking hands, he slid his small camera into the rear compartment of his belt pack, which he had tightly wrapped around his waist. The front compartments contained his wallet, papers, some folded toilet paper and a few pieces of chewing gum. In the middle one he had a dictaphone, pens and Indian coins. He pulled the pack around his waist as tightly as he could, so that the third compartment wasn't visible from the front.

They approached the queue of tourists who were slowly shuffling toward a soldier standing on a ramp. Next to him was a guard booth, in which more soldiers were sitting. A third guard booth could be seen behind it, in the bend of the uphill path. Warning signs about the ban on photography were everywhere. They were drawing near the soldier who made a routine check of everyone's hand baggage. Every rucksack had to be emptied on the table next to the soldier. Eli, Marika and Bashrat passed the check before Michal.

"Open that bag, please," the soldier pointed at his belt pack. Michal opened the zipper on the first compartment, and the soldier asked him to empty it. The soldier nodded approvingly and asked him to open the other compartment. Michal put its contents on the table. The soldier spotted the dictaphone and his eyes lit up like a hunter's when he gets an animal in his sights.

"Do you know photography is forbidden here?"

"I'm sorry, it's just a dictaphone."

"A dictaphone?" The soldier picked up the dictaphone with a digital display resembling a camera. He examined it closely. He didn't like something; he turned to a colleague and said something. Another man came over a moment later, evidently his superior, who took the dictaphone from him and motioned him to continue checking the queue. The superior officer pushed the buttons and the machine started playing sounds that Michal had been recording during his trip. "Are you a journalist?"

"No, I'm not. I'm an ordinary tourist, only I don't feel like making notes, so I record things."

The soldier played with the dictaphone for a while and then returned it to Michal with a smile. "No problem, sir. You may go."

They climbed the remaining steps at a brisk pace. Even Marika seemed to cheer up. It was late afternoon and storm clouds were gathering in the sky. They joined a queue of tourists that were slowly making their way towards the steps leading up to the shrine. On the narrow steps, they made way for those descending, almost exclusively Hindus from the look of their clothes. They didn't see any Muslims. Each one had a dot on their forehead – a benediction from the priest. Michal, Marika and Eli too were given a mark on their foreheads from the two priests who welcomed them to the tiny shrine, about five yards across; the priests also sprinkled a little sweetener in each of their hands. At the center of the room was a symbol of the Shiva lingam, almost seven feet tall and adorned with flowers; one of the priests poured milk over it incessantly.

"Is this a Jewish shrine?" Michal asked in surprise.

"Hindu historians assert that the shrine was founded by Jalluka, a son of King Ashoka, two hundred years before Christ, but the truth is that the shrine stood here at least a thousand years before Christ."

"Is there any evidence?"

"None directly but notice the peculiar shape of the shrine. Everything indicates that those who designed this shrine knew the golden geometry principles. The builders used the golden ratio when building it, similarly to Egyptian pyramids. Such structures are considered to be energy transmitters. According to ancient Vedas, such shapes generate vibrations at a special frequency that enable communication with higher worlds. The shrine has an octagonal footprint. Legends say that King Solomon along with King Hiram were building this shrine at the same time Jerusalem Temple was being constructed. Solomon also allegedly ordered construction of the Martand shrine, the ruins of which are about forty miles from Srinagar. When scientists made a computer reconstruction of it, they found out it was an exact replica of Jerusalem Temple."

They all listened to the doctor attentively. They came to the outer wall, which commanded a marvelous view of the city surrounded with a crown of mountains. The shores of the Dal Lake were lined with hundreds of houseboats, over which black clouds were rallying. Eli leaned over the wall and pointed downward. "Look, that's the reason why no cameras are allowed here."

They walked past the shrine and noticed dugouts in several places, lined with sandbags with small firing ports. "They're machine gun and artillery nests of the Indian Army. It's the ideal place for control over the city." As soon as they stopped for a while, a man appeared by them and asked them politely to not linger by the wall.

"They're nervous. If this one found us with a camera, I don't even want to imagine..."

They walked a little further and Michal produced his camera from the belt pack. Bashrat and Eli nearly yanked it out of his hands. "Please put that away! And don't take any pictures! We could be checked on the way back as well. Maybe we're being watched with binoculars. If they found a picture of a soldier or, God forbid, one of those nests on your display, you'd go to jail for espionage. Michal, please, hide it well."

Michal put the camera back in the belt pack. He excused himself and ran off to the toilet. When he came out, he walked past some thick shrubs, from where he took a few pictures of the shrine. When he heard some voices coming, he put the camera back in the rear belt pack compartment again. He rejoined the others just as there was a distant thunder.

"We should be going now, there's going to be a storm. The corner of Hazratbal Road and Ganderbal Road, from where it's just a few meters to Sahib's home, tends to be quite busy," Eli remarked.

"I don't think there'll be a storm." Marika looked at the sky. Helicopters were approaching the city from beyond the mountain ridge. They noticed people rushing toward the car park. "What's going on?"

Eli went over to the nearest soldier. He came back with a serious face. "I think we should head out for Sahib's as soon as possible. To make it before six."

"What's at six?" Michal asked.

"A curfew has been declared. From six in the evening to six in the morning. It seems the crunch is coming. It's a quarter past five, we've got to get moving."

"What does a curfew mean?" Marika asked worriedly.

"In a normal country it means you can be taken to a police station for no reason during the time. In Kashmir, you can be shot without any reason."

65 Pilate's Proposal

After dark, the centurion and Jesus passed the Sheep Gate, which was just behind Antonia Fortress, where Pilate traditionally resided during his sojourns in Jerusalem. Longinus helped Jesus get off the horse and gave him an encouraging wink. Then he handed him over to one of Pilate's bodyguards, who led him to the Roman prefect.

"Do you know what my name means?" Pilate smiled. Jesus made no reply. "Pilum means lance. I know you've been treating our son secretly. My wife told me. I'm very grateful to you for that. His condition's improved tremendously."

"I hold your wife, a great-granddaughter of Emperor Augustus, in great reverence. She's a loving mother," Jesus said softly.

"Just don't overpraise her, she's also an illegitimate daughter of Tiberius' third wife Claudia," Pilate laughed sarcastically. Jesus nearly took fright at the scary smile: there was nothing human in it. He was watching an impetuous, arrogant and haughty man, who had ordered thousands of his Jewish brethren to die the most terrible deaths by crucifixion. Rumor had it that he'd achieved his appointment as the governor of Judea under pressure from the Praetorian commander Sejanus, who'd convinced him to marry a Roman princess and thus guaranteed himself a career. He was evidently enjoying some form of patronage because normally Roman governors' wives were not allowed to accompany their husbands: Procula was living with Pilate in his splendid residence in Caesarea.

"I've been watching your actions and talks for three years now. You may not be aware of it, but I've repeatedly refused proposals from the Sanhedrin to ban you from public activity. The Jews have half a mind to stone you to death."

"Not Jews, Jewish priests," Jesus corrected him.

"Yes, the priests. They agitate their followers against you." He drank some wine calmly and smiled. "You're thirty-eight, like me. We're not so old that we couldn't be enjoying the pleasures given to us in life." He even offered Jesus some wine, which he politely refused. "I hate these Pharisee priests of yours just as much as you do," Pilate continued. "In public they declare their loyalty to the Emperor, but as soon as I turn my back on them, they start to plot the worst machinations against him. People say I'm cruel. That may be right, but I'm definitely not insidious. Caiaphas has been the high priest since he was eighteen, and although high priests are usually appointed for no more than three years, he's grown so close with some influential people in the Roman court that he's been up there for twelve years, and is slowly beginning to threaten me as well."

"But why are you telling me this?" Jesus asked.

"I like how you criticize and denounce these hypocrites publicly.

Suddenly he burst out laughing. He laughed until he coughed. "Man, did I love it when you thrashed them with that whip. They deserve a good old beating, and maybe much more than that. Do you know what profit they make on Passover?" Jesus said nothing. "Well, count with me. This Passover thing attracts an estimated two hundred and fifty thousand Jews to Jerusalem. Each of them arrives with a full wallet. And this Caiaphas, as the supreme head of the Temple, has a direct access to the temple strongbox. Can you imagine how much those Sadducees make on this? All of these Jewish priests are a gang of thieves. I'm not holy, but at least I don't pretend to be holy. I'm a soldier, I come from an equestrian family in which correctitude was the first rule. These people here are hypocrites without parallel in the world. What I appreciate about you is you haven't incited people against Rome. Your call for people to give the Emperor what's the Emperor's and give God what's God's, is, politically speaking, a correct division of power. But your priests want both power and God. I agree with what you say, that one cannot serve two masters, but they don't respect that." He sipped some more wine from his goblet; it was slowly getting to his head.

"They say you too took money from the temple strongbox to build the aqueduct," Jesus objected softly.

Pilate gave him an angry look, but then grinned broadly. "I did. So what? Doesn't the water serve Jews too?"

"You don't like us..." Jesus remarked.

"I have nothing against Jews who fulfill their duties to the Emperor and our gods. But I hate these hypocritical priests. They've announced that any Jew who joins you must never again enter a synagogue." Then he raised his head. "They've come to see me and demanded your head." He fell silent and played with his cup for a long while, observing Jesus, who stood motionless.

"Are you aware of the danger you're in?" Jesus made no reply. "Non-Romans will receive the strictest punishments. Well, just one in fact: crucifixion. I asked them to state their reasons. They said you declared you're going to demolish their temple and rebuild it in three days and send the priests into exile and sit on the royal throne yourself. Besides, they say you're in contact with Rome and plotting to dispose of me." Pilate made a grin. "They're idiots. I've checked everything, and none of it is true. But I'm also informed – as you are probably too – that men incited by priests are premeditating your death. You're in danger. You know the way to the borders, there's no future for you in this country; run right now, do it before the sunrise. I'll give you enough time." Jesus said nothing. Yes, it would be fair to Mariam, but something was telling him he must first complete what he'd begun in Palestine.

"Run away from this cursed country." Jesus still said nothing, which enraged Pilate. "I'm helping you, and you're ignoring me?!"

Jesus drew a breath. "The Emperor has a good advocate in you. From the earthly point of view, you're right: I should protect my own life, but from the higher objective perspective, your advice is bad. Criminals who've committed something wrong run away from danger. I haven't done anything. I will leave the country, but only after I've completed my work."

Pilate sized him up and down for a long time. "You know that since the beginning of this year, the Roman governor has the right to issue death sentences himself. A year ago, Sanhedrin would have had you stoned to death. The majority of those that I've had crucified since the beginning of the year had done nothing wrong. I had them executed as a warning to others. Your plaintiffs are demanding the same: lest you should be followed, God forbid. Those who're following you loyally are numerous enough as it is. Your death would be addressed to those who might want to join them. I'll give you an equestrian escort that will take you all the way to Damascus. From there you can continue east."

"Going east is my great desire, but... only..."

"Only what?"

"Only... later..."

"If there is a later," Pilate laughed sarcastically.

"Thank you, but I cannot accept your offer just now. I mustn't disappoint my brothers; I must finish what I've started. If I am to die, it will be God's will."

Pilate said nothing for a long while. "Are these your last words?" Jesus nodded.

"Then I'm forced to sentence you and then join forces with those willing to save you. Now go. Longinus will take you safely to the Messalian's house in the Garden of Gethsemane. You can rely on him." The Roman governor stood up, indicating that the audience was over. Jesus bowed slightly and left in the company of a guard. Pilate stared after him for a long time, shaking his head. Then he picked up a bell and rang it. His valet entered.

"Ask them in."

The valet exited and reentered with two bearded men wearing cloaks typical of members of the Supreme Jewish Council. He bowed courteously and informed Pilate, "Dear prefect, the rabbis Joseph of Arimathea and Nicodemus have come at your bidding."

66 Shoes Off in the Grave!

The guest room on the second floor of Sahib's house was small but cozy and clean. Sahib, a man in his forties with dense curly hair falling over his forehead, an aquiline nose and a sharp, uncompromising stare, was obviously not delighted about the visit. Only his respect to the Bashrats senior and junior prevented him from expressing his displeasure more strongly. Sporadic shots or short bursts of automatic carbine fire were heard from beyond the fluttering curtains. Sahib's eyes showed fear, but he was deeply grateful to Doctor Bashrat for curing his daughter's polio. His three small daughters and his wife came only to bow to the guests and then they hurriedly ran into their room.

Marika, Michal, Doctor Bashrat and Eli had to make do with the small room. The floor was strewn with cashmere rugs topped with mats with varicolored cushions and woolen blankets. There was a low table at the center with some cushions around it. Sahib brought a large vat full of hot black tea and flatbreads with jam. It wasn't the tastiest dinner, but they'd grown hungry during the day, so they started eating gratefully. Tension was felt in the house. Sahib had his radio on.

"Only the state broadcast is working, and God knows how much of what they're saying is true."

"What are they saying?" Marika asked, worried.

"The Prime Minister of Kashmir is inviting the rebels to dialogue; he says peace can't be won with guns but only with debate. They've all been saying that for the last forty years. Muslim separatists supported by the Pakistani government have been trying to achieve independence or join Pakistan all this time. From time to time an armed conflict breaks out that turns into war. That's bad. I'm forty-five and I've seen two wars. Fortunately, Khanyaar has been saved from the most violent fighting.

It's an old town and there are no government buildings here that the rebels might want to target. Instead, we have narrow streets that..." he broke off, "... and this."

He went to the window and pulled aside the curtain cautiously. It was seven o'clock and it was getting dark outside. "Roza Bal is just opposite us." He pointed at the low building with a green tin roof and a fenced front yard, sitting at the corner of two narrow streets right under their window.

"You call this a shrine?" Marika shook her head in disappointment. "I thought it would be something like the Holy Sepulcher in Jerusalem."

"You're in a Muslim country, madam," Sahib replied. "My family have lived in this house for eight generations. They've all been guardians of the tomb; we're distantly related to the family of honorable Doctor Ghulam Bashrat. There's no greater honor for us than to be guardians of the tomb."

"Take a good look at the building so we make a clear aim in the morning. Who knows what the situation is going to be like then. I hope they won't put a patrol right outside the house or the shrine. That would be bad. And we can't postpone visiting the tomb anymore. Professor Vaidya insists on starting the fast immediately. So, if we fail tomorrow, then... I don't know when..." Doctor Bashrat shrugged.

"We must succeed," Marika said uncompromisingly.

The sign fastened to the shrine fence strictly forbade photography. Michal read out loud the English translation of the sign in Arabic, lettered on a blue steel sheet: "*What do the Quran and the Bible say about Jesus Christ? The Holy Quran says: They (Jews) boast themselves on having killed Jesus Christ, son of Mary, apostle of Allah. But they neither killed, nor crucified him, the fact is that he revealed himself to them. Those with a different opinion are filled with doubt and uncertain knowledge and only speculate on how to prove they didn't kill him. Allah elevated Him to himself. Allah is All-Mighty, All-Wise. (The Quran, An-Nisa 157-158) Thus spoke the Lord Jesus to them, and he was accepted to heaven and sat by God's right hand.*"

"Incidentally, the Quran mentions Jesus 132 times in deep reverence as a prophet, the son of Mary," Eli added.

"The name Roza Bal is sometimes spelled Rauzabal. It's derived from the word *rauza*, meaning a memorial of a high-status person, a prophet, whereas tombs of saints are called ziarat. But I think we should make a combat strategy for the morning." Sahib walked to the low table and put a blank sheet of paper on it. "Only the four of you are going inside the shrine, I'm staying outside just in case. I've got an old rifle, and a permit from the general police chief to carry it. If any soldiers turn up, I'm simply guarding the tomb," he smiled unconvincingly.

"I know the inside, it's not big but it's important that we don't make a mess in there. Remember it will be dark and we mustn't turn on any lights: nobody goes to the shrine at five in the morning. I don't even want to think about what would happen if a military patrol car went by," Eli added.

Sahib continued, "The tomb looks like this on the inside." He grabbed a marker pen and drew the footprint with confident strokes. He then invited them to the window with it. "Pay attention. On the right side over there is the entrance to the tomb, which was added later. The oak door is barred with a chain with three locks. I've gone and opened the locks so that we don't make a din trying to open them in the morning. Only the fence gate is shut. I'm the guardian and I can go there whenever I please, so there'll be no suspicion there, although…"

"Although what?" Michal asked.

"It'll be during the curfew." He steered away quickly. "Luckily the mosque we go to is opposite the shrine on the other side, but many people go and pray in the new tomb of Sheikh Abdullah, which is nearby. Few Muslims come here these days."

"And non-Muslims?" Marika asked.

"They're forbidden from entering… There's an appliance repair shop next door, but it only opens around eleven." He pointed at a whitewashed house on which somebody had written *Easy Rechargeable* in unshapely letters and drew a battery. "You enter the tiny hallway, where you turn left. That gets you straight to the gallery running around the wooden sepulchral chamber. It's glass, so you'll see the sarcophagus very well. It was once covered with a white-blue cloth with Hebrew insignia; today it's a green cloth, the symbol of Islam. Past the middle window, which is just opposite from here," he pointed at the building, "is a tiny entrance into the sepulchral chamber, which contains the sarcophagus. Visitors are forbidden from entering, but of course I'll let you in." Marika and Michal gave him a grateful look. "As soon as you enter, you come across a smaller tombstone, belonging to Syed Naruddin Rizvi, who was buried there in the 16th century. The bigger stone belongs to Yuz Asaf."

"Who?" Michal shook his head.

"Jesus was given the name Christ by Greeks. His original Hebrew name was Jashua or Jeshua, which the Greek turned into Iesous. It's Iesus in Latin, Issa in Sanskrit and Arabic, and Yuz in Persian. Asaf is Joseph, so it's Jesus son of Joseph. Some Christians have derived the corruption Josaphat from that. I think it will be important for you to take a photo of something that proves almost beyond doubt that a crucified Jew is buried there." Marika and Michal exchanged surprised looks. "When a team of experts led by Professor Fida Hassnain were doing research in the tomb in the seventies, they removed the millennium-old wax off the stone by the tomb and found this." Sahib put down a photo of a rock which clearly showed footsteps engraved in the rock. "It's a custom in Asia that when a saint dies, his death footprints are taken. If I'm not mistaken, you make death face masks of important dead people in Europe. Well, and these are the footprints of the man buried in the tomb. Scars left by crucifixion are visible on them."

"This is what you showed me in Jerusalem…" Marika glanced at Michal. They could barely breathe.

"Allegedly they were carved in the rock by Jesus' companion, Thomas the Apostle. Legends say that he attended Jesus' funeral in person. The world-renowned Christologist Kurt Berna, who cooperates with archeologists, has shown that the stigmas are two thousand years old. They examined the asymmetric footprints, and when they put them across in the computer, it turned out they matched the way Jesus' feet were nailed on the cross. The left foot was nailed over the right one, which is a fact confirmed by the blood stains on the famous Shroud of Turin, in which Jesus was wrapped after they took him off the cross. You have to realize that crucifixion has never been used in India."

"It sounds like a fairy tale." Michal shook his head.

"Both tombstones face in the north-south direction according to the Islamic custom," Sahib continued.

"But I read somewhere that Jesus' tomb is situated west-to-east. Only Jews bury their dead like that. And that was supposed to be the proof of it being a Jew," Michal objected.

"Yes, Kashmir was a Hindu and Buddhist country in the first century. As you know, Hindus and Buddhists burn their dead. Islam didn't exist back then. And that Jewish saint's tomb is really west-to-east, only...hm... unfortunately, you won't get to see it."

"I don't understand," Marika burst out.

"It's underground, and it's been bricked up for about forty years. Look," he took them to the window again. "The entrance to the shrine is on this side now, but originally it was over there, from the side street. The shrine is near the river, and there used to be frequent floods, so the layers of earth and various debris around the tomb have slowly risen. Some of it's been brought by the water, some by people. All that's left of the original entrance is a crevice at the street level, which nobody notices these days. You can look inside the underground tomb through it..." He fell silent for a moment. "Unless the tomb is renovated soon, it's very likely going to be destroyed completely within a few years... That would be the definitive death of Jesus Christ."

"Maybe that's someone's point," Michal remarked.

"To general surprise, the then Kashmiri prime minister Faruq Abdullah permitted research in the tomb in 1984. On the eve of the day when a group of experts was going to enter the tomb, violent fighting broke out around it which left seven people dead. You see, the Khanyaar neighborhood with its labyrinth of narrow lanes is the ideal hiding place for... hm... underground anti-government fighters," Sahib added. "But we're safe," he tried to calm them down unconvincingly.

"And are there no stairs inside the shrine that go underground?" Michal asked.

"There's a ladder there, but that's been bricked up too. To leave our two saints alone," Sahib smiled bitterly. "But the rock with the carved footsteps that you'll see is original. It's on a pedestal in a white frame in the sepulchral chamber. I think it will be good enough for your meditation," Sahib tried to please Marika. She couldn't hide her disappointment.

"Legends say that along with the footprints in the rocks there's also another precious relic in the tomb, allegedly made by Thomas the Apostle himself," Eli added.

"Thomas the Apostle? How could he get here?" Marika asked.

"It has been proven that Thomas was in India in the latter half of the first century. Purportedly, when Jesus felt his final hour was coming, he invited Thomas, who prepared a tomb exactly on the spot where Jesus breathed his last breath."

"So, he actually died in that place?"

"He used to come here to meditate. It was meant to be symbolized by a statue, known as UNUM, marked with the letters J and B."

"I've heard about that," Michal observed.

"The Joachim and Boas statue, or Jesus and Buddha, a statue symbolizing the unity of the two saints and the unity between east and west. It's said to show Jesus meditating in the lotus position. They say the statue has healing powers. Maybe the statue really was there, but someone's taken it. Or maybe it's just a legend, you know how much people can make up..." Eli said

An unusual noise was suddenly heard under the windows: a large group of gesticulating men were hurrying somewhere, raising their fists and shaking them. Sahib opened the window slightly. "They're grumbling because they weren't allowed to see a movie due to the curfew that's beginning in fifteen minutes. The nearby Shiraz cinema's showing a brilliant Bollywood movie with scantily clad girls, and all the men are going crazy about it."

As soon as he finished saying that, shouting and shooting was heard from the street. Michal, Marika, Sahib, Eli and Bashrat were watching the scene from behind the curtains. When the men in the street scattered, two lifeless bodies were left lying in pools of blood on the pavement. A military patrol arrived soon, soldiers tossed the bodies in the pick-up and zoomed away.

Sahib closed the window and pulled the curtain. His hands were shaking. "Fifteen minutes makes no difference in Srinagar... And remember, shoes off in the grave!"

67 Ibis Ad Crucem

It was the beginning of the twelfth day of the Jewish month of Nisan of the year 3795, the momentous year of Tiberius' rule, when a group of temple guards stormed into the Garden of Gethsemane upon orders from former high priest Annas. Several members of the Sanhedrin also arrived with them despite the fact that they were not allowed to take part in the arrest and that no court sessions were permitted after sunset. However, their hatred toward Jesus was greater than their respect for the Mishnah, the Jewish code of law. To their utmost surprise, a hundred Roman soldiers under the command of centurion Longinus arrived in the same garden at almost the same instant. Jesus himself walked up to the temple guards asking who they were looking for. They said Jesus and he proclaimed himself as the one they were seeking, thus the kiss of betrayal that Judas had ready for identifying him wasn't needed.

The group of the temple military servants accompanied by Romans sent by Pilate brought Jesus to Annas, who hated the Nazarene all the more because he couldn't forget his insults back when he was the high priest; in the first place, he was angry with him for his unyielding criticism of his temple swindles. Today, his son-in-law Caiaphas was the number one man of the Sanhedrin, but the arrest of Jesus was initiated by Annas, who had kept control over the priests after his seven years in office.

Jesus knew the Jewish law and refused to testify before Annas, since he wasn't the high priest. Moreover, he was entitled to two witnesses. Annas was forced to send the arrestee to see his son-in-law, who was in the high priests' office for the fifth year. They brought him to Caiaphas' home, thus violating the law, because the law stipulated that court hearings could only be carried out in the court hall on Temple Hill. Caiaphas managed to summon twenty-four of the seventy-one members of the Sanhedrin in his house at night; that was the minimum number required for court to proceed. Thirteen votes were required for sentencing, eleven for deliverance. The accused could be declared guilty by a majority of at least two votes. After hearing Jesus and false witnesses, Caiaphas opened a vote on Jesus' guilt and proposed a death penalty; everybody but two – Joseph of Arimathea and Nicodemus – voted for it. Rumor had it that Joseph was a secret adherent of the Essenes. Nicodemus' wife Martha was an Essene herself and she had a great influence on her husband.

"Wait!" Nicodemus exclaimed in a mighty voice when a satisfied hum and laughter over the sentence filled Caiaphas' hall. "We have no right to judge at night, as we had no right to arrest at night. Three stars were seen clearly when he was arrested, and our law forbids arresting after sunset. You know very well that court hearings must not take place before the morning offering…"

"Shut up, don't spoil it," some of the priests protested, but Nicodemus continued fearlessly, "And the honorable Sanhedrin is not to gather in private spaces."

"This is my space, and I'm the high priest," Caiaphas halted him with a violent gesture that nearly blew off his rich vestments.

"But it's not a temple," Joseph joined Nicodemus and added, "First the accusation has to be presented, but you sentenced him straight away! Everyone may plead for deliverance, but not everyone may push through condemnation! Thus is the law!"

"Why, you two are against," Caiaphas laughed, and others with him.

Joseph fell silent for a while, but Nicodemus continued fearlessly. "According to the Mishnah, the witnesses have to agree in every detail – and these have contradicted each other in almost everything. You proclaimed the sentence at night, whereby you've violated the law, as a death sentence may only be proclaimed by day. You didn't even wait for the legal period of twenty-four hours that have to elapse between the hearing and the proclamation of the sentence! And the worst breach of law has been committed by you, high priest, yourself!" Nicodemus turned to Caiaphas indignantly. "You know very well that voting on the death penalty has to be done individually by each member of the Sanhedrin, starting from the youngest ones so that the elders cannot influence them. But you opened the vote for everyone simultaneously. You have insulted our laws, because you acted on the day of Passover, which the law strictly forbids!"

Jesus stood in silence and watched the dispute.

"Don't bother us with trifles!" Caiaphas burst out angrily. "Do you know who you're defending? This man insists that he has the hereditary right to the throne of David and Solomon, defiles our holidays because he heals and acts on the day of Sabbath, says he'll demolish the Temple and rebuild it in three days, threatens to send Pharisees, Sadducees, Scripture scholars and doctors to exile, and incites against the Emperor! He's declared himself to be a son of God, thus blaspheming God – and that deserves the death punishment, be it at night or by day!" The others nodded approvingly.

"We're all God's children," Jesus said softly. "That's what I meant." But nobody heard him in the hubbub and shouting.

"You have a problem even so," Joseph rejoined the debate. "The Roman Senate has recently withdrawn your right to pass death sentences and gave it exclusively to the prefect. If this man was to die, it could only be done under Roman law, not Jewish, because if you accuse him of inciting against the Emperor, that's a political delict, not religious!" There was hum in the hall. They realized that their decision on Jesus' death wasn't valid without the Roman administrator's approval.

Annoyed, Caiaphas himself headed the procession of temple guards and set off all across Jerusalem to the Roman Antonia Fortress, also known as Praetorium, where Pilate resided during the Easter holidays. To refrain from ritual wrongdoing, he remained outside along with several of the priests.

"So, here they come," Pilate sniggered when he saw the large group of priests and temple guards outside his window, lit with torches.

"Go and get him," he turned to centurion Longinus, who had been informing Pilate in detail about Jesus' actions for the third year. Based on his and other news, Pilate had no convincing reason to give him the most severe sentence. Gaius Cassius Longinus informed him, after all, that Jesus called on people to practice love and understanding. Hundreds of people would indeed listen to Jesus in places where he preached, but nobody had ever heard him utter one word calling for an uprising against Rome or the prefect. The Nazarene rabbi was evidently very popular among the people of Judea, Samaria and Galilee. Gaius would catch himself listening attentively to his speeches made in Aramaic, which he understood well. He would often agree with Jesus internally. Being a Roman soldier, however, he couldn't manifest his liking for the man openly.

"Unfortunately, that won't be possible. Orthodox Jews must not enter your abode before Passover, else they'd become unclean."

"Rattle their bones! What am I to do then? I'll send them off."

"My lord, they're being led by the high priest. Annas would never forgive you. You must see them outside."

"Are you saying Caiaphas, not Annas is leading them?"

"Annas is behind this conspiracy. He makes enormous amounts of money on the temple finance. His son-in-law, the high priest Caiaphas, is just his figurehead."

Pilate was pacing around the hall nervously. "This Jesus is a Jew, not a Roman. Let them handle him."

"They can't. You know well that you're the only one who can decide about the death penalty they're proposing, according to the recently introduced *ius gladii* – sword law."

"However strict their laws, a Roman prefect will not bow to any of their priests. Go and ask them in. If they refuse, bring in just this Jesus."

Only the temple guard commander and Jesus came in eventually. Pilate heard him once again and then told the temple guard commander, "I can find no guilt in him. Take him and judge him under your laws."

"We aren't allowed to kill anyone," the commander objected. "You should judge him because he's incited people against Rome, told them not to pay taxes, and declared himself to be king, thus indicating he competes with the Emperor," the commander objected.

"He did not incite anyone against the Emperor. Conversely, he said that Emperor should get what belongs to him!" Pilate raised his voice. "And as far as the so-called 'his kingdom' is concerned, he maintains it's not of this world! What I'm interested in is threats to the Roman Emperor – and he has not done that."

"That's not true," the commander objected.

Pilate smiled. "And what is true?" He walked around the hall nervously for a while, obviously reluctant to sentence Jesus to death. At that moment it occurred to him that King of Galilee Herod Antipas was staying in Jerusalem during Passover, who had jurisdiction over Nazareth, where Jesus came from. He got a redeeming idea and decided to send Jesus to see Herod, and let Herod decide his fate.

Herod was pleased to see Jesus, as he expected the Nazarene to entertain him with some miraculous acts. And he was afraid of proclaiming a negative verdict over him as he still had a fresh memory of the revolt among his soldiers after the death of John the Baptist, with whom many of them had secretly sympathized. He had no use for more riots among the soldiers in case he condemned Jesus. He knew Pilate and he knew that if he had been clearly convinced of Jesus' guilt, he'd have passed the death sentence himself and wouldn't be sending Jesus to him. But he didn't want to anger him, so he declared Jesus innocent and sent him back to Pilate. He gave a letter for Pilate to the accompanying commander of the escort.

"Reverend Roman governor! I have acknowledged all the charges concerning Jesus of Nazareth, Galilee. Although I could judge this man in the spirit of the Sanhedrin charge, I will gladly pass my rights to you because you are above me in both rank and jurisdiction. Whatever your sentence, I will agree with it. Signed, Herod Antipas, King of Galilee and Perea."

The military escort arrived at Antonia just as Pilate's wife Procula was urging her husband to spare Jesus with respect to the fact that he'd cured their son of epilepsy.

"I'd like to set the man free, but it seems I won't have any other choice but to…" he looked at his wife guiltily. "You know what the situation in Rome is like. The complot against Tiberius initiated by my protector Sejanus has failed, Sejanus is dead, and the Emperor is now vetting everyone who was in contact with Sejanus. The last thing I need is that the Emperor gets news that I let a man live who's declared himself the Jewish king according to Caiaphas. Caiaphas is threatening that if I don't send him to his death, he'll write to the Emperor himself and inform him that I sympathize with a man who incites against Rome," Pilate explained to her and rubbed his temples nervously.

"How egregious," Procula exclaimed. Then a smile appeared on her face. "What if you took advantage of the Jewish superstition that they'll be saved if they load their own sins on the shoulders of a person they sacrifice?"

"I don't see why you're saying that." Pilate looked at her blankly.

"This individual becomes a scapegoat of the nation. That's why they pick one criminal out of every jail before Passover every year, on whom they ritually pile a load of sins of the general populace."

"How's this related to Jesus?"

"I mean you've sentenced to crucifixion those three villains who headed a marauding gang. You could propose to the Jews to pick one of them instead of Jesus."

Pilate stared at his wife for a long while. "That's a good idea. Only I'm afraid this Barabbas ben Jezeia, the rich one, has made security arrangements beforehand and redeemed a pardon with the priests. But I'll give it a try. I'll appear in front of the crowd and propose it to them," Pilate smiled. His wife, who was Jesus' secret sympathizer, gave him a grateful look. "I'll try to hold back the proclamation of the verdict as long as possible." But Caiaphas and his priests were no fools, and when they saw Pilate hesitating to proclaim the verdict, they inferred what he was going to do and only let their loyal people, who had sworn to ask for the death of Jesus, not Barabbas, in the crowd that gathered under the staircase leading to that part of Antonia where Pilate lived. He bribed them with part of the money that Barabbas had redeemed himself with.

Pilate came out onto the staircase, and the crowd fell silent. "I can't seen any guilt in this man. I'll just have him whipped and let him go."

"No, no, no! He's a dangerous criminal and must be crucified!" But Pilate wasn't listening to the crowd and gestured to the soldiers. The commanding officer Pappus raised his hand and one of the soldiers tore off Jesus' clothes, tied his hands to the pole above his head, and started to beat him on the back, shoulders and legs with a flagellum, a short military whip with leather straps each with a lead ball at the end. The onlookers' faces frowned when a pool of blood began forming by Jesus' feet and clotted into black lumps.

When Longinus – who had been present all along – saw that Jesus' legs were beginning to buckle, he gestured for Pappus to end the flagellation. The soldiers made a crown of thorns for him and put it on his head. Pilate was sure that he had pleased the crowd enough and wanted to release Jesus again.

"You're not the Emperor's friend if you release him, because everyone who pretends to be king opposes the Emperor," one of the zealous Levites called. "We want his death!" they repeated after him.

Pilate silenced them with a gesture of his hand, but nervousness could be felt in his voice. "Men of Israel, as is the custom before the feast of Passover, I shall release one convict and give him to you. Barabbas has been found guilty of murdering a dozen people. Let him suffer on the cross," he pleaded more than ordered. But the crowd started whistling and shouting out loud.

"Which one do I release then?" he asked uncertainly.

"Barabbas!"

Pilate grew nervous, pointed at Jesus and cried loudly, "His blood will fall on you. I warn you!"

"Let his blood fall on us and our children."

"As you wish," Pilate resigned a while later and took a bowl of water, in which he washed his hands. "I'm washing my hands of the blood of this just man. You wanted it. I'm releasing Barabbas and giving you Jesus and the other two." Then he turned to his soldiers. "Carry out the sentence immediately."

"You know that nobody is allowed to die on the cross during Passover according to our faith.

Leave him in the jail and crucify him after the Passover," one of the priests objected.

Pilate knew very well that the Jewish religion forbade people from dying on the cross during the most important Jewish feast, and in spite of that, he sentenced Jesus at that time, the most inconvenient for the Jews. "I've decided. Ibis ad crucem. Let him go to the cross!"

68   The Figure in the Tomb

It was three in the morning on May 21, 2010. Marika wasn't asleep. She was tossing and turning on the hard mat, trying to think of the peaceful surface of a lake, as she always did when she couldn't fall asleep, but nothing was helping. It was a dark night; the stars were hidden behind clouds. She stood up, walked over to the window, pulled the curtain aside cautiously and glanced at the shrine. The occasional barking of stray dogs was heard outside the windows, with isolated pistol and rifle shots added to it. She had learned to distinguish the sounds of these firearms during her several hours in Srinagar. The dark green roof of Roza Bal made a mysterious impression on her in the light of a flickering lamp fastened to a post next to the entrance. Bashrat, Eli and Michal were watching her from the corner of their eyes: none of them could sleep either. She lay down again at half past three; her eyes were narrowing with weariness.

In her half-sleep she noticed a female figure by the curtain. The white-haired woman was smoking, looking at the tomb, and saying something with a smile on her face. Marika listened closer: "Cancer's bad, cancer's bad… That's what you deserve, shlomo."

"Mother, please be quiet, the others can't sleep!" Marika yelled, but the figure didn't stop smiling and the words, which she said over and over and over, kept coming. "Go away, away!" she tried to drive her away, but she only hit Michal lying beside her, who'd just managed to fall asleep for a brief moment. He held her hand and calmed her down. The incomprehensible screeching sounds coming out of her throat stopped. She calmed down and fell fast asleep, only to be interrupted by Sahib a while later. "Get up everyone, it's half past four."

The men changed in the room, and Marika went behind a curtain.

"You don't need to put your perfume on," Sahib prodded Marika sarcastically.

"I'm not."

"Who is then?" Sahib looked at the men in surprise. They gazed at each other. "There's such a strange fragrance in here," he sniffed. "Like lavender…"

"More like rose," Eli remarked, inhaling without understanding.

Marika and Michal exchanged puzzled looks, and Marika just shrugged. Michal understood. "Open the window," Bashrat asked Eli.

Sahib gave Eli and Bashrat flashlights. "We'll eat afterwards. Can we go?" The men nodded. They walked down a wooden staircase to the ground floor. Sahib's wife had her bed opposite; she and the children seemed to be fast asleep. Sahib opened the old gate and watched the street. It was deserted, only a cat could be heard meowing somewhere. He motioned them to go, ran first and then the others crossed the street behind him. The fence gate was open, and so was the door to the hallway. Marika noticed a row of graves behind the building.

"A Muslim cemetery," Sahib said softly. "I'll stay here, Eli will lead you."

Eli entered the gallery first, followed by his father, Marika, and Michal last.

Everything inside was exactly as Sahib had described the previous day. Eli's flashlight lit up the glazed wooden sepulchral chamber. He pushed down the handle on the narrow door leading into the chamber. They nearly bumped into the tombstone of the Muslim saint. They walked a few steps and stopped by a tombstone lacking any inscriptions or identifications. It seemed as if it consisted of three parts. The bottommost one was the widest, the central one narrower, and at the top was a stone sloped like a roof. But it was a stone monolith.

"This is it," Eli whispered. "But as is the custom in Muslim tombs, it's just a replica; the actual grave is underground."

"What's this?" Michal pointed at an inconspicuous piece of pipe protruding from the floor.

"Hang on… that's interesting, I've never noticed it before. It seems they remembered the 'nephesh' soul. In Jewish tradition, each tomb had a pipe for souls or a well for spirits. It allows the soul that inhabits the tomb freedom of movement and contact with the outside world," Doctor Bashrat explained.

"That means that down there... hm... is the actual tomb," Marika whispered.

"Yes, only we can't get there."

Seeing that Marika was disappointed, Eli took her to the tombstone and cast a light on the rock where the footprints were clearly visible in the sharp light of his flashlight. "We'll wait outside in the corridor and you can meditate here if you want to. How much time do you need?" He glanced at his watch, "It's five on the dot."

"That's weird." Bashrat listened to the silence. "It's five o'clock, the time the muezzin normally calls for morning prayers. It's totally quiet. Muezzins are very well informed; they might know something. The silence is suspicious." As soon as he finished speaking violent gunfire was heard out of the blue, followed by noises and cries of male voices coming from the street. The voices then started to fade and were followed by the sound of an engine, which stopped after a short time with soldiers jumping off the car. Frightened, Michal, Marika, Eli and Bashrat were looking out onto the street through the tiny window. About ten soldiers were hitting some unarmed men with long sticks; the men were putting up resistance, but vainly. They broke the sticks on them, then heaped the bloodied men on the deck like sacks of potatoes and left. Sahib ran inside the tomb with three big keys in his hands.

"I've shut all the three doors just in case. These madmen could easily run in here and shoot the place into smithereens."

He sat down and wiped his sweaty forehead. Thumping footsteps were heard again, this time followed by gunfire. The booming noise of grenades joined the pistol and rifle fire. The men and Marika were shaking with fear. The soldiers cleared away from the window a while later, but the rattle of engines was heard again a few minutes later and the gunfire around the shrine grew stronger.

"It looks like the rebels have started an offensive," Bashrat noted. "If you can meditate in this atmosphere..." he turned to Marika, who was standing by the tomb; tears of helplessness and indignation were rolling down her face.

"I'm very sorry for getting you in this situation," she apologized.

"Maybe we're lucky to be just here," Sahib remarked. "I guess even the Indian soldiers won't dare break the door of a Muslim shrine. A popular uprising broke out in Kashmir years ago when someone allegedly stole Mohammad's hair from the local Hazratbal mosque. They can't afford to do that again," he tried to appease them.

"I'm afraid they don't care at all," Bashrat replied and motioned the others to go back out to the gallery and leave Marika alone. The gunfire, explosions, shouting, and noise from military pick-up engines were intensifying. Armor-piercing weapons were heard increasingly more often, meaning there were tanks in the streets. The air was thick with smoke, a helicopter flew over the shrine occasionally. The men went back to Marika and prayed together. They shook with fear. Only Marika remained surprisingly level-headed. Heavy detonations of artillery grenades joined the gunfire. The building shook after each grenade explosion. Sahib looked out of the window: his house opposite was alright, but the white wooden house next to it with the *Easy Rechargeable* sign was in flames.

"Maybe, maybe we could go now," Sahib said in a trembling voice. "If Muslims find us here… One of the worst crimes in Islam is defiling a tomb. And a non-Muslim visit in a Muslim tomb is…"

"I'd rather not now. There's a battle outside, and we're safe in here," Marika protested resolutely. Sahib glanced at his watch. "It's half past five, it's beginning to dawn; okay then, we'll wait here."

Just as he said it, a deafening explosion was heard in the street toward the mosque. Roza Bal trembled, and the pressure wave tossed them toward the Muslim tomb, where they fell on top of each other.

Out of fear, Marika seized Michal's hand, wet with sweat. "Aren't you scared?" he asked her.

"You taught me to make friends with death."

The rear part of the building collapsed, but fortunately nobody was hurt. They were sitting in clouds of arid dust, hunched up in a knot. Acrid smoke was mixing with the dust: something was on fire at the back of the shrine. They were waiting to see what would happen. When the dust had settled, Bashrat pointed at the strip of light that hadn't been there before. "Look, the light seems to be coming from below…" The others were also gazing that way. "Oh my God, the missile broke the wall that was blocking the entrance to the underground…"

They were staring down a huge hole that revealed an old wooden ladder running into the underground, lit with light from the street. They were looking at each other with their eyes sunken in faces dirty with sweat and dust.

"Are you alright?" Bashrat asked. Everyone nodded. The gunfire in the street was continuing, and grenade explosions were heard in the immediate vicinity of the shrine. "It seems the fighting is moving from the river to this part of the old town." They were thinking whether to return of Sahib's house or stay in the holy place, which gave them at least some certainty of not attracting the battle.

They stared toward the hole in the ground with curiosity and fear. Marika stepped toward it impatiently, but Eli pushed her aside, knelt down, pointed his flashlight into the hole and looked in. After forty years, it was the first sight of the true grave of the man buried in the tomb. The beam from his flashlight was scanning the dark, stale area, in which Eli's eyes were looking through the clouds of dust at a kind of niche carved in the rock, with a stone sarcophagus protruding from layers of mud and soil, at a right angle to that on the ground floor.

"It's west-to-east," he almost squealed with delight. But suddenly he jumped away and with his face pale with the dust, he cried at the others, who were heaped on his back, trying to peek inside.

"Someone's moving in there. I saw a figure…"

His voice was trembling with fear.

69 I'm Giving You Two Weeks

After Gaius Cassius Longinus' eyesight became impaired due to a cataract in both eyes the cohort commander recalled him from his centurion's post in Rome, and as a loyal Roman soldier who had spent twelve years in various battlefields, he transferred him to the Near Eastern military intelligence. His area of action was Judea, and Jerusalem in particular. The regent Valerius Gratus developed a liking for him and for his loyal service and recommended him to his successor, Pontius Pilate, who took over the office of administrator of Judea after him.

Four years later, during Passover, he proclaimed a verdict in one of his most complicated cases. One of the soldiers threw a red gown over Jesus' shoulders and, with the words, "Here's your royal crown," he put the wreath of thorns on his head: it was made of twigs used for starting illumination fires. To his shoulders they tied a patibulum – the heavy crossbeam of a cross. It was soaked with the sweat and blood of those who had been tortured to death before him. Timber was precious in Judea, so they couldn't afford the luxury of giving each convict a new cross. They drove him to Golgotha – the 'place of skulls' – with a cattle whip.

Jesus was followed by silent Gestas and Dysmas, the two murderers who were going to be crucified along with him. The sorrowful procession was headed by the execution squad, commanded by the successor of Gaius Cassius Longinus, his friend centurion Pappus, with whom he had fought in Syria. Under the burden of the crossbeam and blinded by blood that poured across his eyes out of the wounds caused by the thorns, Jesus reeled a few times, then his legs buckled and he fell in the dirt. Golgotha was situated on a rock promontory near the citadel, by the main road going to Emmaus. The route wasn't long but felt endless for the tortured man walking in the heat of the April sun. The death that was awaiting him at the top of the rocky hill would be redemption for him. He wasn't afraid of it, but his heart was seizing up in terror imagining the torment he would suffer on the cross before he breathed his last. What he didn't know was that the execution squad were men selected by Pappus on Longinus' orders. When Jesus collapsed in the dirt for the second time, Pappus picked a man standing by the road to carry the beam to the top of Golgotha for him. Simon, who had arrived for the Passover celebrations from Cyrenaica in North Africa, took the patibulum and carried it up the hill. Once at Golgotha, they tore off the convicts' clothes and first fastened Gestas and Dysmas on their crosses. They were naked, as was Jesus, as yet another way of humiliating them. Jesus was nailed to a T-shaped cross. The soldiers offered the convicts a mixture of wine and myrrh to mitigate their pain, but Jesus refused to take any, so they pushed him to the beam lying on the ground. The psychic strain he was suffering made him sweat, and his sweat was mixing with his blood. They ran forged nails through his wrists. When his hands were nailed to the patibulum, they lifted him and slid the longitudinal beam under him. His fingers twisted from cramps. In a trained motion, a soldier put his left foot over the right one, twisted it and pierced both his insteps and heels at the same time with a long nail. Another soldier nailed a sign over his head reading INRI – *Jesus of Nazareth, King of the Jews*. Then the soldiers used ropes to lift the cross and plant it in a hole carved in the rock, originally ready for Barabbas. At the explicit bidding of the Sanhedrin, they erected Jesus' cross in between the two criminals' crosses. It was nine o'clock. Hundreds of rubbernecks who had come to Jerusalem for the holiday gathered around the three stones. The crucifixion was a welcome spectacle for them.

Underneath the cross, soldiers were playing dice over his clothes.

"Father, forgive them, they know not what they do." Jesus on the cross was begging God for forgiveness for his torturers. He turned to penitent Dysmas and promised him he would be in paradise with him that same evening.

Mary Magdalene, his mother Mary, Cleopas' wife Mary, Eunice, Sophia, Miriam, Salome, Ruth, Martha were standing under the cross, together with a number of priests, soldiers, and rubbernecks who had joined the wailers. John was the only disciple present.

Jesus looked at him and said softly, "I'm putting my mother under your protection." Then he whispered words that none of the Romans or Jews would have understood even if they had heard them: "Heli heli

Lamah Zabac Tani – Sun, oh sun, why have you forsaken me?" The suffering man's breathing was growing weak. He whispered, "I'm thirsty."

Centurion Pappus gestured to one of his soldiers, who dipped a sponge in a leather bag in which he had some posca: sour wine mixed with some kind of opiate, then placed it on his lance and shoved it up to Jesus' mouth, who eagerly licked the sponge. It was now noon, and the sky was overcast with dense clouds. It was going to rain, and the soldiers didn't want to get wet, so they quickly proceeded to the last part of the crucifixion. They were Jews and knew that nobody was allowed to be on the cross by the beginning of the Sabbath. Picturing themselves having to come back before the dark to speed up the convicts' death, they decided to act immediately. With some iron rods, they went over to Gestas and Dysmas and broke their legs brutally, depriving them of the chance to ease their pain by standing on a wooden pedestal block. They found it impossible to breathe as their lungs had been twisted into an unnatural position. It was evident that their lives would expire within minutes now. As they set out to Jesus' cross, Pappus halted them.

"Halt! I'm giving the honor of coup de grace for the king of Jews to my friend centurion Gaius Cassius." He pointed at the former commander, who was approaching the cross, followed by the soldiers' looks. The sky was now overcast unusually heavily; it was almost dark, so they had to light some torches. The experienced Longinus approached, and without hesitation, he ran the tip of his lance between Christ's fourth and fifth rib. He knew the stab wasn't lethal in that spot. Blood mixed with water ran out of the wound. "The job's done," he said and turned to the captain. He mounted his horse and commanded the other members of the execution squad to follow him. As soon as they disappeared in the bend of the road, a violent storm began, and the crowds of onlookers ran quickly to hide in the city. Only his closest ones, four soldiers, and the centurion Longinus stayed by the cross.

Outside the Praetorium, Pappus met with Nicodemus and Joseph of Arimathea, who had been waiting for him there. As they spotted him, Pappus nodded and then they went to see Pilate together. "Prefect," Joseph addressed Pilate, "we have come to ask you for his body."

"You're his uncle, you have the right to demand the body as his relative. But is he really dead?" he turned to Pappus. He nodded. "But how come? So quick? Did you make sure?"

"Did you break his legs?" Procula asked with a sign of concern.

"We didn't. Longinus thrust his lance in his side. Blood and sweat ran out of the wound.," Pappus informed them.

"Interesting, interesting," Pilate shook his head. "It depends where he thrust it. A stab with a lance isn't always lethal, you know. I'm an old soldier, and I've seen cases of soldiers surviving a stab not only with a lance, but with a spear as well." He turned to Pappus. "You're saying blood ran out of his wound?" Pappus nodded again. "Interesting, interesting," Pilate had no end of wondering. "Have you ever heard of a dead man bleeding? All I know is that when you're dead, blood no longer runs."

"A soldier handed him a sponge with some vinegar. Having ingested the vinegar, he called something in a powerful voice, then his head drooped, and he stopped breathing."

"Have you ever had your mouth full of vinegar? You're choking and panting for breath! You definitely can't call anything in a powerful voice. Only if..." Pilate smiled. "For very hard pain, we used to anesthetize soldiers with Indian cannabis, hemp. We mitigated their pains with it along with vinegar and myrrh. And if the soldier was given an opiate – belladonna or mandrake root, the frequency of his heartbeat dropped so much that he appeared dead... Hm... What use is his dead body to you?"

"Prefect, according to the Jewish law nobody may hang on the cross and nobody may be buried on the Sabbath day. We want to bury him in the tomb that I've had cut in my garden. But you know that very well..."

Pilate smiled secretively. "But if you don't bury him in a place for criminals, as your law orders, you will provoke indignation among the Sanhedrin."

"We voted against his condemnation," Nicodemus said.

"Can you make it before the sunset? It's Friday and your Sabbath begins tomorrow."

"We can make it. We have to."

"He's yours," said Pilate. The men bowed and left the hall. Procula was sitting in the chair and weeping.

"Wait," Pilate halted the men, then thought for a moment and said in a conspiratorial, hushed voice, "I'm giving him two weeks. If he doesn't leave the Roman Empire territory by them, I'll catch him, and then he'll be done for. Is that clear?" The men nodded, bowed and left. Pilate walked over to his wife. "Don't you worry, everything's going to be alright. Things are going exactly as we arranged. But I'm telling you here and now that I'll catch him if he doesn't run. I have to. I'm not going to risk the Emperor suspecting me of neglecting my duties."

70 The Royal Bloodline

Sahib got his courage first, followed by the others. They knelt by the hole and looked into the semidarkness underground. Indeed, a figure in a dark purple cloak was moving about there.

"Jesus Christ…" was all Michal managed. But curiosity overcame fear and they gazed down again. There was a peculiar bluish light in the crypt and a stale odor of mold emanated from it, mixing with an unusual fragrance. There were leftovers of torch holders on the tomb ledges and fragments of candles scattered around. The space resembled a cave. Indeed, some of the walls were made of massive rock with holes carved in them, probably to hold torches.

"Can you smell it? The fragrance… it's exactly the fragrance we had in our room today. Like our oil…" Marika whispered.

Bashrat sneezed. The figure in the crypt stood still and looked their way. Bashrat pointed his flashlight at the figure. It was a bald man dressed in a purple robe.

"I must be dreaming…" Michal said. He couldn't believe his eyes.

"You're not," the man below said, in Slovak.

Michal lost his self-control, went to the ladder, took Eli's flashlight and descended into the crypt carefully. The ladder bore his weight. Michal entered the darkness and pointed the flashlight in the man's face. "Put it down, I can't see a thing," the man protested in a voice that sounded familiar to Michal.

"Oh my God, Tomáš, is it you?"

"It is."

"How did you get here?"

"Down the hole from the street. The explosion blew up a wall with a bit of the foundation."

"This can't be true," Michal shook his head. He started walking toward Tomáš, but Tomáš jumped at him, tore off his glasses, smashed them on the earthen floor and stomped on them with his full weight.

"Hey, what's going on? What are you doing? Are you mad?" Michal tried to stop him.

"I couldn't stand it any longer. There's a lot I have to tell you. A great lot. I worked for them. I worked for them, you see?!" he yelled as if out of his senses.

"For whom? Give me back my glasses!"

"For the Vatican secret service. There was a microphone in your glasses through which you were wiretapped. They knew everything about you two."

"For God's sake, Tomáš," Marika cringed.

"I know, I know, I'll explain everything." He stomped on the glasses so vigorously as if he needed to get out all the anger he had for the world, and, most of all, for himself. The men watched the scene through the hole. Sahib and Eli quickly came down, wanting to help Michal. Eli hit the stranger in the chest. Tomáš faltered but still managed to pick up a piece of broken brick and finish off the glasses. Michal couldn't find his way in the dust and without his glasses, but Tomáš took another pair from his breast pocket and put them on Michal's eyes. The men stared at him uncomprehendingly.

"These are your original ones," he hugged him. "Sorry."

"I don't understand a thing," Michal shook his head. "Can you please explain yourself? What secret service? And where's your hair?"

"I got rid of it. I'm a Buddhist," Tomáš smiled. "I'm sure they're after me, and they'll have a harder time finding me like this." Marika was by him now, and he hugged her warmly. Bashrat, who had entered the crypt, was only staring uncomprehendingly.

"This is our friend Tomáš," he introduced the dusty man in a monastic cassock.

"Namaste," Tomáš greeted them amicably.

"Namaste," they bowed and stared at Tomáš in astonishment.

"I'll explain everything, only now isn't the time for it. I think we've just seen a miracle. If I've read it all correctly, we've just gained access to Christ's tomb thanks to the Vatican."

"Thanks to whom?" Marika asked.

"Tomáš, I'm afraid the explosion's hurt you…"

"It's alright. I suggest we pray together and then…we ought to go, there's not much time. The Afghanis may arrive any minute."

"The who?" They didn't understand.

"They're working for the Vatican. I'll explain everything. And please take the batteries out of your cell phones now. Immediately, please! You too, Marika. You're all being tracked via satellite. They know exactly where you are."

"Sir, you'll really have to explain this." Doctor Bashrat walked up to him.

"I will. But now please pray quickly if you want to, and let's go, because they can get in here very easily through the hole from the street."

"There, there, can you see it?" Marika pointed at the bluish light coming out through the cracks in the stone sarcophagus, the lid of which the explosion had moved slightly.

"That's the ossuary with the dead man's bones," Tomáš said and walked to the lid. "It's a sizeable tomb, meaning whoever had it made must have been in the money." He observed the room in the rock. The sarcophagus was half-embedded in a mixture of mud and earth and slightly tilted.

"Ossuaries were cases for bones used in Judea about three hundred fifty years before Christ until the collapse of the Jerusalem Temple. It seems this ossuary has been damaged by the explosion. Can I have a flashlight?" he asked Sahib and lit the lid. Then he wiped it with his cloak. "Oh God… that's impossible… That's, I mean…" He pointed at the symbols that appeared after he wiped off the dust.

"That's the six-pointed Star of Israel," Marika exclaimed.

"The Star of David is the symbol of Israel today, but originally, it's the Satkona, symbolizing Goloka, the abode of Krishna. Indian students wear it to this day, they say it brings them luck. The Satkona is a center of Indian spirituality. The hexagram inside it is a holy place. It consists of two equilateral triangles, one pointing up, known as the purusa, and the other down, known as prakriti. It's the oldest known spiritual symbol in the world. It means both up and down, man and woman, phallus and vagina, angel and devil, day and night, or birth and death," Doctor Bashrat explained with a surprising calm; he forgot about the violence and shooting near the tomb in the heat of the almost scientific disputation.

"We just need to add that for the Jews, the upward triangle symbolizes the Jerusalem Temple, while the downward one stands for its destruction," Tomáš added dryly. Then his eyes fell on the letters on the lid, clogged with dust and a grey-green patina. "Has anyone got something made of metal?" Without a word, Sahib handed him the biggest of the three keys, and Tomáš used one of its edges to remove the sediment carefully so as not to damage the lid. Some letters appeared. "That's odd... hm... a weird inscription," Tomáš shook his head. "It's in Latin, but written in the Hebrew script."

"Srinagar was an international trade hub in Christ's time, with many languages mixing here, including Aramaic, Greek and Hebrew," Doctor Bashrat remarked.

A burst of submachine gun fire was heard in the street near the tomb. The men looked around nervously.

"What does it say?" Marika urged him.

"*Templum Hierosolym Anno Demolationis*. That means the age of demolition of Jerusalem Temple."

"The Temple was demolished in the year seventy," Michal nearly shrieked.

"Oh God, that's impossible... Christ died in that year according to Sanskrit scriptures!" Eli gasped.

The men swallowed some saliva, but their mouths still felt dry. They had forgotten about the war mayhem around the tomb. The secrets and mysteries that they were unveiling increased their adrenaline levels and they were completely unaware of the danger.

Doctor Bashrat took Michal's flashlight silently and pointed it at the ceiling of the cave. "There, that's the nephesh tube, protruding from the upper part of the sarcophagus."

"The soul tube... a bit narrow," Tomáš said sarcastically and eagerly took the flashlight from Bashrat. He pointed it back at the ossuary lid. "Look at the patina. It shows traces of sample collection. It wasn't that long ago, it seems." He shook his head in surprise.

"Professor Hassnain's team was here forty years ago," Doctor Bashrat remarked.

"Right... so that's clear then," Tomáš calmed down and examined the lid. "The case has suffered a lot of mineral evaporation; many of the signs have been destroyed beyond recovery. Each type of soil and rock deposit contains a specific mixture of magnesium, titanium and trace elements. Over the centuries, the patina has made a chemically significant signature, matching the constellation of the variable conditions, including minerals, bacteria and water. Examining this chemical imprint at the quantum level using an electron microanalyzer determines its age quite accurately. I think the professor did just that and determined the age of the ossuary as the latter half of the first century."

"But why is the star in a circle?" Michal asked, taking the flashlight from Bashrat and pointing it back at the six-pointed star.

"Do you know what the circle means in ancient Jewish and Roman tradition?" They gave him a tense look. "The royal bloodline!" Marika and Michal exchanged surprised looks. However, Tomáš couldn't see their inquisitive stares; he continued wiping the ossuary with the key until he discovered a cross next to the inscription. He frowned and took a deep breath. "There, look… So, we have a Star of David in a circle and a slanting cross."

"As far as I know, the cross didn't exist as a symbol before Emperor Constantine," Michal pondered.

"Hang on, the Christian author Tertulianus mentioned the cross as the Christian symbol already a century before Constantine," Tomáš objected.

"But this one's a bit odd," Marika looked at the X-shaped cross.

"In some conservative Jewish Christian communities, known as Ebionites, the equilateral slanting cross symbolized Jesus carrying his cross to Golgotha. That's why it's at an angle. The fact is that the early Christian movement hadn't accepted the torture instrument as a religious symbol. For the early Christians, wearing a Roman cross on their necks would be like people today wearing the symbol of the electric chair or the gallows. The equilateral cross symbol was even found in Pompeii, which was destroyed forty years after the crucifixion of Christ."

"We've used the equilateral cross symbol since time immemorial," Doctor Bashrat joined the debate again. "I think it was the Ebionite, the earliest Christians who came here with Christ. They didn't believe in his divine nature, they insisted he was an ordinary human being produced by Mary's intercourse with a man. They insisted on adhering to the Jewish Torah, Sabbath and all the Jewish rituals, of course, including the funerary ones."

"Five centuries before Christ, in Ezekiel's time, the equilateral cross was the symbol of justice. Do you know what the cross sign was called in Hebrew? In Revelations, Jesus said the famous words, *'I'm the Alpha and the Omega, the first and the last, the beginning and the end.'* The Alpha and the Omega are the first and last letters of the Greek alphabet. In Hebrew, these would be Aleph and Tav. And in Jesus' time, the letter Tav was written as an X. So that would explain these symbols," Tomáš pondered.

"Look here…" Michal shone the flashlight at some peculiar bones jutting out of the soil layer.

Tomáš bowed down and began to dig up the earth with Sahib's key. He unearthed a strange skull a moment later. "It looks like a small animal. I don't think I'd be very wrong to say it was a lamb's skull. And you all know who the Lamb of God is in the Bible…"

"The light, the light…" Marika shouted, as the thin beam of dark-blue light emanating from the ossuary grew stronger. "The lid's shifted. Help me," Tomáš approached the lid and tried to push it open.

"No, Tomáš, you can't do that," Michal protested.

"Sir, I'm warning you. Disturbing the peace of the dead is blasphemy against God," Bashrat stood in front of him. "Even Professor Hassnain's team didn't do that," Bashrat tried to stop Tomáš, but he too was overpowered with curiosity.

"I'm a priest, I can do it," Tomáš replied. Ironic hyperbole was typical of him, but now genuine curiosity prevailed in him. "Please, then, please…"

"Of course, what are you afraid of?" Sahib came up. "Maybe we'll find something of value to us." He came up to Tomáš and they pushed the lid aside together. The others couldn't control their curiosity either and stepped closer. What they saw inside left them breathless. The stone ossuary, sized about twenty-five by twenty by twelve inches, had bones carefully stored in it. The two longest ones, definitely thighbones, lay crossed on top of them, and the skull was laid over them. Smaller bones, many of them turned to dust, were at the bottom. Michal felt sweat running down his forehead; Marika's whole body was trembling at the idea that these might be Jesus' bones. Tomáš maintained a surprising calm. "A year after the funeral, the Jews took the dead person's bones from the earth and stored them in an ossuary forever. This was an imitation of the Roman custom of storing ashes in urns, only the Jewish religion forbids cremation, so they put bones in the ossuaries instead."

"Can you smell the fragrance?" Marika asked suddenly. There was a magical dark blue light in the ossuary, which emanated out into the darkened room, the scent of roses, lavender and resin came from inside it.

"Let's take out the bones, maybe there's something else underneath them," Sahib asked.

"I don't dare," Tomáš said as he gazed in the ossuary in confusion. "But look, this is interesting." He used the key like a pair of tweezers to lift a rotten clump of fabric. He took it out carefully. "Interesting, you can clearly tell the color more or less. It looks like it was dark blue."

"That was Jesus' mother's favorite color," Marika remarked.

"Interesting, God knows what it could have been." Tomáš shook his head and put the piece of cloth back in awe. "They taught us at the seminary that when they examined Thomas' grave in Mailapur in 1523, under the reign of the Portuguese governor of Goa, they found a bit of dark blue cloth in it... hm..."

"It seems to have calmed down a bit outside," Eli said. "I think we ought to go," Doctor Bashrat said.

"No, no... please, let's stay at least a little longer. A little while," Marika begged. Michal gave Doctor Bashrat a pleading look; he nodded.

But Sahib spoke at the moment, excited. "Here, look what I've got ..." He shone the flashlight in the ossuary and pulled a statue from under the bones. It was made of wood, whose color couldn't be seen because it was covered in a green-grey patina.

At that moment, Marika exclaimed and her legs buckled. Tomáš caught her falling. She was pointing at the statue as if out of her mind. "That's it, that's it..."

Michal went up to Sahib and took the statue out of his hands. "It really seems to be it. It seems to be real."

Tomáš came up to him, gripped the statue and looked at it in fascination. "It seems what Archbishop Athanasius told us wasn't a legend. The JB statue: Jesus and the Buddha." Without a word, they gazed at the statue, about fifteen inches tall. "It's the one. The statue symbolizing UNUM: the oneness and the ONE, the statue expressing the primordial unity of humankind. Jesus sitting in the lotus position is in fact the Buddha." They were looking at the figure of Jesus with his right hand raised, the middle and index finger pointing up and the ring and little fingers pointing down. A gesture of blessing.

"Both up and down, both east and west," Eli noted. "His left hand symbolizes cognition. He is sitting on a double lotus flower consisting of seventeen petals below and sixteen above…"

"Look, look," the excited Marika exclaimed; she was shaking so much that Michal had to embrace her tightly.

"There's a trace of a scar on the right-hand side of his chest," Michal said, almost out of his senses.

Sweat was running down his forehead. Athanasius' words were reeling through his mind. "Only Thomas knew Jesus' three secret statements. When the apostles asked him what Jesus had told him, he replied, *'If I tell you but one of the statements that he whispered to me, you will lift solid rocks and start throwing them at me.'* This is Jesus' greatest secret. Thomas is said to have stored it in the mysterious statue…"

"That would mean that the artist who made this statue, pictured him after he was taken off the cross," Tomáš pondered.

"I think we really ought to go now," Doctor Bashrat said. "It's quiet outside."

"No, no!" Marika almost exclaimed. "I want to pray here. I'll be happy if you join me." She didn't wait for their reaction, she crossed herself and started saying the Lord's Prayer out loud. Tomáš put the statue on the lid and joined her along with Michal. Sahib, Bashrat and Eli began praying out loud in Kashmiri. The silent murmuring of their prayers was overshadowed by gunfire that again resounded in the street. "Our Father in heaven, hallowed be your name. Your kingdom come, your will be done…" They were kneeling and praying.

"Shall we go?" Michal turned to Marika a good long while later. She nodded.

At that moment, a deafening detonation was heard in the immediate vicinity of the shrine. The wooden ceiling with the sepulchral chamber over them moved, creaked and tilted to the side menacingly. "I think it's really high time we went," Doctor Bashrat said.

"Hang on now, we're not! Now that we're within reach of mankind's greatest mystery?" Sahib exclaimed. They stared at him blankly. "Well, there's up to the ossuary with the slanting lid. "No, Sahib, don't touch it," Bashrat exclaimed.

"Why not? The whole of mankind has been waiting for this moment. Do you realize what it will mean for us if they're really proven to be his bones? Can't you see how the world will change? Not Jerusalem, not Rome, but Srinagar – our Srinagar will be the center of the Christian and Jewish world. It won't be Jews and Italians making money on pilgrims, but us! We'll have the DNA tests run, come on! We mustn't ruin such a chance!" Sahib walked up to the tomb, but Bashrat stood in his way resolutely.

"No. This is a holy place, and if we really proved we have Christ buried here, there'd be war. As if there hadn't been enough of that! Do you really think, you silly man, that the power-wielders of the world's religions would allow you to take away their privileges and incomes? What do you think would happen if it really turned out it's Jesus Christ lying here? The leaders of Islam, Christianity and Judaism would blow the place up. People need Christ as an ideal, not a real person! You'll leave those bones alone, whoever's bones they are! Eli, Michal, please help me," he went to the ossuary and wanted to push back the heavy stone slab. However, Sahib pushed him away from the sarcophagus violently, jumped to the tomb, shone his flashlight into it and leaned to take out at least a few bones. "Sahib, don't!" Eli yelled at him.

The men wanted to jump on him, but they were halted when they glimpsed through the crack leading onto the street.

"It's too late," a voice said in the tomb.

71   The Escape

The same soldiers that had crowned Jesus with thorns and whipped him mercilessly a few hours earlier had suddenly completely changed their demeanor. They were taking Jesus down gently, as if he were still alive. They put his body on a shroud prepared by Nicodemus. He bowed down to Jesus' chest and listened to his barely perceptible heartbeat. He looked at Joseph and nodded slightly. As experienced members of the Sanhedrin, Joseph and Nicodemus must have known that before a body was wrapped in the canvas, it had to be washed, its chin fixed, and a scarf applied before wrapping around the shroud. They bandaged Jesus' wounds on his feet and hands with a canvas known as *othonia*. The blood stains remained on the canvas as evidence that Jesus' body was alive when taken off the cross. The Roman soldiers went over to the other two crucifixes. Only the commander and four soldiers stayed with Jesus. Instructed by centurion Longinus, they lifted the shroud, which wasn't sewn up as was the custom; they didn't put the scarf or the chin strap on his face as was customary for the dead but headed with it for Joseph's garden nearby where four servants were waiting. The supreme court spies followed the soldiers' each step. When one of them realized that the men who had taken Jesus off hadn't washed him, he lost control and asked Longinus, who was accompanying the soldiers, "They are just going to leave him like that, unwashed?"

"They say they'll only wash him after Passover. It's after dark now, they might touch him and become unclean. Blast you Jews with your customs," Longinus replied. The spy seemed content with the answer. Assisted by Joseph's servants, the soldiers put Jesus in the new tomb cut in the rock of the garden purchased by their wealthy master previously.

It was in fact a small cave with six niches in which dead bodies could be placed. But they didn't insert him into any of them; they only put him on a stone bench. If he were dead, they'd have slid him in one of the niches. Conversely, they wrapped his body in a hundred pounds of myrrh and aloe, corresponding to the weight of a twelve-year old.

Nicodemus had got that enormous amount. Myrrh was an excellent medicine for wounds. If they were dried herbs, the quantity would require several bags, which would have been suspicious. However, fresh herbs were much heavier and more effective. The opium beverage that he had received on the cross instead of the vinegar sponge was keeping Jesus in a deep healing sleep. When the Sanhedrin spies saw Joseph, Nicodemus and the servants roll a large round rock over the tomb, they returned peacefully to the Hashemite Palace. They informed high priest Caiaphas that Jesus' body had been buried.

"Have you asked Pilate to guard the tomb in case his friends want to take the body at night and then declare it resurrected?"

"Yes, we have. Pilate has given us his own guards. He even sent his scribe to the tomb and had it sealed. Anyone who rolls away the stone will expose himself to the penalty of death for violating a Roman seal."

Caiaphas smiled contentedly. "That's good. Now go to your families and celebrate Passover undisturbed."

It was clear to both Nicodemus and Joseph that they had to get Jesus out of the tomb inconspicuously as soon as his condition would permit. The tomb was guarded by Roman soldiers headed by Longinus, who were clearly instructed by Pilate on how to act. On the third day, shortly after midnight, as Jerusalem was sound asleep after intense celebrations of the second day of Passover, Jesus, braced by two men, walked to the entrance of Joseph's garden, where two other men with two donkeys were waiting for him. They helped him mount one of the animals, the younger one sat behind him and Jesus leaned on him. Joseph of Arimathea sat on the other donkey and motioned to his son to get moving. They passed through the Ephraim Gate and set out for the hamlet of Bet-Basi, where Nicodemus and his friends were awaiting them in a peasant's house. They knew the supreme council spies were scouring the area around Jerusalem and didn't want to take pointless risks. After two weeks, enough time for a little recovery, Jesus decided to leave Palestine for good alongside Nicodemus' son, his loyal disciple

Thomas, and his mother, who had recently had her fifty-fourth birthday. Jesus longed for Kashmir, where he'd left his Mariam. Not only his love for her but also prophecies were commanding him to go where his lost Israeli brothers were awaiting him. They set out for the port of Jaffa, where they arrived on the third day. Mary and Jesus sat on the donkeys, while Thomas and Nicodemus junior walked. They enjoyed a short break in Emmaus. Nicodemus' son parted with them in Jaffa. Jesus, Thomas and Mary continued by boat to Tyre in Lebanon. They chose that way because it was dangerous to go north across the land via Judea, Samaria and part of Galilee, where Caiaphas' informers headed by Saul were just teeming. It was a four- or five-days' journey from Tyre to Damascus. The house of Jesus' former teacher Dositheos stood in the desert by Kokhba south of the capital of the Syria province. He accepted Jesus and his friends for several weeks. Dositheos and his followers washed Jesus' wounds every day and smeared them with a warm ribwort extract dissolved in clove oil, with an addition of birthwort and pricklewort. His condition was improving rapidly, the wounds left by the nails on his wrists, insteps and heels were healing well.

By then, temple guards instructed by the high priest Caiaphas and Roman soldiers instructed by Pilate were searching places and dwellings where Jesus and those who'd taken him out of the tomb could be hiding. The order was clear: catch him whatever the cost. Pilate got a letter from Rome via a quick messenger, in which Emperor Tiberius was asking him for a prompt explanation of the resurrection of some Jesus and information on how he was going to handle the explosive situation following his alleged rising from the dead. He read the letter out loud for his wife, who showed overt joy over Jesus' rescue, to realize the seriousness of the situation. He heard increasing amounts of information that Jews, not only in his province of Judea, but also neighboring Samaria and Galilee, were spreading the idea that Jesus had been saved by God, whereby he had indicated that the crucified man was the Messiah. He decided to catch that man at any cost and have him taken around Judea, Samaria and Galilee in a cage to show everyone that he was just a man, and then have him ultimately executed. His fate would be sealed if the Emperor found out that Pilate had been involved in the conspiracy.

During his stay at Dositheos', Jesus learned that one of his loyal disciples – Stephen – had been stoned to death in Jerusalem. That was why he didn't hesitate for a moment when he received a letter from the king of Nisibis in Asia Minor, asking him to come and cure him from his disease. However, Nisibis was ten days away on a horse, which Jesus didn't have. Therefore, his loyal friend Thomas went to the rich merchant Abanes, to whom he offered up himself as his private healer in exchange for a horse with a cart. Jesus would in no case agree to such a deal, but he was convinced eventually by Thomas' urging and by the looks of his unwell mother. They then set out for Nisibis, a city two days west of Mosul. The seat of an ancient university, it was a busy trading center, receiving many merchants and various other people from Jerusalem, making it unsafe for Jesus to stay longer. Two weeks later, the king's condition improved noticeably, and the rumor of his miraculous healing reached the court of the King of Andrapa in Andrapolis in Paphlagonia, in the north of Anatolia.

Although Paphlagonia was part of the Roman province of Galatia, it was far enough from Jerusalem and neither the administrator of Judea nor the high priest of the Jerusalem Temple had any right to act in the province. Jesus and his mother headed there. To his great surprise, he met Thomas there, who had left Damascus before him. He was just about to leave for Parthia, so they parted shortly after the meeting because Thomas had a place secured in an eastbound caravan. He warned Jesus against staying for long because Temple spies guided by Caiaphas' and Annas' vengefulness had been spotted near the city. Therefore, when the King of Andrapa got better, Jesus asked him for permission to board a boat that would take him and his mother down the Euphrates river to Babylon, the capital of the Parthian Empire, which maintained busy contacts with the Far East. There wouldn't be a problem getting a place in a caravan from Babylon. The king was pleased to satisfy him. Jesus reached the port of Babylon after a two-week boat trip; there, he secured two places in the nearest caravan, setting out a week later. It went east along the ancient Silk Road, running from the Vicus Tuscus, the famous silk market in Roma, to Sian, the capital of China. It continued via Susa, Ekbatan, Zadracarta, Mashag, where he bowed to the grave of Shem, Noah's son, and then on via Herat and Kabul; finally, he reached Takshashila, the capital of the kingdom of Gandhara – from where he'd started his journey home almost six years before.

72 You'll Snuff It Lying Down

Eli, Marika, Tomáš, Michal and Doctor Bashrat looked in the direction the voice was coming from. Five men wearing dirty, sweaty battledresses entered the tomb through the hole from the street. They were aiming their Kalashnikov rifles at them. These were the typical weapons of the Afghan LeT fighters and mostly stolen in combat with Soviet interventionists in Afghanistan.

"Hands above your heads!" cried the man who was most probably in command of the team. Sahib, absorbed by his rummaging in the ossuary, hadn't noticed their arrival. One of the soldiers walked over to him and hit him in the small of the back with the rifle butt. Sahib's legs buckled; the men grabbed him by the belt and tossed him to the others. Sahib remained lying, unable to stand, only crackling: he seemed to have had his spine broken with the blow. Doctor Bashrat tried to help him, but the soldier literally tossed him away from Sahib with a violent kick in his shoulder. Sahib was lying without moving and moaning softly. Bashrat stood up with Eli and Michal's help. One of the men leaned curiously over the ossuary, from where the mysterious light was coming, creating a strange atmosphere in the dark tomb. He waved at the nearest soldier, who had a flashlight in his hand. The soldier walked over to him and shone the light in the ossuary. The other three were aiming their guns at Marika, Michal, Bashrat, Tomáš and Eli, standing with their hands over their heads.

"Tomb raiders on top of this! Yuk, awful!" the soldier aimed the flashlight at them and spat. The man who had entered first produced a ruffled photograph, shone the flashlight at it, and then walked among those present, comparing their faces with the picture. However, Michal's, Eli's, Tomáš's and Bashrat's faces were dirty with dust and sweat. The soldier walked one more time in front of them and then angrily shoved the picture of Tomáš's face with long hair before their eyes.

"Have you seen this man?" Shaking with fear, they all shook their heads. "But we'll find him. Have you come to raid this tomb?!"

"We... I... just... wanted to meditate here," Marika said softly.

"You what?"

"Wanted to meditate," Marika replied with surprising boldness.

"And you others?" The men said nothing. "You've come to raid this tomb!"

"We're friends of this lady's and we haven't come to raid any tombs," Eli protested.

"You haven't? And what about the stone being rolled off?"

"It came off by itself with an explosion..."

"I'll teach you about explosions!" the soldiers yelled and knocked Eli down with his rifle butt.

Tomáš bent down to help him, but the guy grabbed him by the neck and shouted something in his face that Eli didn't understand. Suddenly he fell silent, shouted something at the soldier next to him, took the photo again and passed it in front of his eyes, pointing at Tomáš. The soldier nodded, and they both broke out in an uproarious laugh.

"It is you... Hang on... but, but... You're Dvoran... only I really wouldn't recognize you without that hair... So, you're the traitor. Excellent. We have no kid gloves for traitors. And you backed him. A traitor who's betrayed our friends! When someone betrays our friends, it's like he betrayed us. And those who back traitors are worthless scabs just like him... huh, huh..." The soldier stopped laughing. "To the wall! Come on! You understand?!" He pointed his gun at them and indicated the rock face by which they were to line up. "Come on, quick! Move it! You too!" he shrieked at Sahib, who couldn't stand up. "Help him!" Bashrat, Eli and Michal helped Sahib, whining with pain, to stand up. Shaking with fear, they stood by the wall.

"So, you wanted to steal from a holy Muslim tomb?!" the soldier stood in front of Michal and Marika. "And you, damned dogs, helped them instead of killing them mercilessly? You call yourselves Muslims?!" he yelled at Eli, Bashrat and Sahib.

The soldier who had leaned into the ossuary out of curiosity again suddenly began gesticulating sharply and calling at the others to come over. The commander motioned one of the soldiers to guard the six scared people and leaned into the tomb himself. He then grabbed the statue of Jesus in the lotus position. He examined it curiously and showed it to others. Then he put it on the stone slab of the sarcophagus and again pushed his head and upper body into the ossuary. He then wriggled out and held a few bones in his hands. "Are these the bones of your great Jew?!" he turned to Michal and laughed loudly. He chose the biggest bone and gesticulated with it in front of their faces. "No Jews are going to be buried in a Muslim shrine!" He turned to one of his soldiers. "Take out the bones and throw it to the dogs in the street!" The soldier wasn't very keen on rummaging in the ossuary, but the commander shouted at him again and prodded him with his rifle butt.

The soldier went to the ossuary slowly. "But commander, these are said to be the bones of Saint Isa, one of our prophets..."

"No Jew can be our prophet!" When the commander saw that the soldier wasn't very happy about disturbing the peace of the dead, he shoved him aside and stood by the ossuary resolutely. "I'll do it myself then! Give me the light!" The chief leaned into the ossuary and started throwing decaying bones out onto the earth floor. When they were all in a pile, he kicked it furiously. "Your bones will be found here one day too. Let's finish this," he ordered two soldiers who'd been watching the scene.

They walked over in front of the men and Marika, standing by the rock face. "You out," the chief commanded Marika.

"No! If I'm to die, then with my husband!" she refused and remained on her spot.

"Step out, there's no time for funny business!" the commander yelled and began to pull Marika away from the men.

"Marika, please, listen to him," pale Michal begged his wife.

"Please, please... Let the men go and shoot me," Marika volunteered.

"Hey, hey, look at the hero! Go away!" the commander yelled at her and pulled her away from the wall by her hair. Michal wanted to stop him, but the soldier hit him on the head with his rifle butt.

Michal's knees buckled and blood stained his face. The soldier tossed Marika aside. "Stand up!" he commanded Michal. But Michal lay on the ground with his face bloodied and panted for breath. "Okay, you'll snuff it lying down!" the chief ground out, released the trigger and put the gun to Michal's head.

"No! No!" Marika yelled like a wounded animal. The commander gave her a cynical look and aimed. At that moment, a deafening roar was heard, and wheels of dust rolled into the tomb.

73 Joachim and Boas

King Gondophares welcomed Jesus and his mother to the royal palace in Takshashila with all due honors reserved for the most precious guests.

"Welcome back to Takshashila then. I hope you're back for good this time." Then they spent a long time chatting. Jesus told him about everything that had happened in Galilee, Judea, Samaria, Jerusalem and Damascus. He showed him his wounds on the feet and hands.

"What's happened to my beautiful Takshashila? Many of the palaces are in ruins," Jesus asked in surprise.

"Two years ago, ten days after the spring equinox, we suffered an earthquake. A large part of the city was damaged, more than one half of the university campus destroyed…"

Jesus stood up swiftly. "What? That was the day I was nailed to the cross!"

"Strange. I had a vision that day, I knew something bad had happened to you." The king broke off and his eyes misted over. "That day, dear Isa, wasn't the happiest day of our lives. I don't know how to tell you, but… Your wife Mariam and the child were in the city bath on that day."

"The child?" Jesus sprang up.

"Yes, you had… I hope you still have… a son. She named him Eli. She refused to stay in the palace after you left. I persuaded her, but she eventually ran from the palace. I saw to it that her dwelling in the city was dignified."

"What's happened to them?" he asked eagerly.

"I'm sorry to say so, but I don't know. The baths collapsed during the earthquake. Many died in there… I had the ruins examined, I took part in the search myself; we searched day and night, we pushed aside masses of the debris, found many dead, but her body wasn't found… It's been two years... there hasn't been any news of Mariam since then. They say she was spotted around the holy cave of Amarnath."

"Where's that?"

"About a week's trip east of Srinagar. Her native Pahalgam is halfway up to the cave..." Jesus said nothing for a long while. "I'll set off first thing tomorrow. I must find them!"

"I believe you'll succeed. I'll give you horses, men, everything you'll need."

"How's your son?"

The king frowned. "He died."

"What? Rav Anna?" Gondophares nodded.

"What did he have?"

"He didn't die of a disease. The ship on which he was sailing to Madras with his whole family sank in a storm. The storm was during the fatal earthquake. He died on the same day."

"So... so... his wife Punita and his pretty sons Dev and Sanjan are all dead?" The king controlled himself and didn't weep. He just nodded silently. But his face lit up a moment later and he smiled. "But I have a new joy in life. I'll introduce you to my young protégé, who's replaced my grandchild." He nodded to a servant, who opened a door. Another servant brought a pretty boy, who bowed courteously.

"Well, come here, boy," he offered the boy a seat on a silk sofa. "Introduce yourself to our guest Isa."

"Greetings, my lord. My name is Xenophon, I'm ten years old."

"Do you speak Greek?" Jesus gave him a surprised look.

"It's my native tongue. My father was a Greek, and my grandfather, and my great grandfather, and my great-great grandfather."

"How did they get here?"

"With King Alexander. My great grandfather five generations ago got land from Alexander for helping him defeat King Porus on the Jhelum river, Hydaspes in Greek, and then he stayed in the town of Bucephala, established by Alexander not far from here."

"The boy's amazing," Jesus smiled at the king.

The king said something in Aramaic and the boy then continued in that language. "King Porus refused to surrender to Alexander, and he beat him hollow. But then they became friends. Then an ancestor of our King Gondophares, the King of Takshashila Ambi, or Omphis in Greek, let Alexander in the city because he was Greek as well. The great general repaid him with favor. Then he commissioned my ancestor to teach Greek language and philosophy at the university. Greek kings have ruled here since Alexander's time: Euthydemus, Eucratides, Hippostratus, Menander the Great, Antimaius, Azilises, Spalagadames, Vonones, and King Gondophares was preceded by King Spalyrises."

"Unbelievable," Jesus looked at the king, who patted the boy on the shoulder with praise. "What other languages do you speak?"

"I'm learning Sanskrit. And Bactrian."

"Dear Xenophon, thank you for honoring us with your company," the king thanked him. The boy bowed without a word and left the hall. "He's my greatest joy in my old age. I was friends with his father, but unfortunately, he died. During that terrible earthquake as well... I've been raising the boy since then. I believe he'll grow to become a pride of Takshashila."

"I can see he really fills you with joy. I wish you had more of such joy in your life," Jesus encouraged the pensive king. "Did my friend Thomas arrive in your court? I last saw him in Damascus, he was headed for Parthia and then here."

"Yes, I asked him to supervise the construction of a new royal palace. But to my great surprise, I found out the construction wasn't advancing."

"What happened?"

"Thomas had misappropriated the money."

"Thomas embezzling money? I'm sorry, but I can't believe that."

"Well, it wasn't embezzlement as such... He gave it to the poor. He built refuges for paupers, hospitals and schools with the money." Then the king laughed heartily. "When I wanted to punish him, he said he might have misunderstood me. He said he'd thought he was to build a palace in the heavens for me. You too were reported to say you'd build a temple in three days and everybody misunderstood you. I admit, I misunderstood him too." The king laughed, and Jesus along with him. "Do you want to know what was next? Not only did I not punish him, I even had him baptize me. As a sign that I decided to follow your way."

"What a pity I wasn't here! Is he here now?"

"He's gone south. I have news of him baptizing many people in Mailapur and on the Malabar Coast." Joy played in the king's eyes. "Maybe you'll meet him sooner than you think," he said secretively.

"Dear Isa, I'd like you to stay in my court as long as possible and teach me and young Xenophon your faith." Jesus sat in an awkward silence. "I'd be the happiest if you and your mother stayed here forever. I understand you're drawn to Mariam…"

"Your proposal is magnanimous, but my way leads to Kashmir."

"You still bear traces of crucifixion; my best healers will take care of you. I understand you're drawn to Pahalgam, and I only wish you find your wife and son, but honestly speaking… we didn't manage to discover anyone under those terrible ruins, and many of the bodies were disfigured beyond recognition… Hm… And your mother needs a rest after the long, miserable journey," he tried to convince Jesus.

"Thank you, you're very kind, but my condition is better now so I don't need any care." He drank some tea with a pleasant cinnamon scent. "I'm very grateful to you for your hospitality, but I'd like to set off as soon as possible. Yes, I do want to find Mariam and my son! And I want to see how my ancestors live there."

"Are you sure you'll find them there?"

"I hope to." He looked the king straight in the eyes. "I'd like to see the Throne of Solomon."

"Yes, it's in Srinagar."

"But first of all, I want to see the grave of our father."

"Father?"

"The father of Jews. Moses."

"Is the man so important in your life?"

"He's the leader of the Hebrew tribes, the harbinger of the Decalogue. And maybe he's the father of Indians too."

"Indians?"

"Well, the one who defined the Indian law long ago was called Manu." Gondophares nodded. "The Egyptian lawgiver was named Manes. The Greek lawgiver was Minos, and the Jewish was Moses. Aren't the names somewhat too similar?"

"It is interesting," the king admitted. "Unfortunately, Moses and Manu have another thing in common: they consolidated the despotic power of priests," he added.

"But Moses' greatest merit was leading my ancestors out of Egyptian captivity. Unfortunately, many were scattered somewhere later on. Not a trace has been left of Moses. I'm convinced his grave is in Kashmir."

"I hope you find it. There are indications suggesting it." The king's face spread into a broad smile. "But it won't be an easy journey. I can provide you with protection up to the pass at the bend of the Jhelum river at the foot of the Pir Panjal range. But I can't do that onward from there. Unfortunately, Kashmir isn't part of my kingdom. The aggressive Kushans have pushed me out of there."

"I have nothing and nobody to fear. I know the language of the people and the customs of the Buddhists who live there."

"I advise you to wait until the spring. It'll be warmer. The fall is beginning, now you'd arrive in the winter, the passes will be closed."

"I'm resolved to go as soon as possible so that I can walk over the passes before the winter comes."

"Dear Yuz, wait until the spring. I understand your longing for your wife, but you have your mother with you! Leave her here at least, and then you can pick her up."

"I've spoken with mother. She's resolved on coming with me."

"Are you afraid of the Brahmins?" the king asked unexpectedly.

Jesus made no reply. He remembered well his and Barata's escape from the furious priests at the temple in Banaras. "In spite of being a king, you can't provide me with perfect protection from the Brahmins. Unless I never leave your palace," he laughed bitterly.

The king was still smiling roguishly. "When do you want to leave?"

"As soon as possible."

"I'm afraid it won't be that soon... A messenger from your friend Thomas has arrived."

"Where is he?"

"He'll be arriving any day now. He's coming from Banaras."

Jesus' eyes glinted. "Thomas is coming here?"

"Indeed, I invited him."

"Are you in touch with Thomas?"

"I told you he was here recently."

"What's bringing him here now?"

"You are," the king laughed. "Or more precisely... He's been invited by my brother Gad, the King of Kabul, to wed him. Thomas is travelling to see him via Takshashila to meet you."

"That's brilliant! I'm about to meet Thomas again after many months," he couldn't conceal his joy.

"Are we going to see my brother's wedding then?"

"It's very kind of you, but please understand my heart's calling. I want to go to Pahalgam as soon as possible to try and find Mariam and my son!" Jesus replied so urgently that Gondophares didn't dare talk him out of it. "I'll greet my dear friend Thomas and set off immediately."

"I understand, I understand, dear Yuz Asaf," the king nodded.

"Why are you addressing me like that?"

"It means Jesus of Joseph in my tongue. You ought to use that name. It will be more secure even with respect to the Brahmin's custom. They won't discover you as easily under a new name. I'm worried about you..." Gondophares sighed.

"Don't worry, I've managed more difficult situations. And even so, I'm alive longer than I should have been. You're reborn if you've survived crucifixion."

"News comes from your country that God has resurrected you and taken you to the heavens," the king smiled.

"If it helps them spread the faith in the Father's word, let them say it."

"Dear Yuz, I can see you won't be discouraged from your resolution to go to Kashmir. I have something for you." He stared at Jesus solemnly. He opened a drawer in a solid cedar wardrobe and pulled out a jewel box. It contained a single jewel. The king took it out and handed it to Jesus.

"What is it?"

"My present."

Jesus examined the gift for a long time. "Thank you, you're generous." He turned around the peculiar circular locket of a purple color, less than an inch across, which gave out a pleasant warmth. The front showed clearly a six-pointed star and the reverse depicted two columns linked with an arch. They seemed identical at first sight, but upon closer examination Jesus noticed they differed. The left-hand column had a letter J on it, and the right-hand one a B.

"What is it?"

"Your mother gave it to me when I arrived in Bethlehem at your birth, it had been her gift from your father. I was given it out of gratitude for the myrrh that I'd brought for you."

Jesus studied the locket carefully. "J and B stand for Joachim and Boas, the two columns of Jerusalem Temple."

"And maybe also Joshua and the Buddha," the king looked at him significantly.

74 A Cruel Confession

The rotor of a red-and-white Polaris helicopter beat up the dust and litter around the shrine, and the stream of air broke a few branches off nearby trees. Parts of the tomb wall damaged by an explosion tumbled to the ground due to the deafening noise and vibrations. A few of the older roof tiles fell off Sahib's house, and a few fires were rekindled in the smoldering ruins of the former appliance repair shop. The slowly rising morning sun over Srinagar was clouded over by the swirling dust and garbage. Members of the Kargil elite anti-terrorist paratrooper brigade jumped off the helicopter. They had been given their honorary name in 1999, when they became famous in fights with Pakistan in the demarcation line area around the town of Kargil, about seventy-five miles from Sonamarg, where the brigade had been stationed permanently. They were armed with upgraded AK-47 Kalashnikov assault rifles and Insas automatics, which had proven their worth in the Nepal War and the Battle of Kargil.

Some had scarves tied pirate-style around their heads, others wore ruffled baseball caps, but most boasted the traditional maroon berets that made the blood run cold wherever they arrived. Even Afghan Mujahideen, seasoned by merciless fighting with the Soviet Spetsnaz special units, wiped smiles off their faces when they saw the Kargil paratroopers' berets.

Clouds of dust were driven into the tomb. Both the soldiers and the men awaiting their execution started coughing and rubbing their eyes. Gun fire clapped in the tomb, the wooden lid of the sarcophagus caught fire, which lit the interior of the underground cave at least a little. Michal suddenly felt several strong arms grabbing him and carrying him out of the tomb.

"Run, run!" a bereted soldier waved at Marika, Sahib, Eli, Tomáš and Bashrat, and motioned them to get out as quickly as possible.

Shocked, Eli yelled, "Watch out, the ceiling's falling!"

Bits of wall, ceiling, stone, earth and brick started falling down. They'd been weakened by the explosion and now collapsed right on the ossuary. Two of the Afghans failed to notice the falling pieces of wall and were buried under them. Eli and Bashrat managed to grab Sahib at the last moment and were now pulling him toward the street opening. Their arms were shaking, knees trembling with fear; they didn't know where so much strength came from. They noticed that the chief of the Afghans, who'd been preparing to shoot them was lying in front of the rock face – where they'd been standing but a moment before – his head pierced with a bullet.

"This is God's revenge, God's revenge!" Sahib exclaimed.

To his relief, Michal saw that Marika and Tomáš were out in the street. He was lying on the dirty asphalt, unable to move his left leg. He rolled over and ended up face-to-face with the disfigured face of an Indian paratrooper, lying on the road without a sign of life. His maroon beret had slid off his head. He found the disfigured face familiar. Suddenly, he realized it was the face of the Sonamarg soldier who had blessed him the night before. The red dot on his forehead was darker than he'd drawn it. But when he looked closer, he noticed it wasn't a dot but a hole in the middle of the forehead. He felt sorry for the soldier, but there was no time to think about the cruelty of the place.

Tomáš grabbed him on one side, Marika on the other, and dragged him to Sahib's house with all their remaining strength. Eli and Bashrat were helping Sahib. His wife welcomed them with noisy sobs and theatrical gestures, showing how worried she was. Doctor Bashrat shouted something at her quite loudly; the woman fell silent, slammed shut the front door and slid a solid iron bolt over it. They put the injured – Michal and Sahib – carefully on some mats on the ground floor. Doctor Bashrat and Eli gave them some basic treatment. The situation calmed down less than an hour later.

"Listen, listen," Marika spoke and went to the window. Everybody stared at her uncomprehendingly. "They're summoning a prayer." Indeed, it was unusually quiet in the streets, only disturbed by the peaceful voice of a muezzin, summoning the prayer. The others came up to the windows, Michal leaning on a makeshift crutch made from a piece of old railing, and Eli was holding up the battered Sahib. They were looking at the street. The house opposite was on fire, and the dead soldier had been removed. Some men were walking toward the mosque talking animatedly. They were smiling. Maybe they were just pretending to be going to the mosque and were in fact going to see a Bollywood movie with indecent girls. No one could be surprised after all those grim moments. The silence was pierced by a fire engine, which stopped outside their windows. The firemen started putting out the fires in the house next door and the shrine, although there was hardly any need for it by now.

"Turn on the radio," Sahib asked Eli. Some ceremonial songs poured out of the radio. Eli tuned to other stations.

"Private radios are broadcasting again. They're saying there's been an armistice in all of Kashmir since this morning." The voice on the radio continued: "The Pakistani forces have retreated to the demarcation line and the President of Pakistan has announced that his government is ready to sign an armistice treaty. After many years of tension, fighting and skirmishes, a hope for lasting peace has dawned on this sorely tried region."

Eli, who was interpreting the news for them, listened on. "They say even the fighting in Israel has ceased today."

The men and Marika were sitting on mats and sipping tea, which Sahib's wife had made for them in the meantime. Both Sahib's children were cuddling up to their father. His wife was sitting on the edge of the mat, weeping with relief.

"You took the statue?" Michal gave Tomáš a surprised look. He only realized now that the was holding the precious statue of meditating Christ.

"They'd have destroyed it."

"Once Roza Bal is completely extinguished, I'll go there and put it back in the ossuary," Eli said.

"That will take long," Sahib grinned. "The tomb is ruined." He stood up with some effort, took the statue from Tomáš and put it on a pedestal in the hallway. "You can rest assured that we'll return the statue once the tomb is repaired. It's safe here, but it might be stolen from there. It's too precious to be lost or destroyed, God forbid... And please forgive me for my failure," he apologized.

"I know of a place where it would be perfectly protected," Tomáš said. "It's the Hemis monastery."

"What monastery?" Michal asked in surprise.

"Hemis, Ladakh. I'm about to go there. It's the monastery that stores Jesus' biography. It's near Leh, toward Choglamsar."

"I don't understand this at all," Michal shook his head. "And can you tell me, please, what was that about my glasses? And what are you doing here anyway? How did you get here? And why hadn't we heard from you?"

Tomáš drank a long hot sip of tea and thought about where to begin. "Okay then, listen. It'll be a cruel confession."

75 Moses' Grave

After a moving and cordial greeting with Thomas, the two men had a long conversation. They agreed that after the wedding in Kabul, a week's ride from Takshashila, Thomas would come to see Jesus in Srinagar. It was the fall. Accompanied by four royal riders, Jesus and his mother set out toward Kashmir. Jesus' mother's condition worsened rapidly in the evening of the second day on the way. The road was ascending, and the increasing altitude made her breathing more difficult. On top of it, the air temperature was decreasing. Yuz's small entourage was eventually forced to make a stop in the town of Murree in the Himalayan foothills. Some armed forces were encamped there. It was already freezing in the night and the snow cover was descending from the hilltops to the valleys.

Murree was on an open plateau at an altitude of almost eight thousand feet, and strong wind drove people into their homes. The soldiers provided Jesus, his mother and company accommodation in a barrack designed for visitors. Although Jesus used all the tried-and-tested treatment methods, his mother's condition wasn't improving. Five days later, her body was still gripped by a fever. A local military doctor found an unusually high blood content in her urine and peremptorily forbade Jesus from continuing the journey.

"Her condition requires treatment in a hospital. The nearest one is in Takshashila," the doctor informed Jesus. "But she isn't well enough for us to transport her on a cart for two days in this weather. I've taken the liberty of sending a quick messenger to the royal court with an urgent request for the king's vaidhya Rajana."

"Gondophares' private physician?" The military doctor nodded. "When should he arrive?"

"Any minute now."

As soon as he finished saying that, a tall, noble-looking man entered the room. To Jesus' great surprise, Thomas entered alongside him. "When I heard your mother was seriously ill, I took leave from King Gad right after the wedding and returned to Takshashila. I asked Gondophares to include me in this excellent expert's fast-track team," Thomas smiled. "Rajana, the royal physician," he introduced the man to Jesus and the garrison commander. Rajana greeted those present and walked straight over to Mary. Her eyes were closed, and her face red with the fever.

The doctor took her right wrist in his hand and measured the heart rate. His face frowned. "Her heartbeat is extraordinarily fast. She must have been through a lot recently. We'll give her some medicine from kyuru, arura and baru. It should bring her temperature down quickly. Hand me a bowl of ice water, please." The military doctor gestured to a servant, who brought a jar. Rajana dipped a cotton cloth in it and wrapped Mary's head in it so that only her eyes were showing. She didn't react to the icy compress. The doctor replaced the compresses, but Jesus' mother's head was still red with the fever.

"We must bleed her." He prepared his tools and lit some incense. "It's to encourage heart activity."

Jesus took his mother's hand and measured her heart rate himself. "That's a heart rate at the brink of a stroke."

"Are you a doctor?" Rajana asked.

"A little bit."

"All the better. At least I don't need to explain to you that your mother's in a very serious condition." He turned to the military doctor. "Hold this for me, please." He straightened Mary's left arm, wrapped her forearm tightly with string, and cut open a vein with a gold scalpel. He caught the blood in a porcelain bowl. When the bowl filled up, he wrapped her arm with a cotton bandage.

"If she were conscious, her urine would help us." He opened the mother's right eye carefully and examined her right pupil, then the left one, for a long while. "It's not looking good. We'll apply leeches now."

Rajana motioned to the doctor, who brought a jar with pitch-black leeches in it. He removed Mary's stole, which she had around her neck, to ease her breathing. He took out two leeches and applied them to both her carotid arteries. Jesus, Thomas, the military doctor and the commander of the royal soldiers, who hadn't moved an inch from the group, were tensely watching the thin trickles of blood flowing out of her arteries. Rajana continued to measure her pulse.

"It's so weak now I can hardly sense it." He dipped his fingers in her blood, "It's very thick."

"So, there's little hope for her…" Thomas concluded softly. Jesus said nothing. "I'm sorry, but there's little hope," Rajana sighed.

"Please… please, can you leave me alone with my mother?" Jesus asked softly. The men left the room one by one. "You stay here," Jesus said to Thomas. Thomas sat down by him. The two man were observing the woman for a long time silently; her face was turning pale and began to show signs of a deathly hue. The dawn was slowly beginning. Jesus couldn't sense his mother's pulse, so he put a silver pad to her nose. No trace of breath appeared on its glossy surface. He put his ear to her heart. It wasn't beating.

"She's with the Father now," he stated. He sat and tears rolled down his cheeks. Thomas gripped his hand amicably, and Jesus reciprocated the grip. "I'm glad to have you here with me. You, who trusted me the least."

"She was a precious woman. She gave you to us," Thomas said softly.

"Although you're ten years younger than me, you're like my brother, my Didymus, my twin. When it came to my appeal at the Gethsemane to go out to the world and teach nations you were and are the most successful. You've come with me all the way to faraway India. It's pointless to go on together.

"Let's bury my mother with dignity and then our ways shall part. Our Father's word will spread faster if the two of us spread it in different places. I appreciate it very much that you're willing to come with me to Kashmir, but your place is elsewhere. Please, go back to Takshashila. The university there has great opportunities for you to spread the word among students from every corner of the world."

"I'd like to be with you," Thomas gave him a pleading look.

"You're needed in Takshashila and then you'll go south. I'll try to find Moses' grave and traces of our lost brothers in the north."

"I thought we'd go together."

Jesus embraced his younger companion with kindness. "I'm afraid for you. How like me you are with your obstinacy! I hope you don't end up like I have…"

"I appreciate it very much that you trusted me in spite of my lack of faith. I'll never forget the words you told me in Galilee, forbidding me from telling the others," Thomas embraced him firmly.

"And you did well. Had they known what I told you then, a fire would rise from them…"

Thomas looked at Jesus' dead mother. "My lord, has she entered the Kingdom?"

"Don't call me your lord." He paused for a moment, gently stroking his mother's cold face. "Dear Thomas, we've brought a spark here, and it needs kindling. We're now parting by my mother's remains. She's the silent witness of our brotherhood. My dear brother, I'd be glad if we had the same keepsake from this precious woman."

Jesus lifted his mother's dark blue stole, which Rajana had unwrapped and put on the bed. It was woven of silk, so he had no difficulty tearing it in two. "One will be yours, the other mine. Go south and spread the Word. Climb to the rooftops and don't allow priests and theologians to climb them too."

"My lord, I'd prefer to stay with you. It'll be easier for us to travel if we're together."

"Thomas," Jesus took him around the shoulders amicably, "the south needs to hear the Father's word too. I have concluded you are to go south. And don't try to search for me. There'll be days when you'll want to do it, but you won't find me."

Thomas bowed and hid the precious half of the stole in his bosom. Then they both left the room to bring water and the other ceremonial items to ready Mary for burial according to Jewish customs. The military garrison was situated in an elevated spot over the town, known as Pindi. There, they buried Mary in a grave that they dug in the west-east direction, as the Jewish faith commanded. They parted after the funeral. Thomas returned to Takshashila, and Jesus continued into the hills toward Srinagar.

From Murree he went north to Udabhanda, where the river curved to the south in a deep canyon, and then he reached Uri, the first Kashmiri settlement in the Jhelum river valley. He continued upstream almost to Bandipur, where the river spilled across a wide valley. He hired a guide, with whom he abandoned the river valley and continued north up to the Pisgah range. Despite the fact that the surface of the stream was already freezing over, Jesus was in a fever-like state. He was driven by the vision of Mariam and their son Eli, and the longing to meet his brothers. He disregarded the snowflakes mixed with rain that ran down his face. The horse that the king had given him seemed reluctant to climb the hills. The likable young guide Ghulam constantly urged him to stop hurrying, lest he override the horse. He himself was riding a donkey, because breeding elephants and horses was a royal privilege.

Only members of the royal family or people authorized by them were allowed the ride the animals. However, Jesus wasn't listening to him, and snippets of the Torah kept emerging in his mind: *Then Moses ascended from the Moab steppe to Mount Nebo – the summit of the Pisgah… the Lord's servant, Moses died there in Moab and the Lord buried him opposite Bet-Peor. But nobody knows about his grave to this day…* Driven by his impatience, he was urging the horse, which snorted and panted.

"The original name of the town of Bandipur is Bet-Peor," Ghulam explained. "We'll soon arrive in the village of Aham Sharif, from where Moses ascended to Mount Nebo barefoot. We'll take the same route onto the flank of the Pisgah range. There are hot springs there, by which we will rest."

"There'll be enough time to rest in Bandipur. I want to get to the grave as soon as possible," Jesus objected. Ghulam was refraining from hurrying on purpose, but Jesus was urging both him and his donkey on. They continued to the plain of Mowa, called Moab by locals. The path crossed a swampy meadow. As it started a steep climb, they jumped off their animals and walked beside them. They met young women collecting firewood on the way. After an hour of travelling west they arrived at a group of wooden cottages around which some children were teeming. They welcomed them with noisy shouting. Ghulam quietened them down. "They're the Rishis, guardians of the grave."

"Where is the grave?" Jesus asked impatiently.

"There's only a short climb and we'll be on top of Mount Nebo. The real one, not the one you have in Palestine. I recommend we take a rest before the final climb."

Jesus was seized with fatigue, which was battling with the eager anticipation within him. He eventually accepted the invitation from the locals and entered their dwelling. He nearly lost his breath when he spotted a seven-branched Jewish menorah on a small altar by a window. "Are you Jews?" he asked in a state of shock.

"Yes, I'm Vali Reshi, the guardian of Moses' tomb. And these are my ancestors who've been guarding it for almost five centuries." He pointed at a half-rotten wooden beam by the front door, on which there were unknown names engraved in long columns. "The whole village is our family."

"I'm a Jew too." He briefly told Vali who he was and why he had come. "How did you get here?"

"My ancestors arrived here after the northern kingdom of Israel was destroyed and its people dragged to Babylon. During the reign of King Cyrus, who conquered Babylon, the captive Jewish population was permitted to leave. Some returned, but many continued east. The Bani Israel, the tribes of the Sons of Israel, are located in this region. That was the nickname for the shepherding tribes who settled in this area. We've forgotten our fathers' language, but we've kept their faith."

But Jesus couldn't hear him; he was shaking with impatience. "Please, take me to Moses' grave."

"You can't go see our Father's grave in a bad temper. Appease your soul," the old guardian calmed him down. "Drink some tea first." Jesus was sipping tea, but his hands were shaking so badly that he was spilling it. Vali watched him and smiled.

"Let's go," Jesus insisted.

"We're there now. It's just fifty steps from my house."

They walked to two huge trees, under which Jesus noticed a raised circular mound overgrown with grass. "This is where he's buried."

He stood in front of the grave for a long time. Ghulam and Vali left him alone and returned to the well-heated cottage. The oven gave off a nice warmth, and the men and Vali's family fell asleep fast after the tiring day. When they woke up in the morning, they found out Jesus wasn't in the house.

They ran to the grave. He was sitting on a rock with his face sunken in his hands. There were little stones stacked on top of the mound. He seemed not to be cold at all.

"Isa, come in now. You'll freeze to death out here," Vali roused him. Jesus stood up slowly. Numb, he entered the well-heated cottage. "It's a great pity a prophet like Moses hasn't appeared in Israel yet," Vali said.

Jesus stared at him for a long time. "Why are you saying this?"

"My brothers have been waiting for him. They want to go back home."

76 A False Charge

Tomáš sat in silence for a long time, mustering the courage to tell his story. Marika and Michal sat opposite him, while Doctor Bashrat and Eli were in the next room, packing stuff for their return to Sonamarg. He didn't know how to begin, but he exhaled deeply and finally began.

"I was... hm... how should I put it... I gave them information on some people... you were among them." Michal looked at him, surprised. Tomáš added calmly but convincingly, "I didn't tell them anything important. But still I have a guilty conscience..."

"Who did you give the information to?"

"The Vatican secret service."

"It exists?"

"You'd be surprised," Tomáš laughed bitterly.

"And what did they give you in exchange?"

"Nothing."

"Why did you do it then?"

"They blackmailed me... because of a girl. They threatened to denounce me to my bishop. The love of that woman drove me nearly mad."

"You have a girlfriend?"

"Had... we split up. She said she had to go back to Brazil with her parents, but I think she had suspected something. Maybe she was irritated by my constant inner struggle. Yes, I was on edge back then and sometimes I blew up... I hardly recognized myself. Church against love... Believe me, it wasn't easy. I struggled with it for three years, but then I decided. I'm leaving the church. I won't be blackmailed any longer..." Tomáš paused. "Believe me, I haven't hurt anyone. Everything I told them was information they could have got directly as well. I'm most sorry about the glasses..."

Michal said nothing for a long time; he just stared in front of himself. Tomáš' confession shocked him, but he could understand. Eventually, he put his arm around his shoulders amicably. "You didn't do harm to us, but to yourself." He paused again. Then, in a friendly gesture of forgiveness, he said frankly "I'm glad you came. You should think twice about leaving the church."

"The church is failing…"

"Individuals fail," Michal objected unconvincingly. "We need to fight against those who have cast Jesus away and taken the path of power and wealth. But not everybody in the church is like that."

"I'm not saying they're all like that, but nobody dares speak up." Tears rolled slowly down Tomáš' cheeks. "We don't show people the way, we just control them. That's why we keep them in a constant feeling of guilt, because otherwise we wouldn't control them. You see? We humiliate them so cunningly they're even grateful to us for it."

"Tomáš, that's not how it is. There are great priests too, real ones, like Jesus, who give people hope… It's individuals that fail!" Michal appealed to him urgently.

"It's not a matter of individual failures. If you were inside the church machinery, you'd understand it's a systemic issue. Christ and his teaching are just a pretext."

"But there are many decent and brave priests like you in the church."

"Yes, there are, but those are the most abused ones. Every time the bad ones make some trouble, all the hypocrites in the church start pointing at the decent ones and shouting, "Look at our nuns, at this and that priest, who help people. We give a good name to an institution that doesn't deserve it."

"Every institution consists of people. And people sometimes make mistakes."

"I'm afraid the Vatican are the false prophets, as Matthew identified them, coming in sheep's clothing but they're beasts on the inside. I was like them. You were right in Tiberias back then when you told me I couldn't plant love in people by preaching. Love can only be lived. The world is sick because its cells – people – are sick. I don't have the right to ask anyone for anything, just myself. If every cell of this world is filled with love, this whole world will be filled with love. And I want to love…" Tomáš could no longer control himself and he choked with tears. "It's the worst disappointment of my life." He fell silent, as if ruminating over something important.

"I'll own up. I didn't join their secret service under pressure or blackmail, but out of conviction. But then I started questioning myself: Why does a church need a secret service? Well, tell me, why does an institution that models itself on a man who defended the poor need a bank? Did Jesus have spies and bankers?" Michal stroked him on the shoulder peacefully. "Mišo, Miško, Marika, you can't imagine how much I'm sorry for what I've done! Oh my God, and I believed in it! Please, forgive me…" His stare hardened suddenly. "But that's over! I've decided to finally follow the Holy Book. The Book of Exodus, chapter 23, says, *'You shall not bear a false report; do not join your hand with a wicked man to be a malicious witness. Have nothing to do with a false charge!'* So, I've decided to steer clear from the false way and take a brand-new path. I know it won't be easy; they'll slander me, hate me and persecute me. Those Afghans knew about me. Since I wrote to the Patriarch of Jerusalem that I'm leaving, I've been a traitor to them, and they have no kid gloves for traitors. My path will be like peeling onions. There are many centuries-old false layers in the church. I don't know how many I'll manage to peel off, but I'll take the path of searching for the truth. First, I'll have to leave the path of lies though. For good. I've come to Kashmir and I've decided to stay here. I'll go and concentrate and purify myself in a Buddhist monastery. Pour out this stale, rotten water and make room for the new and pure. I'll try to right my wrongs there somehow. Thanks for listening to me, it's helped me a lot."

"But you don't have to go to a monastery to do that."

"I'm not going to an ordinary monastery. The Kingdom of Heaven is a place that's worth going to. And there are no shortcuts to places that are worth going to."

"So where are you going?"

"Hemis. It contains documents on Jesus' stay in Kashmir. But first I'll meet the Dalai Lama. At least I hope so."

"Meet whom?"

"He has his summer seat in Choglamsar, maybe I'll be lucky. Look at this." Tomáš produced a color photograph printed out of a computer.

"What is it?"

"Take a good look."

Marika and Michal examined the photo and couldn't believe their eyes.

77   The Way of Love

Jesus bid a warm farewell to Ghulam in Bandipur. Srinagar was about a two days' ride from there. The road went on down the Jhelum river valley; Jesus progressed slowly upstream amidst the beginning of a snowstorm. The weather improved unexpectedly past the village of Naugam the next day. The sun revealed itself over the mountains and its warm beams fell on rocks, trees and animals. It was as if nature wanted to bask in the sun for one last time before the winter. He walked slowly beside his horse, not hurrying; he learned in India that time is the greatest value.

When he arrived in Srinagar five days later, he found accommodation with some fishermen on the Dal Lake. The first thing that caught his eyes were their unusually shaped boats: long and narrow, permitting quick movement. He was most surprised at the shape of their oars, though. They were absolutely identical: heart-shaped, like those used by fishermen on Lake Tiberias. He noticed that the locals were very different from other Indian people. They reacted differently, acted differently, their way of life was different; they had different ethics, disposition, language, clothing, and custom.

Kashmiri women called their dances *rof*. The same dance existed in Israel. When the young Kashmiris held each other's hands over their heads in the swaying dance, it reminded him of the two angels touching each other's wings that, according to traditional imagery, were located on the Ark of the Covenant. The most fascinating thing was that the top of the temple that bewitched him and attracted him with its mysteries was the same shape. The Throne of Solomon! It was because of this that he stayed in the city; otherwise he would have continued to Pahalgam. It was situated on a hillock dominating the peninsula between the Dal Lake and the Jhelum River, near the place where he was staying. From a distance, the hillock showed the contours of the structure that had stood in the place since time immemorial: nobody knew the time of its construction. Jesus couldn't stop wondering how much the structure resembled old Jewish tombs in Palestine. As he was climbing the eighteen steps of the temple to the main shrine, he recalled the words of the First Book of Kings: *'The king had a fleet of Tarshish ships at sea along with the ships of Hiram. Once every three years the Tarshish ships returned, carrying gold, silver, ivory, apes and peacocks.'*

When he reached the first platform and walked around the peculiar circular structure, he realized the entrance was in the east. The low ceiling forced him to bow. Filled with awe, he entered. A man was sitting in the tiny shrine, staring fixedly. He didn't acknowledge Jesus' arrival, he only offered him a seat to his right with a gesture. He continued meditating without interruption. Jesus joined him. When the man finished, he blessed Jesus. He introduced himself as the hermit Sangaraksha. He was wearing a long cloak wrapped around using a belt with knots and tassels, identical to those worn by priests of the Jerusalem Temple.

"Welcome, Isa, son of the tribes of Israel," he welcomed the stranger. "I know you have come to search for your brethren as the law commands you to." Jesus made no reply. "You've come to the right place. They came here after they were dragged into captivity. They spread across the holy land of Kashmir. Wherever you arrive in these mountains, you will come across Hebrew names of people, hills, valleys and meadows. This temple was commenced by the great King Solomon, who visited this place during one of his expeditions with King Hiram Abiff of Phoenicia. When their lightweight rowing boats reached the upper Indus, they headed up its right tributary, the Jhelum, up to here. Before the king's arrival, this hill was called Jaishtevara, and was consecrated to the sun. Legends say that King Solomon arrived here wearing clothes made of pure gold that shone more brightly than the sun. He ordered the builder Sandiman to build a temple to honor the sun. The king stayed in Kashmir from the spring to the winter. King Hiram, who arrived with him, had another magical temple built in Martand, south of Srinagar. Its main entrance also faces east. It's on the way to Pahalgam. When you go there, you'll see the temple is unlike any other in all of India."

"This structure reminds me of our prophets' tombs," Jesus remarked.

"Yes, Sandiman was a Persian builder and he knew the tomb of the prophet Ezra, who organized the Jews' return to their homeland in Babylon during the reign of the Persian King Artaxerxes.

"However, many went east, not to Jerusalem. His tomb was Sandiman's model when building this temple. Both temples were also visited by the famous Greek Pythagoras, followed by the great Apollonius, who spent thirteen years at the university in Takshashila."

Jesus sat next to the sage and took in all the details of the interior decoration, dominated by symbols of palm leaves and pomegranates. A while later he realized he was leaning against one of the two columns; Sangaraksha was leaning on the other one. He examined them at length; he found them very familiar. The sage noticed his interest in them.

"They are the Joachim and Boas; Sandiman also built them according to the plans brought by Solomon. They are supposed to be an exact replica of the columns of the Jerusalem Temple. One is milled vertically, the other one in a spiral. One of them symbolizes the number one, the lowest numeral, and the other is number nine, the highest numeral.

"One symbolizes active divine energy, the other one passive. One represents the man and the other the woman, symbolized by the vagina, an equilateral triangle pointing downward. If you combine these two triangles, you get a six-pointed star, symbolizing the perfect human being."

"I'd like to meet one," Jesus said.

"There are some sulfur springs six miles from Srinagar, where you'll find the enlightened Shalivahana, the grandson of Vikramajita, the king who's defeated the Chinese, Parthians, Scythians, and Bactrians. He's created the border between Hindus and non-Hindus, whom he forced to retreat beyond the Indus river. He's a king seeking perfection. Go see him as soon as you can, his time is getting short," the hermit advised him. "The road to Pahalgam starts from there."

* * * * *

When King Shalivahana had a massage after a bath in the sulfur springs, he entered the winter garden to warm his ageing body. Through a peephole between two mango trees, he noticed a pale-skinned man wearing an unusual white robe standing among the people waiting for an audience.

"Who's that man?" he asked his butler.

"He's the famous preacher who teaches modesty and humility. He arrived from Palestine a few years ago, then he went back and now he's here again. They say he's looking for his wife and son. He'd like to bow before you," the butler informed him.

The king had the man summoned. "Are you Isa Putra – Jesus, Son of God – who they say was born of a single mother?"

"My mother's name was Mary," Jesus smiled.

"They say you travel through the country looking for your wife Mariam and your son Eli. I'm the king, but I haven't heard anything about the two."

"I'll go on searching for them until I find them!"

"If you need help, I'll be glad to give it to you. But I'd like to ask you to stay in my court for at least some time. My soldiers will look for the two of them in the meantime. You see, I'm old and I feel that my days are numbered. I'd like to hear the wisdom that you bring before I depart." Jesus said nothing. "Please accept my hospitality," the king pointed at a table filled with Kashmiri delicacies.

Jesus continued to stand politely. "Take a seat." The king pushed a bowl of grapes in front of him. "They say you teach people humility. I like that. Where do you come from?"

"From a country where faithless barbarians oppress believers. The faithless sacrificed me, but I survived my death."

"How can you survive death?"

"With faith."

"With faith? That's difficult. It's easier to doubt."

"For those who have no faith, life is a straight line. They're born in A and end in B. To a believer, life is a circle. You're born in A and after you've gone the circle, you return to A, but you're richer for the experience you got on the way, so it is A, but it's a level higher. Thus, death brings us back to the state in which we were before birth, only richer for the life experience."

"I doubt what you're saying is true. It seems far-fetched to me."

"You should believe it."

"Do you know why I defeated the Chinese, Scythians, Parthians and Bactrians and sent them over the Indus? Because I didn't believe them. Believing is easier than doubting. Belief only requires your decision, made based on your will, but doubt requires reason, you've got to analyze your adversary's words, arguments, look for a trap behind each one. Doubting requires experience, education, wisdom..." The king sipped hot tea from a cup. He offered some to Jesus. "They say people follow you in masses and listen to your words."

"Yes. And they believe me."

"Then you're lucky. If the people weren't silly, they would doubt you. As it is, you can tell them your fairytales and they believe you. They think it's a miracle if you treat people in forsaken mountain valleys using your knowledge from the best university in the world. But your miracles are only based on their silliness," the king laughed. "In a word, belief without thinking is for fools." Jesus drank his tea in silence. "Am I not right?" the king prodded him.

"Your royal highness, a king's always right, because he has power."

"I'm not one of those kings that play wise because they have power. My power stems from wisdom. You don't have to fear my swords but my reason."

"Then use it," Jesus said softly.

"Are you saying that the grandson of the great Vikramajita is a fool?"

"You say belief without thinking is for fools, but so is doubting without thinking." The king thought about the remark for a long while. "Why have you come here?"

"To find my wife and son."

"And when you find them?"

"I will try to use meditation and concentration of the spirit to bring people to God, who resides in each of us and offers us light for the way so that we remove all that is ephemeral."

"What's ephemeral?"

"All evil that tries to instill fear in us."

"Fear?" the king looked at him in surprise. "I know nothing of the kind. I've never fled battle."

"The difference between a hero and a coward is that the hero lasts a little longer in battle. But he fears equally."

The king steered away from the remark. "What are those evils that instill fear?"

"Greed, hatred, envy, impatience, gluttony, lies, theft, killing, laziness, hypocrisy, condemnation, stealing, prejudice, attachment, sadness, pride, disease... Shall I go on?"

The king smiled, "No need. What you're saying is no news around here. But how do you want to get them out of the people?"

"I preach love of one's neighbor. Such tenets as: If someone hits you on the left cheek, offer him the right one. – You look for a speck of dust in your brother's eyes, but you don't notice the log in your own. – Don't judge lest you be judged. – Give God what's God's and the king what's the king's. – Ask, and you'll be given. – Search, and you'll find. – Knock, and the door will open. – Love your enemies."

The king laughed. "That's really clever! I say, if I loved my enemies, there would be no Kushan Empire."

"There'd be an empire of spirit and love. One that is much stronger and more lasting. One Chinese emperor had powerful enemies whom he hated, and they hated him. They fought together all their lives, until the emperor was weary."

"But fighting is the duty of kings and emperor."

Jesus continued without pause. "One day the emperor told his advisors, 'I'll get rid of my enemies forever.' When they came to see him in the imperial gardens sometime later, they saw the emperor walk amid the flowers in a friendly debate with his enemies. 'You said you'd get rid of your enemies,' the chief advisor told him. The emperor replied, 'And haven't I? We've become friends.'"

King Shalivahana said nothing. "When I tell people about the kingdom, they don't understand. But it's up to everyone. I'm just the sower. Some seeds fall into thorn bush, others fall on rocks and dry in the sun, yet others are taken by water, others are eaten by birds. Only a few seeds will fall on fertile land, but if you water and fertilize them, they'll bring a hundredfold harvest."

"You say the same as the Buddha said. Do you have something in common with him?" He sized Isa up. "Gautama said a white prophet would arrive five hundred years after him. Is it you?"

"They say so," Jesus replied.

The king scrutinized Jesus for a long while. "Tell me, Isa, why have you come only now?"

"I've come by myself at the end of the Satya Yuga."

"Why do you think it's the end of the Golden Age?"

"Because Earth is entering the Age of Pisces, which is an age of matter and greed. It will last for over two thousand years. After it will come an age of spirituality and love, the Age of Aquarius."

"How can you forecast the future just like that?"

"Because I know love."

The king gave him an uncomprehending look.

"They thought in Palestine that I performed miracles. But I could simply open the gates of the sick to let in love, which is universal."

The king smiled. "It's been a long time since I was in love. It was the most beautiful thing in my life. The love I was experiencing and getting was beyond description."

"You weren't giving love; love was around your beloved and around you. Love is always here, it's everywhere; it has been, and it will be, only we perceive it just when we manage to open our hearts. She opened yours and you opened hers. It's like a barrier opening in a river and water beginning to flow down every channel. People get sick out of a lack of love. Then, we don't love people, and we don't love nature and animals. We give not love but hatred, and the same returns to us."

"How can I love my enemy, who's done so much evil to me and my people?" the king asked.

"Simple. Forgive him. I'm sure you'll agree that your hatred to him constantly consumes you. King Gondophares, with whom you fought, was consumed by hatred for you. You won't get well unless you forgive him."

"No, no, you're not speaking right. I can't forgive those who killed my closest ones. Maybe I can forget, but not forgive!" the king said resolutely.

"The same sun warms both you and him. Each of us is a ray of the sun. The sun doesn't care if we're good or bad: it does what the creator designed it for. It gives us warmth and light, without which there would be no life. Its duty is to love everyone. Likewise, it's the duty of kings to lead people to love, not to hatred. You won't build a happy future for your kingdom with a clenched fist, but with an open hand. Otherwise we're not going to the kingdom."

"But I have my kingdom," Shalivahana objected.

"I'm not referring to your kingdom, but to the kingdom of souls."

"Where is such a kingdom?"

"It's where people give, not take. Where people live in unity, because giving unites people while taking divides them. It's where people love their neighbors more than they love themselves. This is God's basic law, inscribed in each of us."

Shalivahana made no reply for a long time. "You haven't answered my question. Where is such a kingdom?"

"In your heart."

The king thought, then said softly, as if only to himself, "I don't understand it at all, but somewhere in my heart I feel what you're saying is right. Please, Isa, stay in my court and bring the word closer to me," the king asked him.

Jesus saw in the fading glimmer of the king's eyes that his time was coming fast, and he therefore accepted the king's invitation. In spite of Jesus' effort and those of the royal physicians, Shalivahana didn't live much longer. He died three years after his enthronement.

Jesus went to search for Mariam and Eli immediately after his funeral.

78 Code 1

Marika and Michal examined the photo, which showed a circle divided into twelve sections, with a cross at the center. The first segment showed a crib with a baby over which a man and a woman were leaning and a star glowing above them; the next one showed a boy debating with adult men, the next one an adult man preaching to a listening crowd, another showed a man crucified, and in the last one he climbed the heavens. "It looks like the life of Jesus."

"Correct, it's Christ's circle of life. The Dalai Lama has this picture in his meditation room in Choglamsar."

"The Dalai Lama meditates with Christ?" Marika asked in surprise.

Thomas nodded. "It looks that way. I've found out that he comes to his summer seat in Ladakh two or three times a year. If I don't meet him there, I'll go to see him in Dharamsala in Himachal Pradesh," he smiled. "I've decided I'm going to the hills, where I'll be the happiest man in the world."

"Tomáš, the church also needs people like you," Marika tried to convince him too.

"Maybe I'll come back… one day, but not now. The SIV already knows I'm with you."

"They can't know. All five Afghanis are dead," Michal objected.

"But at least they know you've been informed by me, because you've stopped transmitting, you see?"

"And where did you get the information that they were going to do what they did?" Michal asked.

"There are people at the SIV HQ too who're fed up."

"How do you want to get to the mountains of Ladakh?"

"I don't have the money to fly to Leh, so I'll hitchhike. I hope I'm lucky. Well, it's high time I went. The situation seems to have calmed down. I'll take a rickshaw and get to the main road. So… then, my friend…" Tomáš' voice trembled. "I don't know what to expect in those forsaken parts, so I've brought…this here… just in case. Take it. You've got one half at home. I think the two parts will feel the best when they're together." He fished out of his backpack one half of the UNUM rock that the Coptic archbishop had once given him.

"Is this the rock that saved his life recently? The one whose other half I threw in the trash can?" Marika looked at Michal in surprise. He nodded. She turned to Tomáš. "Have you been carrying it all the way to here?" Tomáš nodded and handed the rock to Michal.

"Wait!" Michal opened his backpack and, to Marika's and Tomáš' surprise, he produced the other half of the rock.

"I knew, I was expecting… I believed… and I still believe we'll meet again." He handed his rock to Tomáš. "I'll think of you."

Tomáš hugged him. "What did Athanasius tell us back then? When you make two into one, when you turn the external into the internal, when what's above will be like what's below, when you make the feminine and the masculine one, then you will enter the kingdom. I think the one who most needs to enter the kingdom, who needs to feel that we're with them, is here." Tomáš took both the rocks and walked to Marika. He handed them to her; she took them in her hands and, unknowingly, she attached one to the other.

"No, no, I can't accept this. They're very precious to you. You take one half each. They'll unite you at least across the distance." She wanted to give each their half, but as hard as she tried, she couldn't separate them. Michal and Tomáš stared at her, then tried to take the rocks apart as well, but they now firmly stuck together.

"It looks like a jasper. Odd. You can't even see where they're joined," Tomáš wondered. He had another go at separating the rocks, but to no avail. "They really won't split."

As soon as he said it, Marika's cell phone rang. It hadn't in a very long time.

"Adelka's calling." She put aside the rock and answered the phone quickly. Her eyes glowed. "Hang on, I'll turn on the loudspeaker, your dad must hear this too."

"So, hello, mommy, daddy. Hans and I want to inform you that you're going to be grandparents. I'm in the third month. It's going to be a girl. And, of course we're therefore coming back home. For good. We'll arrive in September."

"So, dear Marika, gentlemen, we're ready." Bashrat said, entering the room. "I think we shouldn't waste time and get out of the city as soon as possible. It's still quite turbulent here, and it's high time you started fasting," he turned to Marika. His eyes fell on the UNUM rock.

"May I?" Marika nodded.

The doctor took the rock in his hands, examined it at length, played with it, nearly caressing it. "Unum… hm… divided yet joined, joined yet divided…" Marika, Michal and Tomáš were listening to him attentively. "The greatest people are not those who stand at the highest point, but those who know best how to share themselves. Every person has their own frequency, just as everything else around us. We move around a space filled with frequencies that we're capable of perceiving. For example, diamonds, rocks such as this one, and other hard objects have the highest frequencies, and soft objects such as people or air have the lowest frequencies. This seems to us to be our whole world. But it's just the world that we can perceive with our frequencies; there are other worlds here along with us, above and below our frequencies, which we don't perceive and so we think they don't exist. They're the frequencies of angels and spiritual beings. Angels are a normal thing here in Kashmir: we know they live here with us. In the world of our frequencies, the rule is that a being at a higher frequency may affect a weaker human being when their frequency is divisible by that of the person below him…" Bashrat thought. "But we really ought to go now."

"Hang on, doctor," Michal walked up to him. "You're not saying that a low-standing person can influence, or even win over more people than one higher up in the social hierarchy can."

"That's up for a long discussion, I'm afraid we don't have the time for that now…"

"So then Kashmiri angels are those with the highest status?" Marika asked.

"They're those most capable of sharing themselves. Status has nothing to do with it. It's like numbers. The more often a person's frequency can be divided by frequencies lower than their own, the more power the person has. I'll show you on an example with numbers. Take the number sixty. It's a low number in an endless row of numbers, but it's divisible by twelve numbers: one, two, three, four, five, six, ten, twelve, fifteen, twenty, thirty, and itself. Take the number 359, for example. If I can calculate this quickly, I think this number is only divisible by one and itself. Meaning its value is greater than that of sixty, but its real worth is minimal, because it can only be divided by itself. Can you see?"

"A real selfish number," Michal laughed.

"Exactly. A person characterized by this number may be at the very top from the point of view of their power – religious or political – but has no deeper influence on people, because they don't share with them. The number 65,537 is much higher than twelve, but 65,537 is an indivisible prime number, whereas twelve can be divided by six numbers. Such a person, although much higher up with their status, has no spiritual influence on people." Bashrat headed for the door.

"Hang on," Tomáš objected. "But they have a power influence."

"Yes, but only as long as they're in the power. A person's true power is measured by infinity, not by finiteness. Earthly rulers, popes, kings, emperors are alone in fact. It so simple! Only few of us today will remember who Augustus was, but every educated person knows who Virgil, Ovid or Horace was. How many people today know who Lorenzo Medici was? Yet everyone knows about Botticelli, Leonardo da Vinci, Donatello, Michelangelo and others who lived and worked in his era. Few people will recall the Grand Duke Carl August, but Goethe and Schiller, who worked in his court, remain in humankind's memory. They are engraved in human history not thanks to their power that they didn't want to share, but thanks to their art, which they shared with everyone who came into beneficial contact with them." He turned to Michal.

"As you said, the number 65,537 can be termed a selfish number. It's enormously high up, but it's lonely, because it doesn't share itself; it doesn't split or divide itself. You see?"

Tomáš, Marika and Michal made no reply.

"So, a human being's power is not measured by how much they take, but by how much they give. That's why the number one is perfect, symbolizing the highest spirit, or God if you will, indivisible by anyone or anything and yet divided, shared, in every being. Just like the number one. It's in every number, all the way to infinity. It's a perfectly impersonal number. One is the number of God: no other numbers exist without Him.

"He's the beginning. He's the number of fulfillment and infiniteness, he knows no time. One is God's number, expressing constancy, indivisibility, and at the same time, total division, self-sharing. Perfect giving. It's the numeric expression of the meaning of our existence. It's the first code of our lives.

Code 1. It consists in absolute self-giving, which is also unification. The more you share yourself, the more things you unite, the more you embody Unum. You see? The miracle consists in giving..." Bashrat paused for a moment. "But we really must go."

"Doctor, unless I'm wrong, the way to Leh is via Sonamarg." Michal looked at Bashrat. "Could we take our friend Tomáš with us? He'd cover a part of the way."

"Of course we can."

*****

Tomáš said goodbye to everyone the day after their arrival in Sonamarg. Michal saw him off to the end of the village, where the road was beginning its steep climb. They walked in silence side by side.

"And as for the baptism... I hope I'll come..." Tomáš was carrying in his backpack the UNUM rock, which he eventually took with him after Marika's long persuasion. Suddenly he halted, took it out and held it in his hand diffidently.

"You told me about this soldier that gave you his blessing in Sonamarg. I think if anyone needs unity now, it's the Muslims and the Hindus. Please put the rock in the garrison shrine. I hope... maybe... it will help those great people..."

Michal took the rock without a word. "Tell me, are you leaving because you've lost your faith?"

Tomáš gave his friend a wide grin. He bent down and plucked a golden Saint John's wort. "I'm leaving in order to consolidate the faith within me."

Michal nodded and gripped the rock firmly. "I'll take it there straight away." They hugged each other tightly. "We'll be waiting for you."

The top of the hill that the road crossed was still hidden in the morning mist. Tomáš turned around, waved his hand one last time, and set out resolutely toward the paradise that was opening its arms for him.

79 The Cornerstone

After the death of King Shalivahana, Jesus mounted his horse and headed up the Jhelum River to Martand, from where he continued to Pahalgam. His longing to see his beloved wife and son drove him up the inhospitable gorges and sun-scorched footpaths of the Kishtwar range. Nobody had heard about them in Pahalgam. He crossed the area around Amarnath, one hamlet after another from Lalung in the east via Pantacharni, Sheshnag, Marsar and the forsaken farmsteads below the Kaijar Glacier, but nobody had heard about a woman named Mariam and her son Eli. Jesus traveled around the country, which was incomparable to the desert of Israel. Of all the countries he had crossed – from Palestine to Cappadocia, Babylonia, Persia, Bactria, Parthia and many more – this one was without doubt the most beautiful.

Wherever he came, he asked about Mariam and Eli, but nobody had heard of them. He didn't count the days. He didn't count the weeks. He didn't count the months. And he stopped counting the years. He spent his days in Sonamarg herding sheep, staying with the herdsmen in their tents on the riverbank. He couldn't take his eyes off the beauty of the tall peaks covered with snow and lily-white glaciers, from which there flowed springs of gurgling streams that became crystal-clear torrential rivers passing through the endless creeping pines up there, into the dense cedar, spruce, fir, maple, laurel, oak, beech and birch forests below. In the meadows down below, herdsmen, lying in the shade of huge plane trees, were guarding their herds of goats and sheep from lurking black and brown bears, wolves, panthers, jackals, and the occasional leopard and tiger. When the herdsmen fought them off, they turned their claws and teeth against defenseless wild donkeys, which the locals called kiang. They wouldn't back down before a water buffalo or a young elephant either. They shared their leftovers with vultures and eagles, which crisscrossed the Kashmiri sky along with pelicans, ibises, cranes and cormorants. The juicy pastures were strewn with daisies, primulas, edelweiss, gentians, and rhododendrons, which opened their flowers joyfully for butterflies and bees. Even the best honey in Palestine was no match for the golden sweet nectar from the Himalayan meadows. Various kinds of walnut, apricot and apple trees from the area southeast of the Panjal range offered their fresh fruits, which the farmers sold on markets in Srinagar, Kishtwar and remote Udabhanda. Part of the fruits was dried and then taken to the inhospitable Kargil, Zanskar and Ladakh provinces by merchants in difficult caravan crossings.

Jesus was told that one such woman had once passed on the way to Ladakh, so he set out to the inhospitable regions of Zanskar and Leh. There, he met young Xenophon, to whom King Gondophares had introduced him in Takshashila many years before. Xenophon told him news from Srinagar, Lahore and other cities that he'd learned in the royal court. Jesus rejoiced when Xenophon told him some news he had heard from Hindu monks who'd arrived in Takshashila from the south. Thomas had established many Christian shrines on the Malabar Coast of Kerala and in the southeast near Mailapur and disseminated the Father's word eagerly from there. Having established the Church of Christ in Cranganore, he travelled across the Deccan Plateau to Mailapur in the east, from where he sailed to China with a trading ship; he returned to the Malabar Coast four and a half months later. He won thousands of people over to Christ's ideals, from Quilon to Calicut in the north. They included Jews as well as seventy-five Brahmin families. He established church communities in Malankara, Palayoor, Kowa Kayala, Kokkamangalam, Kollam, Niranam, and Nilakeli. When Nero ascended to power in Rome, Thomas returned to Mailapur, from where he went to Ceylon, the land of Tamils, two years later. All the time, he baptized, treated leprosy, exorcised demons, restored blind people's eyesight, mute people's speech and crippled people's walking. After ten years in the south, he set out north to the Sindh river in the Kashmiri foothills, where Jesus preached the Word.

The white prophet was sought by young men and women, chiefly from the poorer classes, who listened to him attentively wherever he went. Amal, Gomer, Raphu and others became Jesus' permanent companions. While travelling around the country, he frequently recalled the words of the Torah: *The Lord planted a garden of Eden in the east...*

A river flowed out of Eden to irrigate the garden, and then it split into four arms... Which made five rivers together, that is Punjab in Sanskrit.

"It sounds almost unbelievable, but this country has much more in common with the description in the Torah than Palestine," Jesus thought out loud as he was sitting alongside Xenophon and his friends high in the reddish massif of the Zanskar hills, where the Zanskar river joins the turquoise-green Indus. "I've been in Kashmir for a long time, and we've had greater or smaller floods almost every year. The whole of Kashmir seems to me like one big pan. If you stick an imaginary plug where the Indus flows out of it, the whole valley will fill up like a reservoir."

"Old women around Leh tell a story that in ancient times the mountains jammed the valley of the Indus and stopped its flow, so that the river then flooded the whole of the Vale of Kashmir. The flood erased all life off the surface," Amal said.

"Do you know what Kashmir means? It's a compound of Ka, which means water in Sanskrit, and shimera, meaning dried up."

"What? That would confirm the idea of an ancient flood." Jesus shook his head.

"Yes, there was a flood in Kashmir about ten thousand years ago. They say Noah's grave is here: the one who built the ship according to your tradition."

"Where is that grave?"

"They say it's in the south of the Punjab range. But nobody has ever succeeded in finding it."

Jesus gave Xenophon a resolute look. "My soul won't have peace until I find it. How happy I would be if Mariam with my son and Thomas were here with me."

* * * * *

Jesus' condition grew worse with his growing age. His psychic condition wasn't improved by the news of the death of the good King Gondophares. His loyal friends Amal and Xenophon tried to distract and cheer him as best as they could. The magnanimous King Gopadatta, who ruled Kashmir at that time, granted the last wish of his predecessor Shalivahana, who had asked him on his deathbed that Jesus might enjoy the hospitality of the royal family in his old age. But Jesus refused to stay in the luxury royal palace in Srinagar; he preferred a modest Buddhist stone cottage attached to the royal palace wall. He went out little in his last years; he only left occasionally for one of the Buddhist shrines commissioned by King Ashoka. His hair turned white, but his eyes retained their boyish look. He was increasingly introvert; often he would be silent for many days, meditating and praying. It was obvious that inside he had begun to get ready for his return to the Father.

"Are you worried about Mariam? I've known you for a few years, and you're ever more taciturn," Xenophon stated.

"Everything in life is the way it should be. We're meant to detach ourselves from everything, including those we love. But even hermits fall to emotions. I'd like to know three things..." he sighed. Xenophon was staring at him.

"Who my real father is..."

"Does it matter? Your father is not the one who begets you but the one who brings you up. And the one who brought you up is your father. He's my father and Amal's as well. The father of us all. Some children have turned out better, some worse. I think he'll be satisfied with you once you return home," Xenophon appeased him. "The other thing?"

"Where Mariam and our son are."

Xenophon and Amal made no reply. In the many years in which they had accompanied him, they had asked about Mariam of Pahalgam wherever they came. Some said she'd gone to a monastery in Ladakh, others said she lived in the mountains near her native Pahalgam with her hermit son. "I'm sure I'll meet my love one day," he said in deep thought.

"And the third thing?" Xenophon asked.

"What my friend Thomas is doing. I hear he's somewhere around the Sindh. How much I'd love to see him one more time!" The wearier he was, the more often he remembered his loyal friend.

When Jesus felt his last days were coming, they carried him over to his beloved coelion on the bank of the Jhelum, where he'd meditated during his stay at Srinagar. The good King Gopadatta sent quick messengers to the Sindh river valley, where Thomas was reported to be at work. When they returned two weeks later, Jesus was lying lifeless on the mat. The king, his physicians and Buddhist healers had spent all his moments with him, they didn't leave him even during sleep. When Thomas entered the room – they hadn't met in almost twenty years – he was lying with his eyes fixated on the scenes from the Buddha's life painted on the cave ceiling. Thomas came to the mat, took Jesus' hands in his, gripped them firmly, leaned over him and looked him in the eyes. Jesus didn't react to his look. "Isa, Yuz, Joshua, Emanuel, my brother and teacher, it's me, your twin. Didymus, Thomas."

"He's very tired, his strength is leaving him," the king said softly.

Thomas stroked his hands. Suddenly he remembered something, He unwrapped the dark blue stole that he had around his neck. He held it in front of Jesus' eyes, which sparkled at that moment.

"My mother's stole. Thomas, is it you?" He tried hard to sit up but failed. Thomas leaned over him and the two old men hugged each other firmly. "My brother..." Jesus undrew his white robe, under which there was the dark blue silk stole that he'd torn in two at his mother's funeral. "And I had you serve the merchant Abanes back then; can you forgive me?" Jesus looked at him pleadingly.

"My dear, you forgive me, please. Forgive me for not believing you when they took you off the cross, and when you tried to convince me that my place is here in India. It was the best decision of my life. I'm very grateful to you for it. I've taken to this country, these great people, Indians, Buddhists, the people of Kerala, Nadu, Mangalore, Karnataka, Takshashila, and Kashmir. Our Jewish brothers from Cochin to Mailapur listen to your words. They follow you and call themselves Christians." Jesus stroked his white hair kindly.

"I'll never forget how I decided to go to Lazarus in Bethany and the Pharisees wanted to stone me. Everyone was discouraging, but you challenged them, 'Let's come along and die with him,'" Jesus recalled with emotion.

"During the last supper, when you told us you'd go to the Father's place to make arrangements for us, I didn't understand what you were talking about, and asked you, 'My lord, I don't know where you're going, how do I know the way?' I thought you'd become angry, but you didn't. When they took you off the cross alive and I said, 'I won't believe until I have seen the nail marks on your hands and put my finger in your wound,' you could have become angry even then, and you didn't." Thomas wept softly, seeing that Jesus' eyes were closing wearily, and the grasp of his hand was weakening. His head dropped onto the pillow, he stared at the steep ceiling of the cave and barely breathed. "When I failed to believe you many more times after that, I thought you'd leave me, but you never did... When I was arrogant and lost my temper, I thought you'd leave me, but you always forgave me."

"Go to the lost sheep of the tribes of Israel," Jesus breathed. His eyes were fading, and his breath slowed down. The cave was silent, only some water was dripping off the ceiling in a corner. Thomas was praying by Jesus' mat when a shadow appeared in the cave entrance. A man about thirty years old, of a paler skin, entered. He walked to the mat and knelt down. He took Jesus' hands in his, raised them to his mouth and kissed them. Jesus couldn't open his eyes anymore, only stroked the man's hair and whispered softly, "I knew you'd come, my son." His hand slid off Eli's head.

"He was the stone that the builders have rejected and that became the cornerstone. I hope people will understand it one day," Thomas whispered.

The doctor came up and took his heart rate. He put down his hand after a while. "He's in nirvana now."

In the year of the destruction of Jerusalem by Emperor Vespasian's troops, Jesus Isa was buried in Srinagar, in a neighborhood known as Khanyaar, in the cave between the Jhelum River and the Dal Lake in which he died. He was buried in the west-east direction according to the Jewish custom.

Before they interred him, Thomas made a death print of his feet as was the custom with saints in Kashmir and carved it in the rock beside the sarcophagus. He carved a statue of his friend from the pale brown wood of the Himalayan cedar, the mightiest of the mountain trees, which he put in a niche in the cave.

Thomas went back to his dearest Christian community in Mailapur Church, where he tried to bring more and more people eager to find the truth to the word of Jesus in spite of his increasing age and fading strength. He was happy to have Eli accompany him on this splendid journey. Eli's mother had died in the earthquake in Takshashila. He had been raised by good people and when he grew up, he started travelling the lands in the Himalayan foothills.

Thomas even baptized the Queen Tertia and her lady-in-waiting Mygdonia in Mailapur. Brahmin temple priests couldn't stand it and convinced the king to have him killed. Two years after Jesus' funeral – on the early morning of July 3, 72 – Thomas was walking down the stone pavement by the temple of the goddess Kali, when two temple priests stood in his way.

"Where are you headed, Thomas?"

"To the coast."

"Why this early?"

"I'm meeting some friends. We want to worship God, the father of us all."

"Our God is Shiva, and this temple is consecrated to his wife. We'll let you go if you worship our goddess with us."

Although it was early in the morning, the stone pavement was already giving off heat, and the hot westerly breeze coming from the mainland drove tears of sweat on Thomas' forehead. His white hair was flowing in the wind.

The priest standing closest to him noticed the sweat on his forehead. "Don't worry, old man, we won't hurt you. We just want you to pay homage to our goddess. We'll treat you to a royal feast after the joint worship."

"I'm not interested in your feast, and I'm not going to sell my soul for a handful of rice."

"It won't be a handful of rice, but the choicest dishes."

"Ones you ripped off the poor?"

"We make sacrifices to both the temple and the poor, but mainly to the goddess," the priest replied irately.

"First, you take their bread and then give them crumbs!" He lost his temper. "You give yourselves the most."

"Watch your tongue, stranger!" The first priest raised his voice.

Thomas wanted to continue his way, but the priests surrounded him menacingly.

"If you insist, I will enter the temple and exorcise the devil from it that seduces you to wrong paths!"

"Don't blaspheme!" the priest shouted. "Are you coming to pray with us or not?!"

Thomas didn't listen to him and walked off resolutely. Then men plunged at him, knocked him to the ground, beat him with clubs and kicked him. He tried to stand up, but he felt blood running out of his side. One of the furious priests took a spear and thrust it in his side. The old man faltered, breathed heavily and blood gushed out of his wound, which was in the same spot as Jesus' stab wound. The frightened priests ran inside their temple. First morning passers-by appeared in the street and tried to help the injured man, but his spirit had left him for good. Eli and Thomas' disciples buried him near the coast, where they'd held their regular gatherings. Eli began to be persecuted, so some time later he set out north to the safe Buddhist areas of his beloved Kashmir.

80 The Secret of the Miracle

It was a full moon on May 28, 2010. Before six o'clock in the morning, when the moon started to wane, Marika began her forty-two-day fasting under the supervision of Doctor Bashrat and with frequent visits by Professor Vaidya.

"Your body will break down the cancer cells during the fasting. Trust the healing powers of your body and spirit. During the fast, your body will eliminate all that is sick and doesn't belong to it. But your faith is crucial," they kept repeating to her.

She drank juices made from beetroot, carrots, potatoes, parsley and celery root. Doctor Bashrat and Eli spent long hours in encouraging debates with her, and she was surrounded by her loving husband and her new Kashmiri friends, who wished her to get well. All of her fasting hours were filled with love and prayer. She meditated in front of the statue of Christ in the lotus position. So much energy emanated from it that from time to time she couldn't stand up on her legs, had to sit down, and burst into tears. For many hours, she gazed at the beautiful smiling man with a scar that told much more than the spear which had made it. She implored him to give her enough power to be able to help herself. She felt she was detoxifying not only physically, but that even the poisons of the spirit that she'd been hiding in the corners of herself for many decades were leaving her. Occasionally, she felt she could smell a beautiful rosy, resin and lavender fragrance. A lightness came into her soul; for the first time in her life she began to feel real freedom. She freed herself of the bad habits that had been implanted in her since her childhood.

She realized she'd been unhappy because she'd expected something from others all her life. Now she knew that happiness consists in giving. She felt as if she'd risen to a higher level of existence in the Kashmiri heaven on earth. From time to time, the image of the unknown woman on a boat crossed her mind. She could only see a few steps ahead with a lantern on the prow, but sunshine helped her see the whole beautiful country.

Ten days after the beginning of the fast, oiling, meditations, repetition of the mantra and use of the special medicine, she could walk for dozens of meters along the river. The distance grew over time, although she didn't eat. When she completed the fast forty-two days later, the pain in her joints and feet was definitely gone. Two weeks after the end of the fast, Marika started to give herself sesame oil enemas every evening before going to bed. The doctor advised her to try to retain them in her for as long as possible. She mostly succeeded to retain the oil in her intestines all night. She did the enemas for an entire month. After a month and a half, Doctor Bashrat added gold to the medicine and took out the copper and the pearl extract.

The time to depart drew near after an almost three-month stay. Professor Vaidya carefully checked Marika's heart rate, pupils, tongue, urine and blood. "Your white and red blood cells are reaching the normal rates. If you observe everything that I've told you, you'll be absolutely healthy within three months. I believe that the return to your old home won't mean a return to your old way of life," he smiled.

The Král's didn't bid Bashrat, Eli and Professor Vaidya farewell. They agreed on a visit to Srinagar in a year's time. Bashrat put a small box in Marika's hand. She opened it. "But it's a compass," she said without understanding.

"Yes, it's a compass. It says, 'as above, so below, as in the east, so in the west'. Let it guide you through your life. And let the compass remind you of the word compassion."

Their plane departed for Dubai at 4 p.m. on Saturday, August 7, 2010; they continued to Vienna from Dubai. That morning, the whole of India awoke in shock to newspaper headlines describing a flood in the Kashmiri province of Ladakh. The flood had destroyed or badly damaged seventy-one towns and villages on August 6. Whereas the average precipitation in Ladakh in August is just 5/8 of an inch, ten inches of rain fell on a single Friday night, which translates into the entire annual rainfall emptying itself on the province in half an hour. The fatal torrents of water surprised people while they were asleep. Leh, the capital of the province located at an altitude of eleven thousand five hundred feet, suffered the worst damage. The swollen surface of the Indus river reached up to thirteen feet above the normal level in some places. The bus station, a hospital, transformer plants, communications systems and dozens of residential buildings in Leh and surrounding villages were destroyed. Several buses were found about two miles away from the station: they were dragged away by the mass of water and mud. Getting supplies to the affected areas was complicated because the main road from the capital Srinagar via Sonamarg and the Zoji Pass was eroded and impassable in many places. Military helicopters brought basic food supplies. Nine thousand people lost their homes. Some media compared the flood to the disastrous biblical one.

According to official information, at least two hundred and sixty people died during the flood, but unofficial sources mentioned three times as many casualties, including six foreigners. One of them drowned near the Hemis monastery. Witnesses described how a man in his forties boldly jumped into the swollen Indus river, which had torn down a bridge connecting the villages of Hemis and Karu just as a group of children was crossing it. The icy stream only threw up the man's disfigured body at the village of Choglamsar, which the flood had destroyed completely. Michal failed to find out through the Slovak embassy whether there was a Slovakian national among the casualties. A lot of identification papers were destroyed during the commotion in the area, so nobody could find out the exact numbers and names of people who had died.

Marika and Michal landed in Vienna around noon on August 8, and they were at home in Bratislava an hour later. A few days after that, Marika went to see her professor at the specialized oncology clinic. The professor ran ultrasound tests but found no lump or nodules. He was reluctant to believe it, so he did a bone scintigraphy and an ultrasound examination of the liver but found no metastases. As if he wanted to prove at any cost that Marika's cancer wasn't gone, he sent her for a mammography. She refused, saying that mammography kills. The professor tried to convince her to have a tissue sample taken for biopsy at least. She resolutely refused that as well, saying she had no cancer. The professor called in his colleagues and showed them the test results.

They shook their heads in disbelief. To make absolutely sure, the professor invited Marika for a checkup in three months' time.

Adelka and Hans returned in late September. They had a daughter on October 15. They named her after Adelka's grandmother. Marika was the happiest person in the world.

She went back for the checkup on November 10. The examinations confirmed that the carcinoma had finally disappeared. The surprised professor invited her to his office.

"Excuse me, Mrs. Kráľová, but this is a miracle. Can you explain it to me?"

"It's a secret."

"What secret?"

"The secret of the miracle. Maybe you'll understand it one day."

"I'd like to understand it very, very much... please... What does the secret consist in?"

"In faith."

"What's faith?"

"Love." The physician stared at her, waiting for an explanation. "I'm sorry, I'll have to be going."

"Please, Mrs. Kráľová, don't go just yet. I'd like to comprehend the miracle."

Marika gave him the nicest smile she was capable of, took his cold hands in hers and held them for a long time. She stared into his eyes silently. He turned down his eyes after a while. "You see, my wife died of cancer. In my hands. The greatest specialist in the disease, I couldn't help my own wife! Can you imagine that?" He held on to Marika's warm hands and wouldn't let go. "I think I'm beginning to understand now. Thank you."

She went out. Michal with Adelka, Hans and her granddaughter Marika in a baby carriage were waiting for her outside the hospital. The first half of November was unusually warm, so they went for a stroll along their favorite Danube riverbank. It was after rain and a beautiful rainbow was shining over the city.

Epilogue – One More Thing I Wanted to Tell You

They baptized me (without my consent) and told me, "You'll be a Christian." But by doing that, they didn't guarantee I'd be a good person as well. The moment I realized I had an intellect, I decided I'd try to become a good person, because to me being a Christian means being a good person. I set out down the hardest path – one of searching for the truth. I understood that if I want to find it, I have to go back to the man whom false prophets took away from us and whose beautiful teaching of love they turned upside town.

There are two possible paths to happiness: via the intellect and via the heart. Most of us take the path of the intellect, of words. He took the path of the heart, of love, of deeds. You must act in order to be able to search. That's why I understand that most Christians don't search, but rather accept as given truths the dogmas of which Jesus didn't have any idea. A dogma is nothing but evidence for lack of evidence. Whoever claims to be an owner of the truth is most likely an owner of a lie. Insisting on dogmas is refusal of intellect, an insult to God.

Why else would God give us intellect if he didn't want us to use it? In my novel *Code 9*, I wrote, 'We're only free when we recognize the truth. And we will recognize it only when we think. Whoever insists on dogmas and does not think, or even worse, prevents others from thinking, is against God, and therefore does not believe. And belief without thinking is not belief but submission to violence.'

Gospels differ from one another in many fundamental statements. If two statements differ, it means that at least one of them is necessarily wrong. That's not good news for those who claim that gospels are from God, or at least inspired by God. God can't be wrong. Besides other truths contained in the gospels, they make it quite clear that Jesus was perfectly prepared for his preaching mission. But where had he acquired his miraculous healing abilities? Where was he between the ages of twelve and thirty? Adding to that a whole range of indications in the gospels that he didn't die on the cross but was instead taken down, healed and forced to escape the Roman Empire, a legitimate interest in his real life arises.

I don't presume that my version of the world's most mysterious story is true, but those who claim that their story of Jesus is true have no evidence either. Unlike them, I'm not forcing my version on anyone. People will search for the truth, although they know they won't find it, because the way is the goal. In spite of that – or because of that – I've set out down the path of searching for the truth. I'm searching for it not because I want to weaken my faith, but conversely because I want to strengthen it. In searching for it, I've built on foreign literature, personal visits to Jerusalem, Bethlehem, Tiberias, Nazareth, Kashmir, Srinagar, Leh, Hemis, Sonamarg, Mailapur, Cochin, Kerala, the Malabar Coast, and other places in Israel and, above all, in India, where both Jesus and Thomas the Apostle stayed according to a lot of direct and indirect evidence. Jews and Christians coexist there to this day, professing their faith in peace.

My ambition was to write a story, not a history textbook; inspire contemplation, not convince; search for the truth, not own it. If a miracle happened and I got the truth as a gift from God, I'd reject the gift and prefer searching for it. If this book has helped at least one person in their search, then writing it was not in vain.

Jozef Banáš

Bibliography

Anthonysamy, S. J: A Saga of faith, National Shrine of St.Thomas Basilica, Chennai, Mylapore, India, 2009
Arias, J.: Ježiš veľký neznámy, Sofa, Bratislava, 2003 Baigent, M.: Ježišove listiny, Remedium, Bratislava, 2006 Banáš, J.: Kód 9, Ikar, Bratislava, 2010
Bernard-Marie: Piate evanjelium, Motýľ, Bratislava, 1998
Berry, S.: From Godess to Mortal, Vajra Publications, Kathmandu, 2007
Biblia, Spolok svätého Vojtecha Trnava, Ikar Bratislava, 2006
Biblia, Tranoscius Liptovský Mikuláš, Slovenská biblická spoločnosť Banská Bystrica, 2000 Black, J.: Tajné dějiny světa, Argo, Praha, 2009
Bricker, Ch. a kol.: Ježiš a jeho časy, Reader' s digest, Bratislava, 2011
Buddhismus a křesťanství, CAD Press, Bratislava, 1996
Davidson, J.: Ježišovo evanjelium, CAD Press, Bratislava, 2004 Dějiny Indie, Lidové noviny, Praha, 2003
Die Bergpredigt, Universelles Leben, Würzburg, 1993
Douglas, J. D.: Nový biblický slovník, Návrat domů, Praha, 1996 Douglas-Klotz, N.: Skryté evangelium, DharmaGaia, Praha, 2009
D'Souza, H.: In the steps of St. Thomas, Disciples of St. Thomas, Mylapore, 2009 England, C. J.: The hidden history of christianity in Asia, ISPCK, New Delhi, 2002 Evangelium Esejských, Kniha první, Synergie, Praha, 1996
Faber – Kaiser, A.: Jesus lebte und starb in Kaschmir, Edition Esteve, Lausanne, 1986 Feinberg-Vamosh, M.: Land und Leute zur Zeit Jesu, Palphot, Israel
Fruchtenbaum. G. A.: Život Mesiáša, MSEJK Bratislava, 2010 Hassnain, F. – Olsson, S.: Rozabal, the tomb of Jesus, Booksurge, 2008 Haywood, J.: Atlas svetových dejín, Slovart Bratislava, 2001 Historická revue, 12/2011
India, DK Travel Guides, London, New York, 2005
Jacobovici, S. – Pellegrino, Ch.: Hrobka Ježíšovy rodiny, Knižní klub, Praha, 2008 Jacobs, A.: When Jesus lived in India, Watkin Publishing, London, 2010

Je Bible zfalšovaná? Earthsave CZ, Praha, 2007 Jeruzalém a Svatá země, Euromedia Group, 2008
Kastein, J.: Eine Geschichte der Juden, Löwit, Wien, 1935 Kersten, H.: Ježíš žil v Indii, Alternativa Praha, 1996
Knight, Ch. – Robert Lomas, R.: Chíramov kľúč, Remedium, Bratislava, 2003 Korán, Odeon, Praha, 1991
Kosina, J.: Světové dějiny, Starověk, Vilímek, Praha, 1929
Kuriakose, M. K.: History of Christianity in India, Serampore College, New Delhi, 2006 Lawrence, R. W.: The Valley of Kashmir, Ali Mohammad&Sons, Srinagar, Kashmir, 2006 Leeming, J.: Jóga a Bible, Votobia, Praha, 1998
Levi: Vodnářské Evanjelium o Ježíši Kristu, Erika, Praha, 1995 Liška, V.: Tajemství Ježíše z Nazaretu, XYZ, Praha, 2011 Malý Biblický atlas, Portál, Praha, 1992
Mattausch, J.: Ladakh und Zanskar, Reise Know How, Bielefeld, 2011
Messadié, G.: Človek, ktorý sa stal Bohom, Bradlo, Bratislava, 1991
Messadié, G.: Jésus de Srinagar, Robert Laffont, Paris, 1995 Messori, V.: Hypotézy o Ježíšovi, Portál, Praha, 1994
Meyer, W. M: Evangelium svatého Tomáše, Volvox Globatorr, Praha, 2007
Moore, T.: A psal prstem do písku, Portál, Praha, 2010
Nandrásky, K.: Ježiš a súčasnosť, Q111, Bratislava, 2010
Notowich, N.: The Unknown Life of Jesus Christ, Dover Publications, New York, 2006 Nový Zákon, Česká biblická společnost, Praha, 1991
Nuzzi, G.: Vatikan AG, Ecowin, Salzburg, 2009
Olsson, S.: Jesus in Kashmir, The lost Tomb, New York, 2005 PM History, 2/2011, 4/2011,12/2012, Collection
PM Magazin 12/2011
Prem Singh Jina: Religious History of Ladakh, Sri Satguru Publications, New Delhi, 2001 Prophet, C. E.: The lost years of Jesus, Jaico, Mumbai, 2011
Roy, L. D: Velké probuzení, Eugenika, Bratislava, 2003,
Samel, G.: Tibetan Medicine, Little, Brown&Comp., London, 2001
Satprem: On the way to Supermanhood, Mira Aditi, Mysore&The Mother's Institute of Research, New Delhi, 2002
Schubert, K.: Ježíš ve světle tradiční židovské literatury, Vyšehrad, Praha, 2003 Svoboda, E. R.: Ayurveda, Penguin Books, New Delhi, 1993
Šuráň, J.: Hvězda Betlémská, Svoboda, Praha, 2011 Tabor, D. James: Ježišova dynastia, Ikar, Bratislava, 2007
Zerbst, M. – Kafka, W.: Seemann's Lexikon der Symbole, Seemann Verlag, 2010 Životopis Svatého Issy z kláštera Hemis, Avatar, Praha, 1994